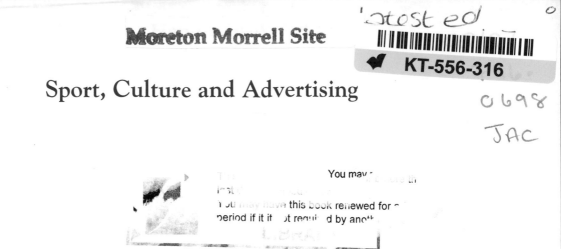

Sport, Culture and Advertising

Advertising is now widely studied yet despite the range of topics explored and positions adopted by cultural theorists, relationships between sport and advertising have been largely overlooked.

Given sport's global popularity and prevalence across the spectrum of cultural and commercial life, it is not surprising that scholars have begun to recognize advertising as an important site for the analysis of power relations, cultural politics and cultural representation in sport and recreation.

Sport, Culture and Advertising presents a first step towards understanding the relationship between advertising and identity with a focus on sport. The book will be useful for scholars across a range of disciplines and will be of interest to students looking for a more critical examination of the commercial realm of sport.

Steven J. Jackson is Associate Professor in the School of Physical Education, University of Otago, New Zealand. He is General Secretary for the International Sociology of Sport Association (ISSA). **David L. Andrews** is Associate Professor in Sport, Commerce and Culture, and is also affiliated to the Department of American Studies, at the University of Maryland, USA. He is Assistant Editor of the *Journal of Sport and Social Issues*.

Sport, Culture and Advertising

Identities, commodities and the politics of representation

Edited by Steven J. Jackson and David L. Andrews

Routledge
Taylor & Francis Group

LONDON AND NEW YORK

First published 2005
by Routledge
2 Park Square, Milton Park, Abingdon, Oxon OX14 4RN

Simultaneously published in the USA and Canada
by Taylor & Francis Inc
270 Madison Ave, New York, NY 10016

Routledge is an imprint of the Taylor & Francis Group

© 2005 Steven J. Jackson and David L. Andrews

Typeset in Goudy by Wearset Ltd, Boldon, Tyne and Wear
Printed and bound in Great Britain by TJ International Ltd, Padstow,
Cornwall

Every effort has been made to ensure that the advice and information in
this book is true and accurate at the time of going to press. However,
neither the publisher nor the authors can accept any legal responsibility
or liability for any errors or omissions that may be made. In the case of
drug administration, any medical procedure or the use of technical
equipment mentioned within this book, you are strongly advised to
consult the manufacturer's guidelines.

British Library Cataloguing in Publication Data
A catalogue record for this book is available from the British Library

Library of Congress Cataloging in Publication Data
A catalog record for this book has been requested

ISBN 0–415–33991–x (hbk)
ISBN 0–415–33992–8 (pbk)

Contents

Contributors

David L. Andrews is an Associate Professor in the Sport Commerce and Culture Program, Department of Kinesiology, and an Affiliate Faculty in the Department of American Studies, at the University of Maryland, College Park. His research and teaching focuses on the critical examination of contemporary sport culture. He has been a guest editor of the *Sociology of Sport Journal*, and is currently Assistant Editor of the *Journal of Sport and Social Issues*.

Alan Aycock is currently on staff at the University of Wisconsin-Milwaukee. He previously held positions as Professor and Chair of Sociology at Cardinal Stritch University and The University of Lethbridge. He has published many articles on play, particularly postmodern analyses of chess using the work of Bourdieu, Baudrillard, Foucault and Derrida. His current research interests include online cultures, advertising as a sociocultural phenomenon, and the sociology of dis/ability.

Debra A. Capon co-authored this chapter while completing her MA at the University of Alberta. Her thesis looked at the hero, representation, media and fans. Since graduating, Debra has worked in community development with 'youth at risk'. She can currently be spotted in Edmonton playing hockey to her heart's content.

Margaret Duncan is a Professor in the Department of Human Movement Studies at the University of Wisconsin-Milwaukee. Her research interests include media representations of female athletes and women's sport. Currently, she is studying the intersections of race, class and gender, and how they shape one's experience of one's body. She is a former president of the North American Society for the Sociology of Sport (NASSS) and a Fellow of the American Academy of Kinesiology and Physical Education (AAKPE).

Michael D. Giardina is a doctoral candidate in the Department of Kinesiology and The Program for Cultural Studies and Interpretive Research at the University of Illinois, Urbana-Champaign. He has published on a variety of topics related to sport, culture and national identity. With David L. Andrews, he is currently editing a forthcoming Special Issue of the journal *Cultural Studies<=>Critical Methodologies* on 'Sport and Cultural Studies'.

Andrew Grainger is a Ph.D. candidate in the Department of Kinesiology, University of Maryland. He completed his undergraduate and Master's degrees at the University of Otago, New Zealand. His research examines how the globalization, commercialization, commodification and corporatization of sport within late capitalism is (re)shaping contemporary identity, understanding and experience.

Michelle Helstein completed her Ph.D. at the University of Alberta and she is currently an Assistant Professor in the Department of Kinesiology at the University of Lethbridge. Her research interests are grounded within feminist poststructural theory and relate specifically to the production and consumption of cultural identities.

Jeremy Howell is an Associate Professor at the University of San Francisco. His research interests focus on the production, promotion and consumption of sport and fitness spectacles, goods and experiences. He has published in the *Sociology of Sport Journal*, *Cultural Studies*, and serves on the editorial board of the *Journal of Sport and Social Issues*.

Steven J. Jackson is an Associate Professor in the School of Physical Education, University of Otago, New Zealand. His research interests include sport media, globalization and sport and sports advertising. He has published in a wide range of scholarly journals including: *Sociology of Sport Journal, International Review for the Sociology of Sport, Journal of Sport and Social Issues*, and *Media, Culture and Society*. He is currently General Secretary for the International Sociology of Sport Association (ISSA) and has served on the editorial board for the *Sociology of Sport Journal*.

Robyn Jones is a Senior Lecturer and Program Coordinator for Coach Education and Sport Development at the University of Bath. He has authored several books including: *Sports Coaching Cultures: From Practice to Theory*, with K. Armour and P. Potrac (Routledge), and *Problematising Sports Coaching: Teaching and Learning in the Sporting Context*, with T. Cassidy (Routledge). He has also published in a number of leading journals including: *Quest, Sport Education and Society, International Review for the Sociology of Sport* and the *Journal of Sport and Social Issues*.

Annemarie Jutel received her Ph.D. in sport history at the Otago and is currently a Senior Lecturer at Otago Polytechnic. Her research interests include issues related to body culture. She has published in the *Journal of Sport and Social Issues* and has authored a number of books on running.

Roger LeBlanc has a Master's degree from the University of Montpellier (France) and recently completed his Ph.D. at the University of Otago. His research interests focus on the experiences of gay athletes and on issues of diversity and human rights.

Mary McDonald is an Associate Professor at the University of Miami-Ohio. Her research focuses on theorizing sexism, racism and classism as interacting forces in contemporary culture. She is the co-author of *Reading Sport: Critical Essays on Power and Representation* (Northeastern University Press) and has published in a number of leading journals including: *Sociology of Sport Journal* and *International Review for the Sociology of Sport*. She has also served on the editorial boards for the *Sociology of Sport Journal* and the *Journal of Sport and Social Issues*.

Jim McKay is an Associate Professor at the University of Queensland. He has authored a multitude of books including: *No Pain, No Gain?: Sport and Australian Society* (Prentice Hall), *Managing Gender: Affirmative Action and Organizational Power in Australian, Canadian and New Zealand Sport* (SUNY), and *Globalization and Sport: Playing the World*, with T. Miller, G. Lawrence and D. Rowe (Sage). Jim is former editor of the *International Review for the Sociology of Sport* and a member of the Editorial Advisory Committee of the *Australian and New Zealand Journal of Sociology*.

Jennifer L. Metz is a doctoral candidate at the University of Illinois at Urbana-Champaign in Kinesiology and Women's Studies and an instructor of Kinesiology at Northern Illinois University. Her doctoral dissertation is an ethnographic exploration of race, motherhood and professional athletics in the WNBA.

Fabien Ohl is a Professor of Sport Management at the Universite Marc Bloch, Strasbourg, France. He serves on the Executive Board of the International Sociology of Sport Association (ISSA) and has published in *Leisure and Society* and *Sciences de la société*.

Nick Perry is a Professor of Sociology at the University of Auckland, New Zealand. He is the author of *Hyperreality and Global Culture* (Routledge, 1998) and *The Dominion of Signs* (University of Auckland Press, 1994).

Jay Scherer completed his undergraduate degree from the University of Western Ontario and his Master's at The University of Windsor. He recently completed his Ph.D. at the University of Otago. Jay has published in the *Sociology of Sport Journal*, and the *International Journal of Sport Sponsorship and Marketing*.

Michael Silk is an Assistant Professor at the University of Maryland. His research focuses on the spaces of sporting production and consumption, the authorship of (trans)nationality and ethnographic research design. He has published in the *Sociology of Sport Journal*, *Journal of Sport Management*, *Journal of Sport and Social Issues*, and has a forthcoming anthology (with David Andrews and C.L. Cole) *Corporate Nationalisms: Sport, Cultural Identity and Transnational Marketing* (Berg).

Brian Wilson is an Assistant Professor at the University of British Columbia. His research interests include youth subcultures, mass media portrayals of race and gender and social movements. He has published in the *Sociology of Sport Journal*, *Journal of Sport and Social Issues* and the *Canadian Journal of Sociology*.

Preface

The idea for this book emerged out of our shared interest in the place of sport in late capitalism and its intersection with many other areas of contemporary social life. Our ongoing discussions with other scholars heightened our awareness that an increasing amount of research and teaching in the field was focusing on and/or being directed towards advertising.

As we developed our ideas for this edited collection it became very clear from the outset that we would struggle to satisfy everyone who we hoped would have an interest in the book. Since this is one of the first books to focus on sport, culture and advertising we were aware of the diverse range of expectations. As such a few qualifications are in order.

Those hoping to use the book for teaching purposes will no doubt wish that we had produced a book that more closely resembled a primer which provided a more structured text with examples, guiding questions and useful resources. However, it was not our explicit intention to fulfil this particular need in this anthology. Still, we certainly hope that students and scholars will be able to draw upon the theories, methods and themes used by our contributors in order to support and enhance their pedagogical pursuits.

Scholars who locate themselves and their work with the area of critical textual or contextual analysis will likely find this book quite useful. Our main thrust has deliberately focused on advertising as texts and sites of communication and identity politics. Researchers who are more focused on aspects of political economy and production, or on audience research, may find that our contributions are limited in these areas. However, where possible most authors have made reference or inference to aspects of production, representation, consumption and regulation, but understandably to different degrees and depths.

To be direct, this book is not intended to be a definitive analysis of contemporary sport advertising. Nor is it focused solely on the political economy of the sport-media-advertising complex. As such those from a sport marketing or sport management background seeking a formulaic text of case studies may find this text less user friendly. Having said that we believe that scholars and practitioners in the aforementioned fields could gain some valuable insights by stepping outside the box and considering a much more critical view of the advertising industry and its role in transforming both sport and other areas of social life.

Ultimately, we offer this collection as a starting point and encourage others to follow up. Indeed, we would suggest a series of books that follow up on sport, culture and advertising by using and looking for links between the production, representation, consumption and regulation of culture. Moreover, we believe this project could be taken up within and across various national contexts in order to locate particular dynamics within the global/local nexus. Ultimately, we envision a succession of studies that would extend this preliminary text in order to gain a better understanding of how advertising as an ideological, cultural, discursive and political-economic force shapes contemporary existence and identity.

Acknowledgements

We wish to thank Sage Publishers for permission to publish a revised version of:

1   Chapter 4: Enlightened racism and celebrity feminism in contemporary sports advertising discourse, Jim McKay
    This is a revised version of an article originally entitled: 'Just do it': corporate sports slogans and the political economy of 'enlightened racism', which appeared in *Discourse: Studies In The Cultural Politics of Education* 16, 191–201 (1995).
2   Chapter 9: Global gaming: cultural Toyotism, transnational corporatism and sport, David L. Andrews and Michael Silk
    This chapter is a revised version of an article originally entitled: Beyond a boundary? Sport, transnational advertising, and the re-imagining of national culture, which appeared in *Journal of Sport and Social Issues* 25 (2), 156–177 (2001).

Introduction

The contemporary landscape of sport advertising

Steven J. Jackson, David L. Andrews and Jay Scherer

> [Advertising] is a commercial tool, a social language, a genre of spectator/reader experience, a technique of persuasion; in fact, it is almost a world in its own right, with its own languages, customs and history, and one that sets the tone and pace for large parts of our lives.
>
> (Davidson, 1992: 3)

From Raymond Williams (1961) to Jean Baudrillard (1975; 1981; 1983), advertising has been conceptualized, defined and vilified by cultural critics from a range of social and political perspectives. As Leiss and colleagues (1990: 17) observe: 'It is difficult to think of another contemporary social institution that has come under such sustained attack from so many different directions.' A cursory view of the myriad ways in which advertising has been characterized highlights its shifting, enduring and inextricable position within contemporary existence (cf. Brierley, 1998; Cook, 1992; Ewen, 1976; Goldman, 1992; Jhally, 1990; Twitchell, 1996).

For example, over the past century, advertising has been varyingly described as: 'a system of organised magic' (Williams, 1980: 186), a science (see Rothenberg, 1999), a hidden persuader (Packard, 1960), a form of subliminal seduction (Key, 1972; 1989), a form of myth making (Barthes, 1972), a language and form of social communication (Goddard, 1998; Leiss *et al.*, 1990; Cook, 1992) 'a discourse *through* and *about* objects' (Leiss *et al.*, 1990: 5), 'an ideational image system' (Lull, 2000: 18), a cultural system (Jhally, 1990), 'the official art of capitalism' (Harvey, 1990: 63), one of the 'fixers of capitalism' (Thrift, 1987), a form of popular culture (Fowles, 1996), a cultural intermediary (Nixon, 1997; 2003), a cultural industry (Lash and Urry, 1994; Sinclair, 1987), the 'most influential institution of socialisation in modern society' (Jhally, 1990: 1), and a 'sphere of ideology' (Goldman, 1992; Williamson, 1978).

The multiplicity and even contradictory nature of these characterizations is both puzzling and intriguing. Arguably, this situation has emerged, in part, because of advertising's changing, but always strategic, location within the circuit of culture and commodification (cf. du Gay, 1997; Johnson, 1986). In brief, the circuit is a conceptual model that traces the life and meaning of cultural commodities as they move through various phases or moments including production, representation, consumption, regulation and, in turn, how they shape our lived experiences and identities. Furthermore, the fervent debates over advertising are also likely due to the historical transformation between a capitalist system driven by production to one based increasingly on consumption (Giroux, 2000; Miller, 1995). Stated another way: 'we used to live in a system where people needed commodities but now commodities need people. This has led Miller (1995: 1) to acknowledge that consumption is now 'the vanguard of history'. If we add to this the dramatic global and technological changes that have accelerated this shift over the past 100 years we may begin to better understand advertising's enduring political, economic and cultural importance. In turn, we may comprehend why different generations of cultural observers have erroneously envisaged their particular historical era to be 'the age of advertising' (Williams, 1980).

The definitive role of advertising as industry, ideology and form of popular culture will remain debatable for the foreseeable future. However, what we can assert with some degree of certainty is that advertising is at the forefront of the expansion of the global economy and postmodern promotional culture (Wernick, 1991). Beyond its purported, yet contentious, role in stimulating consumption (Featherstone, 1991; Miller, 1995), advertising has been identified as playing a key ideological role with respect not only to the legitimation of capitalism and consumer culture (Bell, 1976; du Gay and Pryke, 2002; Ewen, 1976; Lury, 1996) but also within the politics of representation and identity formation (Bonney and Wilson, 1990; Cronin, 2000; 2004; Goldman, 1992; Kellner, 1995; Kilbourne, 1999; Mort, 1996; O'Barr, 1994).

Strikingly, despite the expansive range of theoretical and methodological positions adopted and the wide range of issues and topics related to advertising covered by those in cultural studies, including everything from fashion to body image, sport has been largely overlooked. Given its global popularity and its prevalence across the spectrum of cultural and commercial life it is somewhat surprising that, with a few exceptions (cf. Goldman, 1992; Goldman and Papson, 1996), scholars interested in the cultural politics of advertising have tended to ignore sport; conversely, scholars interrogating the cultural politics of sport have begun to recognize advertising as an important site for the analysis of power relations, cultural politics and cultural representation.

Thus there have been an increasing number of critical sport studies that have at least made reference to the role of advertising in reproducing power relations related to: race (Andrews, 1996; Cole, 1996; Cole and Andrews, 1996; Jackson and Hokowhitu, 2002; McKay, 1995; Wilson and Sparks, 1996), gender (Arsenault and Fawzy, 2001; Cole and Hribar, 1995; Davis and Delano, 1992; Duquin, 1989; Helstein, 2003; LaFrance, 1998; Messner, 2002; Wenner, 1991; White and Gillett, 1994; Worsching, 2000), social class (Renson and Careel, 1986), disability (Maas and Hasbrook, 2001), nationalism and national identity (Jackson et al., 2001; Perry, 1994; Wenner, 1994) as well as the role of advertising in the global economy of sport commodities (Andrews, 1996; Jackson and

Andrews, 1999). In addition, there have been a few studies that have examined the politics and contradictions associated with sport advertising and its confrontations with social policy related to tobacco and alcohol products (Blum, 1991; Crompton, 1993; Dewhirst and Sparks, 2003; Ledwith, 1984) and violence (Grainger and Jackson, 2000; Jackson and Andrews, 2004).

Many of the previous analyses have used advertising for illustrative purposes or as case studies. Others have offered simple deconstructions. However, an increasing number are providing critical contextual analyses that locate their readings and interpretations within wider socio-historical and political economic conditions. It is this type of analysis that underpins the contributions within this book. This anthology examines the politics of advertising *about* and *through* sport and the relationships between representation, consumption and identity. Several questions guide our analysis including: (1) What makes sport such an appealing global commodity for both producers and consumers and the cultural intermediaries (advertising agencies) that are charged with connecting production and consumption? (2) How are particular identities (markets) constructed and represented through sport advertising? and (3) How are particular hegemonies (gender, race, sexuality, class, nation) produced and reproduced by sport, and advertising associated with sport?

Without a doubt this is a rather broad and complex cultural terrain to navigate. What we hope to provide is a preliminary analysis of the ways in which advertising, as a key driving force within consumer capitalism, plays a role in socially constructing and reproducing particular social identities. In doing so it is important to heed Michael Schudson's (1993) reminder that advertising operates as a form of capitalist realism that does not represent society *as it is* but rather *as it should be* according to the logic of capitalism. Thus, the images of idealized lifestyles and identities constructed and represented through advertising are those that contribute to a particular social order, economy and cultural belief system. The consequence is that based on their perceived value to the marketplace certain imagined groups and categories of people are either empowered or disempowered.

Similar to Birrell and McDonald's (2000: 3) *Reading Sport*, we assert that advertising *about* sport and *through* sport offers 'unique points of access to the constitutive meanings and power relations of the larger world we inhabit'. Indeed, perhaps this book could have been called *Reading Sport Advertising* given that most of the contributions examine, in their own particular way, structures of dominance along the 'power lines' of race, class, gender, sexuality, ability and nationality. However, to be fair, some of our contributors address issues beyond representation in order to examine other moments within the circuit of commodification including aspects of production and lived experience/lifestyle.

To put our overall analysis in context the introduction consists of four interrelated sections including: (1) The contemporary landscape of advertising from its political economy to its colonization of public space; (2) a discussion of the appeal and uniqueness of sport as a cultural form and theme within advertising; (3) a brief overview of the chapters in the book; and (4) a summary which includes a call for further projects in this area.

The contemporary landscape of advertising

As a pervasive culture industry reliant on media imagery, advertising plays an integrative role in cultural practices and the process of globalization (Harvey, 1990). Global capitalism, new media technologies and transnational advertising have enormous implications for the economies and cultures of the world. For example, current global spending on advertising is estimated at US$435 billion (Klein, 2000: 8) and is expected to reach US$2 trillion by the year 2020 (Herman and McChesney, 1997). To put things into perspective, according to a United Nations Human Development Report, global ad spending 'now outpaces the growth of the world economy by one-third' (Klein, 2000: 9).

While these figures provide some basic indication of the economic influence of corporate advertising, we should not overlook the structure of the advertising-media complex itself. The advertising industry both mirrors and facilitates global capitalism. Through acquisitions and strategic alliances today's advertising firms have become integrated communication conglomerates (Leslie, 1995). For example, the ten largest ad agencies now have offices in more than fifty different countries with the largest global firm, McCann-Erickson, having over 200 offices in 130 countries. As further confirmation of the increasing advertising-media complex synergy, in 1996 the leading world advertising and broadcasting associations devised a single global standard for the purchase and production of television advertising (Ross, 1996: 3). In combination, the consolidation of these major global political, economic and cultural power brokers is driving a 'new culture of enterprise that enlists the enterprise of culture' (Harvey, 1987; Morley and Robins, 1995). As evidence of advertising's enterprise of culture we only need to scan our everyday surroundings.

Contemporary social life is not only dominated by advertising, it is defined by it. Corporate and even anti-corporate signs, logos and other forms of symbolic representation permeate our personal, organizational, national and global landscapes, leading Jhally (1990) to suggest that we are witnessing the 'colonization of culture'. One effect of this colonization is that almost every conceivable public, private and even virtual space is inhabited by advertising. Consider a few examples:

- Facing ongoing budget cuts many schools have survived by selling space to corporations. For example, in order to reach an estimated 43 million children in the USA with over US$108 billion in buying power, Channel One provides schools with up to US$50,000 in televisual equipment in exchange for the right to broadcast programmes consisting of news along with two minutes of advertising (Giroux, 2000). Moreover, McDonald's and Nike are just two of the many transnational corporations which are now sponsoring curriculum development. According to Henry Giroux (2000: 19), the result of this commercialization of culture is that 'the only type of citizenship that adult society offers to children is that of consumerism'.

- Space platforms that first gained notoriety in director Ridley Scott's futuristic movie *Bladerunner* are now a reality. Advertisers are now capable of buying advertising space on mile-wide billboards that can appear in the sky. Described by some critics as 'intergalactic pollution' it could lead to a situation where 'this sunset is brought to you by Coca-Cola'.

- As one indicator of the power of the relationship between our consumer-based society and advertising we note a recent billboard campaign in Auckland, New Zealand. The campaign, which appeared on twenty-seven city billboards, simply featured a cropped image of the side view of a woman's face and shoulders with text stating: 'NOTHING. What you've been looking for.' A young graphic designer created the billboard as a way of highlighting the absurdity of our consumer-based society. Notably, the billboard company received a number of calls from people wanting to know where they could buy 'nothing'.

These examples verify some of the assertions put forth in Goldman and Papson's (1996) *Sign Wars: The Cluttered Landscape of Advertising*. Increasingly, every conceivable space and strategy is being used in order to attract potential consumers and, just as importantly, to differentiate corporate signs and brands. As a result the advertising industry seeks out cultural sites, images and themes that shock, cannibalize and contribute to a 'haemorrhaging of meaning' (1996: vi). As they note:

> At every turn, the pressure is on to find fresher, more desirable, and more spectacular images to enhance the value of products. . . . As sign value competitions intensify, advertisers invent new strategies and push into fresh cultural territory, looking for 'uncut' and 'untouched' signs. Under such circumstances no meaning system is sacred, because the realm of culture has been turned into a giant mine.
>
> (Goldman and Papson, 1996: v)

Notably, sport, as a global cultural form, practice and institution, has not been immune from advertising's cultural excavation and exploitation. Indeed, for a variety of reasons sport has arguably been at the cutting edge of developments in contemporary advertising technology. A brief discussion of the appeal of sport to the advertising-media complex follows but to begin with let us consider the following examples of 'sporting sign wars'.

The contemporary landscape of sport advertising: sporting sign wars

- The concept of 'virtual' advertising was basically designed for sport. This technology enables global advertisers to have access to a blank canvas in terms of major sporting events. As such beer companies in Brazil, Germany, India, Spain and South Africa have the potential to rent the same virtual space at the same time in order to capture a particular market.

- In addition to sporting events and venues, the bodies and equipment of athletes are now an integral part of advertising and promotion. From Tiger Woods' Nike 'swooshed' golf balls to Adidas' tri-striped logo on the trigger finger of the glove of Winter Olympic biathletes, transnational corporations are constantly seeking brand exposure. The sport of auto racing may be one of the most interesting with respect to sporting sign wars. A strict hierarchy of sponsor signs determines the size and placement of logos on every inch of the car including the driver's suit, steering wheel, even under the hood. Even occasional accidents, though tragic, offer 'advertising opportunities' as announcers fit sponsor soundbites into their narratives. Corporatized bodies are also emerging in professional boxing (McKelvey, 2003) where athletes are permanently or temporarily tattooing their torsos with sponsors' logos for upwards of US$100,000. The fact that there are people employed to measure the visual and auditory exposure of each sponsor during media broadcasts attests to the economy of sporting signs and spaces.
- In 1995 the IOC established the Olympic Television Archive Bureau (OTAB), a repository of over 20,000 hours of film and television footage of the modern games. Astute sponsors, marketing firms and television production companies can now purchase images of the past so that they may be used in advertising and other commercial projects. In this way sporting images of the past become part of the promotional efforts of the present through the marketing of nostalgia. The IOC's new archive is but one example of perhaps the most important development regarding sport, culture and advertising; that is, intellectual property rights (IPR). IPR debates have manifested themselves in many ways both within and outside of sport (Coombe, 1998; 1999; Jackson, 2001; Sebel and Gyngell, 1999; VanWynsberghe and Ritchie, 1998) and highlight the increasingly critical relationship between culture, image and identity. A key issue in a world dominated by images, both past and present, is ownership. As a consequence we find Martin Luther King's 'I have a dream' speech being used to promote telecommunications companies, and indigenous cultures being appropriated to market alcohol and sports teams (Jackson and Hokowhitu, 2002). As Naomi Klein ('Brand Klein', 2001: C13), author of *No Logo: Taking Aim at the Brand Bullies* notes: 'This new kind of branding is not about advertising. It's essentially about creating self-enclosed branding cocoons, which ... is ... all about owning intellectual property. And [he] who has the most intellectual property and the least actual property wins.'

As a result of these examples, and many others, cultural studies critics have incriminated advertising 'as *the* iconographic signifier of multinational capitalism (Nava, 1997: 34). Yet, as with other 'common-sense' institutions, 'we tend to take for granted the deep social assumptions embedded in advertisements. We do not ordinarily recognize advertising as a sphere of ideology' (Goldman,

1992: 1). Conceptualizing advertising as a sphere of ideology provides us with a powerful framework for analysing the links between particular social problems and inequities and the discourses that represent, reproduce and resist them. Indeed, we can think about advertisements as ideological discourses that: (1) reflect the logic of capitalism; (2) promote a normative vision of our world and our relationships; (3) socially and culturally construct our world; and (4) disguise and suppress inequalities, injustices, irrationalities and contradictions (Goldman and Papson, 1996: 18).

Given that advertising is located in the 'pivotal position between production and consumption' (Leslie, 1995: 402), we focus primarily on issues related to representation and ideology and the articulation of particular cultural meanings to commodity signs and by extension socially constructed identities. The role of advertising as representation is important because it is one of the key processes in the circuit of culture that connects meaning and language to culture, thereby constituting socially constructed identities in specific contexts (Hall, 1996). Indeed, because the representations within contemporary advertising are often complex and contradictory they cannot be understood outside of or separated from their context of articulation (Grossberg, 1997). As Hall (1996: 4) notes, it is: 'Precisely because identities are constructed within, not outside, discourse, we need to understand them as produced in specific historical and institutional sites within specific discursive formations and practices, by specific enunciative strategies.'

The focus on texts, discourses and representation is not without its limitations or critics. For example, Frederic Jameson has critiqued the tendency within cultural studies to produce textual analyses of advertising without considering 'real markets' (1993: 264). However, as Sinclair (1987: 97) notes, we must also recognize that: 'Contrary to marketing ideology, markets do not already exist "out there" in social reality but are "constructed": the selection of the advertising medium and the way in which audiences are segmented, that is selected to be addressed by advertising, are both ways in which social categories become transformed into markets.' Thus, while we are fully cognizant that any critical textual analysis of advertising can only be understood in relation to an underlying 'real' political economy we are also aware that the so-called real world market segments of consumption (e.g. 'Generation-X', 'baby boomers') are themselves social constructions (Turow, 1997).

As a final point before we discuss the cultural significance of sport in contemporary advertising it is worth highlighting the important link between representation, cultural theory and the advertising industry. Perhaps the best way to do this is by referring to one of the key innovators in the world of sport advertising. *Wieden + Kennedy* have been the creative force behind Nike, arguably the most successful sports company in history, for the past twenty years. Advertising agencies such as *Wieden + Kennedy* are important because they 'play a pivotal role as cultural intermediaries in articulating production and consumption. This articulation of production and consumption itself constitutes a determinant moment in the circuit of culture: the moment of circulation' (Nixon, 1997: 181). Notably, the company's website provides some key insights into their role as cultural intermediaries and their philosophy about linking production and consumption, commodities and identities:

> Our key strength is brand building. Finding the cultural truths about, or intersections between product, consumer and business. We specialize in understanding cultural trends. As a result we have made Nike, ESPN and Miller Lite part of our shared cultural influence. Once brands are accepted on this level, they are infinitely more powerful.
>
> (www.wiedenkennedy.com)

The very language they use to describe their company resonates with current cultural theory. Thus, while scholars in cultural studies, including sport studies, are working to analyse and critically assess the advertising industry, agencies such as *Wieden + Kennedy* not only draw upon the same cultural theories but they also appropriate and incorporate the critiques levied against them. Needless to say, the question of opposition and resistance is becoming increasingly challenging because the avenues and strategies to do so are disappearing.

Up until this point we have outlined the contested terrain of advertising as an industry and its role as a discourse of ideology that constructs and represents identity. We now turn to sport in order to highlight some of its distinctive features that make it such an attractive avenue to reach consumers as well as a popular cultural theme for the advertising industry.

Sport, culture and advertising

Arguably, sport is a powerful vehicle for transnational corporations and their allied advertising and promotional armatures. As such it has an appeal that stretches beyond the field of sport per se with sporting themes, images, narratives and celebrities located within and across a complex and increasingly global system of intertextual promotional cultures including movies, art, fashion, music and politics. As Clarke and Clarke (1982: 64) note: 'sport has become a significant international currency'.

Even a glance at present-day sport provides insights into its unique and enormous appeal to the advertising industry. Whether it be the Summer or Winter Olympics, World Cup Soccer or Rugby, the Champions League, Super Bowl, World Series or Stanley Cup, major global sporting competitions have become regular features of our emotional calendars. As one macro indicator of the political economy of sport we note that it is now a global industry and accounts for more than 3 per cent of world trade (Blackshaw, 2001), approximately 2 per cent of GDP in the United States, Europe, Japan and Australia (Marqusee, 2000) and more than 1 per cent of the GNP (Gross National Product) of the European Union. As further evidence of the promotional value of global sport, consider the following examples:

- US television network NBC paid US$4 billion for the broadcast rights to the Olympics from 1996 to 2008.
- The current National Football League (NFL) television contract is worth more than $2 billion per year.
- In 2003, Britain's BskyB signed a three-year, US$5.1 billion deal with Premier League soccer.
- In 2000, Tiger Woods signed a five-year deal with Nike worth over $100 million. In 2003, 18-year-old high school basketball player LeBron James signed a deal with the NBA's Cleveland Cavaliers and a $90 million sponsorship contract with Nike. Soccer sensation Freddy Adu at age 13 signed a $1 million dollar contract with Nike. In each case the athlete earns more from endorsements than in salary. It is their manufactured image that truly counts. Thus it is evident that 'within today's multi-layered "promotional culture" (Wernick, 1991), the sport celebrity is effectively a multi-textual and multi-platform promotional entity' (Andrews and Jackson, 2001: 7).

These examples demonstrate the economic value of sport within the global economy. However, important questions remain. *Why* is sport such a valued cultural commodity? And, in turn, why is the advertising industry so enamoured with sport? To begin with, we can simply acknowledge that sport is one of the oldest and most universal forms of performative culture. History and tradition are the cornerstones of many sports. These are important because they provide strong identities that have the potential to form a lucrative consumer base. At the same time it is the strength of local sporting identities (soccer in the UK, Europe and Central and South America, ice hockey in Canada, rugby in New Zealand and South Africa) that make sport such an attractive and powerful commodity for global corporations. As such, sport is an ideal vehicle for capturing 'massive and/or committed audiences with consumption profiles attractive to advertisers/sponsors' (Arundel and Roche, 1998). Moreover, it has the ability to cross spatial, linguistic and cultural divides enabling it to unite distant people, however temporarily. As Singer (1998: 36) notes: 'Only sports has the nation, and sometimes the world, watching the same thing at the same time, and if you have a message, that's a potent messenger.'

Arguably the entire structure of sport as a form of popular culture is ideally suited to advertising and promotional culture. It is global, yet local and particular. It is exciting for consumers because of its *uncertainty* of outcome, yet attractive to producers and advertisers because it is increasingly *certain* in terms of scheduling, rules and commercial breaks. Sport, according to recent IOC advertising campaigns, allows us to 'celebrate humanity' despite the fact that this may occur through violent physical contests. Theoretically it is open and accessible to all, with consideration being given to: gender, race, class, sexuality (e.g. The Gay Games), abled and disabled (e.g. Para and Special Olympics), age (Master's Games), amateur and professional, and it occurs across a vast array of seasons and geographic locations. Of course, these inclusive features operate more in the ideal than in reality. For example, although global sport sponsorship expenditure trebled during the 1990s its distribution was far from balanced, with 37.8 per cent going to North America, 36.4 per cent going to Europe and 20.8 per cent to Asia with South America and Africa hardly registering (Marqusee, 2000). The message is clear: it is not just the size of the consumer market, it is the nature (wealth) of the audience.

Beyond this we suggest that sport is highly desirable because: (1) it attracts large and passionately devoted audiences; (2) in a relative sense it is cheaper to produce than many other types of programming; (3) it is human drama at its finest, providing a stimulus and an acceptable arena for the full range of human emotion; (4) it reveals real people demonstrating the limits of the body; (5) it is sexy and erotic (Guttmann, 1996); (6) it provides us with carefully crafted narratives of heroes and villains (Whannel, 2002); (7) it is associated with positive images of health and nationhood (Rowe, 1996). Finally, it is important to note that sport is an ideal conduit of promotional culture because in many ways it mirrors the idealized version of capitalism; that is, it is based on competition, achievement, efficiency, technology and meritocracy.

In combination, all of these factors provide insights into what makes sport a unique and highly valued cultural commodity. They also help explain why sport sponsorship and advertising have risen from US$0.5 million to $20 billion annually in the past thirty years (Marqusee, 2000). Moreover, these factors confirm why advertising and sponsorship are at the very nucleus of what has varyingly been described as: the sports/media complex (Jhally, 1989), the media/sport production complex (Maguire, 1993) or the media sports cultural complex (Rowe, 1999). There can be no greater model of this complex than Rupert Murdoch. It is almost an understatement to describe his overall media holdings as an empire. Murdoch's sport-related portfolio alone includes: Fox, SKY and Star TV networks and various football, baseball and rugby clubs (Harvey *et al.*, 2001). What is even more striking are his synergistic partnerships which include Star TV (Asia)'s relationship with ESPN which is owned by the Disney Corporation, which itself controls the Anaheim Angels baseball team and the National Hockey League's Mighty Ducks whose name originated with the movie of the same name (Marqusee, 2000).

Clearly the strategic location of sport within the wider media production complex makes it an attractive channel to reach consumers. But it may also be that sport is such a potent cultural force because of its increasing permeability with other areas of social life: fashion, music, movies, television, politics; that is, it has the ability to leak, and be leaked into, key sites and moments that shape our contemporary existence.

Overview of chapters

Taken collectively, the diverse set of studies in *Sport, Culture and Advertising* provide a unique insight into the role of advertising and the politics of representation. Each of our thirteen chapters helps to illustrate a particular set of power relations as they relate to, emerge from and articulate with contemporary advertising. To this extent they highlight ongoing issues of social inequality and identity politics within our increasingly global and market-driven society. Furthermore, each chapter underscores the importance of the links between the author's analysis and wider social conditions. As such, the authors have gone to great lengths to ensure that particularity and context are paramount. We are cognizant of the fact that often specificity limits the extent to which wider generalizations can be made across temporal, geographic, political and ideological terrains. Yet this should not really be seen as a limitation, rather as an accepted and integral part of the work involved in critical sport and culture studies. Indeed, we believe these historically situated analyses of fundamental social problems will not only remain relevant for the near future but will also become significant markers for future scholars who wish to conduct comparative analyses of shifting trends over time.

It should come as no surprise that a book about contemporary sport, culture and advertising includes recurring reference to Nike. Nike has been the most awarded brand at the Cannes International Advertising Festival for the past five years and was Advertiser of the Year for 2002 and 2003. Notably, Festival Chairman Roger Hatchuel said that the awards 'recognised not only the quality of Nike advertising but also its major influence on creativity and lifestyle of the last decade' (Nike, 2003: 2). Furthermore, as Goldman and Papson note in their book *Nike Culture* (1998), the company, in conjunction with their main advertising agency *Wieden + Kennedy*, have become leaders in the 'cultural economy of images'. At times Nike rival Benetton for the title of popular provocateurs in the realm of advertising based on a style 'situated at the intersection between public and private discourses where themes of authenticity and personal morality converge with the cynical and nihilistic sensibility that colors contemporary public exchanges' (1998: 3). As a consequence the Nike trademark swoosh and all that it represents has become 'the sign some people love to love and the sign others love to hate' (1998: 2). While there was no intention of becoming fixated on Nike there was really no way of ignoring it.

The book is not structured into discrete sections but the reader will see an emerging pattern. For example, the first seven chapters take varying tacts on advertising and identity politics related to gender, race, sexuality and disability. In turn, Chapters 8–10 examine the role of advertising between the global and the local. In particular they highlight the strategies used by transnational corporations to appropriate the nation along with the politics, contradictions and forms of resistance to these promotional re-imaginings. The final three chapters drawn our attention to the relationship between advertising, consumers and commodities, and the way in which these shape and define lifestyles.

We begin by noting that the first three chapters examine one of the most intriguing and timely issues of contemporary advertising both from a critical and corporatist perspective: the female consumer. The common thread running through them is the recognition that although various feminist movements have contributed to a growing sense of empowerment for women, their 'potentially alternative ideological force is channelled into the commodity form so that it threatens neither patriarchal culture nor capitalist hegemony' (Goldman, 1992: 131).

In Chapter 1, Mary McDonald highlights the role of cultural criticism as a strategy of intervention (cf. Howell *et al.*, 2002) into the contemporary power relations of consumption. In her analysis of *Women's Sports and Fitness* (WSF) magazine she explores how contemporary women's publications and their advertisements serve as culturally significant discursive sites where new post-feminist ideologies are represented and struggled over. Discussing correlative changes in America's New Right politics in the 1980s to 1990s as they impacted on second-wave feminist movements, McDonald provides important insights into how these were translated into creating new subjectivities for women. Driven largely through consumer capitalism, including sport advertisements featuring athletes such as Gabrielle Reece and Anna Kournikova, these subjectivities served to 'reassure women that the dominant ideological life-choices offered by society at large (heterosexual monogamy, pro-capitalist democracy, aspirational individualism, a high value placed on physical beauty, familial norms, etc.) are indeed' the new Right ones (Sonnet and Whelehan, 1995: 84).

Debra Capon and Michelle Helstein further our understanding of the notion of female subjectivity within the realm of sport advertising in Chapter 2. Tracing the historical basis of 'the myth of the hero' they conceptualize both the myth and the contemporary advertisements that reproduce it as forms of representation at work. Referring to Featherstone's (1992) article 'The heroic life and everyday life', Capon and Helstein identify the juxtaposition between a 'heroic life' which is defined as masculine and the rather mundane 'everyday life' that women are often restricted to. To illustrate the historical and ideological power of myth they focus on Nike because, in their words, 'as legitimate speakers their popular knowledge of what/who the "hero" is continues to increase, so too, does their control of what/who can be constituted or intelligible as the "hero" and vice versa'. Their analysis, like Mary McDonald's, confirms that despite the new economic power of women in the consumer marketplace conventional markers of gender boundaries are reproduced because sport remains an arena for dominant masculinities.

Consolidating themes developed by McDonald, and Capon and Helstein, in Chapter 3 Mike Giardina and Jennifer Metz interrogate contemporary notions of women's empowerment through sport as articulated in Nike's 'Everyday Athletes' campaign. Locating their analysis within current discussions of body politics and in particular the female body within global consumer culture, Giardina and Metz examine the emergence and commodification of empowerment rhetoric. Tracing the discourses surrounding concepts such as 'girl power', they reveal how Nike has successfully merged previously oppositional notions of femininity and athleticism through consumption. In other words, while there is more latitude with respect to the range of sporting practices and bodies that female athletes can occupy, the ideals are still set within a largely white, middle-class, conservative and hetero-normative framework. Thus, social acceptance remains dependent upon, and articulated to, a consumerist lifestyle.

In Chapter 4 Jim McKay provides a contextualized examination of the interrelated processes of appropriation, mythologization, nostalgia and commodification with respect to gender and race in sport advertising over the past thirty years. To do this McKay astutely links Cole and Hribar's (1995) notion of celebrity feminism to Jhally and Lewis' (1992) concept of enlightened racism. As with several previous chapters, McKay focuses on myths which 'disavow or deny their own existence' and which 'accentuate particular versions of reality and marginalize or omit others' providing further transparency into how particular relations of power are naturalized and hence depoliticized. With examples ranging from the 1968 Black Power salute at the Mexico Olympics to Cathy Freeman's role in cleansing Australia at the 2000 Sydney Games, McKay highlights how particular historical moments and celebrities are commodified, thereby transforming human capital into corporate capital (Willis, 1993).

Expanding the analysis of advertising and racial identities in sport, Brian Wilson (Chapter 5) examines the politics of racial representation within the Canadian context. Noting a relative absence of research into sport and racial representation in Canada, Wilson studies African American NBA stars as they are located and defined within a Canadian context. Drawing upon the concept of enlightened racism (Jhally and Lewis, 1992) along with the notion of floating racial signifiers (Andrews, 1996; Jackson, 1998a; 1998b), Wilson sets out to answer a number of key questions including: How are African-American athletes portrayed in Canadian media and how do these depictions compare to portrayals in American media? To what extent has the mass-mediated promotional culture of the NBA spilled over into Canada and what impact might associated images play in perpetuating racism in Canada? The findings reveal that the Canadian media reproduce Wenner's (1995) notion of 'Good Blacks' and 'Bad Blacks' when describing African-American athletes but that these representations are often subtle, shifting and operate within a complex and often contradictory framework.

In a study of the relationship between advertising, market segments and representation of identity, Robyn Jones and Roger LeBlanc (Chapter 6) explore the political economy of the pink dollar. They begin with a basic outline of the growth and economic impact of gay, lesbian and bisexual (GLB) consumers within the world of sport and leisure, including the remarkable growth of the Gay Games. In turn, they discuss a fundamental shift in corporate thinking, strategy and policy concerning GLBs. Noting that corporations and their allied advertising and marketing agencies adopted a rather cautious approach to the gay and lesbian community during the 1980s, Jones and LeBlanc outline the various ways in which the gay and lesbian market segment is both identified and represented. Drawing upon four contemporary advertisements they examine the range of representations of gays and lesbians: from the ambiguous, to the humorous to the openly political. Their analysis, along with the growing list of corporates which deliberately include and/or target gay and lesbian consumers (including Benetton, IKEA, Nike, Toyota, American Airlines, Qantas Airlines and many others), highlight the fact that diversity is now 'not only accepted by the culture industries, it is the mantra of global capital' (Klein, 2000: 115).

While the notion of the pink dollar points to an increasing awareness of the economic power of GLB consumers another group remains largely invisible: the disabled. Focusing on a selection of magazine print advertisements Alan Aycock and Margaret Duncan (Chapter 7) note that we are witnessing a 'radical splitting of hierarchies of attention between those who are always seen and those who are never seen'. Embarking on the type of research that cultural studies scholars have been demanding, Aycock and Duncan examine the media representation of disabled persons, not in isolation, but across a range of other identities including gender, race, sexuality, age and class. In combination all of these configure with a dominant form of 'ableism' which works towards defining the disabled as 'the Other'. According to the authors, sport is a key site for studying the notions of 'abled' and 'disabled' – it is a cultural practice that celebrates not just what the 'normal' body can do but what the superhuman athletic body might achieve. Generally speaking their findings confirm those of Davis (1995; 1997) who found visual representations of disabled people to characterize them as 'dependent, childlike, passive, vulnerable, and less competent than "normal" people' (Davis, 1995; 1997).

In the first of three chapters examining advertising and national identity within the context of globalization, Nick Perry (Chapter 8) examines one particular site to demonstrate how promotional cultures are shaping national re-imaginings. Building on his successful (1994) book *The Dominion of Signs: Television Advertising and Other New Zealand Fictions*, Perry examines the process of national myth making within the context of globalization. Focusing on New Zealand he explores changing notions of popular nationalism within and between the national sport of rugby, broadcasting media and advertising. Specifically, Perry traces the historical development of advances in media technology and how this impacted on the way in which rugby was defined and appropriated by particular power brokers, both political and commercial. According to Perry the 1980s served as a key period for the transformation of the sport, advertising and national identity nexus. As a result of the 1981 South African Springbok tour controversy, rugby was temporarily decentred (Fougere, 1989) as the cultural centre of national populism. Notably, it was the lessons learned from the corporate investment and success with another, unlikely sport that helped restore rugby's national stature. Corporations looking for a vehicle through which to reach the national market astutely shifted their strategy to creating a national market through the 1986 America's Cup challenge in Freemantle. The overwhelming success demonstrated that within the emerging global economy 'representing the nation' became subordinated to building a market' (Perry, 2004: 295). What followed was a reinvention of rugby through major corporate sponsors such as Steinlager which helped develop the first rugby-themed television commercials in conjunction with the 1987 Rugby World Cup hosted by New Zealand. Perry refers to this symbolic transformation as close encounters of a third kind. Perry's analysis, like Gruneau and Whitson's

(1993: 251) previous work, illustrates that: 'What is crucial to the success of such "representational" projects is the linking of national symbols and myths of national character with the ordinary lives of people and with widely shared popular experiences.'

David Andrews and Michael Silk (Chapter 9) examine the role of transnational corporations and their promotional armatures in re-imagining national cultures. They note that although global forces are clearly undermining significant aspects of sovereignty as a cultural object, the nation plays an increasingly important role within the machinations of transnational corporate capitalism. They draw on Manuel Castells' (1996) concept of Toyotism, a system 'designed to reduce uncertainty rather than to encourage adaptability [and where] The flexibility is in the process, not in the product' (Castells, 1996: 158). Developed within the Japanese industrial and economic context, Toyotism has been both imitated by other companies and widely transplanted to other national locations. Andrews and Silk contend that the core aspects of Toyotism in a material production sense – flexible, adaptable and globally contingent regimes of production – can be discerned within the corporation's marketing and promotional strategies; in other words, the realm of cultural production upon which the late capitalist order depends (Jameson, 1991). Andrews and Silk use the concept of 'cultural Toyotism' as a means of understanding the manner in which transnational entities negotiate the global–local nexus, and explicate empirical examples of the contrasting processes whereby sport has been used as a means of constituting the nation. Through a series of global sport advertisements they illustrate the different ways in which various strategies are used to globalize and localize brands within specific national contexts.

While Andrews and Silk provide an analysis of how transnational corporations localize within particular national contexts, Andy Grainger and Steve Jackson (Chapter 10) draw our attention to the power, politics and contradictions associated with the regulation of products and processes at the global–local nexus. Focusing specifically on the context of New Zealand, Grainger and Jackson examine how one particular global media 'product', televisual violence, is regulated and censored. Highlighting several sport-related advertisements banned from New Zealand television screens because they were deemed to be excessively violent, they discuss the politics and contradictions associated with state-policy censorship as located within wider debates about Americanization, globalization and global/local disjuncture. After initially outlining the context of state media policy in New Zealand – including the codes and responsibilities of the two key censorship bodies, the Advertising Standards Authority (ASA) and the Advertising Standards Complaints Board (ASCB) – Grainger and Jackson show how the bans imposed against several American-produced commercials not only reflect the incongruity and uncertainty of Appadurai's (1990) notion of disjuncture, but further disguise efforts to demarcate a unique national 'identity' in a time of growing inter-cultural connection.

In Chapter 11, the first of three chapters addressing the relationship between commodities, consumption, lifestyle and identity, Annemarie Jutel explores how menstrual product advertisements have reproduced menstruation as a restrictive experience for women over the past century. In an extensive study of more than 200 advertisements from the twentieth century, Jutel confirms the enduring taboo against the very mention of the word menstruation with most using euphemisms. This is not to suggest that menstruation products and advertisements have not changed, for they certainly have. For many years menstruation was viewed as a pathological condition that demonstrated women's frailty and vulnerability. Over time advertisements redefined their underlying theme towards products that served as support or solutions to 'the problem'. Nevertheless, Jutel notes that although advertisements no longer focus on the pathological nature of menstruation, they promote discourses of restraint, control and caution. This results in strictly coded rules of feminine behaviour that highlight the female body and its social expectations at the expense of embodied physicality. As a consequence, advertisements that are often intended to enhance sporting and other active lifestyle opportunities for women, potentially end up reproducing existing barriers.

Exactly what does the 'baby boom' actually signify when it comes to health and fitness? What are the key sensibilities that have created, and continue to create, a cultural space in which the fit, active and sporting body is given economic and symbolic value to such a degree that it is seen to define a particular lifestyle formation? And, perhaps most importantly, how does this lifestyle formation turn around and impact upon future fitness and health industry promotional practices? These are the key questions examined in Jeremy Howell's chapter. Citing the dramatic projected changes in marketplace demographics, Howell (Chapter 12) examines the meaning of the concept 'generation' within contemporary health and fitness promotional culture. Drawing upon five key marketing principles that frame his analysis he clearly demonstrates how the meaning of any given 'generation' itself does not exist outside of the very cultural signs, products and practices to which it is articulated. After providing strong empirical data on past, present and future trends, Howell concludes by noting that the way in which sport, exercise, fitness and health events, texts, symbols and activities overflow into the channels of our everyday world, in all their forms and regularities, tells us a great deal about the ways in which meanings, values, and social relations therein are produced, represented and lived.

Our book concludes with Fabien Ohl's analysis that makes the link between representational aspects of advertising, 'markets' and youth consumption (Chapter 13). Drawing upon Goffman's notion of 'the presentation of self in everyday life' in conjunction with Bordieu's concept of habitus, Ohl examines how changes in the nature of our relationships with objects and people are evident in contemporary sport and lifestyle consumption. Using empirical data from France, Ohl analyses more precisely the social context, meaning and ramifications of consumption. Ohl outlines how various segments of youth in France seek to construct identities through sport clothing and related products. Notably, the focus of consumption appears to be on authenticity and difference as a means of defining identity and a form of resistance to the establishment.

Ohl is quick to note that although France serves as the site of his analysis it is important to recognize that globalization is shaping consumer markets and the meaning of commodities worldwide. To this extent France is one of many 'global locals'.

Summary

Advertising, as a privileged form of discourse, provides a cultural kaleidoscope through which we can examine social relations, the construction and confirmation of identities and the appropriation of increasingly shocking and controversial themes through which the logic and power relations of capitalism are negotiated and reproduced. *Sport, Culture and Advertising* presents a first step towards understanding the relationship between advertising and identity with a focus on sport. We have endeavoured to achieve this through a range of contextually specific analyses that highlight the way in which advertising as an industry, ideology and discourse helps us to better understand particular power relations within a consumer-based existence in late capitalism.

While it was not the main goal of this book we do hope that it contributes to some degree of media literacy about advertising. As such we hope that our project, as a form of cultural politics, makes a scholarly, pedagogical and political contribution. Hence we have followed Giroux's premise that 'cultural politics is addressed as a particular practice and way of thinking. It is derived from the relationship between texts and contexts, meaning and institutional power, critical reflection and informed action' (2000: 34). We encourage readers to use and adapt these analyses within their own national contexts for research and teaching.

There is much more work to be done in this area, and we encourage others to critique and extend this modest beginning. In particular there is a need for more ethnographic research that examines the cultural practices of advertising agencies (cf. Dewaal Malefyt and Moeran, 2003; Nixon, 2003). Likewise, there is a need for more work on how audiences read, interpret and resist advertising. We close our introduction with a quote from Graham Murdock that we believe underscores how vital it is for all of us to question the increasingly influential role of the media, and advertising in particular, to shape our identities and lived experience.

> We also need to ask who orchestrates these representations? Who is licensed to talk about other people's experience? Who is empowered to ventriloquize other people's opinions? Who is mandated to picture other people's lives? Who chooses who will be heard and who will be consigned to silence, who will be seen and who will remain invisible? Who decides which viewpoints will be taken seriously and how conflicts between positions will be resolved? Who proposes explanations and analyses and who is subject to them?
>
> (Murdock, 1999: 28)

References

Andrews, D.L. (1996). The fact(s) of Michael Jordan's blackness: Excavating a floating racial signifier. *Sociology of Sport Journal, 13* (2), 125–158.

Andrews, D.L. and Jackson, S. (2001). *Sport Stars: The Politics of Sporting Celebrity.* London: Routledge.

Appadurai, A. (1990). Disjuncture and difference in the global cultural economy. *Theory, Culture and Society, 7,* 295–310.

Arsenault, D. and Fawzy, T. (2001). Just buy it: Nike advertising aimed at Glamour readers: A critical feminist analysis. *Journal of Critical. Postmodern Organisational Science, 1* (3), 80–81.

Arundel, J. and Roche, M. (1998). Media sport and local identity: British rugby league and SKY TV. In M. Roche (ed.), *Sport, Popular Culture and Identity* (pp. 57–91). Achen: Meyer and Meyer.

Barthes, R. (1972). *Mythologies.* New York: Oxford University Press.

Baudrillard, J. (1975). *The Mirror of Production.* St Louis, MO: Telos Press.

Baudrillard, J. (1981). *For a Critique of the Political Economy of the Sign.* St Louis, MO: Telos Press.

Baudrillard, J. (1983). *Simulations.* New York: Semiotext.

Bell, D. (1976). *The Cultural Contradictions of Capitalism.* New York: Harper & Row.

Birrell, S. and McDonald, M. (2000). *Reading Sport: Critical Essays on Power and Representation.* Boston, MA: Northeastern University Press.

Blackshaw, I. (2001). Sports licensing and merchandising. *The International Sports Law Journal, 5/6,* 41–44.

Blum, A. (1991). The Marlboro Grand Prix: Circumvention of the television ban on tobacco advertising. *The New England Journal of Medicine, 324* (13), 913–917.

Bonney, B. and Wilson, H. (1990). Advertising and the manufacture of difference. In M. Alvarado and J.O. Thompson (eds), *The Media Reader* (pp. 181–198). London: BFI.

'Brand Klein: The voice of a generation' (2001). *Sunday Star Times,* 8 July, p. C13.

Brierley, S. (1998). Advertising and the new media environment. In A. Briggs and P. Cobley (eds), *The Media: An Introduction.* Harlow: Longman.

Castells, M. (1996). *The Rise of the Network Society.* Oxford: Blackwell.

Clarke, A. and Clarke, J. (1982). Highlights and action replays – ideology, sport and the media. In J. Hargreaves (ed.), *Sport, Culture and Ideology* (pp. 62–87). London: Routledge & Kegan Paul.

Cole, C. (1996). American Jordan: P.L.A.Y., consensus and punishment. *Sociology of Sport Journal, 13,* 366–397.

Cole, C. and Andrews, D.L. (1996). Look – it's NBA showtime! Visions of race in the popular imaginary. *Cultural Studies Annual, 1,* 141–181.

Cole, C. and Hribar, A. (1995). Celebrity feminism: Nike style post-fordism, transcendence, and consumer power. *Sociology of Sport Journal, 12,* 347–369.

Cook, G. (1992). *The Discourse of Advertising.* London: Routledge.

Coombe, R. (1998). *The Cultural Life of Intellectual Properties: Authorship, Appropriation and the Law.* Durham, NC: Duke University Press.

Coombe, R. (1999). Sports trademarks and somatic politics: Locating the law in a critical cultural studies. In R. Martin and T. Miller (eds), *Sportcult* (pp. 262–288). Minneapolis: UMP.

Crompton, J. (1993). Sponsorship of sport by tobacco and alcohol companies: A review of the issues. *Journal of Sport and Social Issues, 17,* 148–167.

Cronin, A. (2000). *Advertising and Consumer Citizenship: Gender, Images and Rights*. London: Routledge.

Cronin, A. (2004). *Advertising Myths: The Strange Half-Lives of Images and Commodities*. London: Routledge.

Davidson, M. (1992). *The Consumerist Manifesto: Advertising in Postmodern Times*. London: Routledge.

Davis, L.J. (1995). *Enforcing Normalcy: Disability, Deafness, and the Body*. New York: Verso.

Davis, L.J. (ed.). (1997). *The Disability Studies Reader*. New York: Routledge.

Davis, L.J. and Delano, L. (1992). Fixing the boundaries of physical gender: Side effects of anti-drug campaigns in athletics. *Sociology of Sport Journal, 9*, 1–19.

Dewaal Malefyt, T. and Moeran, B. (2003). *Advertising Cultures*. Oxford: Berg.

Dewhirst, T. and Sparks, R. (2003). Intertextual appeal of tobacco sponsorship in adolescent male culture: a selective review of tobacco industry documents. *Journal of Sport and Social Issues, 27* (4), 372–398.

du Gay, P. (ed.). (1997). *Production of Culture: Cultures of Production*. London: Sage.

du Gay, P. and Pryke, M. (2002). *Cultural Economy: Cultural Analysis and Commercial Life*. London: Sage.

Duquin, M. (1989). Fashion and fitness: Images in women's magazine advertisements. *Arena Review, 13* (2), 97–109.

Ewen, S. (1976). *Captains of Consciousness: Advertising and the Social Roots of Consumer Culture*. New York: McGraw-Hill.

Featherstone, M. (1991). *Postmodernism and Consumer Culture*. London: Sage.

Featherstone, M. (1992). The heroic life and everyday life. *Theory, Culture and Society, 9*, 159–182.

Fougere, G. (1989). Sport, culture and identity: the case of rugby football. In D. Noritz and B. Willmott (eds), *Culture and Identity in New Zealand* (pp. 110–122). Wellington: GP Books.

Fowles, J. (1996). *Advertising and Popular Culture*. Thousand Oaks, CA: Sage.

Giroux, H. (2000). *Stealing Innocence: Corporate Culture's War on Children*. New York: Palgrave.

Goddard, A. (1998). *The Language of Advertising*. London: Routledge.

Goldlust, J. (1987). *Playing for Keeps: Sport, the Media and Society* (pp. 78–112). Melbourne: Longman Cheshire.

Goldman, R. (1992). *Reading Ads Socially*. London: Routledge.

Goldman, R. and Papson, S. (1996). *Sign Wars: The Cluttered Landscape of Advertising*. London: The Guilford Press.

Goldman, R. and Papson, S. (1998). *Nike Culture: The Sign of the Swoosh*. London: Sage.

Grainger, A. and Jackson, S. (2000). Sports marketing and the challenges of globalization: A case study of cultural resistance in New Zealand. *International Journal of Sports Marketing and Sponsorship, 2* (2), 111–125.

Grossberg, L. (1997). *Dancing in Spite of Myself: Essays on Popular Culture*. Durham, NC: Duke University Press.

Gruneau, R. and Whitson, D. (1993). *Hockey Night in Canada: Sport, Identities and Cultural Politics*. Toronto: Garamond Press.

Guttmann, A. (1996). *The Erotic in Sport*. New York: Columbia University Press.

Hall, S. (1996). Introduction: Who needs identity? In S. Hall and P. du Gay (eds), *Questions of Culture and Identity* (pp. 1–17), London: Sage.

Harvey, D. (1987). Flexible accumulation through urbanisation: Reflections on 'post modernism' in the American city. *Antipode, 19* (3), 260–286.

Harvey, D. (1990). *The Condition of Postmodernity*. Oxford: Blackwell.

Harvey, J., Law, A. and Cantelon, M. (2001). North American professional team sport franchises ownership patterns and global entertainment conglomerates. *Sociology of Sport Journal, 18* (4), 435–457.

Helstein, M. (2003). That's who I want to be. *Journal of Sport and Social Issues, 27 (3),* 276–292.

Herman, E. and McChesney, R. (1997). *The Global Media: The New Missionaries of Global Capitalism*. London: Cassell.

Howell, J., Andrews, D. and Jackson, S. (2002). Cultural and sport studies: An interventionist practice. In J. Maguire and K. Young (eds), *Perspectives in the Sociology of Sport* (pp. 151–177). New York: JAI Publications.

Jackson, S.J. (1998a). A twist of race: Ben Johnson and the Canadian crisis of racial and national identity. *Sociology of Sport Journal, 15,* 21–40.

Jackson, S.J. (1998b). Life in the (mediated) Faust Lane: Ben Johnson, national affect and the 1988 crisis of Canadian identity. *International Review for the Sociology of Sport, 33* (3), 227–238.

Jackson, S.J. (2001). Global sports marketing, indigenous culture and intellectual property rights: The case of the New Zealand All Blacks Haka. *International Sports Law Journal, 7,* 10–12.

Jackson, S.J. and Andrews, D.L. (1999). Between and beyond the global and the local: American popular sporting culture in New Zealand. *International Review for the Sociology of Sport, 34* (1), 31–42.

Jackson, S.J. and Andrews, D.L. (2004). Aggressive marketing: Interrogating the use of violence in sport related advertising. In L. Kahle and C. Riley (eds), *Sports Marketing and the Psychology of Marketing Communications* (pp. 307–325). Fairfax, VA: Lawrence Erlbaum Associates.

Jackson, S.J. and Hokowhitu, B. (2002). Sport, tribes and technology: The New Zealand All Blacks *Haka* and the politics of identity, *Journal of Sport and Social Issues, 26* (1), 125–139.

Jackson, S.J., Batty, R. and Scherer, J. (2001). Transnational sport marketing at the global/local nexus: The adidasification of the New Zealand All Blacks. *International Journal of Sports Marketing and Sponsorship, 3* (2), 185–201.

Jameson, F. (1993). *Postmodernism, or, the Cultural Logics of Late Capitalism*. London: Verso.

Jhally, S. (1989). Cultural studies and the sport/media complex. In L. Wenner (ed.), *Media, Sports and Society* (pp. 70–93). Newbury Park, CA: Sage.

Jhally, S. (1990). *The Codes of Advertising: Fetishism and the Political Economy of Meaning in the Consumer Society*. London: Routledge.

Jhally, S. and Lewis, J. (1992). *Enlightened Racism: The Cosby Show, Audiences and the Myth of the American Dream*. Boulder, CO: Westview Press.

Johnson, R. (1986). What is cultural studies anyway? *Social Text, 16,* 38–80.

Kellner, D. (1995). *Media Culture: Cultural Studies, Identity and Politics Between the Modern and the Postmodern*. London: Routledge.

Key, W.B. (1972). *Subliminal Seduction: Ad Media's Manipulation of a not so Innocent America*. Englewood Cliffs, NJ: Prentice-Hall.

Key, W.B. (1989). *The Age of Manipulation*. Maryland: Madison books.

Kilbourne, J. (1999). *Can't Buy Me Love: How Advertising Changes the Way we Think and Feel*. New York: Touchstone.

Klein, N. (2000). *No Logo: Taking Aim at the Brand Bullies*. Toronto: Knopf Canada.

Lafrance, M. (1998). Colonizing the feminine: Nike's intersections of postfeminism and hyperconsumption. In G. Rail (ed.), *Sport and Postmodern Times* (pp. 117–139). Albany, NY: SUNY Press.

Lash, S. and Urry, J. (1994). *Economies of Signs and Space*. London: Sage.

Lears, J. (1994). *Fables of Abundance, A Cultural History of American Advertising*. New York: Basic books.

Ledwith, F. (1984). Does tobacco sports sponsorship on television act as advertising to children? *Health Education Journal*, *43*, 85–88.

Leiss, W., Kline, S. and Jhally, S. (1990). *Social Communication in Advertising: Persons, Products and Images of Well-being* (2nd edn). London: Routledge.

Leslie, D.A. (1995). Global scan: The globalization of advertising agencies, concepts, and campaigns. *Economic Geography*, *71*, (4), 402–425.

Lull, J. (2000). *Media, Communication and Culture: A Global Approach*. Cambridge: Polity Press.

Lury, C. (1996). *Consumer Culture*. Cambridge: Polity Press.

McKay, J. (1995). 'Just do it': Corporate sports slogans and the political economy of 'enlightened racism'. *Discourse: Studies In The Cultural Politics of Education*, *16*, 191–201.

McKelvey, S. (2003). More tales of body art and 'branding'. *Brandweek*, *44*, 13.

Maas, K. and Hasbrook, C. (2001). Media promotion of the paradigm citizen/golfer: An analysis of golf magazines' representations of disability, gender, and age. *Sociology of Sport Journal*, *18*, 21–36.

Maguire, J. (1993). Globalization, sport development, and the media-sport production complex. *Sport Science Review*, *2* (1), 29–47.

Marqusee, M. (2000). Sport as apocalypse. *Frontline*, *17* (16), 1–10.

Messner, M. (2002). *Taking the Field: Women, Men and Sports*. Minneapolis: University of Minnesota Press.

Miller, D. (1995). *Acknowledging Consumption: A Review of New Studies*. London: Routledge.

Morley, D. and Robins, K. (1995). *Spaces of Identity: Global Media, Electronic Landscapes and Cultural Boundaries*. London: Routledge.

Mort, F. (1996). *Cultures of Consumption: Masculinities and Social Space in Late Twentieth Century Britain*. London: Routledge.

Murdock, G. (1999). Corporate dynamics and broadcasting futures. In H. Mackay and T. O'Sullivan (eds), *The Media Reader: Continuity and Transformation* (pp. 28–42). London: Sage.

Nava, M. (1997). Framing advertising: Cultural analysis and the incrimination of visual texts. In M. Nava, A. Blake, I. MacRury and B. Richards (eds), *Buy This Book: Studies in Advertising and Consumption* (pp. 34–50). London: Routledge.

Nike (2003). *Admedia Fastline*, 20 February, p. 2.

Nixon, S. (1997). Circulating culture. In P. du Gay (ed.), *Production of Culture: Cultures of Production* (pp. 177–234). London: Sage.

Nixon, S. (2003). *Advertising Cultures: Gender, Commerce and Creativity*. London: Sage.

O'Barr, W. (1994). *Culture in the Ad: Exploring Otherness in the World of Advertising*. Boulder, CO: Westview Press.

Packard, V. (1960). *The Hidden Persuaders*. London: Penguin.

Perry, N. (1994). *The Dominion of Signs: Television, Advertising and Other New Zealand Fictions*. Auckland: Auckland University Press.

Perry, N. (2004). Boots, boats, and bytes: novel technologies of representation, changing media organisation, and the globalisation of New Zealand sport. In R. Horrocks and N. Perry (eds), *Television in New Zealand* (pp. 291–301). Auckland: Oxford University Press.

Renson, R. and Careel, C. (1986). Sporticuous consumption: An analysis of social status symbolism in sport ads. *International Review for the Sociology of Sport*, 21 (2/3), 153–171.

Ross, C. (1996). Global rules are proposed for measuring TV. *Advertising Age*, 12 August, p. 3.

Rothenberg, R. (1999). The advertising century. *Advertising Age*, 70 (13), 9–16.

Rowe, D. (1996). The global love-match: Sport and television. *Media, Culture and Society*, 18 (4), 565–582.

Rowe, D. (1999). *Sport, Culture and the Media*. Buckingham: Open University Press.

Schudson, M. (1993). *Advertising, the Uneasy Persuasion: Its Dubious Impact on American Society*. London: Routledge.

Sebel, J. and Gyngell, D. (1999). Protecting Olympic gold: Ambush marketing and other threats to Olympic symbols and indicia. In R. Davies (ed.), *The University of New South Wales Law Journal: Legal Issues for the Olympic Games*, 22 (3), 691–707.

Sinclair, J. (1987). *Images Incorporated: Advertising as Industry and Ideology*. London: Croom Helm.

Singer, T. (1998). Not so remote control. *Sport*, March, p. 36.

Smythe, D.W. (1977). Communications: Blindspot of Western Marxism. *Canadian Journal of Political and Social Theory*, 1, 120–127.

Sonnet, E. and Whelehan, I. (1995). 'Freedom from' or 'freedom to'. . .? Contemporary identities in women's magazines. In M. Maynard and J. Purvis (eds), *Heterosexual Politics* (pp. 81–94). London: Taylor & Francis.

Thrift, N. (1987). The urban geography of international commercial capital. In J. Henderson and M. Castells (eds), *Global Restructuring and Territorial Development* (pp. 203–233). London: Sage.

Turow, J. (1997). *Breaking Up America*. Chicago, IL: University of Chicago Press.

Twitchell, J.B. (1996). *AdCult USA: The Triumph of Advertising in American Life*. New York: Columbia University Press.

VanWynsberghe, R. and Ritchie, I. (1998). (Ir)Relevant ring: The symbolic consumption of the Olympic logo in postmodern media culture. In G. Rail (ed.), *Sport and Postmodern Times: Culture, Gender, Sexuality, the Body and Sport* (pp. 367–384). Albany, NY: The SUNY Press.

Wenner, L. (1991). One part alcohol, one part sport, one part dirt, stir gently: Beer commercials and television sports. In L.R. Van de Berg and L.A. Wenner (eds), *Television Criticism: Approaches and Applications* (pp. 388–407). New York: Longman.

Wenner, L. (1994). The dream team, communicative dirt, and the marketing of synergy: USA basketball and cross-merchandising in television commercials. *Journal of Sport and Social Issues*, 18, 27–47.

Wenner, L. (1995). The good, the bad and the ugly: Race, sport, and the public eye. *Journal of Sport and Social Issues*, 19 (3), 227–231.

Wernick, A. (1991). *Advertising, Ideology and Symbolic Expression*. London: Sage.

Whannel, G. (2002). *Media Sport Stars: Masculinities and Moralities*. London: Routledge.

White, P. and Gillett, J. (1994). Reading the muscular body: A critical decoding of advertisements in *Flex* magazine. *Sociology of Sport Journal*, 11, 18–39.

Williams, R. (1961). *The Long Revolution*. Harmondsworth: Penguin.

Williams, R. (1980). *Problems in Materialism and Culture*. London: NLB.

Williamson, J. (1978). *Decoding Advertisements: Ideology and Meaning in Advertising*. London: Marion Boyars.

Willis, S. (1993). Disney World: Public use/private space. *South Atlantic Quarterly*, 92, 119–137.

Wilson, B. and Sparks, R. (1996). 'It's gotta be the shoes': Youth, race, and sneaker commercials. *Sociology of Sport Journal*, 13 (4), 398–427.

Worsching, M. (2000). Sporting metaphors and the enactment of hegemonic masculinity: Sport and advertising in the German newsmagazine Der Spiegel. *Journal of Popular Culture*, 34 (3), 59–86.

1 Model behavior?

Sporting feminism and consumer culture

Mary G. McDonald

In exploring the links between advertising and sport, it is impossible to overlook the significance of magazines. Sporting and fitness magazines serve as vehicles for advertisers' messages just as the magazines attempt to construct and deliver demographic segments of the sports/fitness market to advertisers. As many critics have argued, what is actually being created is a highly idealized vision of a reading and consuming audience that is then sold to advertisers. In recent years new sporting and fitness magazines have been developed as publishing conglomerates, and advertisers seek to create and expand a "women's market." Notable among recently constructed sporting and fitness magazines is a venture by the publishing conglomerate Condé Nast, whose other titles include *Mademoiselle*, *Vogue*, *Brides*, *Glamour*, *SELF*, and *Brides* magazines. Executive editor Mary Murray makes clear the economic and cultural logics behind this new venture: "Condé Nast magazines are lifestyle magazines. With the rise of women's sports and fitness, it only seems natural for Condé Nast to appeal to that lifestyle as well" (cited in Vargas, 1999: D7).

With an emphasis on leisure, sport and recreational pursuits, *Condé Nast Sports for Women* launched as a monthly in October 1997 with a circulation rate base of 350,000. Early in 1998, Condé Nast acquired *Women's Sports and Fitness*, a magazine that traces its roots back to 1974 when it was founded by tennis star Billie Jean King. Under King's leadership the early content of the magazine (then called *Women's Sport*) offered advice on how to challenge the lack of organized competitive sport opportunities available to women. In its early years the magazine featured images of women as serious and competent athletes. According to Barb Endel (1991: 130), throughout the 1980s and into the 1990s the magazine gradually shifted focus from sport as a "political activity to personal improvement."

In June 1998, Condé Nast began publishing every other month under the acquired name, *Women's Sports and Fitness* (Kerwin, 1999). Editor Lucy Danziger makes it clear that whatever the title, Condé Nast owns "a sports magazine, but it isn't just a place where the superjocks can find a home. It's open to all players – more akin to a club sport than a varsity program" (Danziger, 1997b: 24). Furthermore, the content includes information for women to learn about "fashion, training, nutrition, health, beauty, travel, profiles – all of that" (Danziger, cited in Lockwood, 1997: 16).

By January 1999, *Women's Sports and Fitness* (throughout the remainder of this paper I use the abbreviation WSF to signify both *Condé Nast Sports for Women* and *Women's Sports and Fitness*) had reached an average circulation of over 500,000 and in October 1999 began guaranteeing a circulation of 650,000 to advertisers (Advertising, 1999). And while WSF is no longer being published, Condé Nast's entry and exit into the domain of women's sport reveals much about the shifting logics of the publishing industry and the never-ending capitalist quest to accumulate profits – in this case by creating a new commodity – an imagined audience of specific demographic characteristics of middle-class women to sell to advertisers. In an attempt to expand this base of idealized consumers in an increasingly saturated sport/fitness market, new desires were thus linked to sporting, recreational and fitness pursuits. These desires were clearly centered on culturally idealized bodies as page after page of WSF is filled with female bodies – young, fit and toned – at the center of the action. Accompanying written texts offer a "new type of attitude" (Danziger, 1997a: 28) in championing fitness and outdoor pursuits in ways that also signify the need to achieve a healthy, sexy and/or glorified consumer lifestyle. Complementing this focus on culturally idealized bodies is a consumer culture paradise complete with images and stories about competent, inspirational women engaging in outdoor adventures and sporting adventure placed alongside advertisements for equipment necessary for similar outdoor and sporting pursuits. Indeed, according to published reports in the first year of operation footwear and athletic wear made up about 20 to 25 percent of the magazine's advertising, with automotive advertising garnering 25 percent. Fashion accounted for between 20 and 25 percent of the advertisements with beauty, food, bottled waters and beverages accounting for the rest (Lockwood, 1997).

In many ways, WSF represents a hybrid media form that combines the content and conventions of glamor and women's magazines with the content and conventions of traditional male-dominated sport and fitness magazines. This concept of hybrid form moves us away from the notion that "women's" sporting magazines focus exclusively on glamor and sexuality while "men's" magazines such as *Sports Illustrated* (whose subscription base is 80 percent male) focus on sport for sport's sake. To the contrary, Laurel Davis' (1997) analysis of the annual *SI* swimsuit issue suggests that the magazine is not really about men's sport as is popularly believed; rather, it is a celebration of a hegemonic masculine lifestyle grounded in heterosexuality via the commodification of (hetero)sexy female bodies (see also Birrell and Theberge, 1994). This conceptualization suggests that there is considerable overlapping content between and among the genres of men's sport and fitness magazines, and women's sport and fitness magazines as well as among women's fashion and glamour magazines.[1]

Yet WSF has also followed a recent trend used by women's glamour magazines in linking concepts such as freedom, autonomy and liberation to the promotion of particular active lifestyles and lifestyle products in order to secure profits. Indeed, within the pages of WSF are repeated suggestions by writers and advertisers that contemporary times allow women to "do anything they please"

(Danziger, 1997a: 28). Women apparently now have the capability to make innumerable choices, to experience success in the workplace and personal fulfillment via numerous leisure or sporting pursuits. In promoting this perspective advertisers and editors of WSF have seized upon and recuperated some of the goals advocated by second-wave feminism. This co-option of feminist ideals in order to sell products is suggestive of the ways magazines promote post-feminist ideologies.

In advocating post-feminist ideologies writers and advertisers infer that feminist activism and feminist movements are no longer necessary. Rather in the pages of magazines like WSF, post-feminist ideologies celebrate women as "nearly there" or having already achieved equality with freedom cast as tantamount to being both sexy and powerful. This perspective especially encourages women to distance themselves from the presumably dour and now out-of-date uniformity of second-wave feminism, and to take pleasure in their bodies and their newly found ability to achieve self-determination (Sonnet and Whelehan, 1995). The result of this advocacy of post-feminist perspectives is a complicated ensemble of texts full of tensions, contradictions and disruptions. Yet, underlying these contradictory images and ideas is a depoliticized process in that post-feminist ideologies represent second-wave feminist social goals as individual lifestyle and bodily choices devoid of historical, cultural or critical contexts (Cole and Hribar, 1995). Esther Sonnet and Imelda Whelehan (1995: 82) are particularly troubled by the version of post-feminism promoted in women's glossy magazines where "the discourse of feminism is turned against itself and mobilized to often antifeminist ends, so that the oft-used terms associated with feminism – such as 'liberation' – are hijacked for quite other purposes" (Sonnet and Whelehan, 1995: 82). Placed within the long history of the American cult of individualism through which consumer capitalism thrives, this post-feminist perspective strips feminism of its origins as a "critique of unequal social, economic and political relations" (Goldman, 1992: 132).

In this chapter I explore *WSF* magazines as culturally significant discursive sites where post-feminist ideologies are represented and struggled over. This exploration into WSF thus offers cultural criticism as a strategy of intervention into the contemporary power relations and social meanings offered for consumption. Critical analysis of WSF reveals a complex interplay of post-feminist discourses about athleticism, gender and sexuality. Still, dominant narratives continue to privilege heterosexuality as the unquestioned norm, a framing long associated with sporting representations and the homophobic world of sport.

Women's magazines, post-feminist inspiration and perspiration

Angela McRobbie (1996; 1997) notes that scholars' engagement with women's magazines has undergone considerable change throughout a variety of stages. Because each of these stages contains considerable overlapping issues and themes, they are best conceived of as dominant ideal types that reflect several shifting frameworks of feminist thought and paradigmatic struggles. According to McRobbie, the first stage of women's magazine criticism is known as the "angry repudiation" stage in which feminists condemned and challenged objectified images of women in the mass media. The goal of this stage was to prevent women from buying magazines and thus liberate them from the most oppressive forms of the patriarchal consumer culture. According to McRobbie, a much more scholarly focus can be identified in the second stage of feminist media analysis, one that drew heavily on Althusser's theory of ideology. This conceptualization noted how all women were interpolated and thus implicated in a complex web of ideological domination. Magazines played a key role in this process, offering subjectivities and definitions of what it means to be a woman in contemporary patriarchal societies. The third stage of analysis was greatly influenced by feminist psychoanalysis and offered theories of female pleasure. This focus on pleasure noted the contradictory effects of women's engagement with patriarchal desires. The pleasure of reading magazines offered women an escape from the oppressive conditions of their daily lives even though these pleasures are based upon ideals often not in women's and/or feminists' best interests. McRobbie notes that there is also a recent scholarly trend in focusing attention on the way readers of women's magazines make sense of the "feminine" images offered for consumption.

Influenced by poststructuralists' insights that explore historically specific relationships between forms of knowledge and the exercise of power, some feminist critics have recently abandoned attempts to determine whether the texts of women's magazines reflect authentic or accurate images of women. Rather these critics explore the ways in which magazine texts assert particular knowledge claims while obscuring the legitimacy of others. Following this school of thought, several scholars have criticized women's magazines for depoliticizing and rearticulating second-wave feminist claims to produce post-feminist knowledges, identities and practices (see Sonnet and Whelehan, 1995). Scholarly criticism has sought to "repoliticize the depoliticized bringing back into the picture, the social and economic relations that are absent" in magazine articles and advertisements related to post-feminism (Goldman *et al.*, 1991: 333).

Post-feminism is not synonymous with the absence of feminism, but rather refers to the growing number of women who now take for granted some of the goals and achievements of the 1970's feminist movement while shunning the label of feminist (Goldman *et al.*, 1991). Furthermore, according to Judith Stacey (1987: 8), post-feminism represents a muted vision through the "simultaneous incorporation, revision and depoliticization of many of the central goals of second-wave feminism." Thus while signifiers of progress, inclusion and equality now circulate freely within popular culture they do so at the expense of feminism's most revolutionary ideas. Whereas second-wave feminism served as a social movement to challenge the structural barriers and belief systems that served to oppress women, post-feminism advocates the status quo through a "seize the power" mindset (Dow, 1996). In proclaiming that women can "have it all," attention is thus shifted away from feminisms' most radical tenants including criticism directed toward sexist practices and ideologies linked to gender, sexuality, race, class and national privileges. Contrary to political feminist critiques of contemporary culture, examples of popular post-feminist mandates are laced throughout United States television programs (e.g. *Roseanne*, *Designing Women* and *Murphy Brown*), Nike advertisements (especially the "Dialogue" and "Empathy" campaigns which ask women to "just do it"), professional sport such as the Women's National Basketball Association, books (including Naomi Wolf's *Promiscuities* and Elizabeth Wurtzel's *Bitch: In Praise of Difficult Women*) as well as via international Western celebrities such as Madonna, the Spice Girls, Oprah Winfrey and Jane Fonda (Cole and Hribar, 1995; Dow, 1996).

According to Cheryl Cole and Amy Hribar (1995), it is impossible to understand the proliferation of post-feminist ideologies without understanding the ways feminism has been reformulated through the most recent backlash against second-wave feminist activism. Indeed, beginning in the 1980s and continuing until today, the Conservative New Right has promoted rhetoric and policies to recast structural and social problems as merely matters of personal lifestyle choices. Thus problems created and elevated by late industrial capitalism, globalization and persistent inequities related to gender, race, class, sexuality are blamed on the inadequacy of particular groups including feminists, gays and lesbians, and the poor. These groups continue to be demonized for members' alleged inability to make moral choices and to instead embody selfish, destructive stances that ultimately result in anti-family values, inner city crime and welfare dependency. In contrast to these "soft bodies," the 1980s and 1990s have witnessed the celebration of hard bodies, those seemingly able to achieve success and happiness through the force of individual will, self-responsibility, personal perseverance and "appropriate" lifestyle choices. With this uncritical advocacy of rugged individualism, the feminist movement is repositioned as troubled, destructive and unnecessary in ways that patriarchy, the gendered division of labor and the New Right are not (Cole and Hribar, 1995; Sonnet and Whelehan, 1995).

By the 1980s advertisers and women's magazines were already well under way in attempting to domesticate the most radical critiques of second-wave feminism. Crucial to this co-optation of feminism is the promotion of an idealized newly liberated woman as self-accepting and successful. Through an appeal to a series of attitudes and visual styles centered on the liberated woman, women's magazines are filled with story-lines and commodities made to stand as equivalent to second-wave goals of independence and freedom (Goldman *et al.*, 1991). In ignoring larger social and cultural contexts that continue to impact upon women's lives, WSF advertisers also promote the New Right's heightened concern with rugged individualism. This framing is clearly evident in every issue of the magazine including an early issue announcing the 1997 Sportswomen of the Year awards. Honorees including surfing champion Lisa Andersen, professional basketball player Nikki McCray, tennis star Martina Hingis, sprinter Marion Jones, wrestler Kristin Stenglein, figure skater Tara Lipinski, mountain biker Missy Giove, and basketball coach Pat Summitt, are all lauded as inspirational embodiments of the American Dream. Despite engaging in different sports, each is praised for her resolve "to achieve their personal best, to redefine what that is, to stay with the program no matter what the obstacles" (Danziger, 1998a: 14).Women athletes are represented as "fearless, accomplished, competitive, alive ... They inspire us, push us to do better in our own pedestrian activities even shame us into action on days we'd normally sit it out" (Danziger, 1998c: 22).

There is a plethora of stories and advertisements connecting female aspirations and success in a variety of workplace, sporting and leisure settings with emotionally charged language and images. Importantly, in an effort to add value and in an attempt to increase profits, this marketing strategy positions Condé Nast and its commercial sponsors as socially concerned advocates for inspirational and empowering visions of women and girls (see also Cole and Hribar, 1995). A State Farm advertisement from Condé Nast composed of a black and white photo outlined by yellow roses is an excellent case in point. The ad features a young figure skater and nostalgic copy linking the youthful athlete's movements with freedom and sheer delight. Here, readers don't learn anything about State Farm insurance policies, but are instead assured that State Farm is a socially responsible, caring corporation that backs women's sport.

> It was there in those first tentative steps that sent her gliding across the ice. And it grew with every lesson and every hour of practice she's taken ever since. It's there in every spiral – every axel and salchow. Joy. Simple intoxicating joy. The same joy that once sent her wobbling across a small frozen pond in Minnesota. State Farm is a proud supporter of women's sports and women's dreams. Little girls have big dreams too.
>
> (Danziger, L., 1998b)

With other advertisers and Condé Nast, State Farm has seized on advocacy rhetoric to market an image as pro-women (Cole and Hribar, 1995).

Discourses of bodily freedom, persistence, and incredible achievement are woven throughout each issue of WSF in other written texts and advertising accounts. These representations reinforce the post-feminist mantra that women have made it, or at the very least things are getting better all the time, for women now enjoy increased opportunities to achieve success in a variety of sporting and fitness endeavors with very little cultural constraint. The September/October 1999 issue provides an excellent site to explore these types of representations. One story lauds the inclusion of the newest Olympic sports such as women's water polo, tae kwon do, pole vault, trampoline, modern pentathlon, triathlon, hammer throw, and weight-lifting. There is also an excerpt from model Christy Turlington's diary detailing her seven-day, 18,500-foot trek to the summit of Mount Kilimanjaro. Her story is narrated as a tale of challenge, personal initiative and perseverance as she and her climbing group overcome problems related to fatigue, weather and altitude. Photo after photo features Turlington climbing, resting and frolicking on the mountainside, yet always dressed in stylish and weather-appropriate climbing apparel. Upon reaching the summit, her goal achieved, Turlington pauses to take a photo of a sign that states "You are now at the Uhuru Peak, the highest point in Africa" (Markus, 1999: 95).

Advertisements in the same issue promote similar themes. For example, Subaru provides a special advertising section for Subaru Outback cars, or "an active women's guide to the great outdoors" (Markus, 1999: 95) that encourages readers to experience freedom, to "take it outback" (Markus, 1999: 95). There is also a six-page WSF fashion spread with active outdoorsy women (and a few men) engaging in active pursuits dressed for success in the latest version of stylish wear brought to you by such companies as Sport Ralph Lauren, Clarks shoes and Wigwam socks. An REI outdoor gear and clothing advertisement features a female rock climber straining as she scales a rock near the headline: "This is no place for doubts. Test your limits. Trust your gear." Here WSF and its advertisers present women as consumers "of objects: objects that symbolize the worth of emancipated women" (Goldman et al., 1991: 340).

As Sonnet and Whelehan (1995) observe, this post-feminist promotional rhetoric of individual achievement and inspirational female success coupled with an idealized consumerist lifestyle means that there is an elusion of harder material realities foregrounded by second-wave feminists including issues of sexual harassment, domestic violence, the sexual division of labor and poverty. Unlike other women's magazines where these and other issues championed by second-wave feminists are at least acknowledged in true-life stories and self-help columns, they rarely appear in the pages of WSF. One exception is the continuing attention paid to women's health issues, especially campaigns alerting women about breast cancer awareness.

The May/June 1999 issues of WSF offer a special advertising section and according to the ad's copy this "important health message is brought to you through the caring and generosity of Ford Division" (Daum, 1998). The advertisement for Ford motor company provides statistical information suggesting that one in eight women in the U.S.A. will develop breast cancer. The section also features a round-table discussion with the female celebrities of the television program *The Practice*. Actresses Lara Flynn Boyle, Lisa Gay Hamilton, Camryn Manheim, Marla Sokoloff and Kelli Williams and an unnamed moderator represent "healthy women from different backgrounds and age groups" (Daum, 1998) sharing opinions about breast cancer "in hopes of initiating a national dialogue among women." Ford's advocacy around this issue supports the efforts of the Susan G. Komen Breast Cancer Foundation in focusing on biomedical research, early detection and treatment. This advocacy encourages women to develop healthy, hard bodies to reduce their risk by maintaining an active lifestyle combined with a low-fat diet and regularly obtaining mammograms after the age of 40. Yet, in contrast to activists who continue to criticize corporations for producing environmental carcinogens and toxins that compromise health, this framing by Ford, WSF, and other commercial sponsors casts an uncritical gaze solely toward medical and research solutions (see Klawiter, 1999). Furthermore this stance remakes the post-feminist focus on individual responsibility in encouraging women to discipline their bodies through fitness and nutritional regiments presumably in an effort to defeat cancer. In encouraging women to provide personal initiative in gaining a healthy lifestyle, these accounts also promote a sense of progress in suggesting that medical science and knowledge about the disease are getting better all the time. Multinational and other corporations that continue to pollute the air and water are let off the hook, as larger environmental causes are not discussed in the pages of WSF and other mainstream accounts (Lafrance, 1998).

One Ford advertisement features a letter from a daughter lauding her mother for being her very own "breast cancer survivor hero." While making visible a stigmatized identity of a breast cancer survivor, this narrative is also consistent with other WSF content offering enticing portraits of inspirational individual women. Overall these representations related to breast cancer do ideological work in creating an idealized liberated consumer while ignoring the deep divisions that exist among and between men and women related to gender, race, class and sexuality. This is an incredibly meaningful absence when related to women's health. For example, Mélisse Lafrance (1998) has demonstrated how post-feminist rhetoric about individual responsibility suggests that all women are equally at risk. Yet poor women are more likely to live in neighborhoods infected with industrial pollutants while Women of Color are less likely to receive early and adequate care in regard to breast cancer. Instead of exploring the hierarchies that exist among women in health care, post-feminist ideologies collude with capitalistic forces. This individualistic framing also remakes the New Right's obsession with hard bodies and promotes the inference that if women don't take personal responsibility, they only have themselves or their inadequate lifestyles to blame (Cole and Hribar, 1995; Lafrance, 1998; Sonnet and Whelehan, 1995).

Playing with gender

The emphasis on the promotion of the liberated woman offers numerous cases where traditional gender expectations are reformulated. First, WSF and its sponsors have at times "turned the tables" and made men the objects of keen scrutiny, a status that women historically have disproportionately been made to endure. For example, a Jockey underwear advertisement features male doctors, surgeons and physical therapists from Los Angles County dropping their pants to reveal their various styles of colorful Jockey underwear. Another story recalls the experiences of professional hockey player Luc Robitaille at Miraval spa in Tucson, Arizona. The text emphasizes Robitaille's apprehensions at being massaged by female attendants: "Oh my God," Robitaille says as the door closes on him and four female attendants. 'What are you going to do to me?'" (Jenkins, 1998: 102). And unlike previous heterosexual romance narratives where women wait for men to save them from impossible situations, personal stories in WSF offer much more agency to women. One such account is "Some like it cold" in which author Pam Houston (1998) leads her boyfriend and hiking novice David on an overnight camping adventure in the Utah desert.

Many representations of women provide activity settings historically defined as male territory. One story about the sport of motocross notes that it is "rough, dirty and dangerous. No wonder some women can't get enough of it" (Dunn, 1999: 131). Another story on extreme sport appears with a photographic image of fourteen extreme sport athletes taken by famed photographer Annie Leibovitz as a headline asks, "Why would otherwise sane women court danger for a living?" (Karbo, 1999: 103). The narrative continues to answer this question by lauding the expressive sport of street luge, hang-gliding, snow-boarding, and wind surfing among other extreme sports. Tales of friends and relatives who met their deaths pursuing the risky elements of these sports help to emphasize the danger extreme athletes face.

In featuring women in daring and non-traditional sports WSF actively promotes itself as pro-women, as the antithesis of unrealistic, unobtainable images traditionally championed by the fashion industry. In doing so WSF editors and writers have followed the lead of Nike in advocating for sport and physical activity as providing sites for responsible, freeing and presumably "authentic" images of everyday women engaged in physical activity, as Cole and Hribar's (1995) analysis demonstrates. Within the pages of WSF magazine authenticity means that women are represented as achievers and adventurers, not as "stereotypical vacuous fashion models" (Goldman et al., 1991: 346). Furthermore, while attractive, toned women grace the magazine pages this achievement-minded editorial position distances the magazine from other magazines that promote unobtainable images of women. According to editor Danziger, WSF:

> is not selling insecurities. We're selling the accomplishments and confidence that an active life brings. In that sense, I don't think we're attached to a direct genealogy of women's magazines. We're looking at our bodies as useful, fun vehicles that can do new things and take us new places.
>
> (Danziger, cited in Way, 1998: 22)

That bodies are conceived of as vehicles to empowering experiences and enjoyable places is most readily apparent in the magazine's focus on exciting travel locales that cater to all sorts of carnal pleasures. "Diving handbook" offers a guide to snorkel and scuba vacations or "ingredients for the perfect winter trip: beaches, steamy weather and fish" (Glock, 1999: 109). The article goes on to detail "seven of the world's top diving and snorkeling sports that also offer great above-water activities" including Walker's Cay, Bahamas and Playa del Carmen, Mexico (Jermanok, 1999: 110). Another exposé combines the daring gender-bending dangers of extreme sport with the picturesque setting of New Zealand, "the adventure capital of the world" (Daum, 1998: 89). The accompanying "thrill seeker's guide to New Zealand" provides all sorts of exciting adventures and physical challenges including sea kayaking on Tasman Bay, horseback riding in Hokianga Hills, and mountain climbing on Mount Cook. But as Cole and Hribar (1995) suggest much as do Nike, here empowerment is narrowly and mistakenly cast as something that can be achieved only by working out the body and through the consumption of lifestyle products and/or travel experiences. Thus in narrating physical activity and travel to fascinating locales as a form of empowerment, Nike and WSF, much like the New Right, promote post-feminist identities that seemingly transcend the weight of history and cultural constraint.

Yet beneath this aura of bodily transcendence are historical conditions and circumstances that continue to impact upon the life chances of women from diverse backgrounds. WSF's post-feminism continues to construct a false sense that women belong to the same group based upon a shared sense of sisterhood, thus suggesting that social class and race are irrelevant to the liberated woman. And yet the glorified distant locales with exciting adventures are of course economically unobtainable for the vast majority of people across the globe. Furthermore, the liberated woman imagined by WSF, as is the case in the majority of mainstream magazines, "is an exclusionary construction: the femininity of women's magazines has been, and remains an identity of white, heterosexual women who are primarily valued for youth" (Currie, 1999: 38).

(Hetero)sexuality and the post-feminist woman

WSF uses *double entendres* that seemingly and playfully make references to sexuality and various levels of sexual performance. For example, "Happy hookers" is actually a story about fishing; "The virgins" talks about the entrance of women's ice hockey into the Olympics for the first time in 1998; "Are you getting enough" deals with the need for exercise. In "Saved: How a sports virgin met Mr. Right and started playing around" (Bolen, 1998) the author's boyfriend tries to ascertain her interest in sport by provocatively asking "What do you do below the neck?" WSF offers references to (hetero)sexuality interwoven throughout stories on celebrities, recreational pursuits and sport. Volleyball star and model Gabrielle Reece has a recurring column where she muses about numerous issues but often discusses her relationship with husband and renowned surfer Laird Hamilton. In one column, "Playing doubles," Reece (1999: 91) argues for the (presumed) naturalness of heterosexuality by proclaiming that "Every Jill has her Jack. Or every Jane her Tarzan." A short piece on heart rate monitors is paired with a picture of a semi-clothed woman and man engaging in passionate sex. Accompanying this text and image are a list of daytime activities with the projected heart rates one might expect from engaging in these activities. Standard week-night sex presumably elevates the heart rate to 90 beats per minute while gossip about a colleague's bad haircut in the ladies' room scores an 87 (The telltale heart, 1997). Another story in the pages of *CN Sports for Women* proclaims that "hard work intensifies sensations. Skinny-dipping in mountain lakes after a long day makes sex seem overrated"

(p. 74). "Play date" chronicles Rachelle Unreich's (1997) date with Baywatch star Michael Bergin and the cut line under the headline promises that "there is grunting. There is groaning. The word love comes up a lot. And this is just the first date. Rachelle Unreich works up a not-so-serious sweat with Baywatch stud Michael Bergin" (Unreich, 1997: 67). The article begins: "My body: hot and sweaty. My attire: next to nothing and that was before I shed my hair scrunchy" (Unreich, 1997: 67). One headline even goes so far as to ask if tennis star Anna Kournikova is "too sexy for her game?" (Coleman, 1998).

There is often a lightness of tone and sense of irony in these renditions of sex and sexual performance. This can be partly understood as a self-conscious attempt on the part of the writers to create feelings of intimacy and friendliness with the readers (McRobbie, 1997). Part of the overall emphasis on sex may also be attributed to the age-old adage that proclaims "sex sells." Yet this adage is inadequate in explaining the contemporary social relations linked to sexuality that support these particular discussions and representations. Angela McRobbie (1997) notes that in the 1990s young girls and women's magazines have broken with a traditional overreliance on romance narratives in favor of (often explicit) discussions concerning sexual foreplay, condom use and sexual pleasure. The result is images and texts of "new sexualities." These "new sexualities" represent lustful women and girls speaking more frankly and sometimes ironically about their own sexual desires and explicit sexual topics once considered taboo for mainstream media consumption. The feminist movement of the 1970s politicized sexuality, arguing for all women to claim sexual pleasure as a crucial right of womanhood. New cultural norms and possibilities around (especially) heterosexuality are continuing to be articulated, some of which suggest that women can obtain sexual enjoyment without the baggage of compulsory childbirth or excessive domestic chores (Weeks, 1989). The extent to which a majority of women enjoy these sexual freedoms and freedom from domestic duty is of course subject to considerable debate.

Despite notable contradictions and exceptions, what is most apparent is the ways in which publications like WSF magazines reinforce post-feminist claims of the "rightness" of monogamous heterosexuality in discussions of female sexuality (Sonnet and Whelehan, 1995). What counts as women within these pages are conventional heterosexual women, and WSF accounts overwhelmingly privilege heterosexuality as the unquestioned norm. This is not to say that lesbians are never acknowledged, since two articles detailing the lives of tennis stars Billie Jean King (Taylor Fleming, 1998) and Amelie Mauresmo (De St. Jorre, 1999) clearly demonstrate that there is lesbian representation within WSF. Yet there are carefully marked boundaries of permissible sexualities within the pages of these and other mainstream magazines as lesbians largely remain connected to liberal discussions about tolerance. There is little acknowledgment of the ways lesbians create legitimate terrains of sexual desire.

Too sexy for her game?

Within the pages of WSF the feminist goals of sexual freedom and self-definition are contradictorily represented and most often linked to the promotion of
self-acceptance and the need for women to hone their bodies to be fit and
active. Furthermore, these notions are imbedded in discourses promoting
beauty, travel and exercise products that draw attention away from social relations to the attitudes and bodily styles of individual women. Furthermore, in
personal stories and many advertisements post-feminist discourses encourage
the rearticulation of personal strength as a means to attain heterosexual attractiveness (Goldman *et al.*, 1991). Or in the words of athlete/model/WSF columnist Gabrielle Reece (1997: 78), "Curves of power are sexy. A little pop of
muscle under a skirt is hot." She continues that it is "also about personality
strength. When we are physically strong we feel more capable and assertive. A
woman who owns her space, who knows who she is and what she can do, is
truly sexy." This is an especially powerful undertone in sport magazines given
the homophobia that underlies competitive women's sport. There is a long
history in which female athletes have been represented in the media in ways
that suggest (hetero)sexual appeal and allure. This represents a defensive
response to the presence of lesbians in sports and a way to recapture the radical
challenge of muscular and aggressive women who dare to transgress patriarchal
notions of appropriate gender behavior (Birrell and Theberge, 1994). WSF promotes post-feminist possibilities by featuring images and narratives of presumably heterosexual, toned and honed female bodies that in turn represent the
iconic new age feminine body. This is a body that has especially gained much
currency among models and celebrities as well as high-profile athletes. Editor
Lucy Danziger (1998b: 12) celebrates this trend, noting that *Terminator 2* movie
actress Linda Hamilton "did more for making muscles sexy than most
Olympians have."

These narratives articulated by Reece and Danziger support Goldman's
(1992) argument that within the pages of women's magazines commodified
images of post-feminism encourage a state in which "meanings of choice and
individual freedom become wed to images of" (hetero)sexuality:

> in which women apparently choose to be seen as sexual objects because it
> suits their liberated interests. The female body gets reframed as the locus of
> freedom as well as sexual pleasure. . . . The commercial marriage of femin-
> ism and femininity plays off a conception of personal freedom located in
> the visual construction of self-appearance. Body and sexuality emerge as
> coincidental signs: the body is something you do to validate yourself as an
> autonomous being capable of will-power and discipline; and sexuality
> appears as something women exercise by choice rather than because of
> their ascribed gender role. The properly shaped female body is taken as
> evidence of achievement and self-worth.
>
> (Goldman, 1992: 135)

Final thoughts

This analysis reveals that cultural forms like magazines are linked to a variety of ideological forces and social practices that in turn create multiple, often contradictory meanings. Yet in the case of post-feminist practices, the very radical goals of feminism "may take on a plurality of faces, but its potentially alternative ideological force is channeled into the commodity form so that it threatens neither patriarchal culture nor capitalist hegemony" (Goldman, 1992: 131). As this analysis has demonstrated, many of the radical goals of second-wave feminism have been rearticulated within the pages of WSF and the wider commodity culture in ways that reduce feminist politics to the status of individual lifestyle choices (Cole and Hribar, 1995). Furthermore, WSF magazine also serves to "reassure women that the dominant ideological life-choices offered by society at large (heterosexual monogamy, pro-capitalist democracy, aspirational individualism, a high value placed on physical beauty, familial norms, etc.) are indeed" the (New) right ones (Sonnet and Whelehan, 1995: 84). Still, cultural processes are fluid, suggesting that there is no guarantee that these visions will remain eternally inscribed within the pages of women's magazines and popular culture. Yet, in contrast to advertisements that mute radical feminist contentions in this contemporary moment, this paper has offered cultural criticism as a strategy to make visible and thus challenge the post-feminist discourses of commodity culture. Such a strategy allows us to construct alternative knowledges to provide an important engagement with the process of political contestation and struggle.

References

Advertising: Young Condé Nast title develops muscle (1999). *The Wall Street Journal*, 23 September, B4.

Birrell, S. and Theberge, N. (1994). Ideological control of women in sport. In M. Costa and S. Guthrie (eds), *Women and Sport: Interdisciplinary Perspectives* (pp. 341–360). Champaign: Human Kinetics.

Bolen, E. (1998). Saved: How a sports virgin met Mr. Right and started playing around. *Condé Nast Sports for Women*, May, 58–65.

Cole, C. and Hribar, A. (1995). Celebrity feminism: Nike style: Post-Fordism, transcendence, and consumer power. *Sociology of Sport Journal*, 12, 347–369.

Coleman, C. (1998). Too sexy for her game? *Condé Nast Sports for Women*, June, 98–101.

Currie, D. (1999). *Girl Talk: Adolescent Magazines and their Readers*. Toronto: University of Toronto.

Danziger, L. (1997a). Start here. *Condé Nast Sports for Women*, October, 28.

Danziger, L. (1997b). Who are we? *Condé Nast Sports for Women*, November, 24.

Danziger, L. (1998a). Happy new year. *Condé Nast Sports for Women*, January, 14.

Danziger, L. (1998b). March on. *Condé Nast Sports for Women*, March, 12.

Danziger, L. (1998c). Star power. *Women's Sport and Fitness*, September/October, 22.

Daum, M. (1998). Adventure 101: Kiwi style. *Women's Sports and Fitness*, May, 86–90, 140.

Davis, L. (1997). *The Swimsuit Issue and Sport: Hegemonic Masculinity in Sports Illustrated.* Albany, NY: SUNY Press.

De St. Jorre, J. (1999). Out in the open. *Women's Sports and Fitness,* September/October, 114–117, 160, 161.

Dow, B. (1996). *Prime-time Feminism: Television, Media Culture and the Women's Movement since 1970.* Philadelphia: University of Pennsylvania Press.

Dunn, C. (1999). Mad about motocross. *Women's Sports and Fitness,* September/October, 130–135, 162.

Endel, B. (1991). *Working Out: The Dialectic of Strength and Sexuality in Women's Sports and Fitness Magazine.* Unpublished doctoral dissertation, University of Iowa, Iowa City.

Glock, A. (1999). Diving handbook. *Women's Sports and Fitness,* January/February, 109.

Goldman, R. (1992). *Reading Ads Socially.* London: Routledge.

Goldman, R., Health, D. and Smith, S. (1991). Commodity feminism. *Critical Studies In Mass Communication,* 8, 333–351.

Houston, P. (1998). Some like it cold. *Condé Nast Sports for Women,* March, 98–103, 129.

Jenkins, S. (1998). Spa cadet. *Condé Nast Sports for Women,* January, 100–105.

Jenkins, S. (1999). Martina's love match. *Women's Sports and Fitness,* September/October, 86–89.

Jermanok, S. (1999). Fantasy islands. *Women's Sports and Fitness,* January/February, 110–112.

Karbo, K. (1999). The extremists. *Women's Sports and Fitness,* January/February, 102–107, 117.

Kerwin, A.M. (1999). Condé Nast title gives circulation bonus. *Advertising Age,* 70 (25), 20.

Klawiter, M. (1999). Racing for the cure, walking women, and toxic touring: Mapping cultures of action within the Bay Area terrain of breast cancer. *Social Problems,* 46 (1), 104–126.

Lafrance, M. (1998). Colonizing the feminine: Nike's intersections of postfeminism and hyperconsumption. In G. Rail (ed.), *Sport and postmodern times* (pp. 117–139). Albany, NY: SUNY Press.

Lockwood, L. (1997). Food for female jocks; Condé Nast Publications Inc. and Time Inc. to launch women's sports magazines. January 24, 1997. *Information Access Company,* 16 (173), 16.

McRobbie, A. (1996). More! New sexualities in girls' and women's magazines. In A. McRobbie (ed.), *Back to Reality? Social Experience and Cultural Studies* (pp. 190–209). Manchester: Manchester University Press.

McRobbie, A. (1997). More! New sexualities in girls' and women's magazines. In A. McRobbie (ed.), *Cultural Studies and Communication: Social Experience and Cultural Studies.* Manchester: Manchester University Press.

Markus, K. (1999). Kili or bust! *Women's Sports and Fitness,* September/October, 91–95.

Reece, G. (1997). Grace in your face. *Condé Nast Sports for Women,* December, 78.

Reece, G. (1999). Playing doubles. *Women's Sports and Fitness,* November/December, 91.

Sonnet, E. and Whelehan, I. (1995). "Freedom from" or "freedom to"...? Contemporary identities in women's magazines. In M. Maynard and J. Purvis, (eds), *Heterosexual Politics* (pp. 81–94). London: Taylor & Francis.

Stacey, J. (1987). Sexism by a subtler name? *Socialist Review,* 96, 7–28.

Taylor Fleming, A. (1998). The battles of Billie Jean King. *Women's Sports and Fitness*, September/October, 130–134, 168, 171.

The telltale heart (1997). *Condé Nast Sports for Women*, November, 50.

Unreich, R. (1997). Play date. *Condé Nast Sports for Women*, November, 67–68.

Vargas, N. (1999). Magazine wars: Women's sports publications battle for uncharted territory. *The San Diego Union-Tribune*, 9 June, D7.

Way, D. (1998). Writing for the new women's magazines. *Writer's Digest*, 78 (3), 20–24.

Weeks, J. (1989). *Sex, Politics and Society*. New York: Longman.

2 "Knowing" the hero

The female athlete and myth at work in Nike advertising

Debra A. Capon and Michelle T. Helstein

The narrative of the hero is one of the most powerful and pervasive of myths, and Western sport media continually use the heroic narrative in reference to athletic performance. The myth of the hero, as a prevailing trend within representations of sport, has inevitably made its way into the cultural politics of sport advertising. Such advertising does not contain itself within the specific spheres of sport; like all advertising its proliferation in contemporary culture is extensive.

> Buses and subways have long been prime advertising spaces.... At least one airline now sells space on the outside of its planes.... Television and radio have long been chock-full of ads.... Ads surround sporting events, both on television and in sports arenas. They arrive in the mail and via fax. We wear advertising logos on our clothes and hum advertising jingles in the shower. In short, ads are so deeply embedded in our environment that we are likely to see [and] hear ... them without thinking twice.
>
> (Croteau and Hoynes, 2000: 182)

Given the frequency of this exposure to advertising, it is imperative that scholars, students, and consumers alike acknowledge advertisements as rich, interesting and significant texts that can and need to be explored for their representational politics. It is the intent of this chapter to illustrate the possibility, importance and potential of such work with respect to a series of Nike advertisements relying upon the pervasiveness of the myth of the hero and directed to female athletes.

To make explicit the politics of representation within this series of advertising, we begin by offering a brief introduction to the characteristics and values associated with the traditional hero myth. Who is and can be defined as a hero within the ancient myth? This section of the chapter details the significance and association of the hero to military and athletic contexts, to masculinity and males, and to femininity and females. These characteristics are acknowledged as influential because it is the remembrance or "knowledge" of the ancient hero myth that contemporary sport media and advertising rely upon.

We then move into a discussion of the form and function of myth.

Traditionally, myth is understood as an explanatory narrative that describes how something came to be as it is. Theorizing myth in this way suggests that knowledge about "the" hero already exists in the world and that this knowledge is simply reflected, explained and transmitted through myth. Joseph Campbell's (1993) common narrative of the hero quest is read according to this traditional understanding of myth to illustrate the effects of such a reading. We argue that in the guise of transmission and explanation, myth reconciles, guides and legitimates actions, values, identities and cultures.

The myth of the hero is not only and simply a case of transmission and explanation. Rather, we conceptualize the myth of the hero as "representation at work" within advertising and explore its functioning through a discursive approach to representation. We have chosen this approach, following the work of Michel Foucault, rather than a semiotic approach to representation (e.g. Barthes, 1972) because it is our intention to investigate the production of knowledge through discourse rather than the production of meaning through language. In other words, we hope to examine and complicate what it is to "know" the hero within Nike advertising directed to female consumers and how power and politics are implicated within that knowledge.

Therefore, the final section of the chapter explicitly examines a series of Nike advertisements. Unlike many other heroic tales within Western culture whose protagonists are powerful, single-minded, courageous men, these advertisements take up female athletes as heroic. We examine the representational politics of Nike's use of the word "hero" as opposed to "heroine" within these advertisements given that myth (including that of the hero) is not only or simply explanatory but rather "representation at work" in producing or reproducing itself, its prevalence, and its significance.

Here it is necessary, interesting and significant to note that many consider advertisements to be the myths of contemporary culture (e.g. Leymore, 1975; Kellner, 1995; Twitchell, 1996). Varda Langholz Leymore (1975) argues that similarly to myth, advertising fortifies accepted modes of behavior and operates as an anxiety-reduction mechanism resolving contradictions in a complex and/or confusing society. Leymore (1975: 156) remarks that "[t]o the constant nagging dilemmas of the human condition, advertising gives a simple solution ... [advertising] simultaneously provokes anxiety and resolves it." Correspondingly, Douglas Kellner (1995: 247) observes that like myths, advertisements attempt to "resolve social contradictions, provide models of identity, and celebrate the existing social order." Seemingly, advertisements today, like the myths of the past, act as a mechanism of socialization. James Twitchell (1996) considers the advertisement as the "Ur-myth" of American commercial culture, in that nothing unites us or the world like the experience of being told how this-or-that product can fulfill our dreams; it is precisely the unification and communion of "us" as consumers that is of interest to the advertiser and their client.

This notion of advertisements as the myths of contemporary culture will be an important consideration throughout this chapter. It is not only the myth of the hero within advertising that is attempting to reconcile, guide and legitimate a particular production of knowledge, but the advertisements themselves. As myths, they too are "representation at work" in the guise of explanation and transmission. Specifically, within this chapter they might be said to be the vehicles for the proliferation and reification of the myth of the hero.

The myth of the hero

Traditionally in the West, the story is an action-packed adventure. The villain(s) is (are) defeated. Good triumphs over evil and in resolution, order is established. The protagonist of the story is the hero, who is presented as an exceptional or superior individual or person. The hero is strong, noble, active and courageous, and is typically a boy or a man. *He* performs brave deeds that go beyond the call of duty. God-like, but not quite a god, the hero transcends the everyday. Kerenyi (1959: 3) states: "What is it to be a hero? It is the glory of the divine ... strangely combined with the shadow of mortality." This transcendence is part and parcel of the moral intended within the hero story: his actions do not only make *his* life better, they make our own lives better and more meaningful. This formulaic narrative, which begins with "once upon a time" and ends with "happy ever after," is a familiar one. It is recounted not just in the ancient stories of Hercules, Odysseus, Jason and the Golden Fleece, and Saint George, but also in the stories of James Bond, Rambo, Rocky, Luke Skywalker, Indiana Jones, and the protagonist in the latest sci-fi film or computer game among others (Hourihan, 1997).

Heroism has predominantly been attached to a military and/or fighting context. This is most apparent within Ancient Greek art and literature. The archetypes of such a tradition are the heroes of Homer's epics, Achilles and Odysseus of the Iliad and Odyssey respectively. Homer was an oral poet and both epics are a product of many years of traditional, oral story-telling. Homeric warriors are consummate "agonal competitors" who are identifiable by an intense spirit of rivalry and competition, a strong sense of individualism, and a questing for fame, glory, honor and excellence (*aristeia*), and who attempted to be "the first amongst equals" (Slowikowski and Loy, 1993: 24).

Although both Odysseus and Achilles possess the similarities of aristocratic lineage and martial prowess, they are also frequently considered to be representatives of a classic brain-versus-brawn dichotomy. Homer constructed two of the great contrasting voices of literature echoing down the ages, "the fiercely uncompromising individual who will be himself whatever the consequences, and the quick-thinking, adaptable, realistic survivor" (Jones, 1997: 18). This suggests some limited variability amongst the qualities associated with traditional heroism.

However, Margery Hourihan (1997: 1) suggests that this narrow range of variability perpetuates heroic "superiority, dominance and success" as essentially a masculine domain. Roger Horrocks (1995), in his book entitled *Male Myths and Icons*, emphasizes that various gender myths bear a close resemblance to the hero myth. Horrocks defines the myths of masculinity as those narratives that assert toughness, stoicism, and courage. For Horrocks such masculine stereotypes permit the disassociation from "soft" femininity that "belongs" to women within the narrative. This sentiment is echoed in Mike Featherstone's (1992) article, "The heroic life and everyday life," in which he juxtaposes the essentially masculine heroic life with everyday life. Featherstone (1992) suggests that everyday life is traditionally linked to women in that it is associated with the routine and mundane, and is the sphere of reproduction and maintenance. "The everyday world is the one which the hero departs from, leaving behind the sphere of care and maintenance (women, children and the old), only to return to its acclaim should his tasks be completed successfully" (Featherstone, 1992: 165).

Within the traditional story of the hero, the heroine is not then the equivalent of the hero. Instead the heroine exists only through her supporting role to the hero. For example, within the Odyssey, Odysseus departs from his home, and by his cunning defeats all foes. He returns home and reclaims his property and status, and in so doing he restores social order. Whereas Odysseus' wife Penelope waits at home avoiding suitors, merely forestalling disaster, until the triumphant return of her husband. Frequently women appear in the narrative as spectators, prizes or victims, and serve only to confirm the heroic status of the protagonist. During the action or on resolution of the action, the hero gets or wins the girl. Indeed, "heroines" often have a secondary role; they are victims who need to be saved. This is exemplified by the stereotypical "heroine" in silent black and white films who is tied to the train track and requires assistance from the male hero.

The "Ancient" masculine ideal of the heroic was not only linked to warfare and defined in opposition to the feminine everyday, but significantly associated with athletics as well. This is illustrated by the inclusion of Patroclus' Funeral Games in Book XXIII of the Iliad. These games were organized by Achilles, who was considered the greatest Greek warrior/hero. The games, which included discus throwing, running and chariot racing, were representative of all the skills considered necessary to be a great warrior. What is important here is that this male warrior-athlete, this Greek/Classical/Ancient/Homeric hero is the "uncomplicated" model for subsequent heroes in Western culture (Cohen, 1990).

According to Flowers (1988), Joseph Campbell laments that in the modern world the ancient heritage of myth is in rapid decay. The contemporary heroic deed for Campbell is at the very least to remember the hero myths of the past, as these stories seemingly serve to remind us of the "lost world" of solidarity and community. With respect to advertising, Twitchell (1996: 7) highlights the importance of drawing on the past: "There is cohesive power in the remembrance of things past. It does link us together." Indeed, Robert Goldman (1992) highlights that advertisers "plunder" already present or remembered meaning systems to get their point across. In so doing, rather than actually creating meaning, advertisements "draw on meaning systems that already have currency with an audience. Ads do not create meanings, but rather provide an arena in which to transfer and rearrange meanings" (Goldman, 1992: 38).

With respect to the hero, it is this remembrance or "knowledge" of things and meanings past that sport advertising is relying upon. Both Susan Josephson (1996) and Robert Goldman (1992) argue that advertising does not construct new heroes or even social values, but rather merely reinforces the ones that exist already. Advertising gives us the means to chase dreams that reflect our desires for such things as social acceptance, rather than creating something that does not already exist on some level (Josephson, 1996: 7). For example, advertising does not give us the desire to be heroic. Such a desire is already established by the society in which we live, and as such, Featherstone (1992) argues that that heroic life remains an important image (as demonstrated in the media, advertisements, literature and films) in Western culture:

> [A]s long as there still exists interpersonal violence and warfare between states [and arguably between and among sporting bodies] there is a firm basis for the preservation of this image, as the risking of life, self-sacrifice and commitment to a cause are still important themes sustained within male culture.
>
> (Featherstone, 1992: 175)

The co-joining of warrior-athlete, at least in the sense of hero as ultimately a "man of action," still has contemporary resonance.

Thus male heroes, including those within sport literature and media, continue to be constructed, to some extent, according to the heroic model offered by mythical protagonists such as Hercules. For example, in *Death of a Salesman*, Willy Loman, talking about his son, a high school football player, says:

> [L]ike a young god, Hercules – something like that. . . . And the sun, the sun all around him. Remember how he waved to me?. . . and the cheers, when he came out – Loman! Loman! Loman! God almighty. . . . A star like that, magnificent, can never really fade away.
>
> (Barlow, 1994: 32)

This speaks to Michael Oriard's (1982) assertion that sport is ideal for the manufacturing and representation of heroes. After all, commonsensically sport heroes survive/exist in that "apolitical, asocial, amoral, even timeless, placeless quality of the athletic contest . . . itself enabling the heroes of the contests to remain unchanged after decades" (Oriard, 1982: 39). For Oriad, the athlete-hero of modern America is associated with the democratic ideal of the "American Dream." This articulates America as the "land of opportunity," possesses the rhetoric that "if you work hard you can be who you want to be" and is attached to the Enlightenment quest for perfection (1982: 48–49). Oriard's "self-made" and "democratic man" is still arguably and ultimately one of athlete-warrior, who in seeking glory is aggressive, competitive, and individualistic. Hence, the supposed timeless, placeless quality of the athletic contest is reinforced by the apparently universal attributes of heroism.

Subsequently, within sport media, the archetypal male hero continues to have exposure and currency. Commentators, journalists and advertisers within North American sport frequently cite (among others) the following as heroes: Jackie Robinson, Muhammad Ali, Bobby Orr, Arnold Palmer, Joe Montana, Wayne Gretzky, Sugar Ray Robinson, Michael Jordan, and Tiger Woods. It is not difficult to recognize that each male athlete on this list is stereotypically placed towards one or the other end of the brain/brawn dilemma articulated by the Homeric heroes Achilles and Odysseus. Whether the hero is the "fiercely uncompromising individual" or the "quick-thinking, adaptable, realistic survivor," the male athlete as hero is celebrated by sport media as a "man of action" who does "battle" in the sports arena. This notion is conformably apparent within some sports that rely heavily on the language of the military. Jansen and Sabo (1994) suggest the "military metaphor" is exemplified by football, which uses such words as *attack, blitz, bombs, flanks, conflicts,* and *territory* within its everyday coaching parlance. In the tradition of the Homeric model, sport, battle and masculinity are once again aligned with the heroic.

In making such statements, we are not suggesting that the various ideals associated with heroism are always consistent or timeless, or that the warrior-athlete is an ideal model. Rather we argue that this dominant myth of the hero continues to be prevalent and pervasive within contemporary narratives, including those within sport and sport advertising. In addition, both Ong (1981) and Strate (1994) suggest the advent of print medium changes the nature of the transmission of the hero story. Ong (1981) highlights that the Greek heroes Achilles and Odysseus are "culturally large" or "heavy figures" in that they transmitted dramatic messages containing important cultural information to "oral-aural" cultures. In contrast, written history means that the hero is "brought down to earth [because as] more information could be stored about any given individual, heroes became individualised" (Strate, 1994: 18). In recent history, print media and mass communication more generally has enabled images to be projected to large numbers of people simultaneously, which in turn has arguably more readily enabled mass hero-worship. With this pervasiveness and prevalence, the myth of the hero has come to occupy a general cultural knowledge that must be interrogated for its politics.

The form and function of myth

Myth as transmission and explanation

As suggested above, the hero exists as part of a narrative, which is myth. Myths are shared meanings, linking individual action into a story. The heroic adventure in which the protagonist encounters the supernatural or the mystical and "good" triumphs over "evil" is often considered the exemplary myth. Traditionally, myth is an anonymous tale that quests for truth, meaning, and significance; locates who "we" are; and ultimately seeks to explain the world (Coupe, 1997).

Myth seeks to communicate how the world or something came to be as it is, through a reflective or mimetic approach to representation. This means that myth is thought to "function like a mirror, to reflect the true meaning as it already exists in the world" (Hall, 1997: 24). In relating the story, myths function to authorize and perpetuate a community's collective values, beliefs and customs. Hence, in narrating/explaining how things have come to pass, myths also seem to be simply a reflection of the way things are. This communication and/or affirmation of social norms provided by myths fundamentally contributes to a society's or a community's sense of solidarity (Campbell, 1993).

Campbell (1993: 30) argues that the myth of the hero has *a* common narrative, that of "separation–initiation–return," which reflects the rites of passage and traverses different times and cultures. Campbell (1993: 30) conceives of this common universal narrative, the journey or quest of the hero, as the "nuclear unit" of the "monomyth." The hero's journey is an escape:

> [F]rom the world of common day into a region of supernatural wonder: fabulous forces are there encountered and a decisive victory is won: the hero comes back from [the] adventure with power to bestow boons on his fellow man.
>
> (Campbell, 1993: 30)

Apparent here are two of the important functions and interrelated facets of myth, namely that of transcendence from mundane life and the hero's actions benefiting the community. In the words of Featherstone (1992), the leaving of the everyday, the sphere of women, for the destiny of the heroic. By living vicariously through the hero, all can share in this glory and transcendence through his return. Although the hero is frequently highlighted as a somewhat isolated individual, the hero, as Jean-Luc Nancy (1991: 51) suggests, "makes the community commune – and ultimately he [the hero] always makes it commune in the communication that he himself effects between existence and meaning, between the individual and the people." Nancy (1991: 51) continues, citing Walter Benjamin to good effect: "the canonical form of mythic life is precisely that of the hero. In it the pragmatic is at the same time symbolic."

Myth as representation at work

In a traditional understanding of myth, knowledge about "the" hero already exists in the world, outside of its explanation: and this knowledge is reflected or transmitted through myth. If this reflection is not transparent, it is at least a symbolic representation of something ("the" hero and the values he upholds) that is. The myth of the hero is understood as a symbolic representation of truth. However, these stories do not simply promote an understanding of the hero (who they are and where they came from). Rather, as Hourihan (1997: 14) suggests, the story is a version imposed upon us, it describes, explains and naturalizes our reality; thus in Western culture, "the hero story has come to seem simply a reflection of the way things are." In the guise of this traditional understanding of myth, as transparent or symbolic explanation, myth is able to function in the service of normalization while the politics of its representation remain uncomplicated. This assertion requires exploring an alternative theorization of myth.

Here we have chosen to turn to Nancy (1991) who offers an interesting and significant account of the concept of myth. In a chapter titled "Myth interrupted," Nancy (1991: 56) suggests that "myth communicates itself, not something else. Communicating itself, it brings into being what it says, it founds its fiction." Within this constitutive approach to theorizing myth, "the" hero does not exist outside of myth. The myth of the hero, as fictional narrative, defines what it is to be a hero. It is in being represented or communicated (in and through myth) that the hero comes to be and have meaning. "[Myth] does not communicate a knowledge [of the hero] that can be verified from elsewhere: it is self-communicating" (Nancy, 1991: 50). The myth of the hero invents itself by uttering itself. In opposition to a traditional understanding of myth, Nancy (1991: 56) suggests that "myth is not simply representation, it is representation at work, producing itself . . . as effect."

Thus what needs to be addressed is not what myth is or means but rather, how "the invention of myth is bound up with the use of its power" (Nancy, 1991: 46). What is involved or invested in the myth of the hero as representation with the power to invent? Critical engagement with this question requires a more thorough examination of what is meant by "representation at work." Primarily this necessitates asking how representation is implicated in broader issues of knowledge and power. To do so, we turn to Michel Foucault and a discursive approach to representation.

Discourse as a system of representation can be defined as "a group of statements which provide a language for talking about – a way of representing the knowledge about – a particular topic at a particular moment in history" (Hall, 1997: 44). Although that object may be a material thing, it only becomes meaningful or an object of knowledge when it is taken up within the rules, procedures, or practices of discourse. Thus, discourse governs the production of what is to count as meaningful knowledge about a particular object or, as Foucault (1969/1972: 49) suggested (echoing Nancy), discourse can be described as the "practices that systematically form the objects of which they speak."

This implies a relation of power. What we "know" cannot be viewed in isolation, it does not exist in a void separate from relations of power. Rather it must be acknowledged that discourse is both constitutive of and constituted by the multiplicity and diversity of power relations permeating through the social. The relation of power and knowledge is such that "there is no power relation without the correlative constitution of a field of knowledge, nor any knowledge that does not presuppose and constitute at the same time power relations" (Foucault, 1975/1995: 27).

It is as a result of this relation that only certain statements can be made within a particular discourse. For knowledge to be recognized as true within the limits of a discourse they must speak to a specific object (as subject) and conceptualize that object in particular ways (Foucault, 1969/1972: 223). In addition, those who utter the statements must be authorized and legitimated speakers within the discourse. Debra Shogan (1999: 12) suggests that "when legitimate speakers of a discourse communicate their knowledge and this knowledge is taken seriously by participants in the discourse, what they say is also understood to be true. In producing knowledge power produces truth." Acknowledging these relations, Stuart Hall (1997: 6) suggests that:

> The discursive approach is . . . concerned with the effect and consequences of representation – its "politics." It examines not only how language and representation produce meaning, but how the knowledge that a particular discourse produces connects with power, regulates conduct, makes up or constructs identities and subjectivities, and defines the way certain things are represented, thought about, practised and studied.

The remainder of this chapter will explore the ways in which the discursive practices and strategies of Nike (specifically in reference to the myth of the hero) are implicated, as representation at work, in relations of power, knowledge and truth.

In a series of advertisements that appeared in a number of popular press magazines (*Sports Illustrated for Women, Women's Sport and Fitness, Fitness, and Shape*) throughout 1999, Nike explicitly takes up the myth of the hero in its marketing to female consumers. Within these advertisements (and in combination with Nike's overall marketing strategy currently directed to female consumers) Nike reproduces the subjects (as objects) it constructs/constitutes and makes them seem natural. By virtue of its corporate success Nike has arguably gained primary positioning among sports manufacturers and has been posited as an expert or "knower" of sport and, specifically within the focus of this project, the sport hero. As legitimate speakers, their popular knowledge of what/who the "hero" is continues to increase; so too does their control of what/who can be constituted or intelligible as the "hero," and vice versa. It is necessary to attempt to make visible Nike's practices and strategies in an effort to illustrate how the discursive formation of Nike constructs subjects ("female athlete," "hero") within the discourse and then subjects them to the power of the discursive formation, framing and delimiting their possibilities. Such work attempts to create an awareness that the statements (including those that support and draw upon the myth of the hero) within the discursive formation of Nike are, to quote Foucault (1969/1972: 120):

> [N]ot like the air we breathe, an infinite transparency; but things that are transmitted and preserved, that have value, and which one tries to appropriate; that are repeated, reproduced, and transformed . . . and to which a status is given in the institution.

The myth of the hero and the statements and images that communicate and support it are "representation at work" in producing or reproducing itself, its prevalence, and its significance.

"Knowing" the hero within Nike advertising

"Knowing" the hero, within the discourse of Nike, is thus not a transparent task but rather one bound up with the politics of representation and thus in need of further exploration. To begin this process of exploration we provide a critical examination of three print advertisements that explicitly and implicitly take up the familiar and naturalized myth of the hero.

Each of these advertisements consists of a two-page glossy spread that is made to resemble a torn old scrapbook thrown open upon a table. The advertisements feature pieces of ragged-looking paper whose phrases ask and speak to questions such as who are your heroes, how do you know you are a hero, and does a hero know she's a hero if no one tells her? The text is accompanied by various images made to resemble photographs including a child wearing a dress and sandals, Cynthia Cooper – a two-time WNBA most valuable player, and a young women holding a baby in her arms. The scrap paper and photographs are arranged on the page as if they had been stapled, taped, tacked, or glued into place. The pages look worn, used, and aged, giving the supposed scrapbook an appearance of history and authenticity.

As already stated, each of the advertisements takes up and relies upon the myth of the hero. In addition, we suggest that read intertextually, the three advertisements parallel Campbell's rendering of the common universal narrative of the myth of the hero, that of separation, initiation, and return. Thus, we propose to look at each of these advertisements individually and intertextually, for the ways in which their use of the myth of the hero produces, publicizes, and authorizes particular ways of "knowing" the hero and thus legitimates particular actions, values, identities and communities. This will require reading myth not as allegorical or as a symbolic representation of truth, but rather as representation at work in both the form and function of these advertisements.

Separation

A young girl stands grinning on a path among overgrown brush. From behind, the sun shines down upon her, lighting up her somewhat disheveled hair that appears to be tied back in a loose ponytail. She wears what could be a home-sewn sundress, a loose and simple design with two pockets sewn on the thighs. Bare feet wouldn't look out of place in the overall image, but of course she wears Nike sandals instead. The scene is a child in the midst of nature. It is a scene that is simple, uncomplicated, and innocent. If a hero's journey begins by "venturing forth from the world of the common day" (Campbell, 1993: 30), from "the sphere of . . . women and children" (Featherstone, 1992: 165), this image exemplifies the place from which that quest begins.

If this is so, the question then becomes: Who ventures forth from this commonality? As the text on the facing page of the image asks:

> Who are your heroes?
> Did you name an actor?
> Did you name an athlete?
> Did you name a woman?
> (Did you name any women?)
> Why don't we think of women as heroes?
> Maybe it's because no one ever shows them to us.
> We have to take the time to find them, celebrate them,
>   and make sure these heroes are seen,
>   so we can find the inspiration to achieve whatever we dream.
> Look around.
> We are surrounded by strong, courageous, accomplished women.
> Any one of them could be a hero.
> A hero could be you.

Arguably those who venture forth are those who are founded within the mythic fiction. Thus, *who are your heroes* might be restated as what or who is produced, normalized and naturalized as hero? What values are produced and reproduced in the statements and images of the advertisement(s)? *Did you name an athlete?* The answer is likely yes, given that the myth of the hero has been normalized and naturalized within sport discourse and therefore highlighted within sport advertising. *Did you name a woman?* The ad suggests that you likely didn't. This is why the next question within the advertisement is posed. *Why don't we think of women as heroes?* Perhaps because within the hero quest the sphere of women is the place from which the male hero departs (Featherstone, 1992). Within the myth of the hero, neither women nor the values of conventional femininity have been represented as heroic. The same could be said about women and femininity in sport.

There are practices that are requirements for success within discourse, and the performance of these practices is both enabling and limiting. Dominant sport discourse, for example, requires strong, aggressive, forceful, space-occupying movements. Adherence (through constraint) to these practices enables (through productive power) the successful "athlete" that is both the subject and the object of the discourse. Dominant gender discourses function in similar ways. Dominant notions of femininity require cooperation and passivity, while dominant notions of masculinity require strength, aggression, and domination. Therefore, to practice dominant sport discourse and a dominant discourse of masculinity is to engage in the same movements and gestures. On the other hand, the practice of conventional femininity and sport is at odds. As Shogan (1999: 55) suggests, "while there is nothing normal about an athletic body for either men or women, male athletic embodiment is an ideal of masculinity, and female athletic embodiment is a contradiction." Thus, a female practicing sport

successfully is a female practicing conventional masculinity. Women who practice conventional masculinity have not been celebrated as heroic, but rather
and often as deviant through an assumed and vilified homosexuality (Cahn,
1994).

Traditionally, acknowledgment of this female embodiment of conventional
masculinity has been resisted. This is most obvious in the refusal of access to
sport for women, and more implicitly in the rendering of women who practiced
sport successfully as abnormal or unnatural. In this second appropriation, it is
thought that the female has to be reclaimed or recovered through attempts to
illustrate hyperfemininity and heterosexuality.

The initial refusal of Nike to create and market a product directly to female
athletes[1] was not unlike the initial hesitation to allow women to participate in
sport. If women could compete in the demands of sport, and simultaneously the
demands of conventional masculinity, then sport and masculinity would be trivialized in a sense. Consequently, introducing femininity into the Nike discourse
would trivialize the "authentic and serious sport image" Nike valued (Cole and
Hribar, 1995: 359).

The advertising text might suggest that Nike is now resistant to this traditional protection of masculinity and sport by encouraging consumers to find and
celebrate *strong, courageous, accomplished women*. In many of Nike's most recent
advertisements, including the hero series, the female who practices dominant
sport discourse (and thus conventional masculinity) is celebrated as inspirational and an indication of progress and evolution. In some respects, we would
not disagree. We value sport in many of its manifestations, and celebrate
women's participation and achievement within it. Representing women as athletic and successful has some important resistive implications. Among others,
when a female can perform the masculine skills of sport, questions should arise
about the supposed "naturalness" of the softness and passivity of the female
body (Shogan, 1999: 61). Arguably this type of representation could begin to
break down the rigid normalizing and policing of gender and sexuality within
sport which connects female bodies to femininity and male bodies to masculinity exclusively. Horrocks (1995: 174) makes a similar contention. When the
female body is presented as honed and muscular, rather than "traditional frills
and curves ... the woman is able to occupy the place of the hero, rather than
the heroine." He goes on to suggest that "gender leakage" is taking place in
popular culture, as "women can be given the role of doughty hero" (Horrocks,
1995: 174).

In a similar mode of thought, Featherstone (1992) suggests that such leakage
is occurring between heroic life and everyday life. He refers to Madonna as
potentially representative of a new breed of hero in that she is "attempting to
redefine her performances as art rather than popular music" (1992: 178). As
artist, she has the qualities of being heroic, in that artists are recognized within
high culture and associated with masculine heroic life in contrast to the popular
or common that is associated with the everyday and thus the sphere of women
(Featherstone, 1992: 177–178). Might an advertisement that represents the

transgression of female athletes as heroes be a potential breeding ground for a similarly new heroic?

We return again to the necessity of investigating representation for its politics. Within this advertisement (and as alluded to above) it is difficult to ignore the significance of the word *hero* as opposed to *heroine*. The text of the advertisement seems to suggest that it is all right for women to aspire to the essential (masculine) qualities of the archetypal hero myth. This aspiration implies a desired emancipation from the status of non-hero or, perhaps more tellingly, from the status of heroine (as the necessary contradiction to the hero). The hierarchy between hero and heroine is reinforced. If, traditionally, the myth of the hero emulates the masculine ideal of sport, then this advertisement still seems to suggest that the female is at odds in sport. If sport is a universal, this universal is masculine.

Thus it is fine for women to aspire to heroism (successful sport, masculinity) but it is still the domain of men and it will be protected. Although the text of the advertisement may connote and celebrate an emulation of the masculine (heroism), there is an implicit and intertextual defense of the boundaries of conventional femininity and masculinity that is staked out within and among these advertisements. Nike operates in subtle ways to reclaim masculinity from the female within Nike discourse (and alongside dominant sport discourse).

In the context of this series of advertisements this maintenance of gender boundaries is largely accomplished by the accompanying images. The females within the hero advertisements are featured in ways that suggest and promote conventional markers of femininity. In the first advertisement the child wears a dress, and a downward camera angle makes her look small and passive. In another of the advertisements a young women holds a baby gently and protectively, connoting a sense of motherhood and conventionally, heterosexuality. Even when an image of an athletic woman in uniform is presented there are no action shots, no images of a woman actively engaged in sport and thus the skills of conventional masculinity.

These images are reinforced by a number of Nike advertisements that seems to suggest that men still hold the "truth" of the skills of sport and masculinity; that although women are increasingly participating, they don't quite get it right. Perhaps the best example of this is a television commercial that features the Nike Fun Police. This police force is made up of various NBA (National Basketball Association) stars that travel around in groups wearing bright yellow coats. In this particular advertisement, a group of young girls playing basketball on an outdoor court are simply going through the motions with little emotion and no fun. The call comes in and the Fun Police, in this case Gary Payton and Moses Malone of the National Basketball Association (NBA), go out to see what can be done. What the Fun Police do is teach the girls to talk trash and play hard. Trained and supervised by the men in yellow coats, the young girls are shown screaming in each other's faces, "come hard or don't come at all." The obvious sentiments of this statement could be said to equate the assumed sexual (or phallic) inability of females with the inability to commensurate females with sport and masculinity. The commercial conveys the sense that successful sport belongs to men and masculinity, and it can only be taken up correctly by girls and women with the instruction or perhaps permission of men, as is evidenced by the final scene of the commercial. As the Fun Police drive away, the young girls are shown again, this time playing with emotion and seemingly having fun.

The "uncomplicated" warrior-athlete model of the hero is reproduced within Nike advertising, and thus is reinforced as the normalized and naturalized heroic model. As such, the heroine is not rescued from being relegated to the train tracks. Thus, one can only be heroic within the discourse of Nike, and by extension, sport, if they embody or at least aspire to the aggressive, competitive, individualistic, and masculine ideal. This is illustrated perfectly in the closing line of the second advertisement, which states, "*Man*, that's who I want to be." Within the heroic journey this suggests "venturing forth from the world of the common" (Campbell, 1993: 30) into "the terrors of the unknown" (Izod, 1996: 185). As the myth of the hero suggests, this separation requires an exceptional or superior individual.

Initiation

This exceptional or superior individual must then encounter and confront "fabulous forces" so that "a decisive victory is won" (Campbell, 1993: 30). This often implies danger, suffering and effort (Izod, 1996: 185). In the second advertisement, this exceptional person is represented by Cynthia Cooper, the two-time MVP of the Women's National Basketball Association (WNBA). In the advertisement, the left-hand page of the scrapbook features a large color photo of Cynthia Cooper. She wears her team uniform, and her smiling face glows from perspiration. Her hands are held above her shoulders as she performs the motion of her signature, in-your-face, celebratory gesture that has become known as "raising the roof." The close-up camera shot means that she fills out almost the entire frame of the picture. The limited background that is visible features the arena fans as a blur behind her. The top left-hand corner of the page contains a much smaller black and white photograph of a small girl wearing a Cynthia Cooper replica jersey over her T-shirt. She sports a hopeful grin and has a basketball tucked tightly under her arm. The right-hand page contains the following text:

> Two years ago, even she didn't know she was a hero.
> How do you know you're a hero? Is there an exact moment –
> when a little girl walks up to you wearing a team jersey,
> and you realize it's yours?
> Is it the first time you hear the sound of a sold out arena?
> Or see your face on the front page of the sports section, instead of inside?
> Two years ago if you asked someone who Cynthia Cooper was,
>   you might get a blank stare.

But after two WNBA championships, two MVP awards, two sparkling
  seasons
Full of enchanted, excited fans, when you ask, you'll hear:
"Man, that's who I want to be."
Just do it.

Given our discussion of the previous advertisement, it is significant that this
advertisement implies that Cynthia Cooper embodies what it is to be a hero.
Perhaps this is because stereotypical or common-sense perceptions of "black"
femininity are more aligned with the masculine heroic ideal of sport than are
stereotypical or common-sense understandings of "white" femininity (or
arguably conventional femininity). Thus, "black" femininity is erased and
replaced by Nike's "just do it" ideal of athletic femininity,[2] which, as discussed
previously, encourages an aspiration to a heroic ideal that, in representation, is
beyond the grasp of the female athlete.

Why, then, does Nike make this appeal to heroism when so few can be the
exceptional or superior individual that "ventures forth from the common day"
and encounters the "fabulous forces" of "supernatural wonder" (Campbell, 1993:
30)? Perhaps because the popular allure of the sport hero is not so much that
people can readily identify with such an individual, but because they *want* to
identify with that individual. It is the desire of the possibility that *a hero could be
you.*

However, as the ad questions, "*How do you know you're a hero? Is there
an exact moment?*" In this advertisement the series of questions that might
define heroism actually serve to make any attempt at a definition more
ambiguous.

How do you know you're a hero? Is there an exact moment –
when a little girl walks up to you wearing a team jersey,
and you realize it's yours?
Is it the first time you hear the sound of a sold out arena?
Or see your face on the front page of the sports section, instead of inside?

The closest thing to an answer that the ad provides is that you know you have
made it when you hear "*Man, that's who I want to be.*" What is significant is that
who I want to be is a reiteration of norms that are founded by the myth of the
hero. These norms may remain explicitly unstated so that heroism can seem to
be all and none of these things. "What it is" requires no explanation because
the norms, which precede, constrain, and exceed the viewer, are invoked as
natural and normal (Butler, 1993). It is the way things are. Thus, Nike can
invoke heroism within its representational images without naming a particular
definition or meaning of heroism. This lack of a referent makes invisible (or at
least slippery) questions of justice, ethics and values regarding what characterizes a hero; who the judges are; and by what authority.

The advertisement, in combination with Campbell's journey of the hero, suggests that heroism is a teleological project. *Two years ago, even she didn't know she was a hero.* Hero then comes to be defined by becoming more than whatever you are right now. In Campbell's formulation, this is undergoing the rite of passage from separation to initiation. Heroism, *who [we] want to be*, is defined ambiguously by its distance from whatever we are right now. Thus Nike's answer to the characteristics of heroism is reference to the similarly non-defined subject of emancipation. Being a likeness of Cynthia Cooper may serve as an example of "*who I want to be*" within this advertisement. However, as the advertisement states, "*Two years ago, even she didn't know she was a hero.*" This suggests that at this moment any one of us may unknowingly be a hero, but it also suggests that it is just as likely that we may have some significant work to do before we can hope to be a hero. Thus, even though the advertisement does not define the precise characteristics of a hero or specify an exact moment when one becomes a hero, we are free to aspire to the non-referential appeal just as we are to assume Cynthia Cooper did. Thus, even though particular values are apparent within representational images produced by Nike, this non-referential appeal means that the politics come to pass as progressive and empowering (encouraging women to aspire to heroism) and therefore to function uncontested.

An aspiration to heroism therefore requires that one tries to diminish the space between whatever you are right now and *who [you] want to be*. Those who embody the greatest contradiction to the norm (*who [you] want to be*) presumably have the most to gain from the emancipatory narrative. The most alienated have the most to gain from aspiring to be more than whatever they are right now, whether that be the young athlete whose skills are significantly removed from the skills of Cynthia Cooper, or the small child wearing a home-made dress and, representationally at least, far removed from sport more generally. What is significant is that regardless of how far removed one is, they must be determined to diminish the gap. As Goldman and Papson (1998: 71) suggest, "signifiers of alienation plus signifiers of determination equals transcendence." You must simply be determined because *a hero could be you.*

This logic suggests that any failure to become more than whatever one is at the moment may be attributed to other desires, interests or circumstances interfering. An individual must not allow prejudices (theirs or others) associated with circumstances of race, class, gender, or physical ability to bias their efforts (as if transcending these things is simply a matter of will and effort!). One must simply work harder to transcend all circumstance, to produce better knowledge or a better effort that will necessarily be purely emancipatory.

This aspiration to heroism and transcendence is what makes emancipation an instance of social control rather than an illustration of emancipation from social control. The relation of power, knowledge, and truth has produced a shared set of values and thus *who [you] want to be* is a reiteration of those values. Thus whatever you are right now becomes the abnormal, the necessary contradiction to the heroic. Emancipation is necessary to make whatever you are right now (alienated identity) into *who [you] want to be* (celebrated norm). In effect, emancipation is necessary to make the abnormal, normal and, following Nike and the myth of the hero, it is all a matter of determination and effort.

It could then be argued that in this context, women are encouraged to continually measure and police their progress toward becoming "*who [they] want to be.*" They come to embody the pursuit so that it feels normal, natural, and innocent to aspire to the prescriptions of Nike advertising. Therefore, the romanticized notion of emancipation becomes an instance of social control. Emancipation is not only enabling or subversive in this instance, but rather limiting and constraining. Thus, although Nike "positions the social as constraining" (Goldman and Papson, 1998: 162), Nike advertising is a regulation and reification of the very types of constraint from which emancipation is sought.

A "decisive victory" over the "fabulous forces" does therefore require a great deal of effort and possibly even suffering. The exceptional individual may have ventured beyond the everyday. They may have transcended the status of non-hero or heroine, but they have not transcended the hierarchical regulation of the status of those terms and their place within sport. The effort and suffering within this heroic victory is in the service of conforming to ideals that link the hero, sport, and masculinity.

Return

In the resolution of the heroic journey, "the hero comes back from [the] adventure with power to bestow boons on his fellow man" (Campbell, 1993: 30). This final stage of the mythical journey is often associated with rebirth motifs, which is significant in light of the image that is featured within the final advertisement. A picture of a young woman holding a baby gently and protectively fills the entire right-hand page of the advertisement. The young woman's face stares away from the camera with a look of solemnity. This may connote that the power of knowing and the possibility of rebirth within the hero quest are taken seriously.

In order for a hero to return to the familiar, bringing with them the "knowledge" of their conquest, they must be recognized within the familiar as heroic. The text of the advertisement speaks to the necessity of this recognition:

> Does a hero know she's a hero if no one tells her?
> Do you know a hero no else knows? A hero doesn't have to
>   save a busload of school kids from certain disaster.
> Or score the winning point in the big game.
> A hero can be anyone who inspires you, anyone you look up to,
> Anyone who cheers you on, makes you better than you were before –
> Just as they made themselves better than they were before.
> Do you know a hero?
> Tell her.
> Then tell everyone.
> Just do it.

Heroes exist only if they are identified as such and are represented accordingly. Heroes are not "found" in sport or in the discourse of Nike. Rather it is in Nike's reiteration and celebration of particular values that heroes can be seen and will be seen, because they have been constituted there. Those who see them, who recognize them as such, will be the community in which the myth is communicated. "[The] hero makes the community commune – and ultimately he always makes it commune in the communication that he himself effects between existence and meaning" (Nancy, 1991: 51).

Therefore, the recounting of the myth builds the community. "Myth represents multiple existences as immanent to its own unique fiction, which gathers them together and gives them their common figure" (Nancy, 1991: 57). There is not an essence to be found or discovered before the hero story. Any number of ways of "knowing" the hero could be suggested but once the myth is spoken only one way is intelligible to those who have communed in the communication of the myth. Myth functions to authorize and perpetuate a community's collective values, beliefs, and customs in relation to naming the hero. *Does a hero know she's a hero if no one tells her?* Arguably no, because without the recitation, communication, and/or affirmation of social norms produced and reproduced by the myth there is no commonality around which to commune.

Being recognized and identified as a hero requires that the individual produces, reinforces, and authorizes that which is already enabled or founded by the recitation that has gathered the community together. The return of the hero and the subsequent bestowing of "knowledge" is in fact a retelling of the myth. In retelling the story, constructed within the discourses that it supposedly informs, the values and identities of the myth are reified and reproduced. Myth, therefore, may be said to:

> [N]aturalize speech, transmuting what is essentially cultural (historical, constructed, and motivated) into something which it materializes as natural (transhistorical, innocent, factual). Myth's duplicity is therefore located in its ability to "naturalize" and make "innocent" what is profoundly motivated.
>
> (Hall, 1997: 182)

The imperative to tell within this advertisement assures the rebirth implied within the return of the hero quest. *Do you know a hero? Tell her. Then tell everyone.* This return or the legitimization of the return of the hero suggests closure. It authorizes, publicizes, and naturalizes the order of things. It confirms the way things should be and reproduces them, affirming them as unmotivated, the common, the everyday.

Of course this imperative to tell is not open to all. The gift or simply the right to speak the story has implications for belonging and exclusion, for publicizing and authorizing what counts as knowledge, and for vilifying all else. What can be "known" and told, who tells, and by what authority is bound, as we have said throughout, to power and politics. For example, within this last advertisement, what is "known" about the hero is once again defined according to their distance from whatever they were before. There is a requirement that they have *made themselves better than they were before*, or alternatively that they *make you better than you were before*. *Better* normally implies morally better, or a movement closer to the accepted or legitimated ideal of the mythic hero. It is bound up in the combination of alienation, emancipation, and transcendence as an instance of social control.

Myth "perhaps says nothing, but says that it says this: myth says that it says, and says that this is what it says" (Nancy, 1991: 48). Myth understood as a mimetic reflection of truth suggests that it "says nothing" that is not already there. Myth asserts itself as explanation and, in the guise of that explanation, "organizes and distributes the world of humanity with its speech" (Nancy, 1991: 48).

Nike's authority to tell is historical and constructed but is often taken up as a gift or ability to communicate the authentic. By aligning themselves with dominant sport and dominant gender discourses, Nike is able to draw on a community that communes in the myth of the hero in similar and complementary ways. Thus, Nike, sport, and conventional masculinity are complementary and intelligible in defining what constitutes the hero. Reconciled by myth this construction is then materialized as natural.

References

Barlow, I. (1994). The worship of the false sports gods. *New York Times*, June 25, p. 32.

Barthes, R. (1972). *Mythologies*. London: Cape.

Butler, J. (1993). *Bodies that Matter: On the Discursive Limits of Sex*. London: Routledge.

Cahn, S. (1994). *Coming on Strong: Gender and Sexuality in Twentieth-Century Women's Sport*. Cambridge, MA: Harvard University Press.

Campbell, J. (1993). *The Hero with a Thousand Faces*. London: Fontana Press.

Cohen, D. (1990). *Being a Man*. London: Routledge.

Cole, C. and Hribar, A. (1995). Celebrity feminism: Nike style: Post Fordism, transcendence and consumer power. *Sociology of Sport Journal*, *12*, 347–369.

Coupe, L. (1997). *Myth*. London: Routledge.

Croteau, D. and Hoynes, W. (2000). *Media/Society: Industries, Images, and Audiences* (2nd edn). Thousand Oaks, CA: Pine Forge Press.

Featherstone, M. (1992). The heroic life and everyday life. *Theory, Culture and Society*, *9*, 159–182.

Flowers, B. (eds) (1988). *Joseph Campbell: The Power of Myth with Bill Moyers*. New York: Doubleday.

Foucault, M. (1972). *The Archaeology of Knowledge and the Discourse on Language*, trans. A.M. Sheridan Smith. New York: Pantheon Books. (Original work published in 1969.)

Foucault, M. (1995). *Discipline and Punish: The Birth of the Prison*, trans. A. Sheridan. New York: Vintage Books. (Original work published in 1975.)

Goldman, R. (1992). *Reading Ads Socially*. London: Routledge.

Goldman, R. and Papson, S. (1998). *Nike Culture*. London: Sage.

Hall, S. (1997). *Representation: Cultural Representations and Signifying Practices*. London: Sage.

Horrocks, R. (1995). *Male Myths and Icons: Masculinity in Popular Culture*. London: Macmillan.

Hourihan, M. (1997). *Deconstructing the Hero: Literary Theory and Children's Literature*. London: Routledge.

Izod, J. (1996). Television sport and the sacrificial hero. *Journal of Sport and Social Issues*, *22*, 173–193.

Jansen, S.C. and Sabo, D. (1994). The sport/war metaphor: Hegemonic masculinity, the Persian Gulf War, and the new order. *Sociology of Sport Journal*, *11*, 1–17.

Jones, P. (1997). The Odyssey is a powerful follow-up to the Iliad – but, asks Dr Peter Jones is it by the same author? *Saturday Telegraph*, October 4, p. 18.

Josephson, S.G. (1996). *From Idolatry to Advertising: Visual Art and Contemporary Culture*. Armonk, NY: M.E. Sharpe.

Kellner, D. (1995). *Media Culture: Cultural Studies, Identity and Politics Between the Modern and the Postmodern*. London: Routledge.

Kerenyi, C. (1959). *The Heroes of the Greeks*, trans. H.J. Rose. London: Thames and Hudson.

Leymore, V.L. (1975). *Hidden Myth: Structure and Symbolism in Advertising*. London: Heinemann.

Nancy, J.L. (1991). *The Inoperative Community*, trans. P. Conner, L. Garbus, M. Holland and S. Sawhney. Minneapolis: University of Minnesota Press.

Ong, W. (1981). *The Presence of the Word*. Minneapolis: University of Minnesota Press.

Oriard, M. (1982). *Dreaming of Heroes: American Sports Fiction, 1868–1980*. Chicago, IL: Nelson Hall.

Shogan, D. (1999). *The Making of High Performance Athletes: Discipline, Diversity, and Ethics*. Toronto: University of Toronto Press.

Slowikowski, S. and Loy, J. (1993). Ancient motifs and the modern Olympic Games: An analysis of rituals and representations. In A.G. Ingham and J.W. Loy (eds), *Sport in Social Development: Traditions, Transitions and Transformations* (pp. 21–49). Champaign, IL: Human Kinetics.

Strate, L. (1994). Heroes: A communication perspective. In S.J. Drucker and R.S. Cathcart (eds), *American Heroes in a Media Age* (pp. 15–23). Cresol, NJ: Hampton Press.

Twitchell, J.B. (1996). *AdCult, USA: The Triumph of Advertising in American Culture*. New York: Columbia University Press.

3 Women's sports in Nike's America

Body politics and the corporo-empowerment of "everyday athletes"

Michael D. Giardina and Jennifer L. Metz

In its latest campaign from Wieden + Kennedy, Nike shies away from provocation, taking the path more traveled. It's a general, red-blooded, upbeat, you-go-girl message, synthesizing every post-empowerment female idea about combining strength and emotion, power and humanity, karate kicks and mascara.

(*Adweek*, 2001: 18)

One author's story

Chapel Hill, North Carolina, USA. Summer, 2001. I am here to take in a Women's United Soccer Association (W*USA) game between the Washington Freedom and the Carolina Courage. Eating lunch before the game at a café near "23," Michael Jordan's theme restaurant located near Franklin Street on the University of North Carolina campus, the sight before me is, at first glance, encouraging: young girls with their parents, most wearing Courage T-shirts or caps, anxiously await their chance to see Mia Hamm play in person; a group of college-aged women, all sporting Team USA soccer jerseys bearing the names "Hamm," "Chastain," or "Overbeck," boisterously discuss the merits of women's pro sports; and an elderly couple, wearing sweatshirts that read "Soccer Grandma" and "Soccer Grandpa," each enjoy ice cream cones before the game. The atmosphere is festive and refreshing; women's professional soccer, like its basketball counterpart – the WNBA – appears to have found a home within the popular imaginary of Middle America.

Making my way toward Fetzer Field – home to both the Courage and the UNC-Chapel Hill Tar Heels soccer teams – the scene from the café replays itself time and again; the Courage are drawing what looks to be a diverse crowd of fans representing the full age spectrum. I also notice a broadcast truck from Turner Network Television (TNT), as well as an "Eyewitness News" van, parked off to the side; the game is being televised nationally on cable and also generating local media interest. I go inside the venue and buy a game program and a T-shirt from one of the vendors, marking both my visit to North Carolina and my support of the Courage (and, by association, women's sports) in perpetuity.

As the teams take to the field, a sellout crowd hovering near 6,000-strong rises to greet them with much cheering and shouts of encouragement. Although the Freedom's All-World superstar Mia Hamm gets the loudest cheer, lesser-known hometown Courage players such as Danielle Fotopoulos and Mikka Hansen receive warm applause. Next to my friends and I sits a high school-aged girl – face painted red, white, and blue, wearing a pink "Girl Power!" lanyard around her neck to complement her "Chicks Rule" basketball T-shirt (the back of which reads "If you don't want to lose to a girl, stay the hell off my court") – who leisurely reads through her game program while engaging her father in conversation.

"Ya know we got practice 'til five t'morrow, right Dad?" the girl asks her father, an athletically built man in his late forties who wears a "Police Athletic League" T-shirt.

"You're OK to practice?" he replies, a mildly surprised grin on his face. "I thought you twisted your ankle yesterday?"

"I did – no biggie; jus'a little sore," she says, rubbing her left ankle for effect. "Playoffs are next week and I'm starting no matter what."

"I just don't want you hurting yourself or anything," her father responds, reaching over to tousle her hair.

"Uh, Dad," she says, a look of mock seriousness on her face and assuasive sarcasm in her voice. "Weren't you the one who told me you played the state championship football game with three cracked ribs and a fever? I think I can stand a little ankle sprain."

Behind us, three couples in their mid-thirties – University of North Carolina alums, judging from their "Alumni Association" polo shirts – talk about their young daughters playing soccer.

"We signed up Jessica and Katy for youth soccer this weekend," says one woman.

"That's great," says one of the men in between bites of his pulled-pork sandwich.

"Jodie played her first season last year and *loved* it. She was running all over the field half the time knocking into people."

"Well, the twins have lots of extra energy to burn off. Maybe this will get them to calm down around the house, too."

"True. And soccer is good for girls, you know, more so than basketball or softball. There's not a lot of contact but they can still be active and get in shape. Besides, they look so adorable in their pigtails."

"Oh, totally," one of the other women says. "All Mitzy wants to do these days is kick the ball 'round the backyard. She even tries to play with her brother and his friends. It's so cute."

In front of me, a couple in their mid-fifties sit with their daughter, a student at nearby Duke University. Both are wearing Blue Devil polo shirts; their daughter wears a Nike warm-up jacket and blue jeans; a Team USA sailing cap sits backwards atop her head.

"Have you seen the new Nike commercial?" her father asks.

"Hmm . . . which one?" she replies.

"You know, the one with the hockey player skating through all those pink balloons," her mother chimes in, adding, almost as an afterthought, "You see, you can play sports *and* like girly things, too."

"You just don't get it, do you?" she says half-heartedly, a sly smile on her face. "In fact, you guys have it all wrong."

Contextualizing women's sports in the 1990s

> Women's bodies and labor are used to consolidate global dreams, desires and ideologies of success and the good life.
>
> (Mohanty, 1999: 368)

Welcome to the Third Millennium, a moment in history when women's sports have risen in popularity to assume a unique position within the popular imaginary of the US. Bolstered by such landmark events as the 1996 Olympic Games (hailed as the "Games of the Women"), the successful launching of the Women's National Basketball Association (WNBA), and the victory by Team USA in the Finals of the 1999 Women's World Cup of Soccer, female sporting successes in the 1990s are routinely pointed to and celebrated as marking a paradigmatic shift toward the widespread acceptance, celebration, and active promotion of female athletes and women's sports. Coming together in a kaleidoscopic opiate of feel-good feminism and post-empowerment jubilation, these successes have been hailed as an inspiration to women and, most especially, young girls, for whom participation in sport is lauded as a major determinant in enhancing self-esteem, physical activity, and overall bodily health.[1] Ranging from Gatorade's "Yes You Can!" message and Nike's "Everyday Athletes" cross-media blitz to more politically oriented deployments such as the US government's "Girl Power!" campaign, the image of the successful female (athlete) and her mythical heir apparent – the American daughter – has come to saturate the landscape of American popular culture. Likewise, a much broader conjunctural view of recent history reveals women's sporting achievements in the 1990s to be reflective of and implicated in a larger socio-cultural milieu characterized by notions of women's empowerment, a call for a "return" to conservative family values and, most importantly, an increased focus on the welfare of the American girl-child.

Consider: at the same time as Teams USA were dominating international competitions (winning Olympic gold medals in basketball, ice hockey, softball, gymnastics, and soccer, to name a few), two sports magazines geared specifically toward female consumers – *Sports Illustrated for Women* and *Amy Love's Real Sports* (later renamed *Real Sports*) – recorded dramatic increases in circulation.[2]

On the playing field, record numbers of women and girls have signed up to play in youth leagues, on high school teams, for competitive intercollegiate programs, or local recreational offerings. However, and contrary to popular belief, women's professional sport in the 1990s/2000s has not been – as some in the popular press would have us believe – the simple progression and natural outcome of female athletic participation since the passage of Title IX in 1972.[3] While mainstream publications such as *Sports Illustrated* or *The Sporting News* and broadcasted sports reportage such as ESPN's "SportsCenter" have been quick to point out that significant strides have been made in addressing gender equity questions, such a position is overly simplistic and remains ignorant of the cultural, political, and economic landscape(s) of the past two-plus decades.[4]

Correlatively, and with the introduction into the popular vernacular of the term "Girl Power!" by the British pop music group the Spice Girls – and more recently with the US Department of Health and Human Services "Girl Power!" campaign of the mid-1990s – the image of the empowered female has not only become central to the construction of national identity but has also become open to co-optation by the interests of corporate America. Whether in the form of vampire slaying, all-American valley girls à la Buffy, cerebral crime fighters such as Special Agent Dana Scully of the X-*Files*, or the mythic warrior-princess Xena, television shows promoting concrete representations of young, empowered, post-feminist characters have shot to the top of weekly ratings, drawing with them a wide-ranging demographic and legitimating their female characters and story-lines as both culturally acceptable and economically viable consumer entities.[5] This trend is also seen quite clearly in the massive success of HBO's "thirtysomething" drama *Sex and the City*, which focuses on the lives and careers of four women in New York City who are clearly presented as forthright owners of both their sexuality and professional status as New Age career women. Sales in the literary community have also recorded similar changes, where books focusing on everything from independent, media-savvy female leads (e.g. Catherine Asaro's *The Radiant Seas* or Vonda N. McIntyre's *The Moon and the Sun*), female hunters (cf. Schultz, 2001), witchcraft, and other sporting novels featuring strong, successful women or girls have become wildly popular with and accrued cultural currency among female consumers of all ages.

Over and against this seemingly progressive cultural transformation, a rhetoric of popular conservatism[6] has remained a strong driving force within mainstream America: unabashedly gendered and conservative programming on channels such as *Home and Garden Television (HGTV)*, *Lifetime Television*, *Food TV*, and *The Disney Channel* has become a ratings winner on cable television; Martha Stewart's elitist Northeastern fashion and lifestyle empire has made its way into mainstream America courtesy of K-Mart (Click, 2001); and Oprah Winfrey – daytime talk-show host and leading guru of self-help consumerism – has come to personify the liberal notion of the self through her apparent literal and physical realization of the American Dream. In particular, Amy S. Hribar (2001: 110) argues that such shifting imperatives unveil the inherent tensions circulating throughout much of late 1990s America insofar as these "positive" images of womanhood (in the form of racial, sexual, and/or gender portrayals) actively promote the fiction "that everyone has equal access to resources and that everyone experiences American culture in the same way." America, we are led to believe, is colorblind, a bastion of gender equity, and heading in the "right" direction. It is this cult of hearth and home in 1990s America – coupled with and articulated to women's empowerment through sport – that has engendered a "new" perspective on the role of women in the USA: the rhetoric now dictates that women can no longer just provide wonderful homes and/or be successful businesswomen – they can *also*, and at the same time, be successful, empowered, sporting participants. The Ancient Greek goddess Diana has now been made corporeal through myriad celebratory images of the women of the WNBA and United States Women's Soccer team, for these women are seen carrying babies, modeling clothing, scoring baskets, and kicking goals, all the while displaying conservative, feminine, and attractive qualities and characteristics. The tacit implication here is that these women are *heterosexual* women, deeply embedded within the cultural logics of what Michael Warner (1993) has called "heteronormative culture"; that is, a public culture organized around and for the active promotion of a heterosexist climate (Berlant, 1997).

Running parallel to such a discursive space, mediated sport has served as one of the pre-eminent sites for the construction of (hetero)normative positions about what constitutes the ideal body and how it is represented within contemporary America (Cole, 1998; Marshall, 1997; Pronger, 1998). It is in this arena that such texts as Nike and Adidas advertisements, sports/fitness magazines, and televised sports programming have become a key site of representational politics (Denzin, 1991; Giroux, 1994; Goldman and Papson, 1998). These texts, operating within the realm of the popular, assist in redefining the articulations of public culture and everyday life to issues of public policy and so-called proper forms of citizenship (Cole and Hribar, 1995; King, 2000).

In this chapter, we critically interrogate the prevailing contemporary notions of women's empowerment through sport as articulated within the context of Nike's "Everyday Athletes" campaign, the latest offering by the footwear and apparel giant that purports to target women of all ages, races, and skill levels. Contextualizing ourselves within the contemporary moment, we (1) discuss the current state of body politics within the USA; (2) articulate empowerment rhetoric to public policy as set forth by multinational corporations; and (3) offer Nike's "Everyday Athletes" campaign as a case study of the pervasiveness of commodified "empowerment" rhetoric. Grounding ourselves in cultural studies, post-structuralist, and postmodern theories, we seek to both illuminate and redefine the current national debate surrounding the image of the American girl-child, while also illustrating the various ways in which we understand "Everyday Athletes" to be indicative of a politics of representation that marks the commodification of women's empowerment discourse as always already entrenched within the white, middle-class, conservative narrative it purports to oppose and resist.

Specifically, within "Everyday Athletes," we focus on the ephemeral embodiment of postmodern subjectivity as located within commodified empowerment rhetoric. Drawing from the current cultural landscape of America's fetishization of and with women's sports, we present a politically motivated and locally particularized interpretation of the way in which Nike – acting in its role as what social theorist and cultural critic Norman K. Denzin (1991: 9) might call a "New Historian" – "perpetuate[s] a hegemonic control over popular culture, defining in every instance proper images of the American dream and the inheritors of that dream." In this instance, the planes of women's sport, empowerment rhetoric, and global capitalism all too easily collide, forming a filiopietistic archive or "body of cultural myth" (Denzin, 1991: 14) whose figures allege to speak the voices of freedom, liberty, and individuality. While the notion of promoting the empowered female *is* socially responsible (and too long in the making), it is precisely the seductive appeal of such promotion that must not pass by unchallenged.

Overall, we seek to challenge the unseen power relations circulating within postmodern America, revealing its "multiple masks" as we "seek to unmask the regimes of truth that structure the experience in any given situation" (Denzin, 1997: 13). Accepting that the meaning of any text is never singular but rather dependent upon its intersecting relationship to a multiplicity of social, cultural, and political vectors (i.e. its intertextuality), we argue that it is the conjuncturally specific planes of effectivity circulating postmodern America which have not only brought the female sporting body to the forefront of everyday televisual life, but have also perpetuated her continued exploitation, overt sexualization, and demonization within popular culture.

Identity politics/politics of the body

> The postmodern self has become a sign of itself, a double dramaturgical reflection anchored in media representations on the one side, and everyday life on the other.
>
> (Denzin, 1991: viii)

Before moving forward to discuss the role of women's sports in the 1990s as articulated to the future of the American girl-child, it would be beneficial to map out the way(s) in which (the) national identity (of the body) has been deployed within the USA during the past two decades. In its most basic formulation, a culture of imploding commodity-signs based on the production of bodily movement, pleasure, and desire "reflects the internalization and incorporation of culture – body culture is embodied culture" (Brownell, 1995: 11). Sandra Bartky (1988: 61) offers a deeper theoretical argument, stating that the body – as a site of contestation and representation – now requires more than "mere political allegiance or the appropriation of the products of its labor: the new discipline invades the body and seeks to regulate its very forces and operation, the economy and efficiency of its movements." It is here that the symbolically hyperreal canvas of the body offers a crucial space wherein all facets of culture – including what Susan Bordo (1992: 13) understands as "the central rules, hierarchies, and even metaphysical commitments of a culture" – are made noticeable through and produced by the consumption of a "constructed narrative ... that implicitly express[es] where the normative center of that discourse should be" (Marshall, 1997: 106). This normative center – displayed most notably throughout the whole of women's professional sports – is at once a fictional middle-ground and also a powerful marker of identity that comes to be seen repeatedly throughout the course of Nike's discursive positioning.

Intimately tying the body to national identity, C.L. Cole (1996) argues convincingly that sport acts as an allegorical locus of "conventional values" that represents hope and possibility for individuals and their community to improve not only the quality of their life but also the quality of their country. Deployed as what Brian Pronger (1998: 277) calls a "project of socio-cultural boundary maintenance," sport – particularly women's sport in the postmodern era – has increasingly become coded as an acceptable (and, more recently, profitable) site for the healthy and productive realization of the American Dream (see also King, 2000). Writing on the "American Dream," Lauren Berlant (1997: 4) contends that:

> [T]he Dream "fuses private fortune with that of the nation: it promises that if you invest your energies in work and family-making, the nation will secure the broader social and economic conditions which your labor can gain value and your life can be lived with dignity."

Naturally, this discursive shift has not occurred within a cultural vacuum. Among others, Berlant (1997) and Susan Jeffords (1994) have argued that the 1990s saw an American populace faced with a crisis of identity, a turbulent period of struggle and strife between who and what counts (and will count) as ideal "American" subjects. This is especially true with regard to the American daughter (or, more accurately, the overwhelming *image* of the American daughter as signifier of the American Dream). "Threatened" at the hands of various bodies operating within the space of the nation (that is, if you buy into the political rhetoric of the day) – each exerting more and more influence on the nation and its citizens – the nation stands at a crossroads of bodily movement. As we argue elsewhere (see Giardina and Metz, 2001), these multiple bodily formations – for example, addicted (Cole, 1998), unhealthy (Cole, 1993), nonheteronormative (Pronger, 1998), racialized (Andrews, 1996; Cole, 1996; Cole and Andrews, 1996), multicultural (Cole and Andrews, 2000; Hall, 2000; Hesse, 2000), and/or flexible bodies (Giardina, 2001; Ong, 1998, 1999) – each frame debates over the present and future of the nation. Throughout much of the late 1980s and 1990s, these bodily images/images of bodies have come to saturate the mediated landscape of American popular culture. In contextualizing this conjunctural epoch, Cole (1998: 261) further argues that one way to understand this exploding focus on the body is by excavating the body/antibody dyad, one that marks "patriotism, race, gender, sexuality, poverty, contamination and threat," as identities in practice. These literal realizations and corporeal embodiments of (post-)Reagan/Clinton ideology are further revealed by Jeffords (1994: 24–25) who posits that:

> In the dialectic of reasoning that constituted the Reagan movement, bodies were deployed in two fundamental categories: the errant body containing sexually transmitted disease, immorality, illegal chemicals, "laziness," and endangered fetuses which we can call the "soft body": and the normative body that enveloped strength, labor, determination, loyalty, and courage – the "hard body" – the body that was to come to stand for the emblem of Reagan philosophies, politics, and economies. It is this system of thought marked by race and gender, that the soft body invariably belonged to a female and/or person of color, whereas the hard body was, like Reagan's own, male and white.

Hence, Reagan's appropriation of "hard body politics," and, more importantly, the constitution of the "hard body" in relation to American national identity, engendered a dialectic relationship whereby the "body" was (re-)articulated with "moral" worth. Arguing that the "televisual politics" of the Reagan Era assisted in shifting the discursive focus of American cultural values from remnants of 1960s/1970s liberal activism toward so-called common sense, All-American values, and ideas, David L. Andrews (1998: 198) states that:

> [T]he New Right's disciplined mobilization of affect encouraged positive popular investment in cultural practices that advanced the discriminatory logics of Reaganism; cultural logics (incorporating neo-liberalism, neo-conservatism, and moral traditionalism) which reasserted a vision of an America dominated by a white, heterosexual, and patriarchal, middle-upper class.

With evocative images of the welfare queen, crack baby, and gun-toting youth entering into the everyday realm of the national image archive (Berlant, 1997), the patriotic hard body was directly set against narratives of weakness, deviance, and subalterneity on the part of raced, gendered, and queer bodies. These images – and the destructive narratives surrounding their histories – subsequently came to be understood with and directly tied to the breakdown of the (mythic) family (Cole, 1998; Coontz, 1992; Denzin, 1991). Such (faulty) logic made it possible to employ issues "previously deemed private such as abortion, sexuality and reproduction, marriage and personal morality as a collective litmus test for one's worthiness as a public citizen" (Hribar, 2001: 18). In other words, one's lifestyle choice was no longer considered as a private issue; it now had implications for public life and the collective well-being of the body politic; the hard, moral, and patriotic body was thus popularly conceived as a site for the recuperation of America's literal and figurative health, where problems of the state (for example, poverty, welfare dependency, and a struggling economy) were blamed on individual shortcomings and the breakdown of the (mythic) family (Cole, 1998; Coontz, 1992; Denzin, 1991; Jeffords, 1994; King, 2000; Hribar, 2001).

However, with the dawn of the Clinton era, we see an explicit shift in the way in which female body politics became inextricably tied to notions of empowerment rhetoric. Of specific interest to us is the way in which contemporary media(ted) sporting culture operates in and produced this shift, particularly as related to Nike, Inc., and its marketing/advertising campaigns. The next section thus focuses on the rise of empowerment discourse generally speaking, and within the USA more specifically. We then move forward and interrogate Nike's latest ad campaign "Everyday Athletes."

Empowering dreams/dreaming of empowerment

> The theme is investing in today's girls, tomorrow's women, and the future. We know that much of what we do, we are doing not for ourselves, but we are doing for our daughters, our nieces, our granddaughters.
>
> (Hillary Rodham Clinton, speech at the NGO forum at the *Fourth World Conference on Women* in Beijing, China)

There has been considerable attention paid to women's empowerment from a *socio-cultural* standpoint; however, public policy and action from the US government has, for the most part, significantly lagged far behind. Fortunately, this has not always been the case in terms of the United Nations (UN), global non-governmental organizations (NGOs), and not-for-profit advocacy groups. Declaring 1975 to be the "International Year of the Women," the United Nations General Assembly marked a significant moment for women's rights on the international stage. This declaration – which offered an agenda for the protection, development, and advancement of women throughout the world, and provided a foundation for future, global, women-centered agendas – kick-started the United Nations' "Decade for Women" (1976–1985). During this time, and with the 1979 ratification of the "Convention on the Elimination of All Forms of Discrimination against Women" (henceforth known as CEDAW), the UN brought women's rights and empowerment discourse to the forefront of its public agenda. Unique in that "it is the only human rights treaty which affirms the reproductive rights of women and targets *culture* and tradition as influential forces shaping gender roles and family relations" (United Nations Press Office, 1995, emphasis added), CEDAW was the first of many politically supported global programs to address the changing nature of male/female relations. The explicit recognition of socio-cultural determinants in the shaping of women's experience, progress, and quality of life is especially telling and obviously important within the frame of the argument we are putting forward; namely, that technologies of media and advertising, government-sponsored yet culturally based programs, corporate-funded sponsorship, and the changing face of American identity politics over the last thirty years has significantly effected the treatments, perceptions, and understanding of the female athlete of the postmodern era.

Ten years after the UN's "Decade for Women" had ended (1995), the Fourth World Conference of Women (henceforth known as FWCW) was convened in Beijing, China, for the purpose of exploring the progress of women's rights in a global world that was about to enter its *fin de millennium*. While the FWCW recognized that there had been important advancements in the status of women in the previous decade, that progress had been uneven at best. Specifically, since 1975, the findings, while ambiguous and broadly reported, noted that significant knowledge and information had been generated about the status of women and the conditions in which they live, helping to create advancement in issues of equality, health, and social-cultural concerns for women and girls. As such, there was set in motion a specific plan of attack to address and enact policy initiatives.

One of these chief outcomes of the FWCW was the enactment of the "Platform for Action," an "agenda for women's empowerment . . . aimed at establishing a basic group of priority actions that should be carried out during the next five years" (United Nations Press Office, 1995). Further, it expressed a call to action for governments, organizations, women's groups, and all others that were interested in the rights of women throughout the world. The Platform reviewed the current state of women's rights in the world and offered twelve critical areas of concern and focus for the next five years, among them, the persistent and increasing burden of poverty on women, violence against women, and the discrimination and violation of the rights of the girl-child.

Of all these areas of concern, perhaps the single most significant and important – especially in light of recent developments related to women's sports – is the focus on the "girl-child." While concern for the female child is not new, a clear and present focus on the girl-child, her rights, and her empowerment became especially noteworthy during the FWCW. In its summation, the FWCW notes that since nearly half of the world's population is under 25 – and with 85 percent of the world's youth being localized in developing countries – the rights and experiences of the girl-child must be protected and enhanced so that women may be players in tomorrow's future (United Nations Press Office, 1995). It is the figure of the young girl and her health – both physical and mental – that has become a key focus for the US response to the Fourth World Conference on Women's "Platform for Action."

The year 2000 marked the five-year expiry date for FWCW's "Platform for Action." Coinciding with this anniversary, the "Beijing + 5" (title of review) found that a "profound change in the status and role of women have occurred in the years since the start of the United Nations Decade for Women in 1976, some more markedly since FWCW" (United Nations Press Office, 2000). Women and women's rights were said to have benefited from the FWCW but, even as progress of women's rights was heralded and applauded, the report cards showed that most countries still have more than a long way to go. In particular, the USA, which has never ratified CEDAW (although 168 nations have seen fit to do so), was given an overall grade of "D" (as in A, B, C, D, and F grades) by US Women Connect, a coalition of women's groups that advocate for women's rights. This report card found the USA's efforts toward the "persistent discrimination against the girl-child and the violation of her rights" (one of the twelve areas of focus) as "severely inadequate" and cited the US government for failing to pass *effective* federal policy that adequately addresses the needs of girls (Carpenter, 2000: 1).

The inability of the USA to score high marks (or, rather, its ability to score low marks, depending on how you look at it) on the US Women's Connect report card has just as much to do with execution as it does with planning. In response to the FWCW and the Platform for Action, the USA created "America's Commitment," a series of federal programs and initiatives alleged to benefit women that were drawn directly from the Platform's call to action. The initiatives were broad in both scope and subject matter, and ranged from a series of objectives to concrete plans such as the development of "The Advisory Council on Violence Against Women" to protect women's rights and to work toward an end to violence against women. While such initiatives were obviously constructed with the utmost benefit of women in mind, they are – as with most public policy grounded in socio-cultural practices – always in flux.

One such example of US policy-making is the "Personal Responsibility and Work Opportunity Reconciliation Act of 1996." Signed into law by President William Jefferson Clinton, this act contained a sweeping, bipartisan plan to dramatically alter the state of America's welfare system; this sweeping welfare reform would deeply affect not only those on welfare but also contribute directly in shaping the types of social programs and messages that young girls and boys would receive over the subsequent five-year period. For our (admittedly simplistic) purposes, the key reform policy limited the amount of time a woman could receive welfare benefits, and carried with it strong work requirements and transition requirements for adults. It also stipulated that "unmarried minor parents are required to stay in school and live at home, or in an adult-supervised setting, in order to receive assistance" (Teen Pregnancy Center Press Office, 2000). The purpose of this reform was twofold: not only did it strive to alter the welfare system as we knew it from an economic standpoint, but it also looked to capitalize on the cultural reception of the reform itself in order to institute a return to the traditional families and family values espoused by both parties; in other words, the blame for societal problems was squarely leveled at the feet of the welfare queen or the teen parent. By coming out swinging against the (image of the) irresponsible welfare queen who had countless babies and lived off the government, while at the same time playing off of the fear that all teenagers would soon be giving birth to babies themselves, this reform and the subsequent teen pregnancy initiatives that followed helped serve to monitor and label as deviant those who were alleged to be caught up in such "risky" behavior as smoking, alcohol abuse, and premarital/unprotected sexual activities.

As a follow-up to the 1996 welfare act, President Clinton (1997) announced a sweeping effort to prevent America's crisis of teen pregnancy labeled the "National Strategy to Prevent Teen Pregnancy" (NSPTP). The main thrust of this strategy was "a comprehensive plan to prevent teen pregnancies and to support and encourage adolescents to remain abstinent," which was seen as a key aspect of avoiding teen pregnancy and helping to shift American culture back to old-fashioned family values. Focused on reclaiming the lives of wild youths and motivating irresponsible adults into becoming productive citizens by deploying such so-called "common-sense" rhetoric as abstinence from sex, hard work, and family values, the multi-million-dollar campaign was hailed as yet another breakthrough in the fight for empowered youth and against unproductive and deviant lifestyles. Despite these aforementioned efforts, there lacks a committed effort to engage positively with young girls and offer something other than such misdirected messages as "abstinence." Enter sport, the popularly conceived bastion of goodness, normalcy, and All-American values.

Girl (em)Power!(ment) discourse

One federal policy that does allege to address the needs of girls is the so-called "Girl Power!" campaign. Popping up in such varied sites as marketing slogans, child welfare programs, cartoons, and mainstream magazines, the term "Girl Power!" and its attendant derivations has become an almost ubiquitous signifier of "Girl Culture" *circa* 2002. Broadly and superficially defined in the popular press as "the empowerment and freedom of young girls from gender stereotyping" (Mesbah, 1998: 26) – an obvious, "common-sense" recitation of its impact – such an interpretation is necessarily bounded within and refuses to challenge the underlying politics of representation that spawn such a pseudo-resistant definition. Moreover, and to the extent that "Girl Power!" writ large relies on "personal self-betterment strategies that mask political and economic conditions of disadvantage and vulnerability" (Geissler, 2001: 329), the lack of critical reflection levied against its commodification and appropriation by corporate America is both disheartening and inexcusable.[7]

Such popular celebration of the girl-child is particularly revealing within the US government's implementation and exploitation of this commodified "Girl Power!" moniker. Under the direction of the Department of Health and Human Services (HHS), and launched in association with Clinton's "President's Council on Physical Fitness and Sports," the stated aim of the alleged politically and socially forward-thinking campaign is to "encourage and empower 9–14-year-old girls to make the most of their lives" (HHS/Girl Power! Official Website). Donna Shalala, Secretary of HHS during the 1996 to 1997 formulation and deployment of this campaign, was quoted as saying:

> With "Girl Power!" we see physical activity as a cornerstone of our strategy to give 9–14-year-old girls the confidence and resilience they need to stay away from the *dangers* like tobacco, drugs, and teen pregnancy and make the most of their lives. . . . Getting involved in sports such as basketball, tennis, and soccer builds self-confidence and self-esteem while also keeping young girls physically active. These are vital skills and attitudes that will help girls throughout their adult lives.
>
> (HHS/Girl Power! Official Website, 1996–1997, emphasis in original)

Of interest to us is the relationship this campaign holds with the construction of national interest *vis-à-vis* the American girl-child, especially with regard to the enactment of sport as a zone of purity from which to better one's life. In the case of athletics in general, and girls' youth sport in particular, we would agree to characterize the discursive alignment brought about by "Girl Power!" – in its multiple incarnations – as a "subversion of stereotypical notions of female body culture whereby binaries of weak/strong, feminine/masculine, and soft/hard are imploded and reconstructed with both empowering and productive results" (Giardina, 2001: 213). While the "empowering" half of the equation should be evident – increased participation by girls in sport, shift in focus to issues surrounding the girl-child, and widespread acceptance of women's sports – it is the productive aspect of power circulating such discursive spaces and masking unequal power relations that, while seemingly embracing all things Girl, further contributes to the status quo rather than challenging it.

Unfortunately, the "Girl Power!" campaign – and the commodified/co-opted narrative of "Girl Power!" in general – has been hailed by many in both the popular press and some in academia (e.g. Carlip, 1995; DeSena and DeSena, 2001; Lound, 1999; however, see also the collection of essays in Maglin and Perry, 1995) as a positive step in the right direction for the future of the American girl-child – a future where she is empowered and on an equal footing with her male counterpart – without fully grasping the socio-political implications and cultural complexities circulating behind its deployment. Such uncritical readings of "Girl Power!" that so casually celebrate its feel-good empowerment message directly buys into the "kernel of Utopian fantasy" offered by such programs while celebrating the overly romanticized notion that overcoming the perpetuation of oppression and domination over women is something that will inevitably occur without the pro-active involvement of dedicated individuals, grass-roots activism and organizations, political action committees, and/or federal legislation.

Everyday athletes *à la* Nike

> When corporate politics is cloaked in the image of innocence, there is more at stake than the danger of simple deception. There is the issue of cultural power and how it works to make claims on our understanding of the past, national coherence, and popular memory as a site of injustice, criticism, and renewal.
>
> (Giroux, 1995: 119)

While successful government-funded and supported programs addressing the current state of women are certainly lacking in most if not all areas, the slack has been picked up (however deleteriously) by the private sector, where women's sport is considered a hot commodity in the advertising and marketing industry. Specifically, corporate America has reached out to embrace women and girls on the level of their problems and concerns in daily life, presenting themselves as organizations and/or corporations that care intimately about these issues. Whether in the form of "global strategic community relations" (GSCR) programs aimed at generating a positive corporate image and which "increasingly help define and direct the values, rights, and obligations of citizenship" (King, 2001), or those advertising/marketing campaigns that extol the virtues of being a girl in postmodern, post-feminist, post-Title IX America, "girls" and "sport" have never before been so intimately intertwined.

One of the most celebrated, oft-criticized, and ultimately complex sites for excavating the underlying power relations circulating in the postmodern era *vis-à-vis* women's empowerment is and has been footwear and sports apparel giant Nike, Inc. Recognized globally as the industry leader in the sports/fitness apparel and footwear market with roughly $9 billion in yearly revenue (Wong, 2001) and positioning itself as a community leader which actively invests in and is responsive to women's issues and concerns, Nike has become synonymous with both women's sports and women's sporting apparel. As C.L. Cole and Amy S. Hribar posited in 1995, Nike, among other leading multinational corporations, has become "deeply embedded in a discursive formation that has generated and legitimated a popular feminism" (Cole and Hribar, 1995: 349).[8] This move, to borrow from Miguel Korzeniewicz (2000: 158), has entailed "the construction of a convincing world of symbols, ideas, and values harnessing the desires of individuals to the consumption of athletic shoes."

After a number of failed attempts to successfully attract female consumers, Nike hit upon a market-share winner when it teamed with global advertising giant Wieden + Kennedy to produce the "Empathy/Dialogue" campaign (often referred to as the so-called "tearjerker" campaign). As Cole and Hribar's (1995: 360) exhaustive critique of Nike's celebrity feminist positioning within the USA reveals, "Empathy/Dialogue" focused on issues of self-esteem and self-affirmation (i.e. not the hypermasculinization of the self found in Nike ads targeting male consumers) wherein "[T]he celebration of the authentic self is heightened through exercising as a strategy for locating, expressing, and caring for the self." The result of this ground-breaking campaign? Sales jumped 25 percent in consecutive years (1991 and 1992), and by 1993, women "accounted for 20% of Nike's $3 billion in worldwide sales" (Cole and Hribar, 1995: 360). Even more impressive is that by 1995, female consumers accounted for $4.7 billion in athletic shoe sales, which represented the largest single market segment (Cole and Hribar, 1995).

On the heels of "Empathy/Dialogue" came "If you let me . . .," which masterfully wove maudlin images of young girls together with such striking copy as "I will suffer less depression," "I will like myself more," and "I will be less likely to get pregnant before I want to." Whereas "Empathy/Dialogue" primarily targeted adult women, "If you let me . . ." shifted the discursive focus to that of the future of America – the young girl.[9] However, while this ad campaign received tremendous popular acclaim (over 500,000 letters and e-mails to Nike in support of it, so the story goes), feminist scholars were quick to point out the problematics of its "blanket request for permission," one that framed such permission as being wielded by the hands of white, middle-class males. As Melisse Lafrance (1998: 128) keenly observes, the

> "If you let me play" ad idealizes and naturalizes post-Reagan conservatism not by what it says, but what it does not say. Discourses of compulsory heterosexuality, "natural" male aggression, the nuclear family, and family planning are presupposed; capitalist productive processes go unquestioned; liberal notions of freedom and choice are both imagined and secured.

However, the mainstream press glossed over this well-reasoned point (imagine that!), choosing instead to focus on the feel-good future of America, American sports, and corporate concern for the physical and mental well-being of children, especially girls. Not only was Nike offering a "solution" to the problems facing women, but it was also, and at the same time, positioning itself so as to authorize and make noticeable the alleged cause of such problems in accordance with its own corporate narrative of consumer affect.

"Everyday athletes" in practice

Foreshadowing Nike's latest foray into women's sports are two coterminous events: Nike's "Helping Girls Become Strong Women" initiative of 1998 and its involvement with the WNBA's "Be Active" program. The former – a collaboration between Nike, Secret Antiperspirant, and the "Partnership for Women's Health" at Columbia University – was undertaken at the behest of Nike to study the issue of low self-esteem and mental health issues surrounding young women. The findings were, to say the least, not encouraging: 50 percent of the more than 1,100 girls surveyed said that they felt depressed or low at least once a week; nearly 29 percent said they felt somewhat or very uncomfortable with their body image; and nearly 40 percent said that they were struggling in school (Nike Press Office, 20 October 1998). What is so disturbing about these statistics is that they point to a trend where girls – despite the popularity empowerment rhetoric holds with them (and with the media) – are still struggling with teenage life and are often without a strong support system. Even more revealing is the finding that more than 20 percent of girls polled said they currently *do not have a strong adult role model.*

Concurrent with this initiative is Nike's sponsorship role with the WNBA and its "Be Active" grass-roots program, one that targets – you guessed it – 9- to 14-year-old girls, and is designed to encourage them to exercise regularly [read: buy Nike shoes] and raise their awareness of how to "play fit and stay fit" [read: buy Nike shoes]. In its current form, the campaign offers fitness clinics for women and youth in eighteen US cities, sponsors a national "Be Active" day, maintains a significant web presence, and contributes financial resources to community projects such as court refurbishment and facilities construction. Felicia Hall, sports marketing manager for Nike's women's basketball division, explains: "Nike has long been committed to the health of America's youth and paving the way to a fit future. Programs such as 'Be Active' and partnerships with exemplary organizations such as the WNBA will allow us to meet that commitment" (Nike Press Office). Needless to say, these two accounts of Nike's recent "charitable endeavors" lead smoothly into its latest pro-woman offering.

This brings us to "Everyday Athletes," the latest attempt by Nike to reach the ever-powerful female consumer market. Bearing ad copy such as "I like pink," "I paint my toenails," and "I've never owned a ball. I sweat," these ads show female athletes engaged in sports ranging from ice hockey and boxing to football and yoga. In tapping into the fashionable cultural discourse of women's empowerment currently dominating the early 2000s, Nike's multi-faceted, cross-media campaign is designed to connect with the "everyday" female athlete and "provid[e] benefits and solutions to the way she lives *now*" (Nike Press Office, 5 February 2001, emphasis added).

Launched on 5 February 2001, "Everyday Athletes" takes its cue from the late Nike co-founder Bill Bowerman's statement, "If you have a body, you are an athlete" (Nike Press Office, 5 February 2001). Along with six televisual commercials and four print executions, "Everyday Athletes" also includes the launching of the NikeGoddess.com website, a chain of retail boutiques catering to women (also called NikeGoddess), and a correspondingly themed monthly publication. Says Jackie Thomas, Nike's director of US women's marketing, about the campaign:

> The definition of "athlete" is very narrow to many women. We'd like women to take ownership of the term and to feel proud of what they do. These ads show the breadth and depth of sports for women, and they show women approaching sports on their own terms.
>
> (Nike Press Office, 5 February 2001)

Most notably, the latest offering from Nike turns and plays on some of the everyday situations, contradictions, and fallacies that surround female athletes. Visually, the images are quite striking, artistically capturing the essence of sport in depicting a football player with blood on her jersey, a hockey player with sweat pouring off her face, and a woman engaged in a complex yoga exercise. These images are meant to signify – positively – the varied sporting enterprises undertaken by women of all ages, appealing to a wide range of lifestyles and tax brackets *circa* 2001. Moreover, since football and hockey are two sports where women have seen recent advances on a wide-ranging scale, they can also be understood as appearing as role models for young girls to look up to and emulate.

Of course, the "proper" role model embodied by the contemporary female athlete and espoused by Nike's philosophy is the fit, disciplined, and contained body. In other words, the body you can have if only you buy (into) Nike. As Michel Foucault (1980b: 56) explains:

> [M]astery and awareness of one's own body can be acquired only through the effects of an investment of power in the body: gymnastics, exercises,

muscle-building nudism, glorification of the body beautiful. All of this belongs to the pathway leading to the desire of one's own body, by the way of the insistent, persistent, meticulous work of power on the bodies of children or soldiers, the healthy bodies.

In this instance, the power invested in and circulating throughout the physically fit body is inherently based upon a white, middle-class fiction that fails to consider other conceptions of fitness or the larger socio-economic forces working on one's body. This fiction assumes the position that one has disposable income, time, energy, and desire to meet the demands of disciplining one's self, which can take the form of everything from membership in a local gym or eating a "healthy" diet to joining a local hockey league or purchasing expensive in-home work-out equipment.

In such cases, the female body is marked by an "unbound" discipline, one that is not bound up in drill sergeants telling one to drop and give them twenty but of the criticism of the hairdresser who tells the overweight girl she has such a pretty face, or the late-night infomercial that promises to reshape and tone one's body into the person one has always wanted to be. This unbound discipline of institutionalized heterosexuality aids in transforming female bodies into attractive objects of desire, while also helping to subordinate other needs and desires in an effort to become physically attractive. Bartky (1988: 75) elucidates this phenomenon, stating,

> [N]evertheless, insofar as the disciplinary practices of femininity produce a "subjected and practiced," an inferiorized, body, they must be understood as aspects of a far larger discipline, an oppressive and inegalitarian system of sexual subordination. This system aims at turning women into the docile and compliant companions of men just as surely as the army aims to turn its raw recruits into soldiers.

Herein lies the genius behind "Everyday Athletes." That one is now able – within the popular matrix of American culture – to both "like pink" and yet "still sweat" re-imagines how the dual consumption of hyperfemininity and tomboy-athleticism is no longer diametrically opposed; the New Age female athlete à la Nike is both "girly-girl" and "athletic."

It is at the core of this liminal space that Nike's "Everyday Athletes" campaign operates from, constructing the physically fit, healthy, and normative female sporting participant of today as both athletic *and* feminine. Further, while appearing to transgress boundaries and engage in sports once consider as wholly male preserves (e.g. football, hockey, hunting), such actions remain framed within and carry with them the trappings of heteronormative politics; the female athlete who plays rugby or ice hockey gains notoriety from and is celebrated because she obeys – whether consciously or not – the tenets of postmodern American culture and its fitness boom, showing how corporate interest in her has made her feel empowered. Through the tacit acceptance of such (seemingly unbounded) boundaries outlined within "Girl Power!," "Be Active," and "Everyday Athletes," the physically fit body becomes molded by and thus exists as a (by-)product of a consumer culture whereby the all-seeing gaze of advertisements, news reports, and dieting books proclaim the fit body as a cure to one's ills, both physical and mental. This gazing eye, one that Denzin (1995: 183) argues "defines and shapes the contours of lived experience," reverberates throughout the entire sphere of the "Everyday Athletes" campaign, while similarly encompassing the whole of women's sports.

Coda

> If power were never anything but repressive, if it never did anything but say no, do you really think one would be brought to obey it?
>
> (Foucault, 1980)

Sport. Politics. Corporate America. The iron triangle of disingenuous rhetoric and civic (ir)responsibility in postmodern America. Tracing out the current trajectory of America's active involvement in and promotion of not only women's sports, but also the (not-so)-subtle construction of a national and political landscape, reveals the complex intersections of sport, media, and social issues that assist in defining the acceptable boundaries of personal subjectivity. In this instance, female athletic participation – while popularly acknowledged as the natural outcome of feminist activism and Title IX – remains predicated on and intimately intertwined with an always already ideology of conservative cultural politics. While Nike, in some fashion, should be credited with trying to advance a dialogue about the future of American girlhood (whether genuine or not), it is ultimately dangerous to sit back, accept, and celebrate that such wonderful social changes are occurring without fully understanding (or challenging) the complex machinations of our conjunctural epoch. As recent findings regarding teen pregnancy, drug use, and self-esteem indicate, there is more at stake with regard to the future of the American girl-child – and American culture in general – than whether or not she has a professional sports league to play in or a yoga class to attend. Ultimately, we as a society must decide whether or not we want our daughters (and sons) to grow up in an environment of blind allegiance to catchy marketing slogans masquerading as political calls to action, or whether we want to advance the promise of a radical progressive democracy where true equality, empowerment, and social awareness are treated as cornerstones of daily life, not afterthoughts.

Acknowledgments

We wish to thank Norman K. Denzin, CL Cole, Amy Hribar, and Synthia Sydnor for their insightful comments on earlier versions of this project, as well as Steven J. Jackson and David L. Andrews for their editorial guidance and helpful words of wisdom during the writing process.

References

Adweek, (2001). Trends, 12 February, p. 18.

Anderson, B. (1983). *Imagined Communities: Reflections on the Origin and Spread of Nationalism*. London: Verso.

Andrews, D.L. (1993). *Deconstructing Michael Jordan: Popular Culture, Politics, and Postmodern America*. Unpublished doctoral dissertation. Urbana, IL: University of Illinois, Urbana-Champaign.

Andrews, D.L. (1996). The fact of Michael Jordan's blackness: Excavating a floating racial signifier. *Sociology of Sport Journal, 13* (2), 125–158.

Andrews, D.L. (1998). Excavating Michael Jordan: Notes on a critical pedagogy of sporting representation. In G. Rail (ed.), *Sport and Postmodern Times* (pp. 185–219). Albany, NY: SUNY Press.

Asaro, C. (1999). *The Radiant Seas*. Mass Market.

Bartky, S.L. (1988). Foucault, femininity and the modernization of patriarchal power. In I. Diamond and L. Quimby (eds), *Feminism and Foucault: Reflections on Resistance* (pp. 61–83). Boston, MA: Northeastern University Press.

Baumgardner, J. and Richards, A. (2000). *Manifesta: Young Women, Feminism, and the Future*. New York: Farrar, Straus & Giroux.

Berlant, L. (1997). *The Queen of America goes to Washington City: Essays on Sex and Citizenship*. Durham, NC: Duke University Press.

Best, S. and Kellner, D. (1997). *The Postmodern Turn*. New York: The Guilford Press.

Bordo, S.R. (1992). The body and the reproduction of femininity: A feminist appropriation of Foucault. In A.M. Jagger and S.R. Bordo (eds), *Gender/Body/Knowledge* (pp. 13–33). New Brunswick, NJ: Rutgers University Press.

Brownell, S. (1995). *Training the Body for China: Sports in the Moral Order of the People's Republic*. Chicago, IL: University of Chicago Press.

Carlip, H. (1995). *Girl Power: Young Women Speak Out*. New York: Warner Books.

Carpenter, M. (2000). Programs to help girls in U.S. found mostly in private sector. *Pittsburgh Post Gazette.com*. Available online.

Carrington, B. (2000). "Two world wars and one world cup, do, dah, do dah": Sport and multiculturalism in Britain and Western Europe. Paper presented to the 2000 Sport and Culture in the Global Marketplace programme. University of Surrey, Roehampton, UK.

Click, M. (2001). Consuming perfection or perfecting consumption?: Martha Stewart's commodification of femininity and affluence. Paper presented at the Women's Studies Network (UK) 14th annual conference on Gender and Culture, Cheltenham, UK.

Cole, C.L. (1993). Resisting the canon: Feminist cultural studies, sport, and technologies of the body. *Journal of Sport and Social Issues, 17* (2), 77–97.

Cole, C.L. (1996). American Jordan: P.L.A.Y., consensus, and punishment. *Sociology of Sport Journal, 13* (4), 366–397.

Cole, C.L. (1998). Addiction, exercise, and cyborgs: Technologies of deviant bodies. In G. Rail (ed.), *Sport and Postmodern Times* (pp. 261–275). Albany, NY: SUNY Press.

Cole, C.L. (2000). The year that girls ruled. *Journal of Sport and Social Issues, 24* (1), 1–6.

Cole, C.L. and Andrews, D.L. (1996). "Look – It's NBA Showtime!": Visions of race in the popular imaginary. In N.K. Denzin (ed.), *Cultural Studies: A Research Annual, 1* (pp. 141–181). Stamford, CT: JAI Press.

Cole, C.L. and Andrews, D.L. (2000). America's new son: Tiger Woods and America's multiculturalism. In N.K. Denzin (ed.), *Cultural Studies: A Research Annual, 5* (pp. 109–124). Stamford, CT: JAI Press.

Cole, C.L. and Hribar, A. (1995). Celebrity feminism: Nike-style post-Fordism, transcendence, and consumer power. *Sociology of Sport Journal, 12* (4), 347–369.

Cole, C.L., Geissler, D., Giardina, M.D. and Metz, J.L. (2001). McPowering adolescence: Consuming girls' sports in Disney's America. Paper presented at the annual meeting of the American Sociological Association, Anaheim, California.

Coontz, S. (1992). *The Way we Never Were: American Families and the Nostalgia Trap.* New York: Basic Books.

Denzin, N.K. (1986). Postmodern social theory. *Sociological Theory, 4,* 194–204.

Denzin, N.K. (1991). *Images of Postmodern Society: Social Theory and Contemporary Cinema.* Thousand Oaks, CA: Sage.

Denzin, D.K. (1995). *The Cinematic Society: The Voyeur's Gaze.* Thousand Oaks, CA: Sage.

Denzin, N.K. (1997). *Interpretive Ethnography: Ethnographic Practices for the 21st Century.* Thousand Oaks, CA: Sage.

DeSena, C. and DeSena, J. (2001). *Girl Power.* Kansas City, MO: Andrews and McMeel.

Elliott, R. and Wattanasuwan, K. (1998). Brands as symbolic resources for the construction of identity. *International Journal of Advertising, 17* (2), 131.

Featherstone, M. (1987). Lifestyle and consumer culture. *Theory, Culture, and Society, 1,* 55–70.

Featherstone, M. (1990). *Consumer Culture and Postmodernism.* London: Sage.

Featherstone, M. (1991). The body in consumer culture. In M. Featherstone, M. Hepworth and B.S. Turner (eds), *The Body: Social Process and Cultural Theory* (pp. 170–196). London: Sage.

Foucault, M. (1977). *Discipline and Punish.* New York: Pantheon Books.

Foucault, M. (1980). *Power/Knowledge: Selected Interviews and Other Writings 1972–1977.* New York: Pantheon Books.

Foucault, M. (1982). Afterword: The subject of and power (pp. 208–226). In H. Dreyfuss and P. Rabinow (eds), *Michel Foucault,* Chicago, IL: University of Chicago Press.

Geissler, D. (2001). Generation G. *Journal of Sport and Social Issues, 25* (3), 324–331.

Giardina, M.D. (2001). Global Hingis: Flexible citizenship and the transnational celebrity. In D.L. Andrews and S.J. Jackson (eds), *Sports Stars: The Cultural Politics of Sporting Celebrity* (pp. 201–217). London: Routledge.

Giardina, M.D. and Metz, J.L. (2001). Celebrating humanity: Olympic marketing and the homogenization of multiculturalism. *International Journal of Sports Marketing and Sponsorship, 3* (2), 203–223.

Giroux, H.A. (1994). Living dangerously: Identity politics and the new cultural racism. In H.A. Giroux and P. McLaren (eds), *Between Borders: Pedagogy and the Politics of Cultural Studies* (pp. 29–56). New York and London: Routledge.

Giroux, H.A. (1995). Memory and pedagogy in the "Wonderful World of Disney": Beyond the politics of innocence. In E. Bell, L. Haas and L. Sells (eds). *From Mouse to Mermaid: The Politics of Film, Gender, and Culture* (pp. 43–61). Bloomington: Indiana University Press.

Goldman, R. (1992). *Reading Ads Socially.* London: Routledge.

Goldman, R. and Papson, S. (1998). *Nike Culture: The Sign of the Swoosh.* London: Sage.

Grossberg, L. (1992). *We Gotta Get Out of this Place: Popular Conservatism and Postmodern Culture.* New York: Routledge.

Grossberg, L. (1997). *Dancing in Spite of Myself: Essays on Popular Culture.* Durham, NC: Duke University Press.

Hall, S. (2000). The multi-cultural question. In B. Hesse (ed.), *Un/settled Multiculturalisms: Diasporas, Entanglements, Transruptions* (pp. 209–241). London: Zed Books.

Hesse, B. (2000). *Un/settled Multiculturalisms: Diasporas, Entanglements, Transruptions.* London: Zed Books.

Heywood, L. (1999). *Pretty Good for a Girl: An Athlete's Story.* Minneapolis: University of Minnesota Press.

Heywood, L. (2001). The girls of summer: Social contexts for the "Year of the Woman" at the '96 Olympics. In K. Schaffer and S. Smith (eds), *The Olympics at the Millennium: Power, Politics and the Games* (pp. 99–116). New Brunswick, NJ: Rutgers University Press.

hooks, b. (1999). Eating the other. In S. Hess-Biber, C. Gilmartin and R. Lyndenberg (eds), *Feminist Approaches to Theory and Methodology: an Interdisciplinary Reader* (pp. 179–194). New York: Oxford University Press.

Hribar, A.S. (2001). *Consuming Lifestyles: Transforming the Body and the Self in Postfeminist America.* Unpublished doctoral dissertation. Urbana: University of Illinois, Urbana-Champaign.

Jeffords, S. (1994) *Hardbodies: Hollwood Masculinity in the Reagan Era.* New Jersey: Rutgers University Press.

Kellner, D. (1991). Reading images critically: Toward a postmodern pedagogy. In H.A. Giroux (ed.), *Postmodernism, Feminism, and Cultural Politics: Redrawing Educational Boundaries* (pp. 60–82). Albany, NY: SUNY Press.

Kellner, D. (1995). *Media Culture: Cultural Studies, Identity, and Politics between the Modern and the Postmodern.* New York: Routledge.

Kellner, D. and Best, S. (1991). *Postmodern Theory: Critical Interrogations.* New York: The Guilford Press.

King, S.J. (2000). *Civic Fitness: Sport, Volunteerism, and the Politics of Generosity.* Unpublished doctoral dissertation. Urbana, IL: University of Illinois, Urbana-Champaign.

King, S.J. (2001). Marketing generosity: Avon's women's health programs and new trends in global community relations. *International Journal of Sport Marketing and Sponsorship, 3* (3), 267–289.

Korzeniewicz, M. (2000). Commodity chains and marketing strategies: Nike and the global athletic footwear industry. In F.J. Lechner and J. Boli (eds), *The Globalization Reader.* Oxford: Blackwell.

Lafrance, M.R. (1998). Colonizing the feminine: Nike's intersections of postfeminism and hyperconsumption. In G. Rail (ed.), *Sport and Postmodern Times* (pp. 117–139). Albany, NY: SUNY Press.

Lound, K. (1999). *Girl Power in the Family: A Book about Girls, Their Rights, and Their Voice.* Minneapolis, MN: The Lerner Publishing Group.

Lowe, D.M. (1995). *The Body in Late-capitalist USA.* Durham, NC: Duke University Press.

McIntyre, V.N. (1998). *The Moon and the Sun.* New York: Simon & Schuster.

Maglin, N.B. and Perry, D. (1995). *"Bad Girls"/"Good Girls": Women, Sex, and Power in the Nineties.* New Brunswick, NJ: Rutgers University Press.

Marshall, P.D. (1997). *Celebrity and Power: Fame in Contemporary Culture.* Minneapolis: University of Minnesota Press.

Mesbah, M. (1998). "Spice Girl Power": Marketers really like it. *Kidscreen* (p. 26).

Mohanty, C.T. (1999). Women works and capitalist scripts. In S. Hess-Biber, C. Gilmartin and R. Lyndenberg (eds), *Feminist Approaches to Theory and Methodology: An Interdisciplinary Reader* (pp. 362–388). New York: Oxford University Press.

Morris, M. (1997). The truth is out there. . . . *Cultural Studies, 11* (3), 367–375.

National Coalition for Women and Girls in Education (2002). *Title IX at Thirty: Report Card on Gender Equity.* Washington, DC.

Nike Press Office (2001). WNBA and Nike to help youth and adults "Be Active." 24 January Available online: Http://nikebiz.com/media/n_active.shtml.

Office of Women's Health (2000). *America's Commitment: Federal Programs Benefiting Women and New Initiatives as Follow-up to the UN 4th World Conference on Women.* The National Women's Health Information Center. Available online: Http://www.forwoman.org/owh/pub/commit/l.htm.

Ong, A. (1998). Flexible citizenship among Chinese cosmopolitans. In P. Cheah and B. Robbins (eds), *Cosmopolitics: Thinking and Feeling Beyond the Nation* (pp. 134–162). Minneapolis: University of Minnesota Press.

Ong, A. (1999). *Flexible Citizenship: The Cultural Politics of Transnationality.* Durham, NC: Duke University Press.

Pronger, B. (1998). Post-sport: Transgressing boundaries in physical culture. In G. Rail (ed.), *Sport and Postmodern Times* (pp. 277–298). Albany, NY: SUNY Press.

Robins, K. (1997). What in the world's going on? In P.D. Gray (ed.), *Production of Culture/Cultures of Production* (pp. 11–66). London: The Open University Press.

Schultz, J. (2001). She got "game": Representations of female hunters in literature, 1998–2000. Paper presented at the XVIII annual conference of the Sport Literature Association, Johnson City, TN.

Spencer, N.E. (2001). From "child's play" to "party crasher": Venus Williams, racism, and professional women's tennis. In D.L. Andrews and S.J. Jackson (eds), *Sports Stars: The Cultural Politics of Sporting Celebrity* (pp. 87–101). London: Routledge.

Teen Pregnancy Center Press Office (2000). *Teen Pregnancy Analysis 2000.* Available online: Http://www.uthealth.com/ut/adolescent/pregnancy_teen.htm.

United Nations Press Office (1995). *Report of the Fourth World Conference of Women* (A/CONF.177/20). United Nations Department for Policy Coordination and Sustainable Development. Available online: Http://www.un.org/womenwatch/daw/beijing/platform/plat1.htm#statement.

United Nations Press Office (2000). *Beijing + 5 Process and Beyond.* United Nations Division for the Advancement of Women. Available online: Http://www.un.org/womenwatch/daw/followup/bfbeyond.htm.

Warner, M. (1993). *Fear of a Queer Planet.* Minneapolis: University of Minnesota Press.

Wernick, A. (1991). *Promotional Culture: Advertising, Ideologies, and Symbolic Expression.* London: Sage.

Wong, E. (2001). Trying new strategies for women; company seeks merger of athletics and fashion. *The New York Times,* 19 June, p. C1.

4 Enlightened racism and celebrity feminism in contemporary sports advertising discourse[1]

Jim McKay

In late twentieth-century America, the cultural capital of corporations has replaced many human forms of cultural capital. As we buy, wear, and eat logos, we become the henchmen and admen of the corporations, defining ourselves with respect to the social standing of the various corporations. Some would say that this is a new form of tribalism, that in sporting corporate logos we ritualize and humanize them, we redefine the cultural capital of the corporations in human social terms. I would say that a state where culture is indistinguishable from logo and where the practice of culture risks infringement of private property is a state that values the corporate over the human (Willis 1993: 132–133).

Prologue: the defiant bodies in Mexico City

The accomplishments of the African American members of the US track and field team at the 1968 summer Olympic Games were astonishing. In winning seven gold medals, the African American men established five world records and tied another. The 400m record set by Lee Evans stood for twenty years, and Bob Beamon's long jump standard was not bettered until 1991. Their women team-mates won three gold medals and set two world records, with Wyomia Tyus becoming the first woman to win the 100m at successive Olympics. Nearly forty years later these remarkable sporting achievements continue to take backstage to the dramatic political gesture of Tommie Smith and John Carlos. Both men had been involved in the civil rights movement and were on athletic scholarships at San Jose State University, where they met Harry Edwards, a civil rights campaigner and former student-athlete at SJSU where he was then teaching part-time. Smith and Carlos became involved with the Olympic Project for Human Rights, an organization that Edwards had formed in order to get African American athletes to boycott the Olympics. Although this goal failed, Smith and Carlos were still determined to make a political statement about racism. The drama unfolded as Smith, who was one of twelve children from a poor Californian farming family, and Carlos, who was born and grew up in Harlem, stepped on to the podium to receive their gold and bronze medals, respectively, for the 200m. Both men had already removed their shoes and rolled up their sweat-pants in order to show their black socks. Carlos wore beads around his neck to represent lynchings of African Americans, and Smith wore a black scarf and carried a boxed olive branch in his left hand as a symbol of peace. Both of them also wore a OPHR badge, as did Australian silver medallist Peter Norman as an expression of solidarity. While the American national anthem played, 80,000 spectators and a global TV audience watched in amazement as both men bowed their heads, remained silent, and held black-gloved fists aloft. Smith subsequently explained the meaning of the defiant gesture:

> My raised right hand stood for the power in black America. Carlos' raised left hand stood for the unity of black America. Together they formed an arch of unity and power. The black scarf around my neck stood for black pride. The black socks with no shoes stood for black poverty in racist America. The totality of our effort was the regaining of black dignity.
>
> (Matthews 1974: 197)

Brent Musberger, who went on to become a leading TV sports commentator, decried the protest as a "juvenile gesture by a couple of athletes who should have known better," and declared that Carlos and Smith were "a pair of dark-skinned stormtroopers ... [who] should have avoided the award ceremony altogether" (Hartmann 1996: 555). Following intense pressure from IOC, the USOC withdrew Smith and Carlos from the relays, where they undoubtedly would have won more gold medals, and sent them home. The IOC, which was unmoved when troops killed hundreds of Mexican students who were protesting the Games ten days before they opened, claimed that Smith and Carlos had been expelled for violating its rule prohibiting "political activity." Yet African American George Foreman, who waved an American flag in the ring after winning a gold medal in boxing, was not censured for his political act. Despite being banished and subsequently receiving death threats, the defiant image of Smith and Carlos became one of the most compelling icons of protest in American history.[2]

It is against this background of race, sport, and cultural politics that I want to examine some recent sport-related advertisements that feature men and women of color. In particular, I will focus on the interrelated processes of appropriation, mythologizing, decontextualization, nostalgia, and commodification that pervade contemporary advertising (Denzin 1987; Howell 1991). My analysis relies heavily on Hall's concept of "articulation" – the historical process by which social texts, identities, and practices are forged out of diverse and contradictory ideological elements. Although Hall eschews both reductionism and determinism by deploying highly nuanced terms such as "disarticulation," "rearticulation," "articulation of difference," and "difference in complex unity," he also insists that social texts, identities, and practices are always *relatively* anchored:

> without some arbitrary "fixing" or what I am calling "articulation," there would be no signification or meaning at all. What is ideology but, precisely

this work of fixing meaning through establishing, by selection, a chain of equivalences?

(Hall 1985: 93)

Similarly, Cowie (1977: 22) points out that:

> the endless possible signification of the image is always, and only a theoretical possibility. In practice, the image is always held, constrained in its production of meaning or else becomes meaningless, unreadable. At this point the concept of anchorage is important; there are developed in every society decisive technologies intended to fix the floating chains of signifieds so as to control the terror of uncertain signs.

Following Cowie and Hall, I argue that the advertisements I analyze below are articulated primarily as *myths* (Barthes 1973; Denzin 1987). Myths are not total delusions or utter falsehoods, but *partial truths* that accentuate particular versions of reality and marginalize or omit others. Myths embody fundamental cultural values and character-types and appeal to deep-seated emotions. In the mythologizing process, events are drained of their historical "truth" and repackaged in ways that serve the interests of powerful groups. Thus, myths depoliticize social relations by ignoring the vested interests involved in struggles over *whose* stories become ascendant in a given culture. Critically, myths disavow or deny their own conditions of existence: they are "authorless" forms of representation derived from specific sites and power relations, but have become so naturalized that people are seldom aware of being interpellated by them. Myths, therefore, are central to the everyday practices of advertising, since they drive the representational and ideological codes that underpin media narratives (Fiske 1987: 5, 135).

I also use the concepts of "enlightened racism" and "celebrity feminism" in my analysis. In their study of *The Cosby Show*, Jhally and Lewis (1992) found that despite appearing to break down racist beliefs, viewing the program fostered what they termed "enlightened racism." This alludes to the fact that white viewers could admire the respectable and affluent African Americans in the program for being "just like us" in striving to attain the American Dream, thus denying the institutionalized class and racial barriers faced by the majority of African Americans. African Americans welcomed the "positive" images in the program, but they too adhered to the American Dream, viewing the Cosby scenario as both desirable and achievable for black Americans. According to Miller (1986: 71), Bill Cosby himself is an advertisement for the American Dream by implicitly proclaiming the fairness of the American system: "'Look!' he shows us. 'Even I can have all this!... I got mine.'" "Celebrity feminism" refers to the welter of contradictory discourses related to corporate populism, promotional culture, the cult of the celebrity, commodity feminism, post-Fordism, corporeal discipline, and individualism that address women as consumers (Cole and Hribar 1995). I argue that in the ads to be considered below, both of these ideological articulations construct comforting, "positive" images of men and women of color, while masking class, sexual, and racial inequalities at both the local and global levels.

Sports advertising, "enlightened racism," and "celebrity feminism"

> Just do it
> There is no limit
> Life is short. Play hard
>
> (Advertising slogans of Nike, Puma, and Reebok)

The first advertisement I want to consider appeared in *Vibe*, a music and fashion magazine aimed at affluent young African Americans, although white audiences also read it. The full-page color advertisement consists of the famous image of Smith and Carlos on the podium at Mexico City. Superimposed on the image is the headline "PUMA SUEDES," followed by writer Alan Light's account of how these shoes were made famous in the 1970s by Walt "Clyde" Frazier, an African American basketball star. The copy states that the "Suedes" (later renamed "Clydes" in Frazier's honor) were popular among hip-hoppers and break-dancers and were recently re-released. It is also noted that the shoes' "legacy of cool" pre-dated Frazier:

> They were introduced in 1968 for the Mexico City Olympics, where they graced the fleet feet of Tommie Smith and John Carlos, who celebrated their gold and bronze medals in the 200-meter dash by giving the Black Power salute on the stand (and, mysteriously, removing their Pumas for the historic moment).

The second illustration is a twelve-page advertisement for Reebok shoes that was inserted into popular running and tennis magazines. The foldout is replete with images and phrases that accentuate freedom, dedication, perseverance, achievement, and individualism, as well as the technological qualities of the Reebok line. Of particular interest is the first page, which contains a sepia-colored, side-on action shot of the upper body of a young, muscular, black man in an athletic vest. The Reebok trademark appears in the middle of the page below the sentence:

YOU'VE COME SO FAR.

The third item is a double-page color Nike advertisement featuring American football superstar Jerry Rice that appeared in *Sports Illustrated*. Like other sportsmen, Rice literally embodies hegemonically masculine ideals, such as competition, discipline, and corporeal power (Messner 1992a; Trujillo 1991). However, the advertisement is ambivalent, because Rice is also an African American, and thus anchored by a constellation of racist stereotypes associated with men of color in general (Boyd 1997) and sportsmen of color in particular (Fleming 2001; Rowe *et al.* 2000; St Louis 2003). On the other hand, the potential for Rice to be read as a "dangerous other" is minimized by several codes. By utilizing chiaroscuro, Rice's face, which takes up most of the top right-hand side and center, is bathed in white light, giving him an ethereal aura. Although Rice looks directly at the camera, he has a contemplative gaze. His hands, which occupy most of the bottom half and right-hand side, are loosely clenched in front of his chest and shoulders, which are barely discernible in the dark shadows. His gesture is generally pensive and non-threatening. Occupying the entire left-hand side is a column of short, exhortatory sentences interspersed with Nike's world-famous advertising motto:

> Mother and father told you repeatedly. Crazy people talk to themselves. Still you heard the voice. Loud and clear. JUST DO IT. Learn how to hit a fastball. Work on your left hand shot. Study harder. Study longer. Get a raise. Crazy people talk to themselves. And still you heard the voice. JUST DO IT. Lose the gut. Master a third language. Swim across the lake. Climb the Tetons. Go to the library and learn how electricity works. Crazy people talk to themselves. And still you heard the voice. JUST DO IT. Bench press your weight. Finish a marathon. Develop a backhand. Switch careers. Crazy people talk to themselves. And finally, you realize, only a madman doesn't listen. JUST DO IT.

In the bottom right-hand corner there is a small photo of a Nike sneaker, and underneath the statement: "Jerry Rice, wide receiver, Mississippi Valley State, enrollment 2,263."[3]

Nike has attempted to maximize its global market share by sponsoring athletes who are: of both sexes (although women are much less prominent than men); both African American and white; from several nations; and represent "the good" (Michael Jordan, Pete Sampras, Wayne Gretzky, Tiger Woods), "the bad" (Jimmy Connors), and "the ugly" (John McEnroe, Charles Barkley) (Goldman and Papson 1998; Wilson 1997; Wilson and Sparks 1996). Nike has also attempted to enhance its image as a "good corporate" citizen via campaigns such as P.L.A.Y. (Participate in the Lives of American Youth Campaign), "NYC-attack," and allegedly women-friendly initiatives like its "If You Let Me Play" ads (Cole 1996, Cole and Hribar 1995; Dworkin and Messner 1999; Lafrance 1998; Lucas 2000; Maharaj 1997; Stabile 2000). In some of these campaigns, Nike has deployed sportswomen of color, most prominently African Americans like Marion Jones, Jackie Joyner-Kersee, and Sheryl Swoopes. Nike's marquee sportswoman of color in Australia is 2000 Olympic 400m champion Cathy Freeman, who has appeared in numerous print and TV advertisements (see Table 4.1).

Sport is a "master metaphor" that subsumes an array of "mini-metaphors" (Balbus 1975; Gozzi 1990). Liberal-democratic societies are suffused with

Table 4.1 Contents of three Nike TV ads featuring Cathy Freeman

Scene number	Image	Male voice-over	Time (secs)
Ad 1			
1	Freeman wearing a black-and-red-colored athletic outfit settling into the starting blocks		3
2	Alternating images of Freeman gazing down the track and in the set position	"You can accept defeat"	6
3	Front-on image of Freeman completing a sprint		9
4	Freeman crossing the finishing line, with the word *Nike* and its trademark "swoosh" displayed prominently on the front of her vest		12
5	*Nike* and its "swoosh" logo appear in the same colors as Freeman's athletic outfit	"Or you can stare at it until defeat blinks and walks away"	15

Scene number	Image	Caption	Time (secs)
Ad 2 (to strains of light classical music)			
1	Grainy black-and-white pan from torso to head of Freeman in an athletic outfit	400 METERS IS NOT A LONG WAY	10
2	Close-up of Freeman's eyes	YOU PROBABLY WALK FURTHER AROUND THE SUPERMARKET	22
3	Freeman's right hand on the starting line	YOU MIGHT RUN FURTHER CHASING A BUS	24
4	Freeman leaving the starting blocks	YOU'D GO FURTHER WALKING THE DOG	26
5	Freeman sprinting down the track	BUT WOULD 19 MILLION PEOPLE HOLD THEIR BREATH WHILE YOU DID IT?	28
6	The "swoosh" logo and phrase "JUST DO IT" in small caps appear in bottom right-hand corner		30

continued

Table 4.1 Continued

Scene number	Image	Caption	Time (secs)
Ad 3 (to strains of light classical music)			
1	Slow pan of six black-and-white stills from a family photo album, showing Freeman competing and training as a child, adolescent, and woman	THE RACE ONLY TOOK 49 SECONDS	15
2	Rapid series of about twenty stills of Freeman competing and winning as an adolescent and woman	THE WIN TOOK A LIFETIME	27
3	Freeman's face on the left and the "swoosh" logo and "JUST DO IT" appear in small caps in bottom right-hand corner		30

sporting metaphors that epitomize liberal definitions of fairness, justice, and equality (e.g. "A sporting chance," "Fair play," "It's not cricket," "Play by the rules," "Abide by the umpire's decision," "Don't shift the goal posts," "A level playing field"). Sport is also commonly cited as *the* exemplar of the purportedly egalitarian character of liberal democracies and frequently invoked as "proof" of the American Dream (Lipsky 1978, 1979; Nixon 1984; Sage 1998; Wenner 1994b). As Rowe (1991: 4, 8) comments:

> the language of sport has a peculiarly strong appeal ... because of the mythology of sport as a privileged site where success or failure are entirely the product of a freely operative meritocracy, where the rules are binding on all and where the only determinants are talent, courage and diligence. In a pluralistic framework of democracy, where the "umpire-state" arbitrates and disinterested reason is held to be the basis of decision-making, the hallowed game is the perfect metaphorical representation of idealized politics.

The Nike and Reebok advertisements alluded to above draw on such myths and metaphors by implying that society functions as "naturally" as a sporting event between strong and weak, and healthy and unhealthy contestants, and that gender and racial backgrounds are inconsequential in competing in a purportedly meritocratic game. However, such articulations disregard both the social inequalities of class, race, age, and gender that pervade sport itself and the global exploitation of labor undergirding the production and consumption of these companies' advertising slogans. It is to these *not-saids* of the texts (Eagleton 1976: 89) that I now turn.

Absences/silences

The Nike and Reebok advertisements exemplify the concept of enlightened racism in that they provide white audiences with "relief not only from fear but also from responsibility" (Jhally and Lewis 1992: 8). After all, if an African American athlete from a tiny college in the Deep South can "just do it," then one implication is that *anybody* can make it to the top. Moreover, if getting ahead is simply a matter of individuals working hard, rather than institutionalized classism, sexism, and racism, then people who fail have no one to blame but themselves. Through the techniques of stereotyping, decontextualization, fragmentation, and nostalgia, the Puma Suedes advertisement reconstitutes a momentous protest as a celebration, expunges the reason why Smith and Carlos wore black socks, and reinscribes an act of dissent as a funky fashion statement. The advertisements also illustrate hooks' (1992: 26) concept of the commodification of otherness: "a sign that progressive change is taking place, that the American Dream can indeed be inclusive of difference."

In short, these representations are *mythical*. For instance, a tiny number of athletes of color, like Jerry Rice and Cathy Freeman, occasionally do manage to escape oppressive conditions by using sport as a vehicle for upward social mobility. However, this needs to be weighed against some other facts in order to obtain a fuller understanding of upward and downward social mobility in sport. One such fact is that the handful of athletes (most of whom are men) who go "from rags to riches" are extremely rare exceptions to the obdurate class, gender, and racial structures of both Australian and American societies. Although a small number of African American men do obtain athletic scholarships, this has little effect on their career prospects, as the majority never graduate (Brooks and Althouse 1999).

Moreover, the astronomical odds against *anyone* securing a career in professional sport mean that only a handful of African American men are eventually signed, and an even tinier number ever coach, manage, or own teams (Coakley 2001). In fact, there is a higher probability of an African American male becoming a dentist, doctor, or lawyer than a professional athlete. As DeFrantz (1991) comments, the career prospects are even bleaker for African American women. The Nike and Reebok advertisements are also silent about the extensive racial inequalities in American professional team sports, where there is evidence of salary discrimination against African Americans in basketball, as well as "stacking" in baseball and football (Coakley 1998). Since professional athletes generally have relatively short careers due to injuries and the high turnover rates of players, they can also experience rapid downward social mobility upon retiring unless they have used sport either to secure long-term economic security and/or obtain skills for the labor market. Consequently, some scholars have suggested that for male athletes from African American and/or working-class backgrounds, sport may be more of a "jock trap" than a "mobility escalator" (Hoberman 1997). Thus, the situation of many young African American male athletes resembles the regime of exploitation depicted in the documentary *Hoop Dreams* (Cole and King 1998; hooks 1995; Jones 1997; Robbins 1997; Sperber 1997) rather than the rags-to-riches mythology conveyed by the Nike commercials.

Similar processes are evident in the ads featuring Freeman, who was once married to an American Nike executive. Contrary to the "pull-yourself-up-by-your-bootstraps" motif enunciated in the Nike ads, Aborigines' experience with sport in Australia has been a microcosm of their treatment in society at large: exclusion, stereotyping, and exploitation. Although Aborigines now face less overt racism in sport than in the past, they still tend to be concentrated in sports that require minimal financial outlay, such as football and boxing, which are male-only sports at the professional level, and absent from or under-represented in sports that require considerable amounts of economic and cultural capital (e.g. golf, skiing, rowing, sailing, swimming, gymnastics, cycling, tennis). Even in football, where Aborigines are over-represented, inequality is manifest in subtle forms. Studies of professional rugby league and Australian Rules football have shown that Aborigines are assigned to peripheral playing positions, suggesting that Aborigines are valued for speed and agility rather than leadership and thinking abilities (Hallinan 1991; Hallinan *et al.* 1999). Hallinan argues that although coaches are not necessarily racist in a personal sense, they operate with a mindset that has been shaped by racist ideologies that have long lingered in the popular imagination of white Australians. Aboriginal football players have also been persistent targets of racial vilification from both players and spectators (Gardiner 1997; McNamara 1988).

The themes of achievement and success in the Nike ads are also at odds with the extremely high rates of morbidity, mortality, and incarceration among Aboriginal people: the life expectancy of Aboriginal Australians is twenty years less than that of the general population and their infant mortality rate is twice as high; about 50 percent of Aboriginal men and 40 percent of Aboriginal women will die before they are 50; Aborigines have the highest incidence of rheumatic fever in the world and are eighteen times more likely than other Australians to die of infectious diseases; less than one-third of Aborigines enrol in post-secondary education; Aborigines are jailed around twenty times more often than other Australians, constitute a disproportionate percentage of the population in correctional institutions, and have an exceedingly high rate of deaths in custody. Meanwhile, both state and federal governments have repeatedly ignored declarations by the UN Committee on the Elimination of Racial Discrimination that both its 1998 amendments to the Native Title Act and sentencing procedures are discriminatory. As is the case with *Hoop Dreams*, the work of the expatriate Australian and investigative journalist and filmmaker John Pilger (1999a, 1999b, 1999c) is instructive. His film *Welcome to Australia* offers a stark counterpoint to the slick Nike ads that showcase Freeman.

As Bruce and Hallinan (2001) note, Freeman has become a national celebrity, and her iconic status has grown exponentially since she lit the cauldron at the opening ceremony of the 2000 Olympics and proceeded to win the 400m. She has been on the cover of every major Australian women's magazine and is regularly featured in advertisements for her major sponsors: Nike, Optus, Qantas, Myer, News Ltd, Channel Seven, and Oakley. Similar to the ways in which Tiger Woods has been acclaimed as "America's New Son" (Cole and Andrews 2001), "Our Cathy" has been hailed as the symbol of national reconciliation in Australia. For instance, immediately after her 400m victory at the Sydney Olympics the front cover of one of the most popular weekend magazines showed a jubilant Freeman with the Australian and Aboriginal flags draped over her shoulders and the headline "United Nation." It is hardly surprising that Freeman has become such a potent symbol of hope to Aborigines and relief to white Australians. Illustrating the concept of enlightened racism, Freeman's biographer notes that:

> White Australia likes to appropriate Freeman, her victories and her cheerful optimism because amid an Aboriginal race so often full of grief she's such a joy because she's one Aborigine we unequivocally don't have to feel guilty about.
>
> (McGregor 1998: 12)

However, only a minuscule number of women athletes, most notably Cathy Freeman, Evonne Goolagong-Cawley and Nova Peris, have ever overcome the class, racial, and gender barriers that face Aboriginal women. As Colin Tatz, the foremost researcher on Aboriginal sport, puts it:

> Cathy Freeman is an aberration. I don't mean she is aberrant. But she is not the symbol or representative of Aboriginal womanhood.... For every Cathy who runs, there are 100,000 Aboriginal women who are not going to get out of the mission or the reserve or the shitty little country town, who are going to lead a life of falling pregnant at 14, living off social service benefits.
>
> (Linnell 2000: 30)

In their analysis of celebrity feminism, Cole and Hribar (1995: 352) note that "Nike gains its identity as a progressive and pro-woman corporation by defining itself over and against what it ... positions as dangerous, unnatural, and even unjust practices." Yet Nike was unrepentant about the strong criticism surrounding its infamous "Sorry" ads that screened in Australia in 2000.[4] As part of a larger project of national reconciliation, Aborigines have continually pressured the conservative Australian government to apologize on behalf of the estimated 100,000 children – about 20 percent of the Aboriginal population – who were forcibly removed from their parents by government agencies between 1910 and 1970. As part of its orchestrated campaign to repudiate what it calls "political correctness" or a "black-armband view of history," the government has: rejected a Human Rights and Equal Opportunity Commission finding that the removal of these children constituted genocide; questioned the number of children who were taken away; challenged the use of the term "stolen generation" to describe this mass removal; and steadfastly refused to apologize, despite increasing public support for an expression of remorse.[5] For instance, in May 2000 an estimated 250,000 people from all sectors of Australian society marched peacefully across Sydney Harbour Bridge in the "Walk for Reconciliation" as a show of support for an apology. A highlight of this unprecedented demonstration was the sight of a skywriter spelling out the word "SORRY" above the crowd.

Shortly afterwards, Nike released a TV ad featuring twenty leading Australian athletes repeatedly saying sorry because of their preoccupation with training. It appears as though all the athletes are addressing Freeman (whose maternal grandmother was a member of the "stolen generation"), as she is the only one who does not say sorry. Instead, she runs by the camera, saying, "Can I get back to you later?" Aboriginal organizations, such as the *National Sorry Day Committee* and the *Journey of Healing*, expressed anger over the ad, claiming that it denigrated and trivialized the campaign for an apology and asked for it to be withdrawn. Nike refused, saying that the ad was just a "coincidence." I now turn to another aspect of what is ignored in all of the above ads – the global exploitation of labour that underpins the production and consumption of the sporting goods industry.

Corporate sport and the global sweatshop

Shaquille O'Neal's Reeboks are stitched by someone; Michael Jordan's Nikes are stitched by someone. . . . Those someones are women, mostly Asian women who are supposed to believe that their "opportunity" to make sneakers for U.S. companies is a sign of their country's progress. . .

(Enloe 1995: 10)

The American-owned sports shoe market alone produces billions of dollars in retail sales. But beneath this all-American facade lies an industry that relies heavily on the labor of women in the non-unionized sweatshops of Third World nations (Miller *et al.* 2001). Nike is the largest and most profitable company of its kind in the world, commanding over 40 percent of the global market in sports shoes and related apparel, which grossed at over $9 billion in 1997 (Goldman and Papson 1998: 4). Originally based in New Hampshire in 1974 (as Blue Ribbon Sports), Nike expanded to Maine in 1978, but shut its American plants in the 1980s and went offshore to Asia. Today, Nike only has several thousand employees in the USA, most of whom are engaged in marketing and design work. The parent firm licenses Asian companies to manufacture shoes to its specifications.

Some of these countries have abysmal records in industrial pollution, human rights abuses, working conditions, wages, and industrial accidents and illnesses (Klein 2000; Sage 1999). The INGI Labour Working Group has accused Nike-licensed factories of: breaking twelve national laws; violating several basic human rights; breaching American law by buying products that are manufactured in contravention of laws on workers' rights; and damaging local and national development. One of the Group's descriptions of the conditions at Nike's factories is worth citing at length:

> There are a thousand dreams that go through a fifteen year old American kid's head when he or she puts on those new Nike pumps. Dreams of the Super Bowl, of the Bulls, of John McEnroe, of the World Series. But for the fifteen year old girl who starts work in one of Nike's licensed factories, it is not thoughts of athletic derring-do, but rather the Sisyphean task of filling her rice bowl. Once she passes through the factory gate at 7.30 am, she will not be allowed out again for at least ten hours. She will work in the same section doing the same simple, repetitive task for six days a week – gluing or cutting or sewing. She will be allowed just one break of between half hour and an hour at lunch when she must go to the factory canteen. At the end of the day she will have earned on average 82 cents. . . . [She] does not own a pair of Nike's. In fact, she owns only one pair of shoes plus the flip-flops she wears for work. And even if the Nike goddess gave her a pair of pumps, she would be unable to play sport in them. Supposing she had the energy after a day on the Nike production line; there are no sports facilities in the spacious factory grounds, never mind the densely packed worker slums.
>
> (INGI Labour Working Group 1991: 8, 15)

In short, the capacity of an American multinational firm to project images of independence and self-expression and to decree "Just do it," rests on its systematic exploitation of some of the most oppressed and vulnerable people in the global market. It is a perversely postmodern "irony" that a First World company uses a Second World nation to exploit workers in the Third World, while deploying images of athletes of color to articulate images of freedom and individualism.[6]

Conclusion

> The object of the stereotype is not so much to crush the Negro as to console the white man.
>
> (Ellison 1964: 123)

> they had much rather see us engaged in those degrading sports, than to see us behaving like intellectual, moral, and accountable beings.
>
> (Douglass 1845/1968: 28)

> If you're not in shape from the neck up, forget from the neck down. Education is *numero uno*.
>
> (John Carlos)

The postmodern "turn," with its emphasis on heteroglossia, polysemy, pastiche, and intertexuality, has been a welcome corrective to essentialist, logocentric, and totalizing readings of social texts. Thus, at one level, the above representations may be read as counter-narratives to the leitmotiv that men of color are "misbehaving" (Messner 1992b), or the pervasive images in the Australian media of drunken and petrol-sniffing indigenous people. For instance, the Nike advertisements explicitly connect initiative, commitment, and success with an African American man and an Aboriginal woman. However, I maintain that these advertisements also exemplify the capacity of the media to mythologize relations of exploitation, and construct ideologies of enlightened racism and celebrity feminism.

This is not to suggest that young African Americans and Aboriginal Australians are "cultural dopes," who have messages about sport hypodermically injected into their heads: "Meaning is always negotiated in the semiotic process, never simply imposed inexorably from above by an omnipotent author through an absolute code" (Hodge and Kress 1988: 12). On the contrary, many young African Americans and Aborigines perceive that sport is one of the few arenas in which there is a chance, however infinitesimal, of "making it." Thus, advertisers have astutely tapped into the pervasive way in which sport embodies what Majors (1990) terms "cool pose" among African American men. However, African American men's concomitant valorization of sporting prowess actually bolsters class and racial domination and reinforces hegemonic masculinity (Messner 1992a; Sabo and Curry Jansen 1992). For instance, Gates (1991: 78) observes that:

> an African-American youngster has about as much chance of becoming a professional athlete as he or she does of winning the lottery. The tragedy for our people, however, is that few of us accept that truth ... the blind pursuit of attainment in sports is having a devastating effect on our people. Imbued with a belief that our principal avenue to fame and profit is through sport, and seduced by a win-at-any-cost system that corrupts even elementary school students, far too many black kids treat basketball courts and football fields as if they were classrooms in an alternative school system. "O.K., I flunked English," a young athlete will say. "But I got an A plus in slam-dunking."

Rowe makes a similar point with respect to Aborigines:

> This jock trap is a real problem. Aboriginal people fall into it themselves. ... But it's a double-edged thing. If we to some degree associate white people with brains and leadership and so on and people of colour with their bodies ... that's really reproducing fairly old racial ideology. Culturally in Australia, because sport is so immensely powerful, the temptation for indigenous people to go into that area, rather than the less glamorous but more important areas where they can get their hands on the levers of

power . . . it's a real danger, You want Aboriginal role models in all spheres. It's a dangerous thing to say to people to try and make it through sport when their chances are infinitesimal.

(cited in Linnell 2000: 32)

To paraphrase Marx, men and women do not make sport just as they please. Nevertheless, they do make it, and it is possible to create alternative sporting practices. Gates has called for professional African American athletes to contribute a share of their income to the United Negro College Fund, and to publicize the value of obtaining an education among young African Americans (also see Edwards 1991). He goes on to state that:

society as a whole bears responsibility as well, Until colleges stop using young blacks as cannon fodder in the big-business wars of so-called nonprofessional sports, until training a young black's mind becomes as important as training his or her body, we will continue to perpetuate a system akin to that of the Roman gladiators, sacrificing a class of people for the entertainment of the mob.

(Gates 1991: 78)

As I have tried to indicate in this chapter, an important part of this struggle over the meaning of sport is to demythologize the ways in which multinational sportswear companies have articulated images of freedom, opportunity, and success with athletes of color, while omitting the exploitative labor practices that underpin their advertising campaigns.

Epilogue: the loyal bodies at Barcelona

Before I won the 200 in Mexico, people used to call me a "nigger"; after Mexico they called me a "fast nigger."

(Tommie Smith)

I'm not black, I'm universal.

(Michael Jordan)

The commercialism of a Michael Jordan is easier to control than the political awareness of a Tommie Smith.

(American sports journalist Robert Lipsyte)

Though Jordan may be a highly popular image and make great sums of money, his status and access to the corridors of power, though obviously higher than most African Americans, are still is subordinate to the corporate interests that he represents.

(Boyd 1997: 108)

The demonstration by Tommie Smith and John Carlos at Mexico City was the apogee of what Harry Edwards called "the revolt of the black athlete" (Edwards 1969; Leonard 1998, 2000). However, the insurrection was short-lived. Since the Mexico Olympics, sport has become increasingly integrated into the media industries, advertising agencies, and multinational corporations of the world market (Miller *et al.* 2001). By the time of the 1984 Games in Los Angeles, the media were saturated with patriotic images of both African American and white American athletes waving their national flag. Instead of seeing rebellious black fists in the air, we saw a double-page color image of Carl Lewis' black body sprinting in front of a huge photo of the Stars and Stripes in a tribute to the Olympics by *Life* magazine. Over the past twenty years, American companies have increasingly employed (usually male) athletes to promote both their merchandise and corporate rhetoric. In the 1970s, Arthur Ashe, O.J. Simpson, Walt Frazier, and Julius Erving became some of the first "crossovers," the marketing phrase for blacks who are popular among African American consumers and also palatable to white clients. The quintessential crossover is Michael Jordan, who is one of the most recognizable people on earth and earns millions for endorsing products by multinational companies such as McDonald's, Coca-Cola, Wheaties, Wilson, Chevrolet, and Hanes, but Nike in particular (Andrews 2001). After winning the gold medal for basketball at the 1992 Olympics in Barcelona, Jordan and his predominantly African American team-mates on the American "Dream Team" also staged a "protest" on the victory podium (Wenner 1994a). Reebok, an official Olympics sponsor, had supplied the American team with warm-up suits with its logo on the jacket. However, Jordan threatened to boycott the proceedings because he did not want to support a rival corporation, claiming that "I don't believe in endorsing my competition. I feel very strongly about loyalty to my own company." His African American team-mate Charles Barkley, also a Nike client, stated that, "'Us Nike guys,' he said, 'are loyal to Nike, because they pay us a lot of money. I have two million reasons not to wear Reebok'" (Baker 2000). At the ceremony, Barkley and Jordan demurred by wrapping themselves in the American flag to cover the Reebok emblem, while the other players unzipped their jackets in order to obscure it. The stark difference between the defiant fists of Tommie Smith and John Carlos at Mexico City and the loyal corporate bodies of Barcelona is a sobering reminder of novelist Milan Kundera's aphorism that part of the struggle of people against power is the struggle of memory against forgetting.[7]

References

Andrews, D.L. (ed.) (2001). *Michael Jordan, Inc: Corporate Sports, Media Culture, and Late Modern America*. Albany, NY: SUNY Press.

Baker, W.J. (2000). If Christ came to the Sydney Olympics, Part 4. Available online at: http://www.abc.net.au/rn/talks/8.30/relrpt/stories/s195324.htm.

Balbus, I. (1975). Politics as sports: The political ascendancy of the sports metaphor in America *Monthly Review*, 26, 26–39.

Barthes, R. (1973). *Mythologies*. London: Paladin.

Bartindale, B. (2003). Famous SJSU Olympic protesters honored. *Mercury News*, 17 October, p. 9.

Boyd, T. (1997). *Am I Black Enough For You? Popular Culture From the 'Hood and Beyond.* Bloomington, IA: University of Indiana Press.

Brooks, D.D. and Althouse, R.C. (eds) (1999). *Racism in College Athletics: The African-American Athlete's Experience* (2nd edn). Morgantown, VA: Fitness Information Technology.

Bruce, T. and Hallinan, C. (2001). Cathy Freeman: The quest for Australian identity. In D.L. Andrews and S.J. Jackson (eds), *Sport Stars: The Cultural Politics of Sporting Celebrity*. London: Routledge.

Coakley, J. (2001). *Sport in Society: Issues and Controversies* (7th edn). Boston: Irwin/McGraw Hill.

Cole, C.L. (1996). American Jordan: P.L.A.Y., consensus and punishment. *Sociology of Sport Journal*, 13, 366–397.

Cole, C.L. and Andrews, D.L. (2001). America's new son. Tiger Woods and America's multiculturalism. In D.L. Andrews and S.J. Jackson (eds), *Sport Stars: The Cultural Politics of Sporting Celebrity*. London: Routledge.

Cole, C.L. and Hribar, A. (1995). Celebrity feminism: Nike style post-fordism, transcendence, and consumer power. *Sociology of Sport Journal*, 12, 347–369.

Cole, C.L. and King, S. (1998). Representing black masculinity and urban possibilities: Racism, realism, and *hoop dreams*. In G. Rail (ed.), *Sport and Postmodern Times*. Albany, NY: SUNY Press.

Cowie, E. (1977). Women, representation and the image. *Screen Education*, 2–3, 15–23.

DeFrantz, A. (1991). We've got to be strong. *Sports Illustrated*, 12 August, p. 77.

Denzin, N.K. (1987). On semiotics and symbolic interactionism. *Symbolic Interaction*, 10, 2–19.

Dilbeck, S. (2003). When raised fists raised nation's ire. *Los Angeles Daily News*, 15 October, p. 23.

Douglass, F. (1845/1968). *Narrative of the Life of Frederick Douglass, an American Slave*. New York: Signet.

Dworkin, S. and Messner, M.A. (1999). Just do . . . what? Sport, bodies, gender. In B.B. Hess, M. Marx Ferree and J. Lorber (eds), *Revisioning Gender*. Thousands Oaks, CA: Sage.

Eagleton, T. (1976). *Criticism and Ideology*. London: New Left Books.

Edwards, H. (1969). *The Revolt of the Black Athlete*. New York: The Free Press.

Edwards, H. (1991). Democratic pluralism: Placing the African-American student-athlete in the context of a new agenda for higher education. *National Academic Advising Journal*, 11, 28–109.

Ellison, R. (1964). *Shadow and Substance*. New York: Random House.

Enloe, C. (1995). The globetrotting sneaker. *Ms.*, March/April, pp. 10–15.

Fiske, J. (1987). *Television Culture*. London: Routledge.

Fleming, S. (2001). Racial science and south Asian and black physicality. In B. Carrington and I. McDonald (eds), *"Race," Sport and British Society*. London: Routledge.

Gardiner, G. (1997). Racism and football: The AFL's racial and religious vilification code in review. *Sporting Traditions*, 14, 3–25.

Gates, H.L. (1991). Delusions of grandeur. *Sports Illustrated*, 19 August, p. 78.

Goldman, R. and Papson, S. (1998). *Nike Culture: The Sign of the Swoosh*. London: Sage.

Gozzi, R. (1990). Is life a game? Notes on a master metaphor. *Et cetera*, Fall. pp. 219–223.

Hall, S. (1985). Signification, representation, ideology: Althusser and the post-structuralist debates. *Critical Studies in Mass Communication, 2*, 91–114.

Hallinan, C. (1991). Aborigines and positional segregation in Australian Rugby League. *International Review for the Sociology of Sport, 26*, 69–79.

Hallinan, C., Bruce, T. and Coram, S. (1999). Up front and beyond the centre line: Integration of Australian Aborigines in elite Australian Rules Football. *International Review for the Sociology of Sport, 34*, 369–384.

Hartmann, D. (1996). The politics of race and sport: resistance and domination in the 1968 African American Olympic Protest Movement. *Ethnic and Racial-Studies, 19*, 548–566.

Hoberman, J. (1997). *Darwin's Athletes: How Sport Has Damaged Black America and Preserved the Myth of Race*. Boston, MA: Houghton Mifflin.

Hodge, B. and Kress, G. (1988). *Social Semiotics*. Ithaca, NY: Cornell University Press.

hooks, b. (1992). *Black Looks: Race and Representation*. Toronto: Between the Lines.

hooks, b. (1995). Neo-colonial fantasies of conquest: Hoop dreams. *Sight and Sound, 5*, 22–23 (reprinted in hooks, *Reel to Real*. New York: Routledge, 1996).

Howell, J. (1991). "A revolution in motion": Advertising and the politics of nostalgia. *Sociology of Sport Journal, 8*, 258–271.

INGI Labour Working Group (1991). Unjust but doing It. Paper presented at the International NGO Forum on Indonesia Conference, Washington, 29 April to 1 May.

Jhally, S. and Lewis, J. (1992). *Enlightened Racism:* The Cosby Show, *Audiences and the Myth of the American Dream*. Boulder, CO: Westview Press.

Jones, L. (1997). Hoop realities. *Jump Cut: A Review of Contemporary Media, 40*, 8–14.

Klein, N. (2000). *No Logo. Taking Aim at the Corporate Bullies*. Toronto: Knopf Canada.

Kundera, M. (1983). *The Book of Laughter and Forgetting*. London: Penguin.

Lafrance, M. (1998). Colonizing the feminine: Nike's intersections of postfeminism and hyperconsumption. In G. Rail (ed.), *Sport and Postmodern Times*. Albany, NY: SUNY Press.

Leonard, D. (1998). What happened to the revolt black athlete? A look back thirty years later: An interview with Harry Edwards. *Colorlines, 1*, 1. Available online at http://www.arc.org/C_Lines/CLArchive/story1_1_01.html.

Leonard, D. (2000). The decline of the black athlete: An online exclusive: Extended interview with Harry Edwards. *Colorlines, 3*, 1. Available online at http://www.arc.org/C_Lines/CLArchive/story3_1_03.html.

Linnell, G. (2000). True colours. *The Bulletin*, 25 July, pp. 28–32.

Lipsky, R. (1978). Toward a political theory of American sports symbolism. *American Behavioral Scientist, 21*, 345–360.

Lipsky, R. (1979). Political implications of sports team symbolism. *Politics and Society, 9*, 61–88.

Lipsyte, R. (1993). Silent salute, ringing impact. *New York Times*, 17 October, pp. 1, 11.

Lucas, S. (2000). Nike's commercial solution. *International Review for the Sociology of Sport 35*: 149–164.

McGregor, A. (1998). A nation's champion. *The Australian*, 26 January, p. 12.

McNamara, L. (1998). Long stories, big pictures: Racial slurs, legal solutions and playing the game. *Australian Feminist Law Journal, 10*, 85–108.

Maharaj, G. (1997). Talking trash: Late capitalism, black (re)productivity, and professional basketball. *Social Text, 50*, 97–110.

Majors, R. (1990). Cool pose: Black masculinity and sports. In M.A. Messner and D.S.

Sabo (eds), *Sport, Men, and the Gender Order: Critical Feminist Perspectives*. Champaign, IL: Human Kinetics Press.

Matthews, V. (1974). *My Race Be Won* (with Neil Amdur). New York: Charterhouse.

Messner, M.A. (1992a). *Power at Play: Sports and the Problem of Masculinity*. Boston, MA: Beacon Press.

Messner, M.A. (1992b). White men misbehaving: Feminism, Afrocentrism, and the promise of a critical standpoint. *Journal of Sport and Social Issues*, 16, 136–144.

Miller, M.C. (1986). *Boxed In: The Culture of TV*. Evanston: Northwestern University Press.

Miller, T., McKay, J., Lawrence, G., and Rowe, D. (2001). *Globalization and Sport: Playing the World*. Thousand Oaks, CA: Sage.

Moore, K. (1991a). A courageous stand. *Sports Illustrated*, 5 August, pp. 62–73.

Moore, K. (1991b). The eye of the storm. *Sports Illustrated*, 12 August, pp. 62–73.

Nixon, H. (1984). *Sport and the American Dream*. New York: Leisure Press.

Pilger, J. (1999a). Fixed race. *The Guardian Weekly*, 21 August, pp. 18–19, 21, 23.

Pilger, J. (1999b). *Welcome to Australia*. John Pilger, director; John Pilger and Alan Lowery, co-producers. Available online at http://pilger.carlton.com/australia/film.

Pilger, J. (1999c). *Australia: The Secret Shame*. Available online at http://pilger.carlton.com/australia/articles.

Robbins, B. (1997). Head fake: Mentorship and mobility in hoop dreams. *Social Text*, 50, 111–120.

Rowe, D. (1991). Player's worktime: Sport and leisure in Australia. *The Australian Council for Health, Physical Education and Recreation National Journal*, Autumn, pp. 4–10.

Rowe, D., McKay, J. and Miller, T. (2000). Panic sports and the racialized male body. In J. McKay, M.A. Messner and D.S. Sabo (eds), *Men, Masculinities, and Sport*. Thousand Oaks, CA: Sage.

Sabo, D.S. and Curry Jansen, S. (1992). Images of men in sport media: The social reproduction of the gender order. In S. Craig (ed.), *Men, Masculinity, and the Media*. Thousand Oaks, CA: Sage.

Sage, G. (1998). *Power and Ideology in American Sport: A Critical Perspective* (2nd edn). Champaign, IL: Human Kinetics Press.

Sage, G. (1999). Justice do it! The Nike transnational advocacy network: Organization, collective actions, and outcomes. *Sociology of Sport Journal*, 16, 206–235.

Sperber, M. (1997). Hollywood dreams. *Jump Cut: A Review of Contemporary Media*, 40, 3–7.

Spivey, D. (1985). Black consciousness and Olympic protest movement. In D. Spivey (ed.), *Sport in America: New Historical Perspectives*. Westport, CN: Greenwood Press.

St Louis, B. (2003). Sport, genetics and the "natural athlete": The resurrection of racial science. *Body and Society*, 9, (2), 75–96.

Stabile, C.A. (2000). Nike, social responsibility, and the hidden abode of production. *Critical Studies in Mass Communication*, 17, 186–204.

Steele, D. (2003). Historic act to be honored. *The San Francisco Chronicle*, 15 October, p. C1.

Trujillo, N. (1991). Hegemonic masculinity on the mound: Media representations of Nolan Ryan and American sports culture. *Critical Studies in Mass Communication*, 8, 290–308.

Wenner, L. (1994a). The dream team, communicative dirt, and the marketing of synergy: USA basketball and cross-merchandising in television commercials. *Journal of Sport and Social Issues*, 18, 27–47.

Wenner, L. (1994b). What's sport got to do with it? *Journal of Sport and Social Issues, 18,* 203–206.

Willis, S. (1993). Disney world: Public use/private space. *South Atlantic Quarterly, 92,* 119–137.

Wilson, B. (1997). "Good blacks" and "bad blacks": Media constructions of African-American athletes in Canadian basketball. *International Review for the Sociology of Sport, 32,* 177–189.

Wilson, B. and Sparks, B. (1996). "It's gotta be the shoes": Youth, race, and sneaker commercials. *Sociology of Sport Journal, 13,* 398–427.

5 Race, representation, and the promotional culture of the NBA

The Canadian case

Brian Wilson

With the introduction of NBA expansion franchises to Toronto and Vancouver in the mid-1990s, Canadian sport media and marketers were forced to respond to the demands of a league defined by its successes linking professional sport with entertainment spectacle.[1] The NBA and affiliated advertisers (e.g. Nike) are renowned for their ability to promote ultra-appealing athletes like Michael Jordan to global icon status, while setting a stage for other notable players to become high-priced celebrities in local and national markets. In Canada, sport journalists and advertisers alike embraced the challenge of educating Canadian audiences about the NBA product and its personalities. Of course, in a league where about 80 percent of the participants are African-American, *this inevitably meant disseminating messages about race*.

There is an abundance of research that describes the construction of racist ideologies about African-American athletes in the media. These ideologies include: articulating common-sense beliefs about the "natural" athletic superiority of African-Americans (Davis, 1990; Wonsek, 1992); constructing subtle images of "enlightened racism" (McKay, 1995); demonizing male African-American athletes (Kellner, 1996; Lule, 1995); and disseminating stereotypes about "dumb jocks" (Sailes, 1993), and "good blacks" and "bad blacks" (Wenner, 1995). Since most of these findings have been reported in the American context, key questions related to race, sport, and the media in Canada have been scarcely considered. For example: How are African-American athletes portrayed in Canadian media and how do these depictions compare to portrayals in American media; to what extent has the mass-mediated promotional/consumer culture of the American-based NBA spilled over into Canada; what role might these images play in perpetuating racism in Canada; what specific role might marketers (who promote the athletes) and sport journalists (who attempt to generate reader interest) play in this audience-socializing process?

The goal of this chapter is to shed light on these topics through a conceptual discussion of race, mass media, and promotional culture (in general and in relation to the distinct Canadian racial context), and through the presentation of findings from research on African-American athlete media portrayals in Canada (via a case study of the Toronto Raptors).

Approaching African-American representation

In an attempt to conceptualize how common-sense beliefs about African-Americans are naturalized through mass media representations, the interrelated concepts of ideology, enlightened racism, intertextuality, and floating (racial) signifier have been adopted. Although the long-standing sociological concept "ideology" has been subject to various applications/interpretations (see Eagleton, 1991), it is nevertheless a useful reference term for understanding the material and symbolic processes by which racial representations are produced and naturalized. For example, in his study of television portrayals of African-American poverty and privilege, Gray effectively links and anchors the concept within race studies, arguing that:

> Media representations of black successes and failure and the processes that produce them are ideological to the extent that the assumptions that organize the media discourses shift our understandings of racial inequality away from structured social processes to matters of individual choice. Such ideological representations appear natural and universal rather than as the result of social and political struggles over power.
>
> (Gray, 1989: 377)

In this way, the historical realities of racism are displaced by celebrations of the African-American middle class using stars such as Bill Cosby and Michael Jackson as fictional and non-fictional representations of "an open class structure, racial tolerance, economic mobility, the sanctity of individualism, and the availability of the American dream for black Americans" (Gray, 1989: 376). These representations are contrasted with non-fictional representations of black urban crime, gang violence, drug abuse, teenage pregnancy, riots, homelessness, and general aimlessness that show the African-American underclass "as a social menace that must be contained" (Gray, 1989: 378). Similarly, Jhally and Lewis (1992), in their study of audience reactions to the *Cosby Show*, proposed that non-stereotypical portrayals of upper-middle class African-Americans, while potentially showing white viewers that the "colour of one's skin can indeed signify nothing," in fact appear to create a false illusion of social equality for these viewers. The authors used the term "enlightened racism" to describe these subtle everyday practices by which the successes or failures of African-Americans are attributed to their ability or inability to take advantage of available opportunities. In his work on sport media, McKay (1995) adapted the concept to study representations of African-American male athletes in advertisements by multinational sporting apparel companies such as Nike, Puma, and Reebok. Akin to Gray and Jhally and Lewis, McKay argued that the advertisements mythologized notions of individualism and meritocracy, thereby allowing white audiences to deny the existence of institutionalized racism both in sport and in American society in general.

Although studies of stereotypical and non-stereotypical portrayals often concentrate on specific genres of media discourse (e.g. television commercials, newspaper sport sections), viewers are believed to make sense of these representations "intertextually," constructing views about race based (in part) on media influences from various sources. As Fiske explained: "knowledge of reality, and therefore, for practical purposes, reality itself, is intertextual: it exists only in the interrelations between all that a culture has written, spoken, visualized about it" (1987: 115). The poststructuralist concept of "floating (racial) signifier" extends and (necessarily) complicates the intertextuality concept in its emphasis on the complex and contradictory nature of social texts, identities, and meanings in "postmodern" societies. For example, in his study of representations of Michael Jordan's blackness, Andrews (1996: 153) identified a "cultural racism" which oscillated "between patronizing and demeaning representations of African-American Otherness." In adopting the concept for this study, however, it is imperative to note that despite a "perpetual slippage of the signifier" (Hall, 1985: 93), social texts, identities, and practices are always "relatively anchored" (McKay, 1995: 192) and that "in practice, the image is always held, constrained in its production of meaning or else it becomes meaningless, unreadable" (Cowie, 1977: 22).

African-American athlete portrayals and advertising

Embedded in the studies noted above are analyses of sport-related advertising specifically. Along with McKay's (1995) work, Wonsek's (1992) research examined the representation of Blacks in all television commercials shown during a sample of 1988 NCAA basketball tournament games, McDonald (1996) and Andrews (1996) studied various promotional schemes in the mass marketing of Michael Jordan, and Wenner (1994) scrutinized television commercials featuring African-American "Dream Team" members that were shown during the 1992 summer Olympics.

Television commercials and other forms of advertising, sport-related and otherwise, contain features that are distinct from other media genres. For example, athletic apparel commercial advertising, which has been described as having a "compressed, rock-video-style narrative" (Wilson and Sparks, 1996: 399), is part of a long and ever-evolving tradition of advertising techniques. As Leiss and colleagues (1990) have noted advertisements in the 1920s tend to espouse the merits of the "product or service" in a straightforward manner, while in the 1960s and beyond, messages were more cryptic and depended on the viewer "relating elements of the ads' internal structure to each other, as well as drawing in references from the external world" (1990: 199). Understanding these industry-based developments is crucial to consider for at least two reasons. First, in semiotic/textual analyses of advertisements, the semiologist who "deconstructs" the ads greatly benefits from understanding the codes and conventions that guide the production of media messages. Although this knowledge might not alter the actual interpretation of the ad, any discussion of the study's relevance to the "sport media complex" (i.e. the relationship between media production, content, and audiences) requires this context. Second, any consideration of the political economy of professional sport, and the impacts of advertisers on the culture of sport (and popular culture generally) requires sensitivity to the specificities of marketing practice (e.g. the strategic use of celebrity athlete spokespersons). Having said this, the extent to which advertising is somehow separate and distinct from other genres of media should not be overstated. As noted above, it is the combination of images and influences from various sources (and mediums) that intertextually impact audiences.

Representations of the Black athlete in Canada: research and context

Compared to the breadth of work in the American context, there is a relative paucity of research on "Black" athlete portrayals in Canadian media. To date, Jackson's (1998a; 1998b) examination of media (racial) discourses surrounding sprinter Ben Johnson and previous work by the author of this paper on the marketing of black culture (Wilson, 1999) and youth interpretations of athletic apparel commercials (Wilson and Sparks; 1996; 1999; 2001) are the only scholarly studies on the topic. Jackson's work demonstrated how Ben Johnson's mediated racial and national identity was unstable and seemingly dependent on the social context of his portrayal (akin to Andrews' (1996) findings), as he explained:

> prior to his world class performances and subsequent to the national shame of the steroid scandal, the media almost always represented Ben Johnson through signifiers that defined him as the "racial other." These demarcations included hyphenated signifiers such as "Jamaican-Canadian" as well as the use of racial stereotypes linked to animal imagery, intelligence and deviance. Conversely, Johnson's mediated representation during his reign as world champion, an achievement which brought Canada world recognition and prestige, reveals a temporary displacement of his racial identity; that is; he was simply referred to as "Canadian."
>
> (Jackson, 1998a: 27)

Wilson's (1999) research, while similarly focused on subtly racist depictions of the race in Canadian media, described how African-American forms of symbolic and cultural resistance (e.g. the "cool pose" described by Majors, 1990) have been appropriated by and incorporated into big business.

While alluding to issues of media production and content, Wilson and Sparks' work focused largely on the impacts of these portrayals on Canadian youth cultures (Wilson and Sparks, 1996; 2001) and on Black and non-Black youths' understandings of race (Wilson and Sparks, 1999). The research showed that commercial advertising along with various other media messages appear to inform youth about style, racial inequality, and race, and moreover that the Black and non-Black groups often interpreted the messages in distinct ways –

differences related to the youths' distinct social locations, racial identities, and the contexts of reception.

Of course, the backdrop for these audience interpretations and the media portrayals of race discussed here is the distinct racial climate of Canada (see also Jackson (1998a; 1998b) for an elaborate discussion of this topic in relation to sport and national identity). Canada has traditionally supported an ideology and resolution to multiculturalism (in contrast to the American "melting-pot"), a commitment that was officially established at a constitutional and legislative level in 1971. These seminal policies led to the establishment of agencies and funded programs that attempted to promote and manage racial and ethnic diversity. More recently, there has been a shift in multicultural directives "from an initial focus on culture and ethnicity ('celebrating differ-ences') to one which emphasizes antiracism and equity ('managing diversity')" (Fleras, 1995: 409). The Multiculturalism Act of 1988 in Canada, what Fleras has described as a "post-multicultural mandate," required institutions under federal control to make appropriate adjustments for minority accommodation through improved entry, access, representation, and treatment (1995: 409). This act was intended to reinforce, reflect, and promote the reality of multi-culturalism in Canada.

For many critics, Canada's movement against ethnic inequality is ineffective and illusory. Research has shown consistently that there are comparatively fewer educational and economic opportunities for visible minorities in Canada compared to those of European (mainly British or French) descent (Agocs and Boyd, 1993; Boyd, 1992; Henry, 1994; Satzewich and Li, 1987). Evidence of unequal treatment, systemic barriers, and failure to accommodate diversity have been well documented in studies of occupations (Agocs and Boyd, 1993; Boyd, 1992; Collinson *et al.*, 1990; Fernandez, 1988; Henry and Ginzberg, 1993). Despite this evidence of overt discrimination and subtle institutional/structural disadvantage for minorities in Canada, the situation appears moderate com-pared to the widespread segregation and racial violence that defines the Amer-ican system (Connelly, 1995; Dyson, 1995; Omi, 1989; Omi and Winant, 1994).

Research method and data

In investigating the relevance of the theoretical concepts mentioned previously, I used the conventional methods of content analysis and social semiotics that were employed in the studies by Andrews (1996), Jhally and Lewis (1992), McKay (1995), and in other related analyses of representations of African-American athletes (e.g. Cole, 1996; Cole and Andrews, 1996; Cole and Denny, 1994; Denzin, 1996; Jackson, 1998a; 1998b; Kellner, 1996; Lule, 1995; Wonsek, 1992). The data came from three sources. The first item was seventeen Toronto Raptors' games that were televised nationally on the Canadian Television Network "CTV" or locally on the *New VR* (an independent station) between 13 February (the first game after the mid-season All-Star game) and 9 April

1996 (the last televised game of the season). The second source was videotapes of five promotional shows called *Raptors Tonight* that were telecast between 18 February and 24 March 1996 on the *New VR*. The goal of the data collection using these first two sources was to obtain information on the portrayals of African-American male athletes in the form of player profiles, social marketing messages (e.g. "Stay in School" promotions), and commercial advertising. The third component was the sports section of one of Toronto's major, non-tabloid newspapers, *The Toronto Star* (referred to hereafter as the *Star*). It was chosen because it contains detailed coverage of the Raptors, whereas its major competitor, *The Globe and Mail*, has a national slant. Two sportswriters had regular columns in the sports section (one contributed four times a week, the other twice weekly) in which they addressed issues other than standard accounts of the games and statistical summaries. This analysis began on 19 September 1995, when tryouts for the Raptors formally began, and ended in December of the same year.

Results

African-American athletes were generally framed as either Good Blacks or Bad Blacks. However, these were not mutually exclusive stereotypes; examples of oscillating representations were also found.

"Good Blacks"

Damon Stoudamire, the Raptors' star player at the time of the study (he now plays for the Portland Trailblazers), and Isiah Thomas, the team's VP and General Manager at the time (he is now General Manager of the New York Knicks) were constructed as archetypal Good Blacks. Thomas, who went from a Chicago ghetto to become a superstar with the Detroit Pistons NBA team, was narrativized by the media as an African-American who used sport as an avenue for upward social mobility. A particularly emphatic example of what Patton (1992; cited in Cole and Denny, 1994: 129) terms "Africanized Horatio Alger trope of athletics," occurred during the telecast of the ceremony prior to a game in Detroit, where the Pistons retired his uniform (New VR, 1996b). The event began with a segment from the news conference that showed Thomas being welcomed as the Raptors' GM, followed by background music and flashback clips of him playing for the Pistons. These images were superimposed by close-ups of a well-dressed (suit-wearing) Thomas talking about his vision for the Raptors, in which he often referred to organizational goals and highlighted the business side of basketball that he was now involved in:

> I think the most important step for us first is to start with people, the people that we bring into the basketball organization, the staffing, the coaching, scouts ... there has to be a certain chemistry. Because the

chemistry that we have as a working organization, as a staff of basketball people is going to be the type of chemistry that we reflect out on the court. It has to be a flexible organization that can encompass and embrace all different types of personalities

The rags to riches' motif was also prominent:

I was just a poor little West Side kid on the Chicago streets. I never dreamed that any of this could have happened ... I'm just fortunate to have met some nice people, not only now but along the way, people who are very important to me and have helped me a lot.

Former coaches and team-mates made speeches about Thomas' work ethic, competitiveness, leadership, and will-to-win. At the end of the ceremony, Thomas brought his family out to center court to share the occasion. This included his brothers, who were known to have fallen victim to the difficulties faced by inner city youth – problems that Isiah had avoided. Some viewers who did not follow basketball until it came to Toronto would have been aware of Thomas' background from newspaper profiles:

Once upon a time Mary Thomas was the matriarch, single-handedly raising her seven sons as best she could ... some fell to drugs, or gravitated to street gangs ... one became an architect, building an NBA team.

(Young, 1995i: E1)

In the *Star*, references were constantly made to Thomas' managerial activities regarding matters much as team finances and player salaries (Ormsby, 1995a; Young, 1995a; 1995e), organizational culture and team chemistry (Ormsby, 1995b; Young, 1995h), and personnel and player management (Clarkson, 1995a; 1995e; 1995f; Ormsby, 1995a; 1995d; Young, 1995a).

Race was notably absent from these portrayals. There was also little mention of the structures that prevent so many inner city blacks from excelling. When problems experienced by the working classes were noted, it appeared that those who failed, such as Thomas' brothers, made the wrong decisions. Thomas, on the other hand, appeared to have made the right choices, taking advantage of available opportunities, and using his extraordinary basketball talent and personality to attain fame and fortune. There was little mention of the large number of players who never escape the poverty of inner city life; the meager number of basketball scholarships available; the impoverished and incomplete education that the few scholarship holders receive, and the miniscule number of African-Americans who actually make it in the NBA (Leonard, 1996).

Although only a rookie at the time of the study, the diminutive Damon Stoudamire's lofty accomplishments (e.g. MVP of the Rookie All-Star game, the team's statistical leader and floor general) drew high praise from Toronto's media. He was described as: "lion heart" (Clarkson, 1995d); a "never-say-die" kind of player, "courageous" (Proudfoot, 1995), a "little big man" (Clarkson, 1995b); an "energizing presence" (Young, 1995); having a "work ethic" (Clarkson, 1995e), and a "Thomas clone" (Proudfoot, 1995). Proudfoot (1995: C1) suggested that Stoudamire is "the kind of energetic little athlete Torontonians have always doted on. They love to watch people beat the odds [referring to Stoudamire's relative shortness] through dedication and defiance." He was often referred to by his nickname "Mighty Mouse" (a cartoon superhero who wears a cape and tights, similar to superman) because he has a tattoo of the character on his arm and because of his small size and superlative ability.

Perhaps the most graphic portrayal of Stoudamire's virtues occurred in a widely shown Nike commercial. Playing on Stoudamire's nickname and tattoo, the commercial begins by showing him emerging from an image of Mighty Mouse. The camera then focuses on Stoudamire's tattoo, which appears to come to life and then flies off his arm. The rest of the commercial shifts between two scenes: one with game clips of Stoudamire making passes and scoring baskets with the Mighty Mouse character superimposed on the screen; the other with him alone in a gym executing fancy moves, dribbling, and shooting baskets while Mighty Mouse glides around. The commercial ends with Stoudamire dribbling the ball and smiling while several cartoon mice run around him and scream excitedly at their superhero. Nike's trademark "swoosh" appears briefly on the screen, and the scene cuts back to Stoudamire. The soundtrack running throughout the commercial is the "Mighty Mouse" cartoon theme song, sung merrily in a deep male voice, with a voice-over (shown in parentheses):

> It's Mighty Mouse (Stoudamire appears and the music begins).... Here I come to save the day (Damon Stoudamire), Mighty Mouse is on the way (what a mouse) when friends of his change wrong to right, Mighty Mouse will join the fight (whenever there's a threat in Toronto). On the sea or on the land, he's got the situation well in hand.

Although Stoudamire's "blackness" is apparent from this television portrayal, the potential for him to be read as "dangerous Other" is minimized by the brightness of the commercial – including the red and yellow colors of the Mighty Mouse character. Stoudamire appears friendly, good-humored, and non-threatening. He was often shown to be low-key, not complacent about his success, and recognizing the need to continually work hard, while at the same time enjoying his new-found fame and fortune. This was particularly evident in his comments during an interview on a boat cruise around the time of the All-Star game: "I feel like I learn something every game. Some times are harder than others but those are the times you fight through it" (New VR, 1996a). While Stoudamire talks, we see clips of him having fun with the driver of the boat and ordering a Margarita. Stoudamire is shown as someone who has recently "made it" and is handling success responsibly. He has worked hard and continues to work hard to achieve, yet is ever playful and non-threatening.

As with Thomas, race is neutralized in these portrayals. While race for Thomas is essentially invisible, race for Stoudamire is non-threatening. Thomas, a former player and still affiliated with a sport dominated by African-Americans, has shed his black identity to become a classic "organization man." Comparable to Michael Jordan, Thomas also "enacts a racially neutered identity, a Black version of a White cultural model," "White America's [and Canada's] solution to the race problem" (Denzin, 1996: 321). In a league that is notorious for "attitude," Stoudamire is a comforting image of blackness. In this sense, Thomas and Stoudamire are somewhat distinct images of the Good Black. Thomas, the businessman, allows white audiences to see that African-Americans can be "just like us," while Stoudamire, the athlete, lets audiences behold that African-Americans can be successful, modest, and "innocent" despite hostile surroundings.

Other "Good" African-American superstars were also featured routinely in commercials during telecasts of Raptors' games, most notably in prosocial and positive ads that the NBA screened to promote staying in school and reducing violence. For instance, two players were depicted in fictional scenes of confrontation as youths. In each case, the athlete's voice-over tells the audience how they kept their cool and avoided potentially violent situations. In another advertisement, a player is shown alone in a gym shooting a basketball, while his voice-over intones about the need to work hard. For him, "if it wasn't basketball it would be something else." He concludes his monologue by suggesting that "without your high school diploma, you don't have a shot." These players are positioned as role models who have succeeded through hard work and good sense. Again, the emphasis is on *individual* choice as the key to overcoming difficulties and achieving successes. These messages acknowledge the everyday problems facing many youth, but do not provide a basis for understanding why so many youth make these "bad" decisions, beyond a standard peer pressure model. Dyson (1995: 167), for example, suggests that "because the situation of black males has become so formidably complex, the horizon of clarity often recedes behind vigorous yet confusing attempts to understand and explain their predicament." Despite the positive intentions and potential impacts of social marketing messages, the audience is still positioned in a way that "blames the victim." Cole (1996: 390) makes a similar argument in her analysis of a series of cause-related Nike advertisements that used Michael Jordan and other African-American athletes to promote "positive" choices for inner city youths. She suggests that "the sport/gang narrative animating [the promotional campaign] imagines sovereign youth who make choices about their fate: those who continue to participate in gangs could have just said no by saying yes to sport." Wonsek (1992) also maintains that such portrayals of African-American role models might influence audiences to think that "only black youth" have these problems.

"Bad Blacks"

Negative portrayals of the Black athlete were evident in both newspaper and television coverage of the Toronto Raptors. For example, a series of articles in the *Star* followed the Raptor Alvin Robertson's charge with "assault in connection with a domestic dispute" (Young, 1995g). Before the incident, Robertson was described in the media as a hard-working veteran player who was trying to revive his career with a new team. After the incident, the "alleged criminal" label was alluded to in most articles that referred to him. When Robertson led his team to a victory in the first game of the season, his accomplishment was described in the following way: "Robertson, who appeared in court yesterday morning and had a charge of assault postponed, more than made up for it with 11 for 14 shooting" (Clarkson, 1995h). A close reading of the article shows that Robertson is actually "making up" for the average play of another team member, a point mentioned in a previous paragraph, although the segment is worded in such a way that Robertson's play seems to "make up" for the assault. Either way, Robertson's name was associated with this charge in the sports pages in both specific and haphazard ways. Other articles treated Robertson's shortcomings more extensively, as in an article with the headline "Robertson Sorry For Past Deeds":

> Yesterday, Robertson referred to past incidents of violence in which he was involved while with other teams. In 1993, Robertson was suspended after attacking Detroit Pistons official Billy McKinney and it's also been alleged that Robertson has been involved in other incidents on and off the court.
> (Clarkson, 1995g: D6)

Robertson was used as an illustration of the "dregs and castoffs that the Raptors have been saddled with in their first year" and of those who have come to the Raptors with "checkered backgrounds" (Young, 1995b; 1995f; 1995g). He was described as the team's "first arrest" in a sports page cover story entitled "Robertson Adds To List with Raptor Bad Boys" (Young, 1995g).

Robertson was the most extreme case in a long list of similar depictions of Raptors and African-Americans on other teams. In an article with the bold headline "Raptor's Father Jailed for 30 Years in Texas Slaying," a detailed description was given of Oliver Miller's father's conviction for murder (*Star*, 1995: E5). Shortly after this article appeared, Miller was reported to have been one day late for training camp as a "result of a court hearing in Phoenix arising out of an old domestic dispute" (Young, 1995f). Another Raptor, Carlos Rogers, was described as "immature," "uncoachable," and "unable to take criticism." He was explicitly associated with the threatening inner city where "he walked the city's meaner side," having "seen his older brother shot on the streets of Detroit" (Young, 1995a). Former Raptor BJ Tyler was said to "carry a lot of baggage," "not follow instructions," and to have a history of "off-court troubles" and drug use. Tyler was said to have been rejected by former coach John Lucas, who is renowned for giving second chances to down-and-out players, or as Young (1995c) put it, had a "personnel policy [that appeared] to be copped from olden days of Ellis Island." Raptor Tony Massenberg, who has been depicted as a "hard worker" at times, was associated with Len Bias, a former college friend and team-mate who died of a cocaine overdose in a highly publicized incident in 1986 (Young, 1995d).

Many of these depictions were reinforced on TV. During a profile in one Raptors' game, Rogers was shown from the neck up wearing a black toque. Black and white images of him sitting alone were intermixed with action shots from games. As with some of the other players, Rogers is shown to be playful, saying that he likes to "joke around." However, Rogers also appears menacing and intimidating during the latter part of the profile, when he begins to speak very seriously:

> I'm a player with an attitude, if you push me I'll push back . . . on the court. I'm 225 pounds, not very much but I'm evil, and that's the key to success, not to care about anybody you're playing against.
>
> (New VR, 1996c)

Miller's profile was filmed in the same close-up, black and white style. He appeared more playful than Rogers, but is shown "losing his cool" on the court by bumping an opposing player with his chest, kicking a basketball and then being penalized for unsportsmanlike conduct. He also talked about protecting his team-mates, saying if you "mess with them," he'll "get you" (New VR, 1996d).

Commercials screened during Raptors' games used African-American athletes to exploit this "life in the ghetto" scenario. In a Reebok commercial, Glenn Robinson, who at the time starred for the Milwaukee Bucks, was shown in a gym, talking about the different moves he uses to beat opponents. While he is talking, clips of Robinson performing these moves are flashed on to the screen. The commercial ends with Robinson saying that he is "not hot-doggin" (showing off), "I'm just marking my territory." Following Robinson's last statement, a playground gate with the Reebok slogan painted on it is slammed shut. All clips of Robinson talking during the advertisement were shown in black and white. Similar to the profiles previously discussed, this commercial shows Robinson as an intimidating individual and arguably a metonym for violence associated with "the hood" (Lull, 1995).

Similar themes were evident in a Nike commercial featuring former Seattle Supersonics player Gary Payton, who is a renowned "trash talker" (someone who tries to intimidate and distract opponents by using insulting language). Payton is shown wearing a blindfold while outplaying an opponent in a dark gym. Once the game is over, Payton takes the blindfold off and pushes his opponent away. The commercial ends with a Nike symbol superimposed on a dark background and the ominous, steady sound of a bouncing basketball. The advertisement contained no music or voice-overs, only the sound of sneakers, a bouncing ball, and the players breathing.

In summary, both print and electronic portrayals stereotyped African-Americans as criminal, arrogant, unruly, undisciplined, and threatening. Although explicit references to race were not made, there were powerful, subtle associations with the inner city, gangs and crime on the one hand, and African-American basketball players on the other.

African-American athletes as a floating racial signifier

Despite the seemingly mutually exclusive categories of Good and Bad Blacks, representations were not always stable. Sometimes Thomas was associated with his former team, the Pistons, which had an intimidatory style of play; at times Stoudamire was shown to be arrogant and brash. Ormsby (1995d) emphasized statements made by Stoudamire early in season on his "quickness," and his power to work "magic" on the court to demonstrate the problems associated with the "NBA's trash-talking element and glorification of self." Stoudamire was said to be "short in stature, but long on rhetoric," as he "unblushingly bragged of his talent." Conversely, Alvin Robertson, who was depicted repeatedly, especially in the newspapers, as an alleged criminal with a history of off-court problems, was shown positively in other instances: "Alvin personifies what a basketball player is. He plays hard for 48 minutes [the length of a game] and makes everyone around him better" (Clarkson, 1995c: D8). Although this article ran before the alleged assault, Robertson was shown to be modest and quiet at other times. In a TV profile, Robertson was soft-spoken and admitted to being uncomfortable talking about himself (New VR, 1996e). His playing ability was praised throughout his "comeback season," but his "fall from grace" has also continued to be prominent. In November 1996 the *Star* reported on his six-month jail sentence for a burglary conviction (Star, 1996: B4). Above this story appeared a half-page picture of Robertson in the courthouse, wearing handcuffs and giving his watch to one of his lawyers after being sentenced.

NBA superstar Anfernee "Penny" Hardaway (who played for the Orlando Magic at the time of this study) was the most striking example of a non-Raptor player whose portrayal was floating and contradictory. In a series of Nike TV advertisements, Hardaway was positioned in various contexts along with a ventriloquist doll known as "Little Penny" – an approximately two-foot-tall, plastic replica of Hardaway that talks and walks on its own and wears Nike shoes. Little Penny is loud, arrogant, brash, and lives a fast-paced life of fame and excess. Hardaway, by contrast, is modest, focused, successful, and conservative. For example, one commercial shows Hardaway driving a car with Little Penny in the passenger seat who yells exuberantly:

> It's a free country. If I want to give interviews, I'll give interviews. You know what your problem is [speaking to Hardaway – Hardaway is shown gritting his teeth and shaking his head, looking frustrated with Little Penny's comments]? You're too modest. I give good quotes [flash to a scene that appears to be in Little Penny's imagination, with him talking on a

cellular phone, acting as a spokesperson for Hardaway) Anfernee Hardaway, greatest player in basketball guarantees championship. Guarantees.

The setting then flashes back to the car, where Hardaway remonstrates that
"you can't say stuff like that." But instead of listening, Little Penny leans out of
the car window and talks to a young woman (actress Tara Banks) in the next
car. Little Penny is attempting to impress her, suggesting that he is the choreog-
rapher for the Orlando Magic dancers, and that he can give her a job as a
dancer. The commercial ends with Hardaway driving away in the middle of
Little Penny's conversation, despite Little Penny's plea: "Stop the car, that was
Tara Banks, fool!"

The other commercials in the series revealed similar character traits. One
commercial showed Hardaway calling his house from a hotel after a basketball
game, where it appears from the background noise that Little Penny is having a
party. Hardaway is angry with Little Penny and tells him to be careful. Little
Penny, oblivious to Hardaway's concerns, abruptly ends the conversation and
the commercial because he has a "meeting" with a young lady in the pool. On
one hand, these commercials inscribe Hardaway as a responsible, cautious,
modest individual, who values a conservative lifestyle. The positive traits are
emphasized while the persona of his alter ego, Little Penny, is exaggerated to
accentuate his status as a Bad Black in a humorous, non-threatening way. On
the other hand, the depiction of Little Penny as a "ladies' man" highlights the
"flamboyant" lifestyles of celebrity African-American athletes such as footballer
"Neon" Deion Sanders, and basketballers Dennis "The Menace" Rodman, "Sir"
Charles Barkley and "Magic" Johnson (Cole and Andrews, 1996; Cole and
Denny, 1994; King, 1993; Lule, 1995; McKay, 1993; Rowe, 1994). His arro-
gance parallels the general stereotypical images of the "dangerous black other,"
which can also be found in sport via depictions of boxers "Sugar" Ray Leonard
and Mike Tyson, baseball players Dwight Gooden and Darryl Strawberry, and
footballers Michael Irvin and O.J. Simpson, who have been variously arrested
for and/or convicted of drug use, wife-beating, rape, and murder (Kellner, 1996;
Kimmel, 1995; Lule, 1995; McKay and Smith, 1995; Messner, 1992; Messner
and Solomon, 1993).

While these alternative portrayals make room for "oppositional" readings
(Hall, 1980), the clear pattern between the Good Black/Bad Black is the most
convincing demonstration of the floating meanings surrounding "Black."
Overall, these overlaps and contradictions establish a "mediated racial identity
that is not stable, essential, or consistent: it is dynamic, complex and contradictory" (Andrews, 1996: 126). The importance of such an analysis in light of
the Good Black/Bad Black dynamic is to recognize in the Canadian context the
existence of the oscillating racism identified by Andrews.

Discussion

These findings support other studies that inscribe African-Americans in an image of "charming, unique and attractive individuals who, we assume, reached their stations in life through hard work, skill, talent, discipline and determination" (Gray, 1989: 382). The noted emphasis on the individual efforts of Thomas and Stoudamire and the absence of structural racist barriers reinforce the view that the failure of the Black underclass is their own fault. Conversely, the images of menace, threat and crime associated with Robertson, Payton and other athletes supports previous research that has documented the enlightened racism which surrounds the everyday representations of African-Americans. As Entman explains: "rather than the grossly demeaning distortions of yesterday, stereotyping of blacks now allows abstraction from and denial of the racial component" (1992: 345). The ideological distortions evident here further reinforce Lule's (1995) view of the media as a place where stereotypes are organized in ways that reinforce negative beliefs about Blacks. In the case of news coverage, the construction of reality is embedded in stereotypical conventions of narration and, like all ideologies, these realities are selected, partial, and incomplete (Lule, 1995).

That these African-American athletes were portrayed in an unstable fashion supports Wenner's (1995) concept of the Good Black/Bad Black dichotomy. The *relatively* anchored Black image, acknowledged by Wenner in his discussion of O.J. Simpson's "fall from grace," is extended by the apparently unstable meaning attached to Thomas, Stoudamire, Hardaway, and Robertson. Similarly, the depictions of these four men also extend Jackson's (1998a; 1998b) and Andrews' (1996) analyses of how signifiers of blackness float. The shifting meanings complicate the Good Black/Bad Black media construction that serves to maintain the ideology of danger and individualism. However, they do not overturn the racist articulations that exist in both cases. These portrayals are embedded in a media culture that "is only too happy" to use a "spectacle of color" to "elevate difference to sublimity," or, to denigrate this same spectacle "to embody negative connotations" (Kellner, 1996: 465).

Conclusions and recommendations

Interrogating media texts is necessary for encouraging readers to develop a critical media literacy, and for "creating alternatives, and asking ourselves questions – about what types of images subvert, pose critical alternatives and transform our world views" (hooks, 1992: 4). The importance of establishing this critical practice is extremely apposite to the current study, when we consider the economic motives of both the sporting apparel companies who market the myths of the inner city, and the NBA promoters who espouse an egalitarian ethic that attempts to mobilize ghetto Blacks, while simultaneously ignoring the racist structures of both college and professional basketball (and American sport and society generally).

While this study has contributed to the literature on media discourses about race, further research is required. Future research could examine whether similar patterns occur in other regions of Canada, and comparative studies could be conducted with portrayals of male African-American basketball players in other countries (Chappell *et al.*, 1996), as well as media constructions of female African-American athletes (Williams, 1994). Researchers have suggested that since textual interpretations are related to the social locations of readers, it is necessary to complement textual work with ethnographic studies (Radway, 1991; Wenner, 1994; Wilson and Sparks, 1996; 1999; 2001). Therefore, reception studies are also needed in order to discern how different audiences consume messages about race and sport, and which groups should be targeted with initiatives derived from this kind of research (beyond the public accountability issues raised with media producers).

This case study of basketball has shown that the concepts of enlightened racism and the floating racial signifier, in particular, which have been useful in detecting racist representations of African-American male athletes in the American context, are also pertinent to the Canadian context. With more critical media work on African-American athletes both in Canada and other nations, a better understanding of the social construction of racism can be attained. Perhaps this will go some way toward redressing Wenner's (1995: 231) concern that "we put an undue burden on sports journalists, a disproportionately white group, to comment on the character of the most publicly visible blacks."

References

Agocs, C. and Boyd, M. (1993). The Canadian ethnic mosaic recast for the 1990's, In J. Curtis, E. Grabb and N. Guppy (eds), *Social Inequality in Canada* (pp. 330–352). Scarborough, ON: Prentice Hall.

Andrews, D. (1996). The fact(s) of Michael Jordan's Blackness: Excavating a floating racial signifier. *Sociology of Sport Journal*, 13, 125–158.

Ang, I. (1985). *Watching Dallas – Soap Opera and Melodramatic Imagination*. London: Methuen.

Boyd, M. (1992). Gender, visible minority, and immigrant earnings inequality: Reassessing an employment equity premise. In V. Satzewich (ed.), *Deconstructing a Nation: Immigration, Multiculturalism and Racism in 90s Canada* (pp. 279–321). Halifax: Fernwood Publishing.

Chappell, R., Jones, R. and Burden, A. (1996). Racial participation and integration in England professional basketball 1977–1994. *Sociology of Sport Journal*, 13, 300–311.

Clarkson, M. (1995a). Raptors' brass set to mull going after free agent players. *The Toronto Star*, 20 September: E3.

Clarkson, M. (1995b). Raptor up-tempo offense starts on defensive boards. *The Toronto Star*, 7 October: E6.

Clarkson, M. (1995c). Raptor hopefuls jockey for jobs. *The Toronto Star*, 9 October: D8.

Clarkson, M. (1995d). Mouse roars over Sixers. *The Toronto Star*, 15 October: B1.

Clarkson, M. (1995e). Raptors' progress pleases Thomas. *The Toronto Star*, 26 October: D4.

Clarkson, M. (1995f). Day of decision for Raptors on bubble. *The Toronto Star*, 2 November: D6.

Clarkson, M. (1995g). Robertson sorry for past deeds. *The Toronto Star*, 2 November: D6.

Clarkson, M. (1995h). How 'bout that NB-eh. *Toronto Star*, 4 November: E1.

Clarkson, M. (1995i). Raptors accept "terrible" call in "lucky" victory over Bullets. *The Toronto Star*, 20 November: E4.

Cole, C. (1996). American Jordan: P.L.A.Y., consensus, and punishment. *Sociology of Sport Journal*, 13, 366–397.

Cole, C. and Andrews, D. (1996). Look – it's NBA showtime! Visions of race in the popular imagery. *Cultural Studies Annual*, 1, 141–181.

Cole, C. and Denny, H. (1994). Visualizing deviance in post-Reagan America: Magic Johnson, AIDS, and the promiscuous world of professional sport. *Critical Sociology*, 20 (3), 123–147.

Collinson, D., Knights, D. and Collinson, M. (1990). *Managing to Discriminate*. London: Routledge, Chapman and Hall.

Connelly, W. (1995). *The Ethos of Pluralization*. Minneapolis: University of Minnesota Press.

Cowie, E. (1977). Women, representation and image. *Screen Education*, 2–3, 15–23.

Davis, L. (1990). The articulation of difference: White preoccupation of racially linked genetic differences. *Sociology of Sport Journal*, 7, 179–187.

Denzin, N. (1996). More rare air: Michael Jordan on Michael Jordan. *Sociology of Sport Journal*, 13, 319–324.

Dyson, M. (1995). *Making Malcolm*. New York: Oxford University Press.

Eagleton, T. (1991). *Ideology: An Introduction*. London: Verso.

Entman, R. (1992). Blacks in the news: Television, modern racism and cultural change. *Journalism Quarterly*, 69 (2), 341–361.

Fernandez, J. (1988). *Racism and Sexism in Corporate Life*. Englewood Cliffs, NJ: Prentice Hall.

Fiske, J. (1987). *Television Culture*. London: Methuen.

Fleras, A. (1995). Please adjust your set: Media and minorities in a multicultural society. In B. Singer (ed.), *Communication in Canadian Society* (pp. 406–430). Scarborough, ON: Nelson Canada.

Gray, H. (1989). Television, Black Americans, and the American dream. *Critical Studies in Mass Communication*, 6, 376–386.

Hall, S. (1980). Encoding/Decoding. In S. Hall, A. Lowe and P. Willis (eds), *Culture, Media, Language* (pp. 128–139). London: Hutchinson.

Hall, S. (1985). Signification, representation, ideology: Althusser and the post-structuralist debates. *Critical Studies in Mass Communication*, 2, 91–114.

Henry, F. (1994). *The Caribbean Diaspora in Toronto: Learning to Live With Racism*. Toronto: University of Toronto Press.

Henry, F. and Ginzberg, E. (1993). Racial discrimination in employment. In J. Curtis, E. Grabb and N. Guppy (eds), *Social Inequality in Canada: Patterns, Problems, Policies* (pp. 353–360). Scarborough, ON: Prentice Hall Canada.

hooks, b. (1992). *Black Looks: Race and Representation*. Boston, MA: South End Press.

Jackson, S.J. (1998a). A twist of race: Ben Johnson and the Canadian crisis of racial and national identity. *Sociology of Sport Journal*, 15, 21–40.

Jackson, S.J. (1998b). Life in the (mediated) Faust lane: Ben Johnson, national affect and the 1988 crisis of Canadian identity. *International Review for the Sociology of Sport*, 33 (3), 227–238.

Jhally, S. and Lewis, J. (1992). Enlightened racism: The Cosby Show, audiences, and the myth of the American dream. Boulder, CO: Westview Press.

Kellner, D. (1996). Sports, media culture, and race – some reflections on Michael Jordan. *Sociology of Sport Journal, 13* (4), 458–468.

Kimmel, M. (1995). Clarence, William, Iron Mike, Tailhook, Senator Packwood, Magic . . . and Us. In M. Kimmel and M. Messner (eds), *Men's Lives* (3rd edn). Boston, MA: Allyn & Bacon.

King, S. (1993). The politics of the body and the body politic: Magic Johnson and the ideology of AIDS. *Sociology of Sport Journal, 10,* 270–285.

Leiss, W., Kline, S. and Jhally, S. (1990). *Social Communication in Advertising: Persons, Products and Images of Well-being.* Scarborough, ON: Nelson Canada.

Leonard, W. (1996). The odds of transiting from one level of sports participation to another. *Sociology of Sport Journal, 13,* 288–299.

Lule, J. (1995). The rape of Mike Tyson: Race, the press and symbolic types. *Critical Studies in Mass Communication, 12,* 176–195.

Lull, J. (1995). *Media, Communication, Culture.* New York: Columbia University Press.

McDonald, M. (1996). Michael Jordan's family values: Marketing, meaning, and post-Reagan America. *Sociology of Sport Journal, 13,* 344–365.

McKay, J. (1993). "Marked men" and "wanton women": The politics of naming sexual "deviance" in sport. *The Journal of Men's Studies, 2,* 69–87.

McKay, J. (1995). "Just do it": Corporate sports slogans and the political economy of enlightened racism. *Discourse: Studies in the Cultural Politics of Education, 16* (2), 191–201.

McKay, J. and Smith, P. (1995). Exonerating the hero: Frames and narratives in media coverage of the OJ Simpson Story. *Media Information Australia, 75,* 57–66.

Majors, R. (1990). Cool pose: Black masculinity and sports. In M. Messner and D. Sabo (eds), *Sport, Men and the Gender Order: Critical Feminist Perspectives* (pp. 109–114). Campaign, IL: Human Kinetics.

Messner, M. (1992). White men misbehaving: Feminism, Afrocentrism, and the promise of a critical standpoint. *Journal of Sport and Social Issues, 16,* 136–144.

Messner, M. and Solomon, W. (1993). Outside the frame: Newspaper coverage of the Sugar Ray Leonard wife abuse story. *Sociology of Sport Journal, 10,* 119–134.

New VR (1996a). Telecast of Toronto at Miami Game, 13 February.

New VR (1996b). Telecast of Toronto at Detroit Game, 17 February.

New VR (1996c). Telecast of Toronto at Utah Game, 22 February.

New VR (1996d). Telecast of Toronto at Phoenix Game, 23 February.

New VR (1996e). Telecast of Toronto at San Antonio Game, 29 February.

Omi, M. (1989). In living colour: Race and American culture. In I. Angus and S. Jhally (eds), *Cultural Politics in Contemporary America* (pp. 111–122). New York: Routledge.

Omi, M. and Winant, H. (1994). *Racial Formation in the United States: From the 1960's to the 1990's* (2nd edn). New York: Routledge.

Ormsby, M. (1995a). Raptors Stoudamire can't wait to get going. *The Toronto Star,* 4 October: B6.

Ormsby, M. (1995b). Raptor rookie eyes top price. *The Toronto Star,* 6 October: C4.

Ormsby, M. (1995c). NBA attitude in 90s: Let us bray. *The Toronto Star,* 8 October: D7.

Ormsby, M. (1995d). Raptors axe hovering over Alexander's head. *The Toronto Star,* 11 October: D6.

Patton, C. (1992). Rock hard. Paper presented at the North American Society for the Sociology of Sport Conference, Toledo, Ohio.

Proudfoot, J. (1995). Stoudamire stands tall as Raptors little big man. *Toronto Star*, 6 October: C1.

Radway, J. (1991). *Reading the Romance*. Chapel Hill: University of North Carolina Press.

Rowe, D. (1994). Accommodating bodies: Celebrity, sexuality and "tragic Magic." *Journal of Sport and Social Issues*, 18, 6–26.

Sailes, G. (1993). An investigation of campus stereotypes: The myth of Black athlete superiority and the dumb Jock stereotype. *Sociology of Sport Journal*, 10, 88–97.

Satzewich, V. and Li, P. (1987). Immigrant labour in Canada: The cost and benefit of ethnic origin in the job market. *Canadian Journal of Sociology*, 12 (3), 229–241.

The Toronto Star (1995). Raptors father jailed for 30 years in Texas slaying. 30 September: E5.

The Toronto Star (1996). Former Raptor gets jail. 5 November: B4.

Wenner, L. (1994). The dream team, communicative dirt and the marketing of synergy: USA basketball and cross-merchandising in television commercials. *Journal of Sport and Social Issues*, 18, 27–47.

Wenner, L. (1995). The good, the bad and the ugly: Race, sport, and the public eye. *Journal of Sport and Social Issues*, 19 (3), 227–231.

Williams, L. (1994). Sportswomen in black and white: Sports history from an Afro-American perspective. In P. Creedon (ed.), *Women, Media and Sport* (pp. 45–66). London: Sage.

Wilson, B. (1999). Cool pose incorporated: The marketing of Black masculinity in Canadian NBA coverage. In P. White and K. Young (eds), *Sport and Gender in Canada* (pp. 232–253). Toronto, ON: Oxford University Press.

Wilson, B. and Sparks, R. (1996). It's gotta be the shoes: Youth, race, and sneaker commercials. *Sociology of Sport Journal*, 13 (4), 398–427.

Wilson, B and Sparks, R. (1999). Impacts of Black athlete media portrayals on Canadian youth. *Canadian Journal of Communication*, 24 (4), 589–627.

Wilson, B. and Sparks, R. (2001). Michael Jordan, sneaker commercials, and Canadian youth cultures. In D. Andrews (ed.), *Michael Jordan, Inc.: Corporate Sport, Media Culture, and Late Modern America*. Albany, NY: SUNY Press.

Wonsek, P. (1992). College basketball on television: a study of racism in the media. *Media, Culture and Society*, 14, 449–461.

York, S (Prod.). (1991). *Selling the Dream*. Television Broadcast, Washington, DC: Smithsonian Institute.

Young, C. (1995a). Raptor Rogers envisions team of "we" warriors. *The Toronto Star*, 19 September: D4.

Young, C. (1995b). Sally perfect tonic for blues of expansion. *The Toronto Star*, 27 September: B1.

Young, C. (1995c). Raptors guard B.J. Tyler carrying a lot of baggage. *The Toronto Star*, 1 October: F1.

Young, C. (1995d). Massenberg follows bouncing ball to Toronto. *The Toronto Star*, 3 October: D6.

Young, C. (1995e). Major money matters loom on Raptor horizon. *The Toronto Star*, 7 October: E6.

Young, C. (1995f). Ex-Sun Miller has Raptor post as centre to lose. *The Toronto Star*, 8 October: D7.

Young, C. (1995g). Robertson adds to list with Raptor bad boys. *The Toronto Star*, October 30: B1.

Young, C. (1995h). Three choice Raptors on the block. *The Toronto Star*, 2 November:
    D1.
Young, C. (1995i). Mom gives Thomas' Raptors her blessing. *The Toronto Star*, 8
    November: E1.
Young, C. (1995j). Stoudamire quickly earns respect of teammates, foes. *Toronto Star*, 11
    November: E5.

6 Sport sexuality and representation in advertising

The political economy of the pink dollar

Robyn Jones and Roger LeBlanc

Introduction

As stated in the Preface, unlike other media texts, advertisements offer rare opportunities for understanding important trends associated with corporate logic and consumer tastes on the one hand, and the cultural politics of representation on the other (Jackson and Andrews, 2001). Indeed, they have been described as "the most pervasive cultural artefact in post-modern society" (Kates, 1999: 28), thus being generally viewed as an integral part of social communication and existence. Similarly, Mistry (2000) considers the medium to have become the "central socialising agent for cultural values." However, in their ongoing exploration for new niche and emergent markets, and how to effectively "reach" them, advertisers are currently considered to be in the midst of a crisis which has forced them into unchartered cultural waters (Goldman and Papson, 1996). Indeed, as the industry constantly strives to update itself, status within it depends "on the ability to set new "innovative trends," and, generally speaking, by being as avant-garde as possible" (Mistry, 2000). In this respect, advertisers' search for unique images and for strategies that construct valuable commodity signs for their products has brought them increasingly into conflict with the politics of identity and representation.

In many cases niche markets have always existed, but it is the perception of their newly acquired economic and consumer power, as expressed in an emergent collective identity, that is initiating change in corporate marketing strategies (Turow, 1997). An example of this has been the increasing attention paid to the burgeoning rise of the economic and political power of the so-called "pink dollar," flowing from gay and lesbian consumers (Wardlow, 1996). Although, in general, the "gay and lesbian populations still remain largely unexplored territory for advertising researchers" (Kates, 1999: 25), recent studies have labeled them "dream consumers" with high disposable incomes and a desire to purchase "quality" items (Kates, 1999). As the stereotype of the "gay spender" (Kates, 1999) has taken hold (a general image which is seen as somewhat problematic in itself), marketeers have, not surprisingly, responded. Since the mid-1990s, advertising has increasingly employed images of sexual ambiguity and distinct homosexuality in an attempt to specifically target the gay community. Such portrayals "are far removed from depictions of the camp gay employed as the comic relief elsewhere in the mainstream media" (Mistry, 2000) as typified in such prime-time comedy shows as *Spin City*, *Will and Grace*, and *Gimme, Gimme, Gimme*. Thus, it has become increasingly acknowledged that the recognition of the gay and lesbian consumer market segment has impacted upon that community's portrayal in the mass media in general, and within advertising in particular.

However, it has been contended that sport marketing remains somewhat outside of this pale of development, since, although it is an area of considerable pink dollar spending, it continues to hold a "privileged" position as a site of dominant masculinities in our society. This concerns both the marketing of sports goods and the use of athletes and sporting personalities to advertise products generally. Hence, although the attention paid to the emerging gay and lesbian market has increased considerably during the past two decades, the related inroads made into sports advertising specifically still appear to be somewhat limited. In this respect, the locker room door is proving particularly difficult to open, since it continues to be perceived as a "world that is probably one of the last bastions of good old fashioned institutionalised homophobia" (Short, 1996: 53).

This chapter examines the presently unfolding interrelationship between sport, culture, and advertising within the context of the pink dollar political economy. Its principal intentions in this respect are twofold. First, to highlight the significance of the gay, lesbian, and bisexual market segment through a brief account of homosexual and lesbian portrayals in the mass media to date, including an examination of the reasons for the recent rise in the consumer power of the pink dollar. Second, an investigation into how the gay population is being increasingly portrayed in advertisements in general, and in sporting and leisure ones in particular, is undertaken. This comprises an illustration of four such ads, two that relate, either directly or through the use of sporting personalities, to the sport and leisure industry.

The ensuing discussion examines the ads in terms of their apparent acknowledgment of sexuality, the sexual ambiguity of their characters, and their general inclusive or exclusive treatment of homosexuality per se. They are also examined in terms of the commonly held belief that homosexual thematic content remains considerably more acceptable and less problematic in mainstream marketing than in the sports and leisure sphere, as the latter continues to be perceived as an "institution of compulsory heterosexuality" (Messner, 1999: 107). In this respect, the analysis is grounded in terms of the continuing socially dominant hetero-normative discourse (Kates, 1999).

Such an investigation is significant as it contributes to the emergent scholarly field of gay and lesbian studies and highlights the importance of media images of homosexuality and the gay and lesbian community as sources of social information. This is particularly so for those persons who are "coming out" as "they search to understand their feeling and sense of difference" (Fejes and Petrich, 1993: 396). Consequently, how the dominant media discourse defines homosexuality continues to have a "significant impact on how individual gay males or lesbians view themselves and their relationship to society" (Fejes and Petrich, 1993: 396–397), in addition to defining the population within, and for, the wider social context. The same could be said of media representations of sport, which remain "particularly powerful in naturalising and normalising hegemonic meanings about the body and social relations" (Wright and Clarke, 1999: 227). Indeed, accepting that the media "frame" events for viewers which emanates a discourse that is anything but neutral (Tonkiss, 1998; Whannell, 1992), sports media texts continue to participate in the production and repro-duction of masculine values and practices. In this way, they contribute to a het-erosexual hegemony as expressed through sexism and homophobia (Wright and Clarke, 1999). Through an examination of selected current advertisements, this chapter aims to go some way to ascertain if this is still the case.

The rise and rise of pink dollar power

Since the 1980s, the gay, lesbian, and bisexual population, particularly in North America, has broadened its leisure activity base. Consequently, opportunities in related gay and lesbian sport, athletics, and fitness activities have multiplied (Pitts, 1989). Indeed, in her definitive "Beyond the bars" study, Pitts (1989) found that in the years between 1976 and 1981, gay, lesbian, and bisexual sports and leisure organizations were founded at an average rate of three per year in the Southern California region. In the period 1982 through 1986, the establish-ment rate increased to an average annual rate of 4.4 (LeBlanc, 1997). Evidence exists that this accelerating trend has not only continued through the 1990s but has also been witnessed in other major centers in America, Western Europe and Australia (LeBlanc, 1997). A consequent appreciation of this emerging niche market has, in turn, prompted a re-evaluation of corporate logic and its accom-panying media campaigns. This has resulted in a reshaping of both the strategies to reach the athletic pink dollar consumer, and of the related representation of the gay, lesbian, and bisexual population.

Fejes and Petrich (1993), in their abbreviated account of how the media have dealt with both homosexual characters and issues during the past century, highlight how the portrayal of homosexuality, both on film and television, has been a history of negative stereotyping. An obvious example of this was Hitch-cock's consistent use of implied homosexuality to "heighten the evilness and alienation of his film villains" (Fejes and Petrich, 1993: 397). Furthermore, although progressive in terms of comparison with the 1960s when "homosexual-ity [on film] was portrayed at best as unhappiness, sickness or marginality," 1990s cinema has continued to obscure and minimize "issues of gay/lesbian culture, community, identity, history, and oppression and discrimination" (Fejes and Petrich, 1993: 398). This has been the case even when gays and lesbians have been presented in a non-problematic manner.

Similarly, television treatment of lesbians and gays has roughly mirrored that of Hollywood movies, with negative stereotypes evident from the earliest days

(Fejes and Petrich, 1993). Although, by the 1980s, positive presentations of gays and lesbians on television were not exceptional, it continued, and continues, to be inadequate. This largely concerns the presentation of a heterosexual view of homosexuality, the desexualization of homosexuals in that they are portrayed as being without desire (Hantzis and Lehr, 1994), and a general reluctance to present gays and lesbians in the context of their own identity and concerns (Gross, 1994). Furthermore, the depiction of adolescent homosexuality on television continues to be particularly taboo (Kielwasser and Wolf, 1992). Although it is generally considered to be an improving situation, gays and lesbians remain rarely presented as members of a larger homosexual community, and thus, alternatively, largely exist peripherally as secondary or occasional characters in a heterosexual world.

Such an "improving" media representation, although continuingly problematic, has been the result of myriad factors. Not least of these was the "increasingly politicised gay and lesbian communities of the 1970s, who began to organise and demand changes in network portrayals" (Frejes and Petrich, 1993: 400). However, a more recent driving force, and one viewed as considerably more potent since it is inherently linked to corporate logic, has been the recognition of the power of the gay and lesbian consumer market segment, as defined by the pink dollar. This has been increasingly pronounced since the early 1990s when gays and lesbians emerged as a statistical category for consumer purposes (Fejes and Petrich, 1993). Indeed, as stated above, gay men in particular are currently considered and portrayed as "dream consumers" by the media, due to their supposedly "higher disposable income, education, good taste and desire to purchase high quality products" (Kates, 1999: 25). To this end, recent studies have concluded that major corporations actively target gay men as consumers (Kates, 1998; Lukenbill, 1995). This has been done through ads featuring gay and lesbian characters and sub-cultural themes, while companies such as Microsoft, Levi's, American Express, and Absolut Vodka commonly use the gay media to advertise their products (Bhat et al., 1998). In addition, some firms (IKEA, Calvin Klein, Toyota, Sony) have gone even further in using definitive homosexual imagery in advertising to more general audiences (Bhat et al., 1998). Although such a strategy has been influenced by cost-effective factors in that it negates the need for separate marketing campaigns to target differing groups (Bhat et al., 1998), it is also considered to be a recognition of more enlightened social attitudes in tandem with the increasing consumer power of gay and lesbian communities.

A principal reason offered for the development of the power of the pink dollar in the sport and leisure industry has been the emphasis upon the physicality of the body within the gay community, linked inevitably to the advent of AIDS. AIDS and HIV brought new health and fitness awareness to the gay community, with body-care consciousness remaining a major method of AIDS prevention and treatment (LeBlanc, 1997; Pronger, 1990). Indeed, in the age of AIDS, health promotion has become an integral part of lesbian and gay culture with many sports clubs and fitness centers catering specifically to gay or lesbian members, thus offering a healthy alternative to the alcohol-dominated world of bars. In this respect, every recognized major gay community can claim several gyms and exercise facilities that cater predominantly to their sports enthusiasts. For example, the LA metropolitan area alone has at least ten different gyms and sports facilities with an almost exclusive gay or lesbian clientele, while the same may be said for New York, Chicago, San Francisco, and Miami (Lukinball, 1995). In New York there is an extensive gay body-building center, the Chelsea Gym, which over a decade ago had more than three thousand active members (Pronger, 1990). Furthermore, evidence exists that, compared to only 8 percent of all Americans, 43 percent of gay men work out systematically (Schulman, 1995), thus spending a disproportionate amount of money, not only on maintaining their mental and physical health in gyms and sports clubs, but also on fitness and grooming products (Drummond, 1995; Miller, 1995; Nudd, 1992).

A second principal factor in the rise to prominence of the pink dollar has been the advent of gay and lesbian national and international leisure and cultural events, as typified by the Gay Games. Although gay, lesbian, and bisexual athletes have always participated in mainstream sport and leisure activities, alienated by homophobia within them and encouraged by the existence and visibility of the Gay Games and similar events, such athletes have increasingly found great refuge and motivation within their own organizations (LeBlanc, 1997). Indeed, it is homophobic hostility that has driven many gay and lesbian athletes to forsake mainstream sports for events like the Gay Games, where "they can be in the majority for once, to 'be themselves' and to feel 'free'" (Hargreaves, 1994: 264). Similarly, according to Pronger (1990: 234), "gay sports are seen by most of their participants as primarily a social enterprise where they can be themselves in a place other than a smoke-filled bar." Such perceived secure places have, not surprisingly, attracted great numbers.

The Gay Games themselves were founded in 1982 by the late Dr. Tom Waddell and the San Francisco Arts and Athletics Organization. Their purpose was to "foster and augment the self respect of lesbian women and gay men throughout the world and to engender respect and understanding from the non-gay world, primarily through an organised international participatory and cultural event held every four years" (Federation of Gay Games, 2000). Today their popularity has grown such that they are currently the world's largest athletic endeavor, with the 2002 Games in Sydney attracting over 14,000 athletes and 100,000 spectators, bringing in more than US$100 million into the local economy (Chicago Area Gay and Lesbian Chamber of Commerce, 2000).

Similarly, popular and lucrative worldwide gay, lesbian, and bisexual celebratory events such as Sydney's Gay and Lesbian Mardi Gras, Atlanta's Hotlanta River Expo, and "world cup" events in soccer, volley ball, tennis, swimming, baseball, and ice hockey among others, are organized regularly. Furthermore, the International Gay Bowling Organization has affiliated leagues in more than sixty-five cities and membership in excess of 25,000, while the North American Gay Amateur Athletic Alliance has member leagues in over twenty-seven cities throughout the USA and Canada (NAGAAA, 2000). The situation in Europe shows a similar pattern of development with the European Gay and Lesbian Sport Federation possessing the equivalent of 40,000 members in sixty affiliated sports groups (Short, 1996). Thus, due to the inability of the sporting industry to embrace outside liberating influences in terms of integrating openly gay and lesbian sports participants, such athletes have moved and are moving away in favor, or in search, of safer, inclusive, and more welcoming environments. As a consequence, they are not only channeling their time and effort into the gay and lesbian sport and leisure market, they are also investing in it, both emotionally and financially.

In recognition of the power of the pink dollar, corporate logic has dictated that many mainstream marketeers are now broadening their appeal to this emerging consumer market. In so doing, however, they face a dilemma. That is, despite an awareness of its growing financial significance and some evidence of increasing social tolerance, the use of homosexual imagery in ads remains controversial (Bhat et al., 1998). This surrounds the continuing diversity in social attitudes towards homosexuals, and the still relatively limited size of the homosexual market. Consequently, advertisers are continually seen to be weighing the advantages "of extending their 'homosexual ads' to a more inclusive audience" (Bhat et al., 1998: 10) at the risk of alienating members of that predominantly heterosexual audience. Such uncertainty has resulted in the portrayal of a range of sexually ambiguous images and messages, stretching from acceptance to inclusivity to exclusivity.

"Integrating" the gay, lesbian, and bi-sexual community into mainstream ads

Following a brief introduction, this section highlights four current advertisements which use homosexual themes. One is used by Sony the electronics multinational, another by the Japanese car manufacturer Toyota, a third by VISA the credit card/financial corporation, and the fourth by Reebok/Finish Line which highlights the merits of a recently released running shoe. Following a brief illustration of all four ads, an analytic comparison is made of their content in relation to the positioning of the issue of homosexuality within advertising in general, and within sports marketing in particular.

Although relatively little research has been done on the issue of athlete sexuality and the commercial impact of "coming out" as gay or lesbian, it is commonly considered that such athletes are reluctant to declare their homosexuality in order to protect their sporting careers, particularly in terms of commercial endorsements (Hargreaves, 1994). Speaking specifically of lesbians, Hargreaves (1994) has noted that because they are made to feel uncomfortable (both emotionally and financially) in the fiercely heterosexual world of mainstream sport, such athletes have tended to hide their sexuality. Accordingly, she concludes openly that "sponsorship opportunities are reduced for lesbian sportswomen who make public their sexual orientation" (Hargreaves, 1994: 206), while the sporting establishment in particular has "failed to create a discourse to explain and deal with discrimination against homosexuals ... and lesbians in sport" (1994: 260). Such a view is echoed by Wright and Clarke (1999: 228), who state that "lesbian athletes have been required to not only hide their sexuality, but also to present themselves as models of heterosexual femininity" to protect their sponsorship incomes. Thus, the pressure to construct and maintain "a socially acceptable image" (Wright and Clarke, 1999: 228) remains, as does the fear of commercial loss for those athletes who "come out." Nelson (1991) similarly supports such a claim in reporting that concerns centering on losing sponsorship dollars, in addition to popularity among their heterosexual fans, were principal factors in the decisions of lesbian golfers to remain "closeted."

Nevertheless, despite such fears, many high-profile athletes in a diverse range of sports have come out in recent years. These include Ian Roberts, Amelie Mauresmo, Martina Navratilova, Billie Jean King, Greg Louganis, Bruce Hayes, Brian Marshall, Muffin Devlin-Spencer, Mark Leduc, and the late Justin Fashanu among others. Many, such as Navratilova and King, who came out in the late 1970s and early 1980s, did indeed lose lucrative sponsorships as a consequence of their declarations, as companies avoided associating themselves with what they perceived as negative publicity (Messner, 1994). However, more recently "outed" athletes, for example, Ian Roberts and Greg Louganis, have not lost out on endorsements. Indeed, when Ian Roberts, the Australian Rugby League player came out, the controversy took him to a broader market. Thus, instead of doing damage control, Roberts' management was busy marketing him as a gay athlete and positive role model (O'Shea, 1995) as he became "a spokesperson for Puma and Telstra, [while] modelling clothes for Ella Bache" (Miller, 1998: 443). Although this could be interpreted as evidence of a gay lifestyle being increasingly acceptable in today's world of sport, Roberts' example would appear to be the exception that proves the rule in this regard, and is thus discussed in depth below. In addition, we can only speculate at what Roberts' commercial value would have been had he remain "closeted."

Alternatively, for most gay and lesbian athletes, coming out remains a contentious issue fraught with anxiety and fear. Indeed, the continuing homophobic sporting culture was recently exposed at the 1999 Australian Women's Tennis Open, when comments attributed to the eventual champion, Martina Hingis, about her openly lesbian opponent in the final, Amelie Mauresmo, caused much tension and resentment. Consequently, although according to former player and current commentator Pam Shriver, "Martina Navratilova and Billie Jean King would probably have liked to have been so open [about their sexuality]; times have moved on and it's a pretty liberal world now" (Wilstein, 1999), a chasm still appears to exist between straight and gay athletes in terms of sexual acceptance and tolerance (Porter, 1999). In the light of such attitudinal diversity, how then are homosexual issues and characters currently depicted in ads in general, and in sports ads in particular? The following provides four examples and a consequent analysis.

Case study ad 1: the Sony MiniDisc

Produced in 1999 by the New Zealand advertising agency Generator, this advertisement is a sales pitch for the Sony MiniDisc player by Sony. It begins by panning between two identical, Sony white radio alarm clocks. Both clocks show 6.59 a.m., with music beginning as the time changes to 7.00 a.m. Two identical-looking males, presumably twins, are then shown shaving, showering, and later dressing in similar clothes. The next camera shot focuses on them eating an identical healthy breakfast in a very modern, minimalistic kitchen/living area, presumably to emphasize the futuristic, enlightened theme of their existence. Each one then copies music from his respective stereo on to his own MiniDisc player. It is at this point that we learn that their names, as noted on the labels of their discs, are Eric's compilation and Derek's compilation. Having recorded their music Eric and Derek head for the door where they stand side by side at the curb as if waiting for a ride. Up until this point neither twin has spoken a word, and indeed there is no dialogue in the entire advertisement, although a number of "looks" have been exchanged. Next, a silver Mercedes convertible sports car pulls up, driven by a beautiful blonde young woman. The first twin (though the audience does not know which one) puts on his headphones and begins listening to "Never knew a girl like you before" before getting in beside and being driven off. Once they leave, an identical sports car pulls up driven by what is seemingly intended to be a stereotypically looking gay man: with bald head, thick moustache, tattoos and wearing a black wrestling singlet. The remaining twin puts on his headphones listening to "Mad about the boy" by Dinah Washington. The man winks at the remaining twin, who smiles back before getting into the car in a position where the driver has his arm draped over the passenger's seat. The closing caption of the advertisement then appears on the screen: "Very individualistic: Very Sony."

Case study ad 2: Toyota

The ad begins with three young children in the back seat of an old yellow Toyota estate car, complete with kayak on the roof. They are loudly counting the kilometers on the car's odometer as it ticks over from 299,000 to 300,000 to the opening strains of the classic 1970s hit "Everyday people" by Sly and the Family Stone. The high kilometer count is presumably meant to hint at both the reliability of the car, and the averageness of the "working" family within it. The ad then progresses to display a series of scenarios illustrating "normal" people both at work and at play to the song's continuing verses, the lyrics of which include "We've got to live together" and "I am no better and neither are you, We are the same whatever we do." Meanwhile, the scenes switch quickly from a teenager learning to drive, to parents taking children to an after-school activity, to separate portrayals of Asian families, in an attempt to emphasize the inclusiveness and appropriateness of Toyota vehicles to all types of social circumstances, incomes, and needs. Included in this mosaic of depictions is that of a young man leaning on his car with his arm around a girl. The words "Kev" and "Sal" are writ large on the windscreen above the driver's and passenger's seats respectively. The next shot is of the same man with another girl, while the name on the windscreen has changed from "Sal" to "Sue," presumably indicating that he has a new girlfriend. This happens again, as "Sue" is replaced by "Val." Finally, the name above the passenger seat is changed again to "Ron," as "Kev" is seen emphatically hugging a man cheek to cheek, presumed to be "Ron." The ad continues at pace with further inclusive images of "everyday" people, while the final caption further emphasizes the campaign's theme through the words "Toyota: Everyday."

Case study ad 3: VISA

This comparatively short advertisement begins with former NFL San Francisco 49ers star quarter-back Steve Young being portrayed in a number of tragic-romantic scenes obviously pining for a lost or absent love. He is seen looking longingly out of a window as the rain falls heavily, gazing at a man and woman kissing in a street café, walking alone along a beach, and sitting in a coffee bar, again alone, as an older bartender shakes his head with pity. The scene then switches to a shot of Young and another man, walking away together out of a shadowy area into one illuminated by streetlights. Young is then heard to say to his companion, "Jerry, don't tell the guys about the flowers"; an obviously veiled reference to the friendship and professional relationship that Young had with his wide receiver at San Francisco, Jerry Rice. Finally, a shot of a gridiron stadium with the VISA logo evident at the top of the screen is displayed, accompanied by the closing caption: "VISA, official card of the NFL and everywhere you wanna be."

Case study ad 4: the Reebok/Finish Line DMX training shoe

This advertisement is for a Reebok running shoe, which may be purchased from Finish Line stores. The ad begins when two male buddies out hiking decide to leave a trail and take a short cut through a heavily grassed area. While crossing, the second character, who was a little reluctant to leave the trail in the first place, is bitten by a snake high on the calf. As he yells in pain and fear, the camera closes in on the wound, while his partner dramatically takes control of the situation ("Hunker down man, you're going to be fine!"). After informing his snake-bitten partner that he once saw this "on a survival show," he drops to his knees and begins to suck the wound, in an attempt to eject the poison. The camera now pans away slightly, thus displaying an image of a man kneeling in a field with his head in another's groin, while the latter is heard to wince and moan. At this point an attractive female jogger passes by on the nearby trail looking inquisitively, and with a hint of concern, at the action taking place. Once the snake-bitten character is aware of her presence, he unceremoniously pushes his partner away on to the ground, while trying to regain his masculine composure with a deep-voiced "Hi" to the passing runner. The closing caption is of the runner jogging away to the voice-over: "Want better advice? Get Reebok with DMX technology at Finish Line. Shoes to absorb the shock."

Discussion

In comparing the content of all four advertisements, what is immediately obvious is their fundamental differing treatment of homosexuality per se, in that they appear to range from inclusivity and acceptance to total exclusivity. For example, in the Sony advertisement, albeit at a superficial level, homosexuality is deemed to be acknowledged and recognized as one twin enters a car driven by a male, stereotypically represented by various signifiers, as gay. Although this twist in the "story-line," having witnessed the first twin leave with a beautiful girl, is undoubtedly meant to be the metaphorical "barb" that hooks the consumer to the company and product, in contrast to earlier media portrayals, the image does not imply a negative one. Indeed, perhaps the mere fact that a homosexual theme has been adopted by a leading multinational company for its advertising campaign may be seen as an indication of how far the issue has come to being normalized in recent years. Naturally, it also carries the message that Sony is an enlightened company with a conscience when it comes to sexuality, thus making a pitch at the wider young, in addition to the gay and lesbian, market. A similar conclusion could also be drawn from the gay content included within the Toyota ad, and perhaps, although to a lesser extent, from the VISA ad. Indeed, such advertising content could be seen as leading multinational companies legitimizing gay relationships and consequently "bestowing respectability on gay culture" (Kates, 1999: 30); a potentially exciting thought for the gay consumer community with an apparently high disposal income. Seen in this light, the Sony and Toyota ads in particular could be viewed as encouraging social tolerance, and perhaps even open acceptance, in terms of an individual's preferred sexuality.

However, on deeper analysis, the image portrayed of the gay twin in the Sony ad is not without its problems. For example, the direct inevitable comparison with the apparent heterosexual twin, in that the only difference between them is the gender of the person they left with, appears to promote and "privilege a masculine notion of homosexuality (white, male, affluent, macho, yet gay)" (Kates, 1999: 27). Likewise, "Kev's" final choice of a similar gay partner in the Toyota ad, having earlier had several girl-friends, carries the same message. Indeed, a more critical reading of this particular aspect of the ad would suggest that it reproduces myths about sexual uncertainty and confusion among gays and lesbians. Overall, critics have argued, specific forms of gay, lesbian and bisexual experience are marginalized, while an "unproblematically unified, centred and naturalized gay and/or lesbian identity" is created and promoted (Kates, 1999: 27). Hence, a hetero-normative discourse is seen to inform representations of gay men in advertising. Thus, while on one level, homosexuality is perceived to have become much more acceptable in social thinking, as witnessed by the content of the Toyota and Sony advertisements, its stereotypical portrayal remains heterosexually problematic in terms of gay identity. Even through gay representation therefore, the heterosexist status quo remains.

What appears to be happening here is that heterosexuality and homosexuality are being merged into a commonality through mediated discursive practice, driven by the potential of the pink dollar. In this way, the twins in the Sony ad wear the same clothes, use the same grooming products, and naturally use the same model "MiniDisc." They appear to exactly mirror each other except in their suggested sexuality. Consequently, the ad demonstrates that gay and straight men have much more in common than not, particularly in terms of luxury items, as it makes an attempt to integrate the gay community into the wider mainstream consumer market. The gay twin is, therefore, positioned as another version of normal, with his sexuality being just another social option. Kates (1999: 30), commenting on a different advertisement, describes this phenomenon as a "reconciliation of opposites, [which] occurs when gays and heterosexuals see aspects of themselves represented by two respectable men inhabiting the [same] space."

Such an apparent acknowledgment of homosexuality as a social option appears even more evident in the Toyota ad where the gay depiction is only a minor part of the totality. In this way, the social inclusivity of homosexuality, together with myriad other scenarios portraying "everyday people," is confirmed. However, although encapsulated within a theme of everyday normality, what both the Toyota and the Sony ads are also "selling" is the fashion of individuality (Mistry, 2000). According to Mistry (2000), what is really emphasized here is the coolness of "being different;" what Mort (1988: 204) has described as "stressing the plurality of signification" as opposed to a fixed masculine identity. Indeed, the closing caption of the Sony ad ("Very individualistic: Very Sony") openly confirms such a hypothesis. Thus, both companies, through publicly demonstrating their apparent acceptance of homosexuality per se, are not only aiming to become known as openly tolerant organizations, but also marketing themselves along the lines of radical chic. The "queer representation" is thus limited to an aesthetic (Mistry, 2000), with the homosexual content included more for its exotic appeal for the spectator than for any aspect of "gay sex" (Crimp and Warner, 1993). Such "queer chic" gives heterosexual consumers a "special flavor, an added spice" (hooks, 1992: 157) which allows them to "identify with an appropriate queer style [while] the actual practice of queer is rejected or, at the very least, overlooked" (Mistry, 2000). By reducing gender and homosexuality to the level of fashion rather than identity, as is done particularly in the Sony ad, it is exposed as a superficial but visible "put on" (Schwichtenberg, 1993). According to Mistry (2000), what has happened is that "advertisers have embraced queer representation with a consumer driven motivation rather than with a conscience. And inevitably the politics underneath the look are falsely represented, if at all." Such themes and images are thus merely presented at the level of style.

Kates (1999: 33), in applying queer theory to deconstruct such advertise-ments, questions the apparent need for "positive images" of gay men in the media, as represented in both the Toyota and Sony ads in particular. He con-cludes that when deconstructed, such ads "betray themselves as representational whitewash," as it appropriates acceptable "mass media images associated with heterosexuality and diffuses them into the gay men's community." For Kates (1999), through deconstruction, we are able to expose the politics of gay representation, as a hierarchy of respectability emerges with the masculine, affluent, well-dressed, white male at its apex. Consequently, other gay possi-bilities are marginalized or denied. As Kates (1999: 34) concludes, "in theo-retical terms, such ads have a performative function: [they] construct a particular gay subject, and produce what [they] purport only to describe. In brief, such representations illustrate the market sanitization of homosexuality [while] by importing positive images of gay men stripped of any hint of feminin-ity or sexual perversity, marketers contribute to the heterosexualization of homosexuality."

If the Sony and Toyota ads depict a somewhat positive, although ultimately problematic, stereotype of gay men, the Reebok/Finish Line advertisement may be interpreted as not even presenting a positive facade of the issue at all. Indeed, although giving the most graphic instance of perceived homosexual fel-latio yet seen in advertising, the theme is definitively anti-gay with the snake-bitten main character pushing his partner's head away from the bite on his leg in a particularly macho fashion as he perceives a passing female runner thinking that they are engaged in an act of homosexual oral sex. The obvious and imme-diate textual message is read as fear of being caught in what appears a compro-mising situation with a male partner, and thus of being labeled gay. This is accentuated by the deeper voiced "Hi" our hero half-heartedly yells at the dis-appearing female runner in a seemingly vain attempt to reassert his perceived lost masculine heterosexuality. The final catchy message of the ad, "Shoes to absorb the shock," is further proof of the portrayal of homosexuality as the abnormal perceived shocking "other" in society.

The Reebok/Finish Line ad presents homosexuality within a typical hetero-sexual male buddy culture, whereas although acknowledgment of such issues is made, it screams out that "we are not homosexual!" In essence the snake-bitten character is involved in "doing heterosexuality" (Messner, 1999); that is, engag-ing in identity construction. In this way, he seeks to avoid the stigma, embar-rassment and ostracism associated with gay suspicion within the sporting culture (Messner, 1999). One could interpret such a message, which appears divorced from the image presented in both the Sony and Toyota ads, particularly in terms of the bluntness of its rejection of homosexuality, as emanating from a homophobic sport culture and discourse. Thus, the simulation of homosexual activity is something to be joked about between mates, while the general message is one of reaffirmed unambiguous heterosexuality. In this way, the por-trayal of sports culture within the ad serves to further "construct and perpetuate compulsory heterosexuality" within sport (Wright and Clarke, 1999: 228).

While the VISA ad appears not to reject homosexuality as blatantly as the Reebok/Finish Line one, several similarities are evident. These are seen most notably in the "tongue-in-cheek" approach adapted to the issue, since it appears to poke fun at the apparent consistent speculation that both Young and Rice are gay. Consequently, by engaging in what is perceived as self-deprecating humor with regard to the rumors, both characters are involved in a process of confirming their heterosexuality. Indeed, the quirky, jokey treatment given to homosexuality in this context echoes the informal "humorous" references constantly made to gays and lesbians within the general sporting culture (Sabo, 1994). Such "humor" can be principally explained in terms of a superiority theory; that is, as an expression by a dominant heterosexual culture of a "form of hierarchical differentiation between in-groups and out-groups" (Snyder, 1991: 125). Indeed, according to Sabo (1994), the lessons on homophobia in sport are principally learned and acted out through teasing and ridiculing, while the "pervasiveness of anti-gay jokes reinforces the general impression that homosexuality is not welcome" (Pronger, 1999: 188). Such "humor" often includes gay slurs, disparages the homosexual out-group, while simultaneously developing the status, recognition, and prestige of the perpetrator within the larger and more powerful heterosexual "in-group" (Jones, 2002). Action of this nature inevitably creates the concept of separate identities, complete with the associated notions of inclusion and, more importantly in this context, exclusion. Homophobia, therefore, appears to remain an integral strand of sporting group relations and locker room subculture.

Such an apparent social hegemony stems from the view that in mainstream sport, heterosexuality is viewed as the "only rational, 'natural' and acceptable orientation" (Hargreaves, 1994: 169). This relates not only to anxiety regarding the "effeminization" of males, but also the masculinization of women (Hargreaves, 1994). Consequently, although there has been a broadening in the definitions of sexuality in general during recent years, heterosexual criteria continue to form powerful frames of reference, particularly in the world of sport. Thus, the discourses that construct heterosexuality as the only form of sexuality within sport remain pervasive (Wright and Clarke, 1999).

The power of the images of compulsory heterosexuality is "essentially ideological" as they "reflect a common system of values and meanings" (Hargreaves, 1994: 172). In this respect, sport exists in the vanguard of a fiercely heterosexual, tough, and competitive system, into which young males are induced and which embodies a fear of effeminate gay men (Hargreaves, 1990; Pronger, 1990). Similarly, Messner (1987: 54) views the situation as sport, in relatively liberalizing times, being "one of the last bastions of male power [having] superiority over – and [being] separate from – the feminization of society." Consequently, "while over the last twenty years homosexuality has taken a higher profile in popular mainstream culture – in films, on television, and fashion – in men's sport it has remained anathema" (Pronger, 1999: 189). Both the VISA and, to a greater extent, the Reebok/Finish Line ads appear as continuing evidence of this.

In investigating further the sexuality discourse and attitudes evident in both the sporting and wider Australian media, Farrell (1999) contrasted the general reception given to the gay-themed film *The Adventures of Priscilla, Queen of the Desert* with that given to the "outing" of Australian Rugby League star Ian Roberts in 1994. While the former was greeted with much critical acclaim and an American Academy Award, Roberts was subjected to a whole range of responses, ranging from the supportive to the violently hostile. However, Roberts' case remains unique in many ways, since he didn't lose sponsors as a result of his outing. Farrell (1999: 163) argues that this seeming acceptance of Roberts' sexuality lay not in the liberalization of the Australian Rugby League establishment or general culture, but because "his body performed hegemonic masculinity so well that its effectiveness for queer politics was numbed." In short, it was only his considerable ability to play rugby league that allowed him continuing status within the game, as "it was not the acceptance of homosexuality that won him a place in the rugby league world but rather his ability to perform heterosexual masculinity" (Farrell, 1999: 159). In this way, as Farrell (1999) notes, a queer subjectivity is reconciled with hegemonic heterosexual performance and contained within the broader concerns of heterosexual maintenance and identity. Consequently, while this apparent sexual "alternative" remains contained within a hegemony of heterosexual masculinity (Farrell, 1999), homosexuality continues to be defined as a "stigmatised, abnormal and marginal identity, that is socially threatening to the norm"(Wright and Clarke, 1999: 229).

Conclusion

This chapter has attempted to address the commonly held assumption that society is liberalizing as witnessed by many social trends, one of which is the perceived increasing homosexual content of advertisements. Such a change, however, has also resulted from the considerable economic and political clout of the emerging pink dollar and its recognition by corporate logic. However, although mainstream ads in general containing homosexual themes appear to have diversified, the image portrayed of the gay man in particular remains problematic. In essence, he has been heterosexualized, thus presenting a "normalized" and sanitized alternative to a mainstream audience. Indeed, according to Mistry (2000), what the "incorporation of the queer aesthetic into the mainstream media has led to [is the] watering down of its political edge – to what Paul Rudnick and Kurt Anderson call the creation of the 'world of heterosexual camp, Camp Lite.'"

The consumer jury however is still out on such inclusive advertising campaigns like the Sony and Toyota ones discussed in this chapter. Indeed, we agree with Bhat *et al.*'s (1998) suggestion that a future area of research should concentrate on the effectiveness of such inclusive campaigns that aim to target multiple audiences, where the salience of the homosexual images used is reduced. Although perhaps more acceptable to a perceived liberalizing mainstream culture, they could be viewed as overly simplistic, patronizing, and a crude token attempt to get at the pink dollar by critical gay consumers. Consequently, perhaps as Bhat *et al.* (1998: 24) suggest, companies which employ such inclusive ad campaigns should be aware of the need to "become more sophisticated in their definition of sub-markets and selection of ad messages" in order to maximize their marketing campaigns.

Conversely, using homosexual themes in sport advertising remains less problematic, than simply homophobic. As Cole (1993) has lamented, sport remains a site where the boundaries between being sick and homosexual, and being healthy and heterosexual, meet (Pronger, 1999). Thus, the line between homosexuality and heterosexuality is as demarcated as ever within the sports world, with advertising images continuing to deny the legitimacy of the gay presence in an ultra-masculine arena. Sport ads therefore persist with images of men doing heterosexuality, often in attempted humorous situations, portraying homosexuality as being beyond the pale of normality.

References

Bhat, S., Leigh, T.W. and Wardlow, D.L. (1998). The effect of consumer prejudices on ad processing: Heterosexual consumers' responses to homosexual imagery in ads. *Journal of Advertising*, 27 (4), 9–28.

Chicago Area Gay and Lesbian Chamber of Commerce (2000). Chicago 2006 committee formed to bring Gay Games to Chicago. Available online at http://www.glchamber.org/chicago2006.html.

Cole, C. (1993). Resisting the canon: Feminist cultural studies, sport and technologies of the body. *Journal of Sport and Social Issues*, 17 (2), 77–97.

Crimp, D. and Warner, M. (1993). No sex in *Sex*. In L. Frank and P. Smith (eds), *Madonnarama: Essays on Sex and Popular Culture* (pp. 93–110). Pennsylvania: Cleis Press.

Drummond, T. (1995). Vamping for new visitors. *Time*, 25 September, pp. 54–55.

Farrell, K. (1999). (Foot)Ball gowns: Masculinities, sexualities and the politics of performance. *Journal of Australian Studies*, 63, 157–164.

Federation of Gay Games (2000). Concept and purpose. Available online at http://www.gaygames.org/.

Fejes, F. and Petrich, K. (1993). Invisibility, homophobia and heterosexism: Lesbians, gays and the media. *Critical Studies in Mass Communication*, 10, 395–422.

Goldman, R. and Papson, S. (1996). *Sign Wars: The Cluttered Landscape of Advertising*. New York: The Guilford Press.

Gross, L. (1994). What is wrong with this picture: Lesbian women and gay men on television. In R.J. Ringer (ed.), *Queer Words, Queer Images: Communication and the Construction of Homosexuality* (pp. 143–156). New York: SUNY Press.

Hantiz, D.M. and Lehr, V. (1994). Whose desire? Lesbian (non) sexuality and television's perpetuation of hetero/sexism. In R.J. Ringer (ed.), *Queer Words, Queer Images: Communication and the Construction of Homosexuality* (pp. 107–121). New York: SUNY Press.

Hargreaves, J. (1994). *Sporting Females: Critical Issues in the History and Sociology of Women's Sports*. London: Routledge.

hooks, b. (1992). *Black Looks: Race and Representation*. Boston, MA: South End Press.

Jackson, S. and Andrews, D. (eds) (2004). *Sport, Culture and Advertising: Identities, Commodities and the Politics of Representation*. London: Routledge.

Jones, R.L. (2002). The Black experience in English semi-professional football. *Journal of Sport and Social Issues*. 26 (1), 47–65.

Kates, S.M. (1998). *Twenty Million New Customers! Understanding Gay Men's Consumer Behavior*. Binghamton, NY: Harrington Park Press.

Kates, S.M. (1999). Making the ad perfectly queer: Marketing "normality" to the gay men's community. *Journal of Advertising*, 28 (1), 25–37.

Kielwasser, A.P. and Wolf, M.A. (1992). Mainstream television, adolescent homosexuality and significant silence. *Critical Studies in Mass Communication*, 9 (4), 350–374.

LeBlanc, R. (1997). The "pink dollar" in sport. Unpublished paper presented at the University of Otago, January.

Lukinball, G. (1995). *Untold Millions*. New York: Harper Business.

Messner, M. (1987). The life of a man's seasons: Male identity in the life course of a jock. In M. Kimmel (ed.), *Changing Men: New Directions in Research in Research on Men and Masculinity* (pp. 53–67). Newbury Park, CA: Sage.

Messner, M. (1994). AIDS, homophobia and sport. In M. Messner and D. Sabo (eds), *Sex, Violence and Power in Sports* (pp. 120–126). Freedom, CA: The Crossing Press.

Messner, M. (1999). Becoming 100 percent straight. In J. Coakley and P. Donnelly (eds), *Inside Sports* (pp. 104–110). London: Routledge.

Miller, C. (1995). The ultimate taboo. *Marketing news*, 29, 14 August, pp. 1, 18.

Miller, T. (1998). Commodifying the male body: Problematizing "hegmonic masculinity?" *Journal of Sport and Social Issues*, 22 (4), 431–446.

Mistry, R. (2000). From "hearth and home" to a queer chic: A critical analysis of progressive depictions of gender in advertising. Available online at http://www.theory.org.uk/mistry.htm.

Mort, F. (1988). Boy's own? Masculinity, style and popular culture. In R. Chapman and J. Rutherford (eds), *Male Order: Unwrapping Masculinity* (pp. 193–224). London: Lawrence and Wishart.

NAGAAA (2000). What's NAGAAA? Available online at http://members.aol.com/scslpgh.html.

Nelson, M.B. (1991). *Are We Winning Yet?* New York: Random House.

Nudd, K. (1992). Profit v prejudice: Why it pays to target gays. *Ad/media*, 8, 24–26.

O'Shea, P. (1995). Out on the field. *Advocate*, October, 4–6.

Pitts, P.G. (1989). Beyond the bars: The development of leisure-activity management in the lesbian and gay population in America. *Leisure Information Quarterly*, 15 (3), 4–7.

Porter, D. (1999). Don't ask, don't tell: Mauresmo flap raises issues women's tennis would rather avoid. Available online at http://www.foxsports.com/cgi-bin/email.pl.

Pronger, B. (1990). *The Arena of Masculinity: Sports, Homosexuality and the Meaning of Sex*. Toronto: Summerhill Press.

Pronger, B. (1999). Fear and trembling: Homophobia in Men's sport. In P. White and K. Young (eds), *Sport and Gender in Canada* (pp. 182–196). Ontario: Oxford University Press.

Sabo, D. (1994). The politics of homophobia in sport. In M. Messner and D. Sabo (eds), *Sex, Violence and Power in Sports* (pp. 101–112). Freedom, CA: The Crossing Press.

Schulman, S. (1995). Gay marketeers. *The Progressive*, 59, 28–29.

Schwichtenberg, C. (1993). Madonna's postmodern feminism: Bringing margins to the centre. In C. Schwichtenberg,(ed.), *The Madonna Collection: Representational Politics, Subcultural Identities and Cultural Theory* (pp. 129–145). Boulder, CO: Westview Press.

Short, B. (1996). Playing it straight. *Gay times UK*, July, 52–54.

Snyder, E.E. (1991). Sociology of sport and humour. *International Review for the Sociology of Sport*, 26 (2), 119–132.

Tonkiss, F. (1998). Analysing discourse. In C. Seale (ed.), *Researching Society and Culture* (pp. 245–260). London: Sage.

Turow, J. (1997). *Breaking up America: Advertisers and the New Media World.* Chicago, IL: University of Chicago Press.

Wardlow, D.L. (1996). *Gays, Lesbians, and Consumer Behavior: Theory, Practice and Research Issues in Marketing.* Binghamton, NY: Haworth.

Whannel, G. (1992). *Fields in Vision: Television, Sport and Cultural Transformation.* London: Routledge.

Wilstein, S. (1999). Post match fall out continues. Available online at http://www.foxsports.com/cgi-bin/cmail.pl.

Wright, J. and Clarke, G. (1999). Sport, the media and the construction of compulsory heterosexuality: A case study of women's rugby union. *International Review for the Sociology of Sport*, 34 (3), 227–243.

7 Fitting images

Advertising, sport and disability

Margaret Duncan and Alan Aycock

Introduction[1]

Works on advertising seldom deal with disability;[2] works on disability rarely speak of advertising.[3] When such intersections occur, scholars routinely point out the obvious: because there is so little advertising that includes persons with disabilities, it follows empirically that there is scarcely anything to write about (Nelson, 1996; Hahn, 1997).Thus, although there are many well-argued and thoroughly documented studies of stereotypic images of race, gender, nationality, indigenous peoples, and colonized populations in advertising (Barthel, 1988; Pieterse, 1992; Kern-Foxworth, 1994; O'Barr, 1994; Pinkus, 1995; Goldman and Papson, 1996; Kilbourne, 1999), there is no comparable study of stereotypic images of disability in advertising. Conversely, there are several magisterial studies of television, photographic, and cinematic images of disability (Klobas, 1988; Schuchman, 1988; Hevey, 1992; Norden, 1994; Pointon *et al.*, 1997), but none of these deal specifically with advertising. This gap in scholarship appears unbridged.

This chapter attempts to address the deficit that we have described: we are writing about disability, advertising images, and stereotyping, specifically in the context of sport and leisure, where representations of ableism are perhaps the most commonly found. By no means do we regard our data or analysis as definitive – there really are not much data available on stereotypic images of disability and advertising. On the other hand, we think that we can offer some intriguing hypotheses that are consistent both with the limited data that we have secured, and with a variety of theoretical paradigms that describe and analyze pervasive cultural themes associated with disability. These hypotheses may suggest directions for further examination of significant issues in disability, sport and leisure, and advertising.

Ableism

Our own challenge in critiquing these images is to show some of the messages of ableism in North American society. For our purpose here, we define ableism as a perspective in which nondisabled experience and point of view is central and dominant (Linton, 1998). Ableism has many significant, concrete effects on the disabled. Ableism contributes to systematic institutional discrimination in favor of nondisabled persons, both in North America and abroad (Wendell, 1996; Charlton, 1998). The "spread effect" of ableism supports the idea that one's overall abilities or characteristics are determined by a particular disability; thus, ability becomes a key status, often the sole key status for those with disabilities (Russell, 1998). Finally, since people with disabilities may differ visibly from mainstream norms of competent appearance and/or behavior, ableism assumes that the disabled, both as individuals and as a group, are inferior (Aycock and Duncan, 1996).

The assumption that difference is equivalent to inferiority leads ableist textual or visual representations of disability to portray the disabled as more dependent, childlike, passive, vulnerable, and less competent than "normal" people (Davis, 1995; 1997). Differences among the disabled themselves, such as distinctions of race, gender, sexual orientation, or age, are minimized by reference to their key status as "the disabled" or worse "the handicapped." More broadly, ableism constructs people with disabilities as the "Other" of normal humanity (Thomson, 1997). The social and psychological dynamics of exclusion are clear (Wendell, 1996): those designated as Other become mere objects of perception upon whom are projected a wide range of anxieties and fears. Such objects cannot, must not speak for themselves (Booth, 1996; Linton, 1998); indeed, Others are precisely those with whom full identification as authentic, independent, active agents is impossible (Gill, 1994).This notion of disabled persons as Other leads to the cultural stereotyping of the disabled, especially through exaggerations of their heroism, depravity, suffering, and dependency. Such stereotypes evoke the admiration, disgust, pity, and charity of those who see themselves as nondisabled (Cole and Johnson, 1994; Whyte and Ingstad, 1995).

Nowhere is ableism more prevalent than in sport (Stewart, 1991). Sport routinely privileges those whose reactions and movements rise above mainstream (ableist) standards of performance; sport celebrates a certain form of achievement – and, indeed, measures that achievement in the most minute increments in order to do so – as an ideal to which all persons should aspire (Rabinbach, 1990). Anything less is at best merely normal. More to the point, sport authorizes the body as fully human or even superhuman, and relegates its Other, the "abnormal" body, to an object of pity, disgust, and finally denial in case any others should be "reduced" to a comparable fate (Duncan and Aycock, 1997). For this reason, an analysis of disability advertising in a context of sport or leisure is a particularly effective way to display the nuances of ableist stereotyping.

Methods and texts

Our work in this area began with an earlier study of images of disability and sport of more than a hundred sites on the World Wide Web (Duncan and Aycock, 1997). Our findings in this study – to be reviewed below – were clear.

Prejudicial stereotyping of disability online in a context of sport and leisure was more blatant than we wished to imagine in a post-ADA (Americans with Disability Act) world. Upon reflection, however, we wondered whether our findings reflected bias (Moore *et al.*, 1998). Were we seeing Web images of persons with disabilities *intended* by persons with disabilities, or were these images produced online by well-meaning Webmasters unwittingly imbued with ableist perspectives? Were the organizations that paid for these websites run by and on behalf of persons with disabilities, or were they instead – the Muscular Dystrophy Association is a notorious instance – managed by the "temporarily abled," pursuing a "Jerry's kids" agenda for motives both charitable and financial (Johnson, 1994; Longmore, 1997)? The latter seems more likely to us, but we require empirical verification of our hypothesis.

Accordingly, we decided to focus on advertising images of sport and disability in hardcopy magazines. Our reasoning is that magazine advertising, by contrast with Web imagery, is less ephemeral in a capitalist regime (McCracken, 1993). The institutional arrangements that produce mass-marketed or niche-marketed glossies (i.e. magazines that can afford the more expensive production costs of glossy covers and pages) usually involve identifiable organizations and individuals equipped with specific marketing goals and concrete resources (McAllister, 1996). Almost anyone can post to the Web and claim to fairly represent a given perspective; that is both the advantage and disadvantage of Web publishing. However, not just anyone can publish a magazine that appears on the shelves of major chains such as Barnes & Noble. This requires that in some respects an organization must legitimize itself – and its claims to represent a particular point of view – in a formal and routinized setting (Lears, 1994; Ohmann, 1996). The nature of modern cultural and economic capital is that it is simultaneously symbolic and tangible (Jhally, 1987; Goldman, 1992); thus, we have chosen to examine its influence in a hardcopy mode of expression.

We have selected three glossies – *Mainstream*, *Abilities*, and *Accent on Living* – that are commonly subscribed to in the USA and Canada. We find it highly suggestive that although the disability-oriented glossy *We* did not begin publication until our study had already been completed, our observation of its pages showed that its advertising remained clearly within the patterns that we identify in this chapter. In fact, nearly all of the advertising that we had selected for our present study was still being circulated by *We* a full year after we had completed our data selection. This implies, in our view, not only that our findings are predictive, but more to the point, that in this marketing niche the rate of advertising turnover is relatively slow (even glacial by comparison with ableist sport advertising). This suggests in turn that the advertising images of sport and disability are socially stable and economically rewarding to a degree that would be improbable in a Nike or Speedo campaign.

We have defined our sample by choosing advertising photos rather than their surrounding text, though where the text is necessary for clarification of the images, we refer to it minimally. These advertising photos are few, however, and the repertoire of images in disability glossies is narrow. Thus, we expanded our original sampling protocol to include the magazine covers as well, simply because to do otherwise would mean that we would have little to say about key areas such as persons of color and even children with disabilities. Finally, we have chosen only advertising images that occur in a context of sport or leisure (though as we will show, disability advertising in a workplace setting is so rare that this did not constrict our choice). After we discarded multiples – images that appeared in more than one magazine, or in more than one issue of the same magazine – we wound up with thirty-eight distinct images of sport or leisure and disability. These images are categorized as A1–2, A5–8, A12–15 (*Abilities*), AL1–10, 12–13 (*Accent on Living*), M7–17, M20–24 (*Mainstream*).[4] This set of images comprises our sample. Had we not removed "multiples" from our sample as indicated above, it would have been approximately twice as large from one month to the next; that is to say, an advertisement that appeared in one of the three magazines we examined was likely to appear in at least one of the others.

We note that this sample of sport and leisure advertising images in disability glossies is clearly biased. Magazines published by radical disability activists, for example, the well-known activist magazine *Disability Rag* (Shaw, 1994) or the Madison, WI magazine *Dykes with Disabilities*, contain very little advertising. Thus, our study uses advertising images only from "glossy" disability magazines that are politically moderate. This is obviously not a coincidental linkage, since advertisers are unlikely to risk controversy by investing their capital in radical magazines. As a further instance of bias, we have found no advertising content related to mental disabilities. This may partly reflect the three magazines' emphasis on mobility-related disabilities, despite their implicit claim to represent all persons with disabilities. It may also reflect the extent to which mental disability has been relegated to a "ghetto" of specialized areas such as special education, which has its own array of publications (Linton, 1998). Finally, we have decided not to use the TV clips. We chose photo stills instead of moving images to maintain our analytical focus.

Analysis and discussion

We have organized our findings into three categories that reflect the overall composition of advertising photos – focus, setting, and visibility – and into five categories – gender, race, age, sexual orientation, and class – that constitute common social attributes of photographic models. In this way we provide a grid of photographic background and foreground that places ableist imagery in its fullest context.

Focus

We find a pattern repeatedly in disability advertising that is extremely rare elsewhere: the disabled person who would normally be the focus of the ad is positioned facing partially or wholly away from the camera, creating a distance between the model in the ad and the reader of that ad. For instance, we found three ads for vans that were being sold as specially modified for wheelchairs: in one, the model is positioned in his wheelchair as if he were about to be elevated into the van, but he is facing off to the left, not looking directly into the camera; in another, the model is positioned next to the van, her face visible only from a three-quarters back profile; in a third, the model is about to be elevated into the van by his partner, but while *she* is smiling full face at the camera, the model's back is his only visible feature!

These ads, we believe, function subtly in several ways to reinforce stereotypes of persons with disabilities. First, they produce a strong sense of the person as an object – in the ads described above, an object is simply placed next to another object, the van that is to be purchased. It is as if the disabled person is merely a sort of cargo that requires movement from one place to another. Second, the ads emphasize the passivity of the disabled. Instead of being presented as fully social agents, they are accompanied by large prostheses – the vans – that visually overwhelm their presence. Third, along these same lines the van ads described seem to be addressed to a primary caregiver, a more active and entirely autonomous social agent, who would purchase the vehicle on behalf of the disabled person. Fourth, the photographic conventions of disability advertising reinforce the strong social taboo on looking directly at persons with disabilities, since the magazine reader is not positioned completely face to face with the model. Finally, since the model is not looking at the reader, the reader is not invited to identify her/himself with the model. Overall, this device of disability advertising emphasizes the social distance of anonymity as a marker of difference, and by so doing relieves any implicit concern that the reader might become disabled as well (Davis, 1995).

Setting

The setting of the photos in our sample is almost invariably rural, or at least non-urban in the sense that a humanly constructed environment of buildings, sports arenas, crowded gathering places, and pavements are rigorously excluded. This does not imply that people with disabilities are portrayed in wilderness settings, since this might suggest that they could be confronted with overwhelming obstacles or even dangers. Instead, in thirteen – one-third – of our photos the persons with disabilities are located in well-manicured grassy parks, wheeling along neatly cropped pathways, or situated pleasantly on beaches or in camp grounds with unthreatening waves at a safe distance, or quiet streams in the background. One memorable ad shows a man using a wheelchair submerged up to the tops of the wheels in a stream where he is fishing, but he is smiling comfortably to signal the reader that he is in no danger. One ad shows a child in a wheelchair being pushed across sturdy bridges by an able-bodied caregiver; the pace of the caregiver is sufficiently sedate and her lack of effort clearly evident to demonstrate that the disabled person is in no peril. Park-like settings seem to offer a conventional image of relaxation in a way that city environments cannot (Lewis and Catterson, 1994; Urry, 1995). The incredibly low population density of disability advertisements segregates persons with disabilities from the productive world of speed and labor for which they are implicitly ill-equipped. It also mirrors, ironically, the actual isolation of the disabled from desirable but mainly inaccessible urban environments such as business offices, schools, factories, shopping malls, theaters, and restaurants, all of which are highly relevant to ableist experience and perspective, but which – even long after the passage of the ADA – often remain sites for struggle by and on behalf of persons with disabilities (Shapiro, 1994).

Visibility

Another pattern which seems specific to disability advertising is the use of camera shots that make the disabled person less visible, or altogether invisible. For instance, two ads for vehicles focus textually on the independence, freedom, and safety of their passengers, all values that might be expected to appeal to persons with disabilities. Both of these ads, however, involve scenic outdoor vistas – mountains and trees – in which the vehicle that is presumably carrying a disabled person is a small, distant component of the picture. An ad for wheelchairs shows the empty wheelchair as its only feature, substituting the machinery of disability for the persons who would presumably be using it. An ad for sailboating shows the (presumably disabled) person far out on the water – of course, the model's face and the front of the body is turned away from the camera – much too far away to discern whether in fact s/he is disabled. Similarly, an ad for parachuting depicts the chutist dangling beneath the canopy, again too far from the camera to be able to identify the chutist as a person with a disability.

The effect of the ads described above is to sanitize disability by separating the desire to buy the product advertised from the perhaps unpleasant reminder that its purpose is to serve the needs or pleasure of a person who is disabled. The message seems to be that fun and adventure are acceptable pursuits, but the actual presence of disability may diminish the anticipated experience. This would be particularly relevant, of course, if the person with a disability were *not* the target audience (i.e. potential consumer) addressed by the advertisement. Instead, when we tried to identify the targeted audience for these ads we were left with two likely conclusions. One is that persons without disabilities are assumed always to be active social agents and caregivers when paired with disabled persons; of the pair, the caregiver would be the target consumer rather than the disabled person. This indeed appears to be a convention of disability photography in the glossies we examined. A second conclusion is that advertisers themselves may dislike, and assume that others may dislike, seeing or being reminded of persons with disabilities. In other words, the advertisers are merely conforming to their ableist socialization by producing "normality dramas" of disabled persons (Darke, 1998).

Gender

Gender stereotypes are pervasive, in fact far more common in disability advertising than in other kinds of advertising (Goffman, 1976). The rules are simple and familiar as indicated above, and consistent with previous gender studies of sport and media images (Duncan and Messner, 1998): male athletes are almost always active competitors, while women athletes are almost always presented more passively (Duncan, 1993). Female athletes are often presented in cheesecake costumes and positions (Duncan, 1998); disabled women, like all women photographed in advertising, are far more likely than disabled men to be presented in ads with children nearby. Here are some examples.

Four advertisements show close-up shots of elite male athletes waterskiing or wheelchairing in intense concentration. There are no ads that show women involved in waterskiing or racing cycle competitions. Nonathletic-looking men are also depicted in our sample, but they are shown as being active: one is seated in a wheelchair hurling a bowling ball down an alley, while the other is hauling in a large fish from the upper deck of a fishing boat. Four ads for exercise machines portray women sitting passively on the machine, doing nothing. One ad shows an elite female athlete, a member of the US Olympic Women's Wheelchair Basketball team, sitting quietly next to a vehicle, handing a basketball to a gaggle of nondisabled boys.

We include three ads in our sample that show close-up shots of women in swim-suits next to or in a swimming pool. In none of the ads is any of the women actually swimming, even in the ad that is captioned "Keeping Fit." In two of the ads the women are dressed in provocatively tight swim-suits, one of the suits high-cut on the thigh; in both of these ads the women are smiling into the camera, and their bare legs are prominently displayed. Again following photographic convention (Goffman, 1976), the women in disability ads are far more likely to be shown smiling than men in disability ads. This is particularly emphasized if males are performing physically, since men are more often shown frowning with physical exertion than women. A typical example is the contrast between an ad that shows a man, mouth open and struggling to breathe, grimly concentrating on his wheelchair race, versus another ad that shows a smiling woman idly sitting on a golf cart, apparently about to putt.

Finally, in addition to children in the ad, mentioned above, featuring an elite female wheelchair athlete, we also include in our sample several other ads that take place in leisure settings in which disabled women are accompanied by children. One such ad displays a woman in a wheelchair on a beach with waves breaking nearby. The woman is pointing out something in the distance to the nondisabled girl who is standing next to her. Other typical ads show women in family contexts, while men are more likely to be shown in ads alone. All of these clearly underscore well-documented stereotypes of women and men in advertising (Kilbourne, 1999).

Race

The racial composition of advertising in disability magazines is unambiguous. Almost all persons depicted are white and Nordic. Even dark-*haired* models are extremely rare, let alone dark-*skinned*. The sole persons of color we were able to include in our sample are extremely light-skinned, one black woman and one Hispanic girl, both with classic Anglo features. We note that these persons of color are on the covers of magazines, not in advertisements (though being on the cover is at least *some* improvement over total invisibility). Black males – even with the stereotypically hip "bad male" glower of black male athletes (Johnson and Roediger, 1997) – simply do not appear in disability advertising.

We suggest that this is consistent with our earlier internet research (Duncan and Aycock, 1997) that shows disproportionate representation of white people with disabilities on websites devoted to sport and disability. There is considerable empirical evidence which suggests that the actual distribution of disability in the population at large includes relatively *more* persons of color than white people (Livingston, 1994; Belgrave, 1998). There are many reasons for this. Persons of color are likely – due directly or indirectly to racial discrimination – to be working under dangerous, even toxic conditions (Storck and Thompson-Hoffman, 1991; Branche-Dorsey *et al.*, 1998). Persons of color are more likely to be subject to such disorders as adult-onset diabetes and CVAs resulting partly from lack of preventive care and other medical treatment comparable to that of white people, partly from environmental stress and unhealthy lifestyle patterns arising from racial oppression, partly due to genetic differences in susceptibility (Semmes, 1996; Belgrave, 1998). Finally, persons of color have less access to preventive or rehabilitative programs, and fewer persons of color have insurers willing to cover the cost of special leisure-capable prosthetics (Belgrave, 1998). Thus, we believe that the occasional appearance of persons of color in disability advertising, rare as it is, substantially disguises the even bleaker actual practices of discrimination against disabled persons of color.

Age

The distribution of age in disability advertising is at best a mixed blessing. Even "Tiny Tim" figures of pitiable innocence and victimization, so characteristic of nonprofit advertising campaigns, are rare in disability glossies. Teenagers and twentysomethings also make very few appearances, although the rate of disability among young male motorists and motorcyclists is relatively high in the actual population. It may be that prosthetics don't lend themselves readily to youth-oriented consumers, perhaps because wheelchairs are at odds with our stereotype of the idealized young, active consumer immersed in rock concerts, style-conscious clothing, and sexual escapades.

On the other hand, elderly persons figure prominently in our sample of disability ads, very often in the company of children without disabilities. This is consistent with the medicalization and infantilization of the elderly, who are stereotypically assumed to be infirm (Morgan and Kunkel, 1998). Prosthetics such as wheelchairs are considered, in this worldview, to be a normal, though disheartening, part of the life cycle. It is noteworthy that our advertising almost always shows elderly persons alone rather than in cross-sex pairs, the asexual stereotype of disability reinforced by an analogous stereotype of aging. One advertisement shows an older man by himself, wheeling slowly along a well-groomed path with a woodsy background. Another advertisement shows an elderly man with a cane seated on a recumbent bicycle with a child perched behind him; the bicycle is canted in the photo, as if it were careening around a corner. The elderly man wields the cane as if he were steering with it, perhaps to show both that he is disabled, yet also to demonstrate reassuringly that he really doesn't need the cane since he brandishes it so playfully. In some ways this ad is anomalous in our sample: the image of "rest" is very strong in most of the advertisements that involve older persons. The elderly persons in our sample have little to do other than to smile at children gamboling in their vicinity: one standard ad shows an older man in a wheelchair posed next to young kids who are admiring his fishing prowess.

Sexuality and sexual orientation

The sexual orientation of persons with disabilities in advertising highlights an interesting and important issue (Wade, 1994). On one hand, a pervasive ableist stereotype maintains that persons with disabilities are, or should become asexual, because they are physically "inferior" and "unattractive" (Shakespeare et al., 1996). On the other hand, numerous persons with disabilities have argued that their sexual needs are often unacknowledged or even actively prohibited (Waxman, 1994). It is not surprising to learn that sexuality is strongly down-played in disability advertising, and that sexual orientation – insofar as it is acknowledged at all – is presented in very conventional terms that would presumably be less threatening to the nondisabled reader.

For instance, lesbians and gays are never represented as such in our sample (as noted, the lesbian disability magazine Dykes with Disabilities attracts no mainstream advertising). Yet there is no evidence that we are aware of to suggest that gays or lesbians have fewer disabilities than heterosexuals. Nevertheless, same-sex intimates are invisible in disability advertising: males are not usually photographed with males, or females with females, unless one is adult and the other a young child.

What sexuality may be inferred from the ads is always depicted in traditional mainstream terms. For instance, several ads in our sample show males and females together but always in circumstances suggesting a married or marriage-able couple of approximately the same age. A standard female–male ad shows the models looking into one another's eyes and smiling, unless they are smiling at their children, almost always one male and one female child, the perfect nuclear family. The ads, moreover, are rarely shot in an intensely romantic or sexualized setting such as a night-club or resort. Most often, the background is bucolic, resembling a camp ground. As far as sexuality goes, disability advertising remains firmly in the 1950s.

Class

The advertising in our sample makes several assumptions about social class, some more direct than others. We have already noted that white people, who as a category have far more disposable income than persons of color, are most often depicted in the ads. One ad in particular shows two women, one in a wheelchair and one standing, smiling at each other after a hard day of shopping. Immaculately coiffured, manicured, and stylishly dressed, they clutch shopping bags displaying brands such as Eddie Bauer and Williams-Sonoma. The women have paused in a driveway that includes a fountain fronting a glamorous portico, obviously an upscale shopping mall. The sole signal of disability in the ad is that one of the women is sitting in a wheelchair, but she is positioned in such a way that it seems equally plausible to the reader that she merely sat there casually, as she might have sat on any other horizontal surface, just because she became tired after a hard day of shopping. Other "typical" disability settings include golf courses and private swimming pools, both icons of high-class lifestyle.

A second, and more subtle signal of social class is that the disabled persons in advertising are always slim and conventionally attractive (unless they are elderly, in which case they have full heads of fluffy white hair). Attractive physical appearance is a powerful signal of social acceptability; thus, no unsightly disabled persons appear in advertising (Schell and Duncan, 1999: 33). The standard linkage of "normal" intelligence to social competence and hence, social attractiveness, also functions in disability advertising as a marker of social class. There are no persons with mental disabilities in disability advertising in the glossies we sampled. This is again consistent with the findings of our earlier Internet study (Duncan and Aycock, 1997), where mental disability was represented only as Down's syndrome, and then only among appealing children who could serve as possibly redeemable Tiny Tims (Shapiro, 1994; Castles, 1996).

A third element of social class in disability advertising is the most subtle, and perhaps the most hypocritical of all. We had no difficulty finding advertising that shows disabled persons at leisure, because in stark contrast with other advertising genres, there is virtually no advertising that portrays persons with disabilities at work! Even school work and housework are invisible in disability advertising. One favorable interpretation of this phenomenon is that advertisers want to show the disabled as persons who are relaxed and happy in their leisure surroundings. A somewhat less flattering interpretation is that disabled persons are widely assumed to be unproductive and to require responsible caregivers who supply them with their needs. Least charitably, we suspect that this absence of work in any guise from disability advertising reflects an actual social condition, the extremely high rate of unemployment and poverty among the disabled by contrast with the general population (McNeil *et al.*, 1991; Bryan, 1996; Barnes *et al.*, 1999). If disabled persons are not to be imagined in the workplace, then of course they must be supported by able-bodied caregivers. This interpretation is perhaps too cynical, but the pattern is unmistakable in our sample.

Summary and conclusion

Our sample of sport and disability images associated with advertising in disability-oriented glossies strikingly confirms our earlier generalizations about sport and disability images on the Web. Our findings in both cases strongly suggest that conventional stereotypes – gender, race, age, sexuality, sexual orientation, and social class – predominate in the media. These stereotypes reinforce existing social hierarchies by privileging the needs, attitudes, activities, and experiences of middle-class white male athletes with disabilities. When we refer to reinforcement of social hierarchies, however, we are not alluding to a straightforward "media effects" claim that what is viewed on the Web or seen in magazines directly shapes the world of everyday experience.

A slightly different type of media effects claim provides an opportunity for us to reflect on the significance of the photos in our sample: we wish to discuss media effects as a *process* and not merely as a *product* (Corrigan, 1997). We perceive the social hierarchies that are so clear in our current sample (and in our earlier internet study as well) primarily as hierarchies of "attention" that portray some persons with disabilities as socially exemplary while marginalizing Others with disabilities by making them invisible, segregating them entirely from the public gaze. For instance, attractive, well-built white men epitomize active athleticism in our sample, while black men – attractive or not, athletic or not – simply do not exist. Mobility disorders predominate in the world of disability glossies, while cognitive or emotional disabilities vanish altogether. In each of these cases the sport and disability photos in our sample emphasize the former and utterly deny the latter. No effort is spared photographically to normalize good-looking white men with mobility disorders, while by contrast, black male Others are placed so far outside the realm of normality that they literally cannot be seen, at least in disability glossies. Yet in real life black men with disabilities do exist, and white men with disabilities are not always attractive or athletic. What sort of media effects might this photographic version of schizophrenia produce?

In daily life, people interact on a basis of enduring cultural expectations that are acquired through socialization. During routine cultural encounters, people transact the human business of trust, common feeling, mutuality, and recognition. These cultural practices of daily life are inextricably linked to the numerous mediated images that express human nuance in a given society. Yet our sample of sport and disability ads in disability glossies seems to divide mediated image from real-world interaction, to separate these mediated discourses from the practices they project. Thus, we are examining here the *decoupling* of practice and media discourse by a radical splitting of hierarchies of attention between those who are always seen and those who are never seen. This could easily have concrete, though unpredictable, consequences. To be made invisible may remove a key source of self-esteem and social standing; to be made invisible may isolate and disenfranchise; to be made invisible may problematize the competence – athletic and otherwise – of those excluded from view. We want to be careful about our media effects claim at this point: we are not assuming either that reality is prior to its images, or that images refer directly and simply to an unadorned real world. Reality and imagery are always contested (Hogan, 1999). Gays and lesbians, after all, have fought for decades to sustain their rights by making gay pride visible, yet the enactment of "defense of marriage" legislation is one unfavorable consequence of this heightened visibility. If disabled lesbians and gays are excluded as such from the advertising in disability glossies, they are nonetheless able to purchase and use wheelchairs without direct restriction. So what are the consequences, if any, of the separation of image from practice?

The marketing of the culture of sport and disability, by which we mean both the production of its cultural images and their transformation into commodities to be consumed, entails a continuous circulation of disability images throughout disability culture. This constant flow of images does not begin or end with the photos in the disability magazines we have studied. By themselves, the photos in our sample are static, only one moment in the process of producing and consuming disability culture. To understand what these photos and their accompanying stereotypes *mean*, we must place them also in the social context in which they are consumed: actively read and interpreted, then aligned with social practices (du Gay *et al.*, 1997). Moreover, the social context of image consumption is not uniquely determined by the photographic repertoire arrayed by our sample, since many consumer contexts of practice can be sustained by the same repertoire of images (Lurie, 1996). For instance, to see a photo of an elderly disabled woman enjoying herself with her granddaughter at the beach may imply one context of reading from the viewpoint of elderly consumers who are too poor to travel; quite another, from the perspective of a young caregiver who finds it boring to imagine sitting idly on the seashore. The social context suggested by an advertising photo of an elderly man on the upper deck of his cabin cruiser powerfully hauling up a big fish is again very different from the social context implied by an elderly man photographed wheeling himself alone down an empty path in the park. Readers are not likely to construe those two images in quite the same way, or fit them comfortably into a single unproblematic context of consumption (Fiske, 1996).

In turn, shopping practices – another key moment in the consumption process – are constitutive elements of the modern postindustrial economy. We use shopping to define ourselves in much the same way that religious sacrifice produces an experience of transcendence in a preindustrial economy (Miller, 1998; Twitchell, 1999). Shopping is a cultural occasion finely attuned to the circumstances of shoppers *vis-à-vis* the consumer goods depicted in advertising. How do shoppers move from consuming the ads in disability glossies to consuming the items themselves? For instance, are caregivers who purchase such items also acquiring the social standing conferred by upscale disability ads such as the ad we described that shows two attractive women chatting idly in front of a shopping mall? Or are the caregivers culturally defining the social class of the disabled persons for whom the items are purchased: mom looks much better in jeans purchased at Eddie Bauer's or Banana Republic than in jeans bought at Walmart or Dress for Less! The images of sport and leisure disability in the glossies are thoroughly targeted to older consumers; we note above that teenagers with disabilities are never depicted in our sample. Does this mean that teenaged shoppers with disabilities cannot experience the same cultural affirmation, the "swoosh," as non-disabled teenagers who buy Nikes?

Equally as basic is the space in which shopping occurs. Nearly all store displays are organized to attract and serve an idealized consumer who fits a model of "ability" (Underhill, 1999). During the national debate over passage of the ADA, disability activists pointed out that a person who uses a wheelchair cannot get to the mall, or, once arrived at the mall, cannot enter and browse the store that sells an advertised item (Shapiro, 1994). How does this interruption of the process of consumption define the cultural competence of persons with disabilities at the level of daily practice? When we think of media effects from the perspective of the social spaces they occupy, those media images are much more difficult to interpret than is suggested by the simple stereotypes they invoke. For example, at one level of abstraction it is obviously important to debate why women's worth should be judged by their appearance; yet at another, if women *must* live in a society that measures them visually, their disappearance from view as real persons and their reconstruction as stereotypes in full public view is doubly or trebly demeaning (Kilbourne, 1999). Women in disability ads nurture children or smile reassuringly at the camera, or both, if they are to be photographed in anything resembling athletic attire. Women who are athletic but who do not fit conventional standards of allure must not be seen at all. The competence of sweat is symbolically a male domain in disability glossies.

The media effects model that we recommend here for further research problematizes not merely the photos of sport and disability that permeate disability glossies, but the way in which those photos influence the *process* by which images and practices circulate in disability culture. We argue that the photos we have analyzed turn image against practice because the culture of disability *images* is far narrower than the range of practical encounters with the disabled. Intimacy, for instance, is always photographically established by disability advertising in the domain of the heterosexual nuclear family, though there are many disabled who are neither married nor heterosexual. We also believe that the process of consumption – considered for better or worse as the foremost rite of celebration now available to us (Twitchell, 1996) – symbolically excludes many from its domain by stereotyping persons with disabilities. In more concrete terms, the development of commodified "difference" – the "ad-sponsored cultures" which are a central signifier of identity and community in modernity

(Branston and Stafford, 1999) – is denied to many, who thus are disenfranchised in a variety of ways that matter. Consequently, there is some urgency in investigating whether this hierarchy of attention has unforeseen but important consequences as it becomes situated in daily practice. If persons of color have little access to sport and leisure facilities, photographing them in a park is a lie that forestalls an attempt to do something about the situation. We have tried to sketch a plea here for examining media effects as a process in itself, rather than merely an end of that process (Morley, 1995).

There is one final remark that arises ineluctably as we step back and look at our sample as a whole. Advertisers have found so many different strategies to make people appear normal. Sometimes these strategies are subtle: the advertisers focus the camera away from the face of the model or else place the models at a physical distance that makes their disability unidentifiable. More often the strategies are not so subtle: the advertisers photograph only people who are conventionally attractive, or avoid photographing people with disabilities who lack the money that makes them desirable consumers. This relentless obsession with normalcy is *precisely* what removes the humanity – diverse, intriguing, unendurable – from disability advertising. Those who are interested in a photographic decentering of their sense of these norms should consult the classic works of Diane Arbus, or more contemporaneously, the disability photography of Rasso Brückert (http://www.bildagentur-querschnitt.de/). The co-authors of this study are both disabled (Gill, 1994). We wonder: would it be so awful if disability ads reflected something closer to the truth of our lives?

References

Aycock, A. and Duncan, M.C. (1996). Situational competence: Another look at leisure, sport, and disability. Research paper given at the annual meeting of the North American Society for the Sociology of Sport (NASSS), Birmingham, AL, November.

Aycock, A. and Duncan, M.C. (1998). Wheelies and walkies: Race and gender in media images of disabled athletes. Research paper given at the annual meeting of the North American Society for the Sociology of Sport (NASSS), Las Vegas, November.

Barnes, C., Mercer, G. and Shakespeare, T. (eds) (1999). *Exploring Disability: A Sociological Introduction*. Cambridge: Polity Press; Malden, MA: Blackwell.

Barthel, D. (1988). *Putting on Appearances: Gender and Advertising*. Philadelphia, PA: Temple University Press.

Belgrave, F.Z. (1998). *Psychosocial Aspects of Chronic Illness and Disability Among African Americans*. Westport, CT: Auburn House.

Booth, T. (1996). Sounds of still voices: Issues in the use of narrative methods with people who have learning difficulties. In L. Barton (ed.), *Disability and Society: Emerging Issues and Insights* (pp. 237–255). New York: Longman.

Branche-Dorsey, C.M., Russell, J.C., Greenspan, A.I. and Chorba, T.L. (1994). Unintentional injuries: The problems and some preventive strategies. In I.L. Livingston (ed.), *Handbook of Black American Health: The Mosaic of Conditions, Issues, Policies, and Prospects* (pp. 190–204). Westport, CT: Greenwood Press.

Branston, G. and Stafford, R. (eds) (1999). *Media Student's Book* (2nd edn). New York: Routledge.

Bryan, W.V. (1996). *In Search of Freedom: How Persons with Disabilities have been Disen-franchised from the Mainstream of American Society*. Springfield, IL: C.C. Thomas.

Castles, E. (1996). *We're People First: The Social and Emotional Lives of Individuals with Mental Retardation*. Westport, CT: Praeger.

Charlton, J.I. (1998). *Nothing About Us Without Us: Disability Oppression and Empower-ment*. Berkeley, CA: University of California Press.

Cole, J.S. and Johnson, M. (1994). Time to grow up. In B. Shaw (ed.), *The Ragged Edge: The Disability Experience from the Pages of the First Fifteen Years of the Disability Rag* (pp. 131–136). Louisville, KY: Advocado Press.

Corrigan, P. (1997). *The Sociology of Consumption: An Introduction*. Thousand Oaks, CA: Sage.

Darke, P. (1998). Understanding cinematic representations of disability. In T. Shakespeare (ed.), *The Disability Reader: Social Science Perspectives* (pp. 181–197). New York: Cassell.

Davis, L.J. (1995). *Enforcing Normalcy: Disability, Deafness, and the Body*. New York: Verso.

Davis, L.J. (ed.) (1997). *The Disability Studies Reader*. New York: Routledge.

du Gay, P., Hall, S., Janes, L., MacKay, H. and Negus, K. (1997). *Doing Cultural Studies: The Story of the Sony Walkman*. New York: Sage.

Duncan, M.C. (1993). Beyond analyses of sport media texts: An argument for formal analyses of institutional structures. *Sociology of Sport Journal, 10,* 353–372.

Duncan, M.C. (1998). The body in question: Women, girls, and the sport media. Borghild-Strand Distinguished Lecture, Tucker Center for Research on Girls and Women in Sport, University of Minnesota.

Duncan, M.C. and Aycock, A. (1997). Border crossings on the web: Rhetorics of sport and disability. Research paper given at the annual meeting of the North American Society for the Sociology of Sport (NASSS), Toronto, November.

Duncan, M.C. and Messner, M. (1998). *The Media Image of Sport and Gender*. In L.A. Wenner (ed.), *MediaSport* (pp. 170–185). New York: Routledge.

Fiske, J. (1996). *Media Matters: Race and Gender in US Politics*. Minneapolis: University of Minnesota Press.

Gill, C.J. (1994). Questioning continuum. In B. Shaw (ed.), *The Ragged Edge: The Dis-ability Experience from the Pages of the First Fifteen Years of the Disability Rag* (pp. 42–49). Louisville, KY: Advocado Press.

Goffman, E. (1976). *Gender Advertisements*. New York: Harper and Row.

Goldman, R. (1992). *Reading Ads Socially*. New York: Routledge.

Goldman, R. and Papson, S. (1996). *Sign Wars: The Cluttered Landscape of Advertising*. New York: Guilford Press.

Hahn, H. (1997). Advertising the acceptably employable image: Disability and capital-ism. In L.J. Davis (ed.). *The Disability Studies Reader* (pp. 172–186). New York: Rout-ledge.

Hevey, D. (1992). *The Creatures Time Forgot: Photography and Disability Imagery*. New York: Routledge.

Hogan, A. (1999). Carving out a place to act: acquired impairment and contested iden-tity. In M. Corker and S. French (eds), *Disability Discourse* (pp. 79–91). Philadelphia, PA: Open University Press.

Jhally, S. (1987). *The Codes of Advertising: Fetishism and the Political Economy of Meaning in the Consumer Society*. New York: St. Martin's Press.

Johnson, L. and Roediger, D. (1997). "Hertz, don't it?" Becoming colorless and staying black in the crossover of O.J. Simpson. In T. Morrison and C.B. Lacour (eds). *Birth of* a Nation 'hood: Gaze, Script, and Spectacle in the O.J. Simpson Case* (pp. 197–239). New York: Pantheon Books.

Johnson, M. (1994). A test of will: Jerry Lewis, Jerry's orphans, and the telethon. In B. Shaw (ed.), *The Ragged Edge: The Disability Experience from the Pages of the First Fifteen Years of the Disability Rag* (pp. 120–130). Louisville, KY: Advocado Press.

Kern-Foxworth, M. (1994). *Aunt Jemima, Uncle Ben, and Rastus: Blacks in Advertising, Yesterday, Today, and Tomorrow.* Westport, CT: Greenwood Press.

Kilbourne, J. (1999). *Deadly Persuasion: Why Women and Girls must Fight the Addictive Power of Advertising.* New York: Free Press.

Klobas, L. (1988). *Disability Drama in Television and Film.* Jefferson, NC: McFarland.

Lears, T.J. (1994). *Fables of Abundance: A Cultural History of Advertising in America.* New York: Basic Books.

Lewis, J.F. and Catterson, P. (1994). Selling the good old days: Images of rural utopia in contemporary American advertising. In L. Manca and A. Manca (eds), *Gender and Utopia in Advertising: A Critical Reader* (pp. 145–153). Lisle, IL: Procopian Press; Syracuse, NY: Syracuse University Press.

Linton, S. (1998). *Claiming Disability: Knowledge and Identity.* New York: SUNY Press.

Livingston, I.L. (ed.) (1994). *Handbook of Black American Health: The Mosaic of Conditions, Issues, Policies, and Prospects.* Westport, CT: Greenwood Press.

Longmore, P.K. (1997). Conspicuous contribution and American cultural dilemmas: Telethon rituals of cleansing and renewal. In D.T. Mitchell and S.L. Snyder (eds), *The Body and Physical Difference: Discourses of Disability* (pp. 134–158). Ann Arbor, MI: University of Michigan Press.

Lury, C. (1996). *Consumer Culture.* New Brunswick, NJ: Rutgers University Press.

McAllister, M. (1996). *The Commercialization of American Culture: New Advertising, Control, and Democracy.* Thousand Oaks, CA: Sage.

McCracken, E. (1993). *Decoding Women's Magazines: From Mademoiselle to Ms.* New York: St. Martin's Press.

McNeil, J., Franklin, P. and Mars, L. (1991). Work status, earnings, and rehabilitation of persons with disabilities. In S. Thompson-Hoffman and I. Storck (eds), *Disability in the United States: A Portrait from National Data* (pp. 133–160). New York: Springer Publishing.

Miller, D. (1998). *A theory of Shopping.* Ithaca, NY: Cornell University Press.

Moore, M., Beazley, S. and Maelzer, J. (1998). *Researching Disability Issues.* Philadelphia, PA: Open University Press.

Morgan, L. and Kunkel, S. (1998). *Aging: The Social Context.* Thousand Oaks, CA: Pine Forge Press.

Morley, D. (1995). Theories of consumption in media studies. In D. Miller (ed.), *Acknowledging Consumption: A Review of New Studies* (pp. 296–328). New York: Routledge.

Nelson, J. (1996). The invisible cultural group: Images of disability. In P.M. Lester (ed.), *Images that Injure: Pictorial Stereotypes in the Media* (pp. 119–125). Westport, CT: Praeger.

Norden, M.F. (1994). *The Cinema of Isolation: A History of Physical Disability in the Movies.* New Brunswick, NJ: Rutgers University Press.

O'Barr, W.M. (1994). *Culture and the Ad: Exploring Otherness in the World of Advertising.* Boulder, CO: Westview Press.

Ohmann, R. (1996). *Selling Culture: Magazines, Markets, and Class at the Turn of the Century.* New York: Verso.

Pieterse, J. (1992). *White on Black: Images of Africa and Blacks in Western Popular Culture.* New Haven, CT: Yale University Press.

Pinkus, K. (1995). *Bodily Regimes: Italian Advertising under Fascism.* Minneapolis: University of Minnesota Press.

Pointon, A., Davies, C. and Masefield, P. (eds) (1997). *Framed: Interrogating Disability in the Media.* London: British Film Institute.

Rabinbach, A. (1990). *The Human Motor: Energy, Fatigue, and the Origins of Modernity.* New York: Basic Books.

Russell, M. (1998). *Beyond Ramps: Disability at the End of the Social Contract: A Warning from an Uppity Crip.* Monroe, ME: Common Courage Press.

Schell, L.A. and Duncan, M.D. (1999). A content analysis of CBS's coverage of the 1996 paralympic games. *Adapted Physical Activity Quarterly, 16,* 27–47.

Schuchman, J. (1988). *Hollywood Speaks: Deafness and the Film Entertainment Industry.* Urbana, IL: University of Illinois Press.

Semmes, C.E. (1996). *Racism, Health, and Post-industrialism: A Theory of African-American Health.* Westport, CT: Praeger.

Shakespeare, T. (ed.) (1998). *The Disability Reader: Social Science Perspectives.* New York: Cassell.

Shakespeare, T., Gillespie-Sells, K. and Davies, D. (1996). *The Sexual Politics of Disability: Untold Desires.* New York: Cassell.

Shapiro, J.P. (1994). *No Pity: People with Disabilities Forging a New Civil Rights Movement.* New York: Times Books.

Shaw, B. (ed.) (1994). *The Ragged Edge: The Disability Experience from the Pages of the First Fifteen Years of the Disability Rag.* Louisville, KY: Advocado Press.

Sivulka, J. (1998). *Soap, Sex, and Cigarettes: A Cultural History of American Advertising.* Belmont, CA: Wadsworth.

Stewart, D. (1991). *Deaf Sport: The Impact of Sports Within the Deaf Community.* Washington, DC: Gallaudet University Press.

Storck, I. and Thompson-Hoffman, S. (1991). Demographic characteristics of the disabled population. In S. Thompson-Hoffman and I. Storck (eds), *Disability in the United States: a Portrait From National Data* (pp. 15–33). New York: Springer Publishing.

Thomson, R.G. (1997). *Extraordinary Bodies: Figuring Physical Disability in American Culture and Literature.* New York: Columbia University Press.

Turow, J. (1997). *Breaking Up America: Advertisers and the New Media World.* Chicago, IL: University of Chicago Press.

Twitchell, J. (1996). *Adcult USA: The Triumph of Advertising in American Culture.* New York: Columbia University Press.

Twitchell, P. (1999). *Lead Us Into Temptation: The Triumph of American Materialism.* New York: Columbia University Press.

Underhill, P. (1999). *Why We Buy: The Science of Shopping.* New York: Simon & Schuster.

Urry, J. (1995). *Consuming Places.* New York: Routledge.

Wade, C.M. (1994). It ain't exactly sexy. In B. Shaw (ed.), *The Ragged Edge: The Disability Experience from the Pages of the First Fifteen Years of the Disability Rag* (pp. 88–90). Louisville, KY: Advocado Press.

Waxman, B.F. (1994). It's time to politicize our sexual oppression. In B. Shaw (ed.), *The Ragged Edge: The Disability Experience from the Pages of the First Fifteen Years of the Disability Rag* (pp. 82–87). Louisville, KY: Advocado Press.

Wendell, S. (1996). *The Rejected Body: Feminist Philosophical Reflections on Disability*. New York: Routledge.

Whyte, S.R. and Ingstad, B. (1995). Disability and culture: An overview. In B. Ingstad and S.R. Whyte (eds), *Disability and Culture* (pp. 3–37). Berkeley: University of California Press.

8 Close encounters of another kind

Nationalism, media representations and advertising in New Zealand rugby[1]

Nick Perry

Introduction

There is a Mexican folk saying that exhorts us to 'Pity poor Mexico, so far from God and so close to the United States'. New Zealand lies on the other side of the Pacific, far away from both Mexico and the USA; hence references to it as 'God's Own Country' might be said to exhibit an endearingly antipodal symmetry. Austin Mitchell's (1972) satirical but affectionate *The Half Gallon, Quarter Acre Pavlova Paradise* signalled that this claim to have been divinely blessed was at one time both semi-official and thoroughly popular; part of the stock-in-trade of the nation's politicians as well as an article of faith for some of its more complacent citizens. Small size, low population density and great scenic beauty all played a part in providing the legitimating grounds for such an assertion. It was, however, their homeland's remoteness from the assorted Babylons to the North that was arguably most crucial to New Zealanders' disposition to accredit their country with Eden-like properties. The associated assumption was of a nation that was largely exempt from the troubles of both the Old World and the New; an assumption that, through the contrasting binaries of cultural nationalism, was formalised as the doctrine of New Zealand exceptionalism.

Since the 1950s, however, the country's living standards have slid from third highest on the planet to the mid-twenties and below, and an egalitarian income distribution has given way to accelerating inequalities and social divisions. As a result, the phrase 'God's Own Country' (and even its ironic offspring, Godzone) – and with it the presumption of being uniquely blessed – has now all but disappeared from popular usage. The scenic beauty remains, but as the rest of the world has moved closer, it would appear that God – not unlike many of the country's intelligent young – has chosen to go offshore. Or to put this point in terms that are both more secular and less sardonic, the pattern of national myth making has been, and is being, transformed by the local implications of the current phase of globalisation. Popular nationalism, official ideologies and their interrelations are all subject to realignment. This chapter interprets the changing patterns within and between New Zealand rugby, the broadcasting media and advertising as a cultural tracer of that process.

Distance, then and now

In McKenzie Wark's (1994) account of the virtual geographies that are made possible by the dense infrastructure of global communications media, he suggests that we now have aerials rather than roots and terminals rather than origins. As a consequence neither 'here' nor 'there' are any longer what they were. The plausibility of Wark's aphorisms should, however, be moderated by Manuel Castells' (1989) axiom that although power now moves in flows, people continue to live in places. In this sense, the notions of distance and remoteness are a crucial point of intersection between the now colliding, now colluding forces of globalisation and the construction of local identities. Yet in New Zealand some conception of 'distance' has been seen as consequential ever since the country was first constituted as a settler capitalist, First World colony; as simultaneously a part of 'the West' yet geographically removed from it. From such a location there therefore seems to be something peculiarly Euro- or America-centric about the focus on globalisation as if it were a somehow novel or recent phenomenon. For bit players in the global script, what appears to be novel is not the notion of power flows, but rather their density, their plurality and the prospect that they are no longer to be interpreted as axiomatically moving in, or from, one direction.

Thus in New Zealand the West is both close to hand and far away – both immediately familiar and spatially remote, both locally grounded and critically distant. Hence the term *distance* has not only been invested with a generic geographical meaning but also with a historically and culturally specific one. These meanings have become so intertwined as to be all but inseparable. Distance at once signals a discursively located, materially significant, purportedly universal, global fact and the construction of a socially consequential, purportedly idiosyncratic, local myth. Such a combination has effectively been constituted as a cultural given, a taken for granted aspect of the discourse of New Zealand nationalism. It thereby occupied a position that is somewhat analogous to that played by 'the frontier' in American historiography, albeit one that foregrounds deeply ambivalent attitudes to linkage rather than a desire for, and promise of, discontinuity. The associated concerns were typified by Keith Sinclair's editing of *Distance Looks Our Way* (1961) and authorship of *A Destiny Apart* (1986), or by Malcolm McKinnon's (1988) *The American Connection* (across the Tasman, the Australian exemplar of this tendency was Geoffrey Blainey's (1968) *The Tyranny of Distance*).

If New Zealand is viewed from a metropolitan standpoint, then a glance at any reliable world map is sufficient to confirm the 'fact' of distance. New Zealand is not just the most far flung of Britain's former colonies, it is also (according to the US Postal Service) further away from the USA than any country on earth. To be sure, the stability of those verities that remoteness had once seemed to secure is now routinely subverted. The dense and expanding overlay of global networks and processes has led to realignments in the relations of time and space, such that the term *distance* has been invested with new sets of meanings. But whether interpreted as problem or as opportunity, there is nothing new in the notion of powerful external forces acting to shape how New Zealand as a nation is constituted (and has come to constitute itself). As a British colony, New Zealand's physical remoteness from global centres had not, of course, precluded its subordination to their interests. Almost from the beginning of European settlement, the development of the country's small and vulnerable economy was driven by the imperatives of a leading colonial power on the other side of the globe. In geographical terms New Zealand may have been a farm in the South Pacific, but its structural location was tantamount to somewhere in the Irish Sea. For with the advent of refrigerated cargo, New Zealand was charged with the task of providing a flow of cheap food to, and through, British ports. Capitalist expansion and colonisation thus laid the basis for a political economy that was (and still is) heavily dependent upon export receipts from primary production. The family farm was to become the engine of this economy, but the establishment of the relevant infrastructure was orchestrated by a centralised and continually interventionist state.

Beginning in the 1930s, the (still) fledgling nation's policy makers sought to counteract the narrowness and vulnerability of this economic foundation through the elaboration of a state-sponsored strategy of import substituting industrialism. With the working out of the post-war global settlement and attendant realignments in the international division of labour, however, New Zealand has perforce been repositioned within a very different web of dependencies. Against a background of gradual expansion in the level of overseas ownership of economic resources, the once dominant, but presumptively secure, single (British) destination for exports has been displaced by a less stable, but more pluralistic, range of possible markets. Moreover, by the beginning of the 1980s the import substitution strategy had run its course, the domestic cost structure associated with small-scale, protected local producers having eroded the competitiveness of the exposed, but functionally indispensable, export sector. Import substitution thus gave way to a programme of restructuring in which the economy was rapidly opened up to the full forces of globalisation. At the same time what had always been a precarious, British influenced and literary derived high culture has progressively yielded to a more explicitly populist, and more obviously mass-media-based, American cultural hegemony.

Nation, here and there

This is an exceedingly condensed sketch of the context within which notions of nation building and national identity acquire their significance. In the New Zealand context that significance is both empirical and conceptual. This is precisely due to the extent and import of those dilemmas and paradoxes that conceptions of national identity at once help to construct but are nevertheless obliged to address. Consider, for instance, the contradictions that gather around, and are gathered together by, the notion of 'dominion subjects'. Meaghan Morris (1992) has pithily described those subjects as 'dubiously post-

colonial, prematurely postmodern, constitutively multicultural but still predominantly white ... who oscillate historically between identities as coloniser and
colonised' (p. 471). The notion of the New Zealand nation is that invented
place where the associated dilemmas are (dis)played (out). As such it is constitutive not only for its subjects but also for criticism – generative of ambivalence,
a location that is at once enabling and limiting. In this sense, the willingness of
Melbourne-based New Zealander Simon During (1990) to promote and identify
with the axiom that Australian intellectuals '"ought to be nationalistic" would
seem to be no less pertinent for their counterparts in his birthplace' (p. 139).

This is in contrast to the academic suspicion that notions of a national imaginary tend to invite in Britain, being viewed for the most part as axiomatically
conservative formulations that serve to direct attention away from the divisions
of class, gender and ethnicity.[2] In the corresponding American literature, the
tendency is for 'nation' to be rendered more visible, even to be explicitly
invoked. It is invested with especial strength by the willingness to rely upon,
even to embrace, that diversity associated with the theme of a nation of immi-
grants. Yet here too, in what Seymour Lipset (1963) identified as the first new
nation, a distinctive inflection of the traditional combination of mythic sanction and historical amnesia is at work, most obviously with respect to the usurp-
ing of America's own first peoples. A further unspoken proviso is that the USA
offers a normative template, whose correlate is either the implicit assumption
that all other nations aspire to be more like (the) USA, or a bemused puzzle-
ment whenever they do not.[3]

Yet no matter whether a concept of the nation is made invisible or made
explicit, repudiated or embraced, what deserves to be contested is such a univer-
salising of its attributes and the presumption that their generic social import is
already known. For as befits the location that provided the setting and inspiration for Samuel Butler's *Erewhon*, New Zealand has proved to be neither here
nor there (as these terms are likely to understood in metropolitan centres). Yet
in New Zealand (as in Australia), the meanings of nation are nevertheless of
immediate social and political consequence – and they are not yet fixed,
prompting the country's most accomplished cultural critic to entitle his col-
lected essays *How To Be Nowhere* (Wedde, 1995). What deserves the attention
of both metropolitans and marginals, however, is not (or at least, not just)
whatever might be understood as distinctive about the content of New Zealand
national meanings, but (also) the forms through which they find expression. It
is in this respect that sport, the media, advertising and the relations within and
between them assume an especial significance. Such an emphasis on forms is a
way of resisting any reduction of the unstable and avowedly idiosyncratic features of the New Zealand case to the status of the anecdotal, explicable as a
more or less exotic, quirky anomaly, a deviant footnote to an otherwise secure
and secured general model.

A questioning of the presumption of such general models has proved to be an
incidental, but general (*sic*), effect of the intensification of transnational flows.
This chapter is knowingly complicit with this development. It is a development

that has not only revealed and enhanced an awareness of the global complexity of the local. It also points to the sometime parochialism of those cosmopolitans whose conceit was to extrapolate a purportedly totalising approach from the(ir) particular.[4]

Benedict Anderson (1991) is among those who have proved to be receptive to national differences. In the revised edition of *Imagined Communities*, his influential account of the development of nationalism, he suggests that the dynastic nineteenth-century states of Europe did not – and could not – provide the direct model for the official nationalism of the colonised new states of Asia and Africa. For as colonial states they were typically and overtly *anti*-nationalist in policy and ideology. Nevertheless, the grammar of those institutions through which such states orchestrated and imagined their domains, such as the census, the map and the museum, served to construct – respectively – subjects, territory and history as national. I do not doubt that such a state-sponsored trio of forms of representation and control was, and is, relevant to the New Zealand case (Dibley, 1997). But my interest is in a nationalism that is grounded in popular enthusiasm, as much as in nationalism that derives from state power. Hence my intention in selecting sport, broadcasting and advertising as a nation-building trio is precisely to bring into play the tension between – respectively – the institutions of civil society, the state and the economy from which these three – respectively – derive their origins. For such a purpose a consciously ambivalent relation to nationalism, of the kind that During and Turner promote, would seem to more nearly be a methodological prerequisite than it is an incidental effect.

Sport, civil society and popular nationalism

Sport *really* matters in New Zealand. Whether measured in terms of participation or spectatorship, it attracts high levels of involvement among all sections of the populace. Some degree of interest in sport is therefore widely assumed to be a cultural given, so that when strangers meet socially, there is typically the expectation that a shared awareness of local sporting performances will provide a basis for conversation. Sport and talk about sport is thus an important social lubricant, an integral feature of social life as it is locally understood. This taken for granted role of sport in the weaving together of the very fabric of everyday life and the shaping of the pattern of social relations is one of the reasons that it has also come to matter for government and business. Hence in New Zealand as elsewhere, sport and the range of political and economic interests that have coalesced around it can now only be separated analytically. Yet what merits emphasis is that when it comes to identifying the origins of such enthusiastic support for sport, it is civil society that enjoys historical and conceptual priority. In a reversal of the categorisation made famous by Steven Speilberg, close encounters of this first kind were constituted through face-to-face social interaction and active participation. Let me briefly develop just how this has been consequential for the emergence of nationalist sentiment and the form that it takes.

In contemporary New Zealand it is the women's sport of netball that attracts the highest number of regular participants. There are presently an estimated 120,000 players, most of whom are schoolgirls (thereby constituting a majority of the relevant age cohort). Hence on Saturday mornings throughout the winter, rain or shine, a continuous stream of teams occupy the country's netball courts. The game is represented at the national level by an accomplished side known as the Silver Ferns. The statistical dominance of netball players does not, however, transcribe into a position of centrality within the national imaginary. The latter was, and in large measure still is, a man's project. It is a project within which the predominantly male game of rugby, and especially the All Blacks as the national side, has come to occupy a privileged position. Rugby may thus be interpreted as a tracer of those forces acting upon, and through, the society and its culture, and those processes of inclusion and exclusion by which national self-definition has been constructed.

Rugby did not arrive in New Zealand until 1870, but within twenty-five years there were more than 50,000 players and some 300 teams affiliated to the Rugby Union (Phillips, 1987, p. 88), at a time when the entire male workforce was perhaps 250,000 strong. As in its country of origin, it was initially an upper- and upper-middle-class sport with an urban base, but it was to spread rapidly from the cities and towns to the rural areas and across occupational differences and social class divisions. Maori[5] were also quick to take up the game. It is just such developments that prompted Geoff Fougere (1981; 1989) to identify rugby in New Zealand as acting as an exemplary mechanism of social integration. First of all, the game induced individual participation, and the accompanying processes of identification, through a relatively egalitarian team structure. Local teams competed with each other, but at the same time they also constituted a source from which players were selected to play for the provincial sides. The resulting unification at the provincial level provided the basis for inter-provincial competition. This latter, in its turn, constituted the recruitment pool for the national team that would eventually become known as the All Blacks. Rugby thus acted so as to combine social and textual representation. In this way, distinctions between social classes, between town and country, between regions, between colonisers and colonised, were both dramatised and bridged.

The provinces were formally abolished as administrative units of the state in 1876, but nevertheless continued to serve as the basis for sporting competition in rugby, netball and cricket. As a result, their names are familiar to all but the most reclusive or the most recent of the country's citizens. It is thanks largely to sport that the provinces have been central to the construction, pertinence and persistence of regional identity and the intensity with which it is asserted. But more than that, the establishment of a pattern of inter-provincial competition was integral to the very process of nation building. In Fougere's (1981) concise formulation, 'Before we had anything resembling a national market, or even a very effective national state, rugby tied together the collection of localities and provinces into a national body' (p. 12). This process was powerfully reinforced – and the sport itself newly mediated through telegraphy and press reports –

by the success of the national side that toured Britain in 1905. For in winning all but one match they did not just beat the colonial power on its home grounds and at its own game. They did so through a sport that was understood by the local male population to be socially *inclusive*, as distinct from those socially *exclusive* and elite associations that distinguished English and Scottish (but not Welsh) rugby.

The introduction of rugby thus not only provided a platform for the construction of a particular nation; it also linked this process to a particular construction of masculinity. Rugby represented a kind of dialogue between the rough and the respectable, between a frontier ethic and a civilising mission. Hence Jock Phillips (1987, pp. 81–130) interprets the game as having acted to manage, although not to resolve, the tension between these tendencies. Thus the establishment of the New Zealand Rugby Football Union, and with it the consolidation and elaboration of a system of rule(s), exemplifies the second term in these couplets. This official system nevertheless represented an accommodation to the persistence of a more or less unofficial, more or less imperfectly suppressed, frontier-style code of drinking, swearing and womanising. Conceptions of the national imaginary and of masculine identity were thereby made mutually constitutive.

Contra Benedict Anderson, it was therefore not so much literacy as sport that had ushered in those allegiances that contributed to the development of popular nationalism (Rowe and Schelling, 1991). The press and the telegraph had, to be sure, been implicated in its subsequent mediation, elaboration and consolidation, but they were not themselves foundational. As for books and novels *vis-à-vis* the popular at this time, there is not much to be said as there was little to be read (McCormick, 1959). A literary-based and marginal high culture was subsequently to construct both itself and the notion of 'the New Zealand tradition' around a mythology of Man Alone – as in John Mulgan's novel of that name. Sam Neill's documentary *Cinema of Unease* may be read as an attempt to update and recycle this thesis – within another medium and for an international audience. Yet both the myth and the book on which it was based had been pre-dated by a popular cultural practice, whose taken for granted premise was the principle of Men Together. It is therefore not surprising that what had shaped the anxious subtext of this Man Alone mythology was an uneasy suspicion that Real Men Don't Read Books – let alone write them (Jensen, 1996). However, in the very same year (1937) as Mulgan had begun to work on his Man Alone manuscript (Day, 1977), a maverick sports commentator called Winston McCarthy had begun to induce men in general to gather together around the radio (Day, 1994).

'Listen . . . listen. . .': McCarthy's mantra and close encounters of the second kind

With the advent of radio broadcasting in the 1920s and its extremely rapid growth during the 1930s, the airwaves provided the terrain on which high and popular nationalisms would engage not only with one another, but also with a succession of governments that were determined to closely regulate them both. At first, broadcasting had been based upon a regional and private enterprise format. However, its success with audiences soon prompted government to not only establish commercial and non-commercial variants – and the associated structural tension between them – but to subordinate them both to a system of national coordination and control. The structural form through which television would subsequently be introduced into New Zealand is explicable only by reference to the pattern by which radio had developed.

Rugby broadcasts were an early initiative on radio, with a 1927 inter-provincial game representing the very first occasion on which the fledgling medium had organised transmission on a nationwide basis (Day, 1994). The various provincial rugby unions and the national body were initially ambivalent about broadcasting, being somewhat fearful of the effect on gate receipts – concerns which were to establish the basis for subsequent payment to sporting bodies (Day, 1994). Not unexpectedly, transmissions of rugby and other sports were popular with audiences from the outset. Under a centralised broadcasting regime – and what was to become its attendant (but altogether much less independent) local permutation on a BBC-style Reithian broadcasting project – sport on radio was, however, ad hoc and slow to acquire institutional support. In such a context the medium's endemic and enduring subtext would prove to be the contested and shifting relations between high and popular nationalisms as they were refracted through realignments within the framing political system.

Thus in 1935, the incoming first Labour government saw in a national radio system a counterweight to a regional and conservative press, and Colin Scrimgeour, a street-wise, left populist Methodist minister turned broadcaster, was charged with running and developing the entire commercial network. In a characteristic New Zealand reversal, it was therefore precisely the commercial stations that a left-of-centre government was concerned to champion. British ex-patriot James Shelley, an education professor with Reithian but, in context, broadly progressive sensibilities, was recruited to be head of the New Zealand Broadcasting Service. He was given responsibility for integrating the commercial and non-commercial stations and for fostering national loyalties. Shelley (unlike the BBC's Reith) proved reluctant to contest direct governmental control and use of radio for its own ends (Carter, 1993), whereas Scrimgeour's rise – and indeed his fall – was actually based upon it (Day, 1994). It is also possible to interpret the subsequent Scrimgeour/Shelley relation and its policy consequences as a permutation on the high/popular contrast; as a radio version of rugby's earlier dialogue between the rough and the respectable, albeit at an altogether more 'developed' stage within the civilising process. If Shelley had envisaged radio as pedagogy in a new key, then for Scrimgeour, it was politics by other means. For both men, however, it was nevertheless recognisably politics as usual, played out on the terrain of the state and with civil society understood as not so much the source, but more as the prize, for its successful praxis.

It is within such a state-centred and increasingly populist-inflected milieu that the voice of Winston McCarthy came to assume significance. Whereas Scrimgeour had shaped New Zealand broadcasting's representation of politics, the contribution of sports commentator McCarthy was to the politics of representation. Put another way, although McCarthy may not have aspired to speak *for* the (male) working class, he knowingly spoke *from* it. In his autobiography, McCarthy (1973) indicates that the traditions on which his broadcasts drew were the music-hall, workplace humour and the institution of mateship. Hence 'Listen...' became a kind of catch phrase, with which he was identified as a result of his commentary on a penalty kick during a rugby international in 1945. This was the first occasion on which a sporting fixture was broadcast directly from England to New Zealand. The penalty kick in question seemed unlikely to succeed. McCarthy's (1973, p. 11) own transcript reads:

> Then I added, 'There will be a terrific roar from this vast crowd if it goes over. I'll let you judge for yourselves how he goes. Here he is moving onto the ball. He has kicked it and, LISTEN.... As the ball soared goalwards the roar from the crowd swelled and swelled, and as it crossed the bar I came in again with my piercing voice cutting over the top of the crowd – "It's a goal!"'

The effect was to evoke a response that was at once congruent with the traditions of popular culture and drew upon the dramatic and imaginative possibilities of the new medium. The (imagined) action on the field of play, the (hush-to-roar) sound of the crowd, the commentator's own vernacular-informed implication in the occasion and the listeners at home were thus encouraged to assemble together, to articulate (into) a community of response. It thereby simulated, yet nevertheless functioned in accordance with, what Basil Bernstein (1973) has called the 'sympathetic circularity' of the restricted code. That is, the language acts primarily as a means of constituting or reinforcing a like-minded social collectivity, rather than as a means of constructing or displaying differentiated individualised subjectivities. One measure of McCarthy's iconic import is that his voice and most famous phrase reappear in 1990s television commercials for both Ford and Steinlager. 'Listen...' became McCarthy's call sign and calling card, the signifier of a cultural code that was constructed somewhere between the plain, matter-of-fact intimacy of Roosevelt's fireside radio talks (an initiative emulated by New Zealand Labour prime minister Michael Savage) and the call-and-response of the gospel tradition (and Colin Scrimgeour's recognition of radio's rhetorical possibilities). The dynamics of the rugby/nation nexus continued to be grounded in, and draw their energy from, the direct social relations and representations of civil society, but were now mediated through the (increasingly obligatory) passage points of a state-controlled broadcasting system.

With the state in play, the state of play was thus transformed; new interests and new players had become involved. The transformation was slow at first, because the broadcasting of sport, although popular, was initially regarded as incidental both to the interests of governments and to the cultural mission of those in charge of the radio medium. No less decisive was that rugby was now being 'played' not just on fields of grass (and mud), but in multiple new locations in living rooms across the country. The changing structure of interests and the novel technology of representation thus acted together. Radio brought rugby into a domestic setting, where it took up a place in among other kinds of programmes with other agendas and other sorts of listeners. Thus McCarthy's mantra had its female counterpart in 'Aunt Daisy' Basham's 'Good Morning, Good Morning, Good Morning'. Daisy Basham rose to national pre-eminence as a star saleswoman, advertiser and radio announcer on the commercial network, where she introduced an affirmative, personality-based form of consumer-oriented broadcasting to a daytime female audience. It was not just that the accommodations between the high and the popular began to assume somewhat different forms. With the double movement of men's sport into the home and of women's domestic activities into a forum on the airwaves, the traditional contrast between public and private began to blur, as did the distinction between the audience as citizens and as consumers. Women's relation to rugby (understood both as a sporting activity and as a nation-building forum) had been defined and mediated by and through their relation to men. What radio programmes like Aunt Daisy's offered them as a subject matter was their own socially isolated domestic activity, but what radio as a medium provided was the sense of a shared social condition. No matter whether this is understood as a preamble to, or a substitute for, social action, as a reinforcement of consumerism or as an embryonic politics, what radio therefore represented for women was both a different channel and a channel for difference.

Rugby had been built from the ground up, on a platform of popular participation, gathering men together in a live drama of their own. Radio was understood as an aspect of infrastructure and as an instrument of government, perceived as a top-down technology for facilitating centralised state policies. New Zealand rugby and New Zealand radio thus derived from different foundations and were based upon contrasting logics of socio-political representation. Each had its own kind of imperative. If both of these tendencies were to be accommodated, then the dilemma this posed was that of how to unify the *textual* representation of the game via such a medium. Sport in general and rugby in particular may have only been part of a range of practices through which civil society constituted itself, but they were also widely recognised as especially consequential and therefore as prospectively the object of state regulation. Through what kind of discourse and on what kind of terrain could such community-derived activities and broadcasting as a state agency engage with one another? What emerged was the combination of a commercial form and a vernacular idiom, a pattern which pre-figured a widening of the field of forces and the range of interests that would come to coalesce around sport. For although it was a pattern that developed within a hierarchically ordered control structure, it was nonetheless congruent with the operation of a market system. The general process by which radio delivered its listeners to the state could also deliver them to the blandishments of market actors. As radio broadcasting developed it thus became the terrain for the elaboration of conceptions of nationalism that derived from the relations of civil society, the policies of the state and organised economic interests – at the same time as it acted to blur the boundaries between them. This in turn constituted the institutional configuration, discursive matrix and cultural setting within which television was introduced into New Zealand.

From 'listen. . .' to see/hear and see here: encounters with television and facing up to commercials

The terms under which television was developed were shaped by the radio broadcasting system from which it grew. National television was first introduced in 1960. From the outset the system through which it was delivered was a hybrid, part state-sponsored, part commercial, yet nevertheless fully owned and regulated by the government. It was unlike either the type of full-fledged public service model that is exemplified by the BBC, or a purely commercial system along the lines of the American networks. With a total population of less than three million it could not have been funded through a licence fee alone. At the same time, nation-wide coverage was regarded as a well-nigh absolute political imperative. Yet in this long, narrow country with a spatially dispersed audience, such coverage would not have been achievable – or, at least, not at that time – by way of a purely commercial system. Thus New Zealand's quirky geo-politics, the available level of technological development, the economics of transmission and the cultural and institutional precedents provided by radio broadcasting all combined to generate a hybridised system whose funding depended upon both advertising revenue and an annual licence fee. Within such a system, it proved difficult for programme makers (especially, but not exclusively, those with nationalist agendas) to assert occupational autonomy or to aspire to organisational control. Initially, it was the engineering problems associated with achieving national coverage that proved to be pre-eminent. That era (and that technology) has now passed, but throughout its forty-year history New Zealand television has been obliged to confront what have proved to be the more intractable problems in and around the issue of local content. The term 'dismal science' might almost have been invented to describe the economics of producing for the local television market versus the purchasing of imported programmes. Because the latter have routinely recovered their costs (and characteristically made their profits) in their own much larger domestic markets (typically Britain, the USA or Australia), locally oriented programmes cannot begin to compete either on price or on production values.

This basic dilemma is endemic to small nations, but it has been exacerbated by the policies of successive New Zealand governments (Farnsworth, 1992). Hence New Zealand television is now a fully commercial system in all but name and restrictions on overseas ownership of television channels have been lifted. Although the two largest free-to-air channels remain state owned, they are charged with making a profit (with the possibility that one or both may well be sold off). The public service component of broadcasting has been rendered progressively more marginal over time; its beleaguered rump now resides in a commissioning agency called New Zealand On Air. It is therefore symptomatic that in a recent ten countries' study of small producers, New Zealand television had the lowest proportion of local content (Norris and Pauling, 1999). Sport looms large within this latter (both in its own right and within the newscasts), together with low-budget clones of overseas game shows and related formats. During prime time, approximately twenty minutes of every hour are devoted either to commercials or to station identification. It is above all the commercials and sports programming which, between them, appear to most clearly and to most routinely contest the constraints under which local production is understood to operate. Global branding can and sometimes does mean that 'global' commercials are shown, and the increased integration of the Australian and New Zealand economies can and does mean that Australian commercials are shown.[6] But the most popular commercials are those that have been expressly conceived and designed to catch the attention of local viewers. Hence the commercials on New Zealand television are not only more likely to incorporate local content than the programmes which interrupt (*sic*) them, but the best of them are also technically and formally accomplished, incorporating higher production values than many of the locally made programmes and offering funding and opportunities to local film makers.[7]

A commercial form of broadcasting with a vernacular idiom had grown inside, but remained subordinate to, the state structure of radio. Yet the associated popular nationalism should not be seen as indicative of state capture. Rather it represented an articulation of specific and sectional interests in both state and civil society – an articulation in that it both effected a link between them and spoke from, and for, the cultural position(s) thus constituted. Thus before television was introduced, a popular version of the national imaginary, to which sport was integral and in which commercialism was incipient, was already in place. What was effected through the development of the medium was the reconstruction and elaboration of that imaginary on new terrain, via a discourse that served to prioritise the hitherto subordinated economy.

The cost structure of local production, combined with the reluctance of governments to provide funding, was such that New Zealand television was driven to at once identify and *confirm* the society's pre-existing centre of cultural gravity (so as to maximise audiences) and yet nevertheless driven to *remake* that centre in a commodified form (so as to secure revenue). Sport exemplified the former; advertising exemplified the latter. The engine of sport was a (by now thoroughly mediated) pattern of popular participation and spectatorship; the engine of advertising was the local large firm system; an institutional imperative for television was how to construct a discourse that might somehow bring the differing priorities of these two constituencies together. Rugby, especially rugby at test match level, televised live and duly bracketed by match preambles and post-mortems, generated the audience. The large firm advertisers that it attracted provided the revenue. In such a small economy the large firm system was not that large. It consisted of that handful of economically significant local companies and subsidiaries of overseas multinationals that had emerged and grown inside the shield provided by the import-substituting industrialism strategy of the New Zealand state (Perry, 1992).

During the two decades following the introduction of television in 1960 there was both a decisive enhancement in the structural power of these large capitals and a gradual, but no less decisive, erosion of rugby's hitherto taken for granted claim to occupy and to exemplify a nation-defining position. Rugby's problems were administrative, political, economic and cultural. Administratively, there were the first signs of a challenge to a tradition of amateur and gerontocratic control by advocates of professional management. This contrast imperfectly mapped on to another – which was between the priorities of assertive, younger players and the policies pursued by the game's officials. Politically, the maintenance of a sporting connection with an apartheid-based, rugby-loving South Africa had lead to increasing pressures at home and abroad (Thompson, 1975). Other New Zealand sports teams and individuals were subject to international sporting boycotts, and a once marginal protest movement within New Zealand had gathered broad-based support. Economically, the persistence of this South African connection began to induce a measure of publicly expressed anxiety among exporters. Within the game, exposés of 'shamateurism', the increasingly transparent fiction that top-level rugby was an entirely amateur code, signalled the buildup of pressures to extend the professionalisation of the sport to include players and coaches as well as administrators. The existence, and attractions of, rugby league reinforced these pressures. This professionalised version of the game was popular in Australia. In New Zealand it had a developing social base among the various Polynesian communities in particular and the working class in general. Culturally, the diffusion of aspects of second-wave feminism, the political and cultural resurgence of Maoridom and the expansion of an urban, purportedly more urbane (and hence explicitly more consumerist) middle class, were all indications of an ever more visible gap between rugby's social base and the characteristics of the society that it claimed to represent.

This latter became all too apparent in 1981. The scale and intensity of the protests that accompanied the 1981 tour by South Africa's national side indicated how deeply and how evenly the country was divided. For week after week the imagery of a society in turmoil appeared in streets and stadiums throughout New Zealand – and on its television screens (Chapple, 1984). Far from symbolising national unity, rugby had come to signify social division.

Its subsequent reconstruction during the 1980s was based on the forging of a more direct alliance between the interests of some of New Zealand's larger corporations and the game's administrators, with television providing the terrain on which this new union would (eventually) be textually consummated. In 1986, the corporations had seen the economic benefits that derived from aligning themselves with New Zealand's challenge for the Australian-held America's

Cup, an international yachting competition wholly dependent upon corporate sponsorship and deeply congruent with corporate interests. Yet it had not only proved possible to orchestrate something resembling the kind of popular enthusiasm that had once been reserved for All Black rugby, but also to extend it beyond the sectional appeal with which the latter sport had come to be identified (Perry, 1994).

Like the yachtsmen, the All Blacks had proved to be an internationally competitive team – but rugby had problems. Given the extent of the realignments in the field of social forces from which it had developed, then if All Black rugby was to be able (once again) to represent the nation, it would have to be made over. Only now 'representing a nation' was to be subordinated to 'building a market', and hence a possible or incidental effect rather than an intrinsic objective. Whether or not the furtherance of the economic goal shared an envisaged common referent with the practice of nation making was a matter of contingency. Inasmuch as the nation that 'imagined community moving through time' (Anderson, 1991) had derived from the policies of the state and the relations of civil society, then the state (axiomatically) and civil society (conventionally) were understood as spatially delimited and territorially defined. Economic activity was not subject to any such formal limitation. Indeed, with the demise of the import substitution strategy and the ascendancy of large capitals, the removal of such constraints was positively valorised in theory and powerfully supported in practice.

Reconstructing rugby so as to render it congruent with such interests depended upon combining the textual possibilities made available by television as a medium with the material extension of commodification as a process. Telecasts of important games had always been, and could no doubt continue to be, relied upon to deliver audiences to advertisers. Nevertheless, up until the 1980s the relation between the representations of televised rugby and the content of those television commercials with which they alternated air time was one of, at best, affinity rather than necessity. Any similarities between them were explicable as a by-product of their appeal to, or targeting of, a common demographic category. But beginning with the buildup to and screening of the first Rugby World Cup competition in 1987, the television commercials for Steinlager as sponsor and the televised contests themselves each moved into more explicitly symbiotic formats, into close encounters of a third kind. The commercials initiated a trend of knowingly eroticising and stylising the bodies of All Black players and of dramatising the action of the game so as to broaden the demographic to which both the game and the product would appeal (Perry, 1994). Incremental changes in the narrative emphases and visual imagery employed in telecasts of games (Star, 1992), the trailers for forthcoming transmissions, the discussion programmes, even the feature stories in women's magazines, all signalled the growth of intertextuality and of representations that were compatible with this emergent commodity aesthetic. The audiences were intrigued, enchanted even. But the (economic) genie was now out of the (state-sponsored) bottle – and about to go global.

The sky's the limit

Up until the early 1990s All Black rugby was screened on free-to-air television in real time. The associated sponsors and advertisers were either New Zealand's own fledgling multinationals or local branches of overseas-based companies that were prepared to play the nationalist card as an indicator of their good corporate citizenship. But with the development of cross-media and planet-wide communications companies such as Rupert Murdoch's News Corporation, All Black rugby's traditional sponsors, such as the aforementioned Steinlager, literally began to look like small beer. No less significant was that the scale of the rewards available to players in the fully professionalised, and hence more clearly commercialised, league code was accelerating dramatically and drawing an increasing number of top players into changing codes. Thus in 1995 the officialdom of New Zealand rugby narrowly averted a crisis when the entire All Black team seemed set to jettison their links with the national administration in order to participate in the development of a lucrative, global rugby circuit that was expressly oriented towards television audiences. Hence by 1996 the game's administrators had been obliged to transform the All Blacks – and the game's upper reaches – into a sport that was as fully professionalised as rugby league (Fitzsimons, 1996). Transmission rights had been sold to Murdoch, who onsold them to a local (but US-owned) pay network called Sky (in which INL, another Murdoch company, subsequently bought an interest).

A Sky commercial on the free-to-air channels served to signify the resulting newly preferred relationship between rugby and its supporters. The establishing shot shows what looks like a stage set containing half a dozen rooms on two levels. Each room contains a small group of people who seem to be settling in (and looking towards the camera) as if about to watch television. Both the rooms and the 'viewers'' clothing are highly stylised and distinctively colour-coded. As the commercial begins to build a sense of occasion and excitement, one or two group members succeed in establishing contact with those on the other side of the partitions which divide them. The camera starts to pull back and we now see that they are surrounded by many more such similar-sized rooms, each of which contains would-be viewers. As the camera pulls yet further back the rooms dissolve into the simulated shape of television sets that seem to move up and down in an excited fashion. Before going to the Sky logo/pack shot the sequence concludes with a simulated long-distance view of a packed sports stadium in which the stands are filled with these selfsame 'excited' television sets.

Technically, this dance of technological artefacts in an imaginary space might thus appear to be a kind of reversed version of the famous docking sequence in Stanley Kubrick's 2001: A Space Odyssey. Culturally, however, it points to a close encounter of quite another kind, one that is fully within the realm of simulation. As such it signals that the merchandising of rugby as a global game and the All Blacks as a global brand overrides and conditions the terms under which a national team may now act in relation to the very national imaginary that they helped to constitute. Further evidence of this trend is exemplified by the new sponsorship deal signed between the All Blacks and global sports company Adidas in 1999. Yet, while the deal provided Adidas with a powerful global brand and provided the All Blacks with some desperately need financial support, there were clear implications with respect to local cultural identity. Consider, for example, the long-term sponsorship deal with local company Canterbury which came to an end. Moreover, signs of resistance emerged as debates surrounding Adidas' use of the haka in one of their television advertisements focused on issues of intellectual property rights and indigenous culture (Jackson and Hokowhitu, 2002).

The All Blacks' role as agent and symbol of national identity formation had initially been grounded in direct relations as mediated by social and linguistic rules (with print occupying a subordinate role). They provided the platform for those subsequent processes of cultural sedimentation, layering and elaboration that derived from the encounters with national radio and television respectively. As such, All Black rugby has followed a trajectory that is an antipodal confounding of the sequence identified in Steven Speilberg's *Close Encounters of the Third Kind*, in which the first encounter is an auditory signal, the second a visual sighting and the third face-to-face (*sic*) social contact. And whereas in the Speilberg movie it was making music together that had provided the basis for communication and social exchange, in the All Black drama the introduction of music as a sound-track for the commercials[8] might better be seen as an indicator of, and substitute for, the progressive closing down of any such reciprocal relation. Put another way, such differences might be said to signify a distinction between communicating with aliens and the alienation of communication.

The All Blacks, together with the top layer of New Zealand provincial teams who compete in the 'Super 12' (a twelve-team, tri-nation competition between South African-, Australian- and New Zealand-based sides) are now globalising. There are some five New Zealand sides involved in the Super 12 and the All Black team is recruited exclusively from their ranks. Taken together these five franchises cover the whole country. They are, however, the product of a market-driven mapping that is based upon a 'virtual' media footprint rather than corresponding to any pre-existing political or administrative boundaries 'on the ground'. The decisive determinant of such mapping is prospective market size rather than historically derived local loyalties. This is a process whose logic extends to, and weakens, the traditional pattern of the All Blacks/national nexus. Is this process to be interpreted as 'de-territorialising' or as 're-territorialising', as indicative of the dark underside to Wark's (1994) notion of virtual geography, or as a movement towards a bright spotlight on a global stage?

What such globalisation seems to mean for a small nation is that – like the past – it is now another country. Moreover, with the shift from the sociopolitical to the virtual-simulated – there is the prospect that it will become someone else's. For where Rupert Murdoch goes has been a pointer to the path that All Black rugby has followed since 1995. And Murdoch, in order to better compete as a global player in his chosen game of media control, had shown himself willing to forgo his initial citizenship and national affiliation.

References

Anderson, B. (1991). *Imagined Communities* (rev. edn). London and New York: Verso.

Bernstein, B. (1973). *Class, Codes and Control, Volume 1*. London: Paladin.

Blainey, G. (1968). *The Tyranny of Distance: How Distance Shaped Australia's History*. Melbourne: Macmillan.

Carter, I. (1993). *Gadfly: The Life and Times of James Shelley*. Auckland: Auckland University Press.

Castells, M. (1989). *The Informational City*. Oxford: Blackwell.

Chapple, G. (1984). *1981: The Tour*. Wellington: Reed.

Day, P. (1977). *John Mulgan*. Wellington: Oxford University Press.

Day, P. (1994). *The Radio Years*. Auckland: Auckland University Press.

Dibley, B. (1997). Museum, nation, narration: The museum of New Zealand – Te Papa Tongarewa. *Culture and Policy*, 8, 97.

During, S. (1990). Literature – nationalism's other? The case for revision. In H. Bhabha (ed.), *Nation and Narration* (pp. 138–153). London and New York: Routledge.

Farnsworth, J. (1992). Mainstream or minority: Ambiguities in state or market arrangements for New Zealand television. In J. Deeks and N. Perry (eds), *Controlling Interests; Business the State and Society in New Zealand* (pp. 191–207). Auckland: Auckland University Press.

Fitzsimons, P. (1996). *The Rugby War*. Sydney: HarperCollins.

Fougere, G. (1981). Shattered mirror. *Comment*, November, pp. 12–14.

Fougere, G. (1989). Sport, culture and identity: The case of rugby football. In D. Novitz and W.E. Willmott (eds), *Culture and Identity in New Zealand* (pp. 110–122). Wellington: Government Print.

Grossberg, L., Nelson, C. and Triechler, P.A. (eds) (1992). *Cultural Studies*. New York: Routledge.

Hechter, M. (1975). *Internal Colonialism: The Celtic Fringe in British National Development, 1536–1966*. London: Routledge.

Jackson, S.J. and Hokowhitu, B. (2002). Sport, tribes and technology: The New Zealand All Blacks *Haka* and the politics of identity. *Journal of Sport and Social Issues*, 26 (1), 125–139.

Jackson, S.J., Batty, R. and Scherer, J. (2001).Transnational sport marketing at the global/local nexus: The adidasification of the New Zealand All Blacks. *International Journal of Sports Marketing and Sponsorship*, 3 (2), 185–201.

Jameson, F. (1995). Cultural studies. In J. Munns and G. Rajan (eds), *A Cultural Studies Reader* (pp. 614–645). London and New York: Longman.

Jensen, K. (1996). *Whole Men: The Masculine Tradition in New Zealand Literature*. Auckland: Auckland University Press.

Lipset, S. (1963). *The First New Nation: The United States in Historical and Comparative Perspective*. New York: Basic Books.

McCarthy, W. (1973). *Listen. . .! It's a Goal*. London: Pelham Books.

McCormick, E H. (1959). *New Zealand Literature: A Survey*. London: Oxford University Press.

McKinnon, M. (ed.) (1988). *The American Connection*. Wellington: Allen & Unwin.

Mitchell, A. (1972). *The Half Gallon, Quarter Acre Pavlova Paradise*. Christchurch: Whitcombe and Tombs.

Morris, M. (1992). Afterthoughts on 'Australianism'. *Cultural Studies*, 6 (3), 468–475.

Norris, P. and Pauling, B. (1999). *Local Content and Diversity: Television in Ten Countries*. Wellington: Report for New Zealand on Air.

Perry, N. (1992). Upside down or downside up? Sectoral interests, structural change and public policy. In J. Deeks and N. Perry (eds), *Controlling Interests: Business, the State and Society in New Zealand* (pp. 36–58). Auckland: Auckland University Press.

Perry, N. (1994). *The Dominion of Signs: Television, Advertising and Other New Zealand Fictions*. Auckland: Auckland University Press.

Phillips, J. (1987). *A Man's Country?* Auckland: Penguin.

Rowe, W. and Schelling, V. (1991). *Memory and Modernity: Popular Culture in Latin America*. London and New York: Verso.

Rushdie, S. (1988). *The Satanic Verses*. New York, NY: Viking.

Sinclair, K. (ed.) (1961). *Distance Looks Our Way*. Hamilton: Paul's Book Arcade.

Sinclair, K. (1986). *A Destiny Apart: New Zealand's Search for National Identity*. Wellington: Allen & Unwin.

Star, L. (1992). Undying love, resisting pleasures: Women watch telerugby. In R. du Plessis, P. Bunkle, K. Irwin, A. Laurie and S. Middleton (eds), *Feminist Voices: Women's Studies Texts for Aotearoa/New Zealand* (pp. 124–140). Auckland: Oxford University Press.

Thompson, R. (1975). *Retreat From Apartheid: New Zealand's Sporting Contacts with South Africa*. Wellington: Oxford University Press.

Turner, G. (1993). Introduction: Moving the margins: theory, practice and Australian cultural studies. In G. Turner (ed.), *Nation, Culture, Text* (pp. 1–13). London and New York: Routledge.

Wark, M. (1994). *Virtual Geography: Living with Global Media Events*. Bloomington and Indianapolis,: Indiana University Press.

Wedde, I. (1995). *How To Be Nowhere: Essays and Texts 1971–1994*. Wellington: Victoria University Press.

9 Global gaming

Cultural Toyotism, transnational corporatism and sport

David L. Andrews and Michael Silk

According to Held and colleagues (1999: 16), globalization is "a process (or set of processes) which embodies a transformation in the spatial organization of social relations and transaction – assessed in terms of their extensity, intensity, velocity and impact – generating transcontinental or interregional flows and networks of activity, interaction and the exercise of power." While most contemporary commentators (Hirst and Thompson (1996) apart) would concur with Held *et al.*'s assertion as to the existence of globalizing economic, political, cultural, and technological processes, there is widespread disagreement as to their effects. This is particularly true when considering the ramifications of globalization for the future of the nation state. While many learned commentators decry the demise of the nation at the hands of rampant globalization, some display a steadfast belief in the enduring relevance of the nation as a source of identity and differentiation. This fracture is equally evident among those working in the global marketplace, particularly those within the marketing and advertising nodes of transnational corporations (i.e. Sony, Volkswagen and Disney), whose corporate footprints transcend the boundaries of nation states, and who operate "simultaneously in different countries around the world, on a global scale" (Morley and Robins, 1995: 223). Located as it is in the "pivotal position between production and consumption, the advertising industry plays a key role in constituting the geographic boundaries of markets and in the internationalization of consumer culture" (Leslie, 1995: 402). Consequently, it is the strategizing developed within the promotional arm of transnational corporate entities that provides our present focus.

Clearly the commercially inspired reinvigoration of the nation represents a telling economic, political, cultural, and technological issue, yet one that has thus far received little intellectual interrogation within the broader field of sport studies. Moreover, such a project is of particular interest to the sociology of sport community, since sport (either in terms of sporting practices, spectacles, or celebrities) is frequently used within advertising campaigns as *de facto* cultural shorthand delineating particular national contexts. As such, this discussion problematizes the *end of the nation* rhetoric that punctuates the globalization debate, by demonstrating the apparent contradiction exposed by the continued presence and importance of the nation as a cultural entity, within what Albrow (1996) describes as the "global age." This chapter examines the role played by transnational corporations and their promotional armatures in re-imagining national cultures; introduces the concept of cultural Toyotism as a means of understanding the manner in which transnational entities negotiate the global–local nexus; and explicates empirical examples of the contrasting processes whereby sport has been used as a means of constituting the nation within the advertising discourses of transnational corporate entities.

Globalization and the demise of the nation?

In order to decipher its contemporary form and influence, it is necessary to provide a brief genealogy of the nation, whose historic veneer – steeped as it is in tradition and mythology – belies what are relatively recent origins within the history of human civilization. According to Smith, the nation is a multidimensional, ideal-type concept incorporating a *"named human population sharing an historic territory, common myths and historical memories, a mass, public culture, a common economy and common legal rights and duties for all members"* (Smith, 1991: 43, emphasis in original). The prototypes for modern nationhood emerged within the dominant powers of Western Europe during the sixteenth and seventeenth centuries, specifically England, Spain, and France. Within these geographic spaces, ethnic communities congealed into nations around such interconnected forces as the construction of a state bureaucracy, the formation of a market economy, and the instantiation of secular institutions, all of which contributed to the establishment of the political, economic, and cultural boundaries of the burgeoning national community (Smith, 1991). From these roots in early modern Western Europe, the nation – and its ideological accomplice, nationalism – became the unquestioned design for the socio-spatial organization of modern humanity, such that the globe has currently been dissected into more than 210 national entities. As Hannerz noted, the "idea of the nation is ubiquitous, itself globalized, as well as pervasive" (1996: 82).

While not wishing to deny the importance of the political and economic forces in shaping the modern nation, it is within the cultural realm that the nation has had its most enduring influence and effects. The very experience of modern nationhood was realized through the politically and economically motivated creation of national cultural identities, that acted as sources of collective identification and reassuring communion for the – frequently disparate – populations living through the transition from agrarian- to industrial-based societies. Within this context, the modern nation state emerged as a cohesive political, economic, and cultural entity designed to consolidate and regulate capital accumulation within the boundaries of a specific geographic location. It is in this sense that Anderson famously conceptualized the nation as an imagined community: a collective mythos that is *"imagined* because members of even the smallest nation will never know most of their fellow-members, meet them, or even hear of them, yet in the minds of each lives the image of their communion" (Anderson, 1983: 15). Not that national imaginings emerged organically from the collective experiences of national populations; rather, in the first instance, the political institutions of the nation state sought to nurture a cohesive sense of *authentic* common cultural heritage and affiliation, through what Hobsbawm and Ranger (1983) referred to as the invention – perhaps the more appropriate verb is selection – of particular national traditions (e.g. symbols and practices such as flags, anthems, heroes, ceremonies, dress, architectural aesthetics, and sporting pastimes). From the eighteenth century onwards, this hijacking of national cultural memory worked to such an effect that the nation has become the most potent of collectivities: "Other types of collective identity – class, gender, race, religion – may overlap or combine with national identity but they rarely succeed in undermining its hold" (Smith, 1991: 143).

Prefigured on the logic of increased interdependence and interconnectedness, contemporary conditions of advanced globalization have seriously undermined the economic and political autonomy that helped constitute the modern nation. Although its roots can be traced further back, this process of "the withering away of the nation" (Hannerz, 1996: 81) began in earnest during the 1970s, whence the confidence in Fordist/Keynesian economic policies that had held sway in many Western economies since the end of the Second World War began to unravel. At this time, the state regulation of national economies focused primarily on industrially based production was fatally undermined by "rising wages and declining productivity, overcapacity and market saturation, competition from low-wage countries, [and] increasing costs for public services" (Morley and Robins, 1995: 27). In the wake of this crisis of economic confidence, many major corporate entities shifted from focusing on commodity production and capital accumulation within individual national economies (a strategy which largely existed within and helped constitute national boundaries), to a more flexible and dynamic approach within which the corporate footprint transcended national borders in the search for more rational and efficient commodity chains. Hence, the transnational corporation was born; those nomadic economic institutions (i.e. Toyota, Philips, Sony, Nike) that scour the globe for the ever cheaper labor costs and under-exploited markets that would ensure expected rates of growth. Working beyond national boundaries, these transnational corporations evidence the degree to which "'The nation' today is visibly in the process of losing an important part of its old functions, namely that of constituting a territorially bounded 'national economy'" (Hobsbawm, 1990: 173). Of course the rise of transnational corporations has been aided and abetted by concomitant shifts in the geo-political landscape, particularly those inspired by the neo-liberal economics that emanated from the USA and the UK in the 1980s. Both the Reaganite and Thatcherite regimes espoused a superficially *laissez-faire* approach to economic development centered on the primacy of free markets, deregulation, and unfettered international trade (Sassen, 2000), which has been institutionalized by the formation of transnational political structures, alliances, and treaties (such as the World Trade Organization, the International Monetary Fund, and NAFTA).

To many commentators it would appear that the death-knell has been rung for the nation, since transnational forces appear to be undermining significant aspects of sovereignty once held by nations, thus rendering them increasingly obsolete economic and political entities within the all-prevailing global marketplace. Yet, as a cultural object, the nation plays an increasingly important role within the machinations of transnational corporate capitalism. Hence, it is possible to refer to the contemporary nation as an enduring "space of identity" (Morley and Robins, 1995), whose symbolic resonance has continued far beyond the nation's shelf-life as a largely autonomous and distinct political and economic formation, and in spite of the cultural threat posed by the cosmopolitanism that accompanied the increased transnational flow of products, capital, images, and institutions. As Raymond Williams famously narrated:

> There was this Englishman who worked in the London office of a multinational corporation based in the United States. He drove home one evening in his Japanese car. His wife, who worked in a firm which imported German kitchen equipment, was already at home. Her small Italian car was often quicker through the traffic. After a meal which included New Zealand lamb, Californian carrots, Mexican honey, French cheese and Spanish wine, they settled down to watch a program on their television set, which had been made in Finland. The program was a retrospective celebration of the war to recapture the Falkland Islands. As they watched it they felt warmly patriotic, and very proud to be British.
>
> (Williams, 1983: 177)

As ever, Williams discerned the complexities and contradictions implicit within cultural existence, in this instance, with regard to the conditions of accelerated global interconnectedness operating within contemporary Western life. Despite the cosmopolitan (and indeed hybridized: see Pietersee, 1995) nature of much of contemporary existence, Williams identified a residual attachment to the nation as an "imagined community and source of identity" (Hannerz, 1996: 81). According to Smith (1991), this is attributable to a number of factors, including: the implausibility of a global culture conclusively extinguishing national difference; the degree to which national discourses are ingrained, and thereby reinforced, within the practices of everyday life; the relief from existential angst offered by one's location in the ongoing project of national regeneration; and the repeated affirmation of collective histories and bonds through ceremonials and events ranging from national holidays to sporting contests. All of which help explain why national affiliations "have proved so durable, protean and resilient through all vicissitudes" (Smith, 1991: 163) accompanying the spread of transnational global capitalism.

The transnational re-imagining of national cultures

The transnational corporations that drive the global economy have clearly acknowledged, and indeed sought to capitalize upon, the enduring cultural resonance of experiences of national belonging within the various national markets they seek to penetrate. Rather than using uniform and invariant global marketing and advertising initiatives that attempted to negate entrenched national cultural boundaries (something tried and failed by many in the fledgling stages of the transnational era), transnational corporations seek increasingly to represent national cultures in a manner designed to engage the nationalist sensibilities of local consumers. In this scenario, the locus of control in influencing the manner in which the nation and national identity are represented becomes exteriorized through, and internalized within, the promotional strategies of transnational corporations.

Our central argument is that the *context* in which, and the *processes* through which, national cultures are produced and reproduced is being transformed (Held *et al.*, 1999). Not that the internal political forces previously responsible for harnessing and contouring national cultural identity have been rendered obsolete; rather, their position of influence is being eroded by external, commercially driven, forces. To reiterate, the logics and practices of transnational corporate capitalism are playing an increasingly influential role in the shaping of national cultures. The penetration of local cultures by the economics and imagery of global capitalism represents the latest, and most sophisticated, attempt by transnational corporations to command the widest possible market base, and thereby accrue, the benefits derived from the realization of colossal economies of scale. In the early stages of corporate globalization, companies operated "as if the entire world (or major regions of it) were a single, largely identical entity" and subsequently attempted to sell the "same things in the same way everywhere" (Levitt, 1983: 22). While such global naivety persists in some corporate (and indeed academic) circles, most soon realized the impracticability of treating the global market as a single, homogeneous entity.

Although the advancement of capitalism has always been about the overcoming of spatial constraints as a means of improving the flow of goods from producer to consumer (Hall, 1991; Morley and Robins, 1995), the intrinsically rationalizing logic of market capitalism initially came unstuck when faced by the "warm appeal of national affiliations and attachments" (Robins, 1997: 20). So, rather than attempting to neuter cultural difference through a strategic global uniformity, many corporations have realized that securing a profitable global presence necessitates negotiating with the local, "and by negotiate I mean it had to incorporate and partly reflect the differences it was trying to overcome" (Hall, 1991: 32). It is in this sense that Robins acknowledged "Globalization is, in fact, about the creation of a new *global–local* nexus" (1997: 28); it is about the ability of transnational corporations to seamlessly operate within the language of the local, simultaneously, in multiple locations (Dirlik, 1996). As Dirlik (1996: 34) proposed, "The radical slogan of an earlier day, 'Think globally, act locally,' has been assimilated by transnational corporations with far greater success than in any radical strategy." Yet the *locals* produced within this context are routinely little more than transnational corporations' commercially inspired inflections of local cultures. As such they are liable – though certainly not preordained – to be superficial and depthless caricatures of national cultural differences. Dirlik continues, "The recognition of the local in marketing strategy, however, does not mean any serious recognition of the autonomy of the local, but is intended to recognize the features of the local so as to incorporate localities into the imperatives of the global" (1996: 34). According to the logics of global capitalism, transnational corporations that seek to be "part of that culture too" (NBC's Vice-president J.B. Holston III, quoted in Morley and Robins (1995: 117)) are effectively involved in the production of localized spaces, identities, and experiences (the national cultures) that facilitate the "continuity of flow" (Harvey, 1985: 145) between global production and local consumption. Hence, it is possible to refer to transnational capitalism's role in the delocalization (Castells, 1983), detraditionalization (Luke, 1996), or decentralization (Robins, 1997) of national cultural production. In this sense, the material has been superseded by the cultural – the physical by the symbolic – as new televisual, satellite, digital, internet-based technologies play an ever more central role in the mapping of national cartographies. As the key mechanism in the reconstruction of national spaces, cultures, and identities, new communications technologies are thus deeply involved in the "ongoing construction and reconstruction of social spaces and social relations" (Morley, 1992: 272). In cultural terms, the global mass media can thus be argued to have created new electronic spaces (Robins, 1990; 1997), whose presence has prompted some to argue that the *space of flows* has superseded the *spaces of places* (Castells, 1996; Luke, 1996; 1999).

While it is difficult to assess the precise impact that transnational corporate capitalism is having upon the nature and efficacy of national cultures, it is easier to point to the processes through which such changes are occurring. Given their preoccupation with knowledge-intensive, dynamic, and flexible "think work" (Allen, 1992), the marketing and advertising armatures of the new culture industries have become the core vehicles of surplus value production, and therefore capital accumulation, within late capitalist economies. In order to realize the goal of creating global–local markets for their products, transnational corporations concentrate increasingly on the promotional nodes of their respective commodity chains, thereby manipulating "the image which crosses and recrosses linguistic frontiers much more rapidly and more easily, and which speaks across languages in a much more immediate way" (Hall, 1991: 27).

The global–local logics of "cultural Toyotism"

Following Tomlinson (1999), rather than viewing the power of transnational capitalism as distributing a "capitalist monoculture," we see the global strategies of post-industrial leviathans involving a greater degree of engagement with the local than is credited by many commentators. Of course within some intellectual quarters the resilience of the nation is widely acknowledged, yet this recognition has tended to be expressed in terms of the localized consumption of global cultural products. Arguments are thus made pertaining to the necessarily varied processes of translation, adaptation, and indigenization of various cultural texts as they are appropriated within particular national locales (Appadurai, 1990; Morley, 1992; Robins, 1991; Tomlinson, 1999). The efficacy of the local is equally evident (though perhaps less researched) within the realm of global cultural production. Most significantly it is the denizens of Madison Avenue – spiritual home to the marketing and advertising armatures of the new culture industries – who clearly recognize (and have sought to capitalize upon for their transnational corporate clientele) the mainstream populace's residual attachment to the nation. In order to recover a corporation's escalating production costs by exploiting the maximum possible market base, this new class of cultural intermediaries (Bourdieu, 1984; du Gay et al., 1997) must create global images and campaigns that resonate with local experience and sensibilities. As such, they understand the importance of "achieving a real equidistance, or equipresence, of perspective in relation to the whole world of their audiences and consumers" (Morley and Robins, 1995: 113). Far from transcending or eradicating difference, today's global advertisers recognize the central and prefigurative importance of the local, and routinely incorporate difference and particularity within their strategizing (Dirlik, 1996; Morley and Robins, 1995). What we appear to be witnessing is the capitalization upon, and redefinition of, national belongingness by the promotional and marketing agents of transnational corporations intent on inserting their products into the diffuse and diverse markets they seek to penetrate.

Manuel Castells (1996) proposed the concept of Toyotism to refer to a new and flexible management system that organized material production in a manner which allowed it to respond effortlessly to the inherent, yet unpredictable, dynamism of advanced economies. This was a system "designed to reduce uncertainty rather than to encourage adaptability. The flexibility is in the process, not in the product" (Castells, 1996: 158). Developed within the Japanese industrial and economic context, Toyotism has been both imitated by other companies and widely transplanted to other national locations. Moreover, it is our contention that the core aspects of Toyotism in a material production sense – flexible, adaptable, and globally contingent regimes of production – can be discerned within the corporation's marketing and promotional strategies; in other words, the realm of cultural production upon which the late capitalist order depends (Jameson, 1991).

With the aggressive globalization of the automobile industry in the 1970s, Toyota recognized that its overtly Japanese corporate identity was a significant hindrance to future growth. Therefore, in order to begin to accrue the benefits of colossal economies of scale derived from successfully penetrating markets outside of Japan, Toyota's marketing and promotional strategies had to incorporate and reflect the very differences that earlier phases of global corporate expansion had sought to neuter, or overcome (Hall, 1991). Rather than attempt to sell the "same things in the same way everywhere" (Levitt, 1983: 22) – rationalizing their products through single globally focused directives and thus treating the world as if it were a single homogeneous space – Toyota's promotional initiatives effectively sutured the corporation and its vehicular products into the various national contexts in which they sought a tangible market presence. Somewhat reconfiguring the work of Castells (1996), in order to begin to explain to transnational corporations' re-imaginings of national cultures, we have developed the nascent concept of cultural Toyotism.

As a "local" branch of what has become a truly transnational car corporation, Toyota New Zealand exemplifies the practices and processes associated with cultural Toyotism. Within numerous campaigns and strategies, Toyota New Zealand has sought to redefine this potentially incongruous brand into the local culture. For instance, Toyota's latest car product, the *Yaris*, styled in Germany and engineered and built in Japan, has been renamed the *Echo* and marketed in a way designed to appeal to the sensibilities of the New Zealand consumer (Sloane, 1999). Toyota's advertising initiatives have been the most effective vehicles for creating a space for the corporation within the New Zealand popular imaginary. By evoking symbolic representations of both urban and rural New Zealand, Toyota's commercial narratives have appealed to the core national sentiments that constitute New Zealand identity. This was particularly evident in a campaign involving Barry Crump, a best-selling author and rural nomad who came to embody the mythos of the New Zealand nation. Despite the popular perception of the nation as a rural idyll, New Zealand is one of the most urbanized countries in the world, with 83.8 percent of the population defined as urban (Perry, 1994). Crump became the central character in a series of commercials for small pick-up trucks, which, according to Toyota, are equally at home in the city as in the country. Thereby, through Crump, Toyota involved itself in the renegotiation between the rural and the urban within New Zealand society, effectively bringing these locations, physically as well as symbolically, closer together (Perry, 1994). As such, Toyota positioned itself – even by association – as a valid contributor to the ongoing national dialogue.

The Toyota New Zealand scenario, as with its subsequent "Everyday People" campaign that ran simultaneously in numerous national markets (same music and sentiment, different people and experiences), evidences the degree to which transnational corporations have come to acknowledge, exploit, and indeed accentuate the enduring cultural relevance of the nation to the process of identity formation. Of course, Toyota is certainly not alone in adopting such transnational promotional initiatives. Morley and Robins (1995) identified a comparable stratagem in Sony's (the global media conglomerate) practice of "global localization," which seeks to gain insider status for the Sony brand through the tailoring of its global promotional strategies to the cultural contingencies of local markets.

Having introduced the concept of cultural Toyotism, our preliminary investigations have unearthed two primary designs whereby transnational corporations have attempted to engage national market sensibilities through global–local promotional schema. First, they develop campaigns designed to ingratiate brands within the specificities of targeted national cultures, through appropriately adapted marketing initiatives. This stratagem was exemplified in the pre-Christmas 1999 worldwide release of the computer game *Tomb Raider IV: The Last Revelation*. Herein a global cultural product was explicitly, and simultaneously, marketed to varied local contexts. In specific terms, the computer game was adapted in various ways, so as to appeal to the perceived cultural sensibilities of particular nationally bounded markets. Thus, the gun-toting heroine, Lara Croft, deemed too "tall and too British to appeal to the Japanese market," was modified appropriately. Similarly, the swastikas and other Nazi iconography that appeared in some renditions were removed for the German market, whereas for the US market a naked priestess and zombies were clothed in order to satisfy America's puritanical veneer (Chadbourn, 1999: 14). Second, in terms of strategies adopted by transnational corporations as a means of engaging local markets, in recent times many major brands have sought to rationalize their worldwide marketing strategies, through global advertising campaigns – constructed around single, multivocal, multinationally oriented texts – that attempt to engage a multitude of national markets at one and the same time. These initiatives simultaneously exhibit both the global and the local demeanor of the brand in question. The most vivid example of this monotextual, yet multivocal, global–local stratagem may be gleaned from the Ford Motor Company's "Just Wave Hello" global anthem, that first aired on Monday, 1 November 1999. Starting at 9 p.m. in New Zealand and playing at that time in various marketplaces throughout the world (including Britain, France, Italy, Germany, USA (on thirty-eight channels), Canada, and Australia), Ford sought to fight through the cluttered commercial media landscape, and thereby reach an audience exceeding one billion. The commercial exhibited all seven of Ford's automobile brands and, in a montage of nationally grounded vignettes (including a US war veteran riding in a Ford Mustang convertible in a home-coming parade, an Italian couple embracing in front of a Volvo, a well-dressed English woman putting her dogs in the back seat of a Jaguar, and Japanese girls playing in cherry blossom orchards near a Mazda), illustrated how its vehicles were ingrained in the everyday experience of peoples around the globe.

In the remainder of this chapter we aim to unearth these two primary strands of cultural Toyotism, particularly in relation to the ways that sport practices, celebrities, and spectacles have been appropriated by transnational corporate capitalism, as culturally resonant vehicles used in the commercially motivated process of national re-imagining. According to Bell and Campbell (1999: 22), sport has become one of the "world's biggest obsessions." Clearly, advertising and promotional innovators have operated under the assumption that, and indeed capitalized upon, the stylized excitement and glamor that characterizes most contemporary consumer-oriented sporting forms. As leading sport marketing agency, ISL's Daniel Beavois has indicated, "Sport is probably the only thing that fascinates everyone in the world.... Many people now feel more concerned by sport than almost anything else in their lives" (quoted in Bell and Campbell, 1999: 22). While clearly an over exaggeration – what else would one expect from an employee of one of the world's largest and most influential sport marketing agencies? – this quote does suggest the way in which the corporate world has come to view sport and its potential as a means of engaging and mobilizing consumers around the globe. It is argued, then, that prefigured within the logic of cultural Toyotism, sport is mobilized as a major cultural signifier of nation that can engage national sensibilities, identities, and experiences. As such, sport is used as *de facto* cultural shorthand delineating particular national sentiments. That is, within the logics of transnational corporate capitalism, sport is seen as a globally present cultural form, but one that is heavily accented by local dialects. It is this notion of sport as a globally present, but locally resonant, cultural practice that advertisers seek to mobilize within this process of cultural Toyotism.

Multivocal transnationalism I: acting globally, thinking locally

During earlier phases in the process of globalizing consumer capitalism, the aspiring giants within the global marketplace – most, if not all, of whom originated in the USA – treated the international market as a uniform and homogeneous entity. Hence, and here one is thinking of Coca-Cola, Disney, and McDonald's in particular, globalizing corporations routinely adopted standardized advertising campaigns regardless of the national context within which consumption was being encouraged. This frequently meant the indiscriminate running of advertising campaigns originally produced for the "home," American, market. Whether intentionally or otherwise, this inevitably led to charges of a cultural imperialism being waged by American corporations. This is perhaps better expressed as an America-flavored Coca-Colonization; a bringing of "America to the world through Coca-Cola," Disney, McDonald's *et al.* (Leslie, 1995). While the hawking of Americana (the symbols and products readily associated with American culture) continues to be a profitable strategy (especially in efforts targeted at engaging the global youth market), many mature global corporations have acknowledged the pitfalls associated with such blanket strategizing, and have modified their approaches accordingly. In this vein, Coca-Cola began to soften its American edge, initially by producing nationally ambiguous and thereby globally inclusive advertising campaigns, such as the "I'd Like to Buy the World a Coke" television commercial that first aired in 1971 (Prendergrast, 1998). Latterly, in an attempt to further distance its brand image from its storied American roots, certain Coca-Cola campaigns provided an even narrower focus on specific regional and national cultures. In terms of the former, the "Eat Football, Sleep Football, Drink Coca-Cola" campaign is of most relevance to this discussion. In separate pan-North American (American Football), pan-European (Association Football), and pan-Australasian (Australian Rules Football) television advertisements, Coca-Cola was unselfconsciously conjugated with regional sporting cultures through commercial narratives which focused on the passion, intensity, and excitement of the various football codes and, by inference, that of drinking Coca-Cola itself.

Coca-Cola's subsequent incursion into the realm of national cultures is most graphically, and indeed beautifully, illustrated in the 1996 "Red" commercial developed by Wieden and Kennedy, Portland, as a means of furthering Coca-Cola's presence on the Indian subcontinent. The very real poverty experienced by much of India's vast populace would suggest little consumer interest in a carbonated soft drink that to many would represent an unattainable luxury. Nevertheless, the sheer volume of the Indian population (approaching one billion) means that – although small in percentage terms of the total populace – the potential market for Coca-Cola, namely India's middle and upper classes, is sizable enough to encourage global corporations into the Indian market. Such was the rationale behind Coca-Cola's recent foray into Indian popular consciousness, as realized through the "Red" commercial. This sixty-second depiction of the vibrancy and complexity of Indian culture keyed on the byline "Passion has a colour." The color in this instance being red: the red of chillis drying in fields; the red of a Rajasthani man's turban; the red of the *bindis* adorning women's foreheads; the red of the *dupata* drying on river banks; the red of the cricket balls that regularly punctuate the visual narrative; and, of course, the red of the Coca-Cola brand symbolism so subtly, and seamlessly, inserted into this panoramic sweep of Indian culture. With the backdrop of the late Nusrat Fateh Ali Khan's hypnotic Sufi-inspired devotional "Mustt Mustt" (himself a Pakistani but with a considerable following in India), the commercial brazenly synthesizes India's passion for cricket (red ball) with a desired passion for Coca-Cola (red logo). Through this association with the cricket thematic, Coca-Cola sought to thrust itself into the mainstream of Indian culture by providing itself with a seemingly natural place within local culture and experience. To be sure this stunning commercial warrants article-length analysis in its own right (something we are currently working on). However, for our present purposes it is sufficient to state that Coca-Cola's "Red" represents a vivid example of the way in which national sporting practices have been mobilized by the symbolic processes, and, through the mediated products, associated with the transnational corporate *modus operandi* that we have characterized as cultural Toyotism.

As well as mobilizing the sporting practices associated with particular nation cultures, corporations adopting the cultural Toyotist approach regularly appropriate sporting celebrities as mechanisms of identification with a particular locality. Nike, now also seeking to shed its overt American demeanor, has been noticeably promiscuous in forming relations with national sporting heroes. As an exemplar of this type of initiative, Nike developed a television advertisement in which the Australian cricketer Shane Warne bowled a chainsaw, rather than a cricket ball, toward a cowering batsman. In this example, Nike "selected" a national sporting "hero" and a national sporting pastime, and attached its commodity sign (brand identity) to these potent national cultural signifiers. Through its liaison with Warne, Nike sought to nurture an authentic sense of national affiliation (Hobsbawm and Ranger, 1983) for the company, which could still be perceived as something of an interloper into Australian culture. Using a widely acknowledged aspect of Australian cricket culture, namely the aggressive style of Warne's spin bowling, the ad illustrates the precise way in which transnational entities seek to ingratiate a global brand (Nike) within a local context (Australia). In doing so, and in the true spirit of cultural Toyotism, Nike crafted a highly engaging, yet superficial and depthless, representation of Australian national sporting identity: effectively, a construction of Nike designed to fit unselfconsciously into Australian culture. Of course, Warne is by no means Nike's only nationally bounded sport celebrity, as evidenced by the considerable promotional work the company has put into nurturing such national sporting icons as Ian Wright (the English footballer), Jeff Wilson (the New Zealand rugby player), Christian Vieri (the Italian footballer), and of course America's Tiger Woods (golf) and Michael Jordan (basketball).

McDonald's is perhaps the most common signifier of transnational capitalist expansion, as well as being among the most (along with Nike) targeted recipient of anti-capitalist "demonstrations." Having long nurtured its explicitly American demeanor, in recent times, and like both Toyota and Nike, McDonald's appears more concerned with melding its brand identity into the superficial vagaries of the local culture. In Britain, perhaps unsurprisingly, McDonald's has regularly drawn upon British footballing heroes in order to cement its place within the British national imaginary. Within one noted television commercial Alan Shearer, then England's football captain, embarks on a nostalgic journey through his native Newcastle, visiting among other places his old school, football boys' club and, of course, a McDonald's restaurant. Significantly, the advert draws upon what are perhaps the best-known cultural signifiers of Newcastle: Shearer himself, the football club for which Shearer plays and the evocative Tyne Bridges. Hence, McDonald's invokes the cultural specificities of an English locale as it embeds itself ever deeper within the experience of everyday British life. A more recent promotional offering operates more explicitly at the national level. McDonald's revises and resites, as an element in the commercial production process, the 1966 Soccer World Cup final between England and Germany. The ad commodifies history and reinvents a "reality" that could never have existed – a simulacrum of the non-existent, a place in which space, time, and place boundaries have been collapsed, and fact fused with fiction (Harvey, 1993). The ad depicts Geoff Hurst, mythologized in English history for his three goals in the 1966 World Cup final, scoring his third goal in the game, a goal made even more immortal in English consciousness by the accompanying commentary from Kenneth Wolstenholme: "There's some people on the pitch, they think its all over, it is now!" Rather than the ball entering the net for Hurst's third goal, the ad revises history by showing a streaker running on to the pitch, causing Hurst to miss the shot. The advert concludes with Hurst consuming the new product in McDonald's range, the *McDonald's Triple Burger* with "*twisty fries*," the narrative defining the revised footage as "a triple with a twist." The Shearer and Hurst campaigns, however parodically, are attempts to insert the global brand (McDonald's) into the imaged recollections of the national psyche. Specifically, the ads use selected imagery, both concrete signifiers and sporting celebrities, to nurture the distinctly local (national) demeanor of the global brand.

Multivocal transnationalism II: global anthems/local sensibilities

Thus far we have proposed that cultural Toyotism is characterized by the local being incorporated and reflected in the promotional processes of global capitalism. Extending Castells (1996), we suggested that cultural Toyotism could point to the degree to which transnational corporate forces, rather than internal or regional politico-economic forces, have begun to reconstitute the tenor of popular national sensibilities and imaginings. Up until this point, we have addressed the ways in which transnational corporations have inserted brands within specific local cultures, initiatives that thus fuse the global with the local. However, the advertising and promotional denizens of transnational corporations, which actively endorse the implausibility of a global culture conclusively extinguishing national difference, have also constructed initiatives that seek to engage a multitude of markets at one and the same time. Specifically, these campaigns rationalize the escalating costs implicit in reaching the maximum market base by producing single, multivocal, multinationally oriented texts. These texts appeal to a number of different local markets and thus simultaneously exhibit both the global reach and the local resonance of the brand in question. Despite the globalizing cosmopolitan logic underpinning such campaigns, the producers of these initiatives are aware that the particularities of place and culture can never be absolutely transcended. Rather, they recognize that:

> Globalization is, in fact, also associated with new dynamics of re-localization. It is about the achievement of a new global–local nexus, about new and intricate relations between global space and local space. Globalization is like putting together a jigsaw puzzle: it is a matter of inserting a multiplicity of localities into the overall picture of a new global system.
>
> (Morley and Robins, 1995: 116)

Following Dirlik (1996), these campaigns reflect the ability of transnational corporations to operate within the language of the local, simultaneously, in multiple locations. For example, the Ford "Just Wave Hello" ad, described above, provides a set of global products (some tailored specifically for local markets) that are appropriated within a number of different physical places (complete with national cultural referents, such as a home-coming parade).

Through its transnational advertising agency Wieden and Kennedy, which has offices in Portland, New York, London, Amsterdam, and Tokyo, Nike has produced a series of global multivocal promotional campaigns that select various "authentic" national traditions (in the form of sporting "heroes") and combine them to exhibit both the global ubiquity and the local pertinence of the brand. This trend it most evident within Nike's insurgence into the nationally charged global football marketplace: an initiative prompted by Nike's recognition that if it were to become a truly global sport corporation, it would need to secure a global presence within what is unquestionably the global game (Giulianotti, 1999). Initially, Nike's multivocal football campaigns selected specific physical locales and corroborated them with images of complementary national football heroes, as they sought to engage the national sensibilities and affiliations of multiple and dislocated consumers. Nike's first incursion into global football was realized in its 1994 "Wall" campaign, created within Wieden and Kennedy's main office in Portland. Within this spot Nike selected a series of football "heroes," hijacked from the cultural memory of particular localities, and positioned them as representatives of their respective nations. Significantly, the ad depicted these celebrities within their own localities and it was a football that orbited a time–space compressed "Nikeworld." The advert highlighted various footballing celebrities, moored, quite literally, in the bricks and mortar of their own locales, while kicking a ball around a compressed globe. The advert depicts Eric Cantona, a former French international and Manchester United player on a billboard next to Paris' Eiffel Tower. Cantona, adorning a Manchester United shirt, perhaps to engage the French and the global Manchester United marketplace at one and the same time, beats a nondescript opponent also moored on to the billboard and kicks the ball over the English Channel, past the Houses of Parliament and into a billboard in London's Leicester Square. Here, Ian Wright, then of Arsenal and England, controls the ball and fires it past Tower Bridge. The ball continues its flight around the world, passing between various national symbols and heroes, such as a Rio de Janeiro beach and the Brazilian player Romario, finally ending up in Mexico City where the ball is saved by the Mexican goalkeeper, Jorge Campos.

As Nike's global football strategizing evolved, explicit representations of place would appear to have been discarded in preference to a sole focus on football heroes as signifiers of national cultural difference. In 1996, Wieden and Kennedy's Amsterdam office produced the direct successor of the "Wall" campaign. According to Nike UK spokesperson Graham Anderson, the 1996 advertisement, titled "Good versus Evil," highlighted football "stars" from a whole range of countries demonstrating how the game can unite the planet against the forces of evil (www.auto-server.com/newsroom/sports). "Good versus Evil" did not define the other (opponents) as place-bound; rather the selected "heroes" were pitted against opponents that were both temporally and spatially ambiguous. Set in a Roman Amphitheater, the ad depicted the selected celebrities (good) playing, and ultimately beating, a team led by a representation of the devil and his underlings (evil). Herein, Nike complicated local affiliation, for some players adorned their national team uniforms, others, their club uniform. Paolo Maldini and Ronaldo, for example, wore their Italian and Brazilian national team shirts respectively. However, Ian Wright (Arsenal), Patrick Kluivert (Ajax), Luis Figo (Barcelona), and Eric Cantona (Manchester United) adorned their club shirts, arguably, to appeal not only to a multitude of markets, but also in an attempt to capitalize on the market within which the player was best known. Cantona, resplendent in Manchester United livery, proved the central figure in the ad, by destroying "evil" with his deadly penalty kick. At the time of the ad, Cantona was better known for his exploits with Manchester United than with the French national team. Nike capitalized upon the global appeal of Manchester United (and indeed Barcelona, Ajax, and Arsenal) as symbols that would better engage a multitude of markets than the national team uniforms of most of the assembled players. And yet, given Italy and especially Brazil's globally acknowledged, and indeed celebrated, football heritage, Maldini and Ronaldo wearing national team uniforms could be seen as an attempt by Nike to constitute a global (as well as an implicitly national) market for these universally admired national football dynasties.

Like Nike, Adidas has produced transnational campaigns that are multivocal in nature through selecting particular national "heroes" and events with which audiences in different localities can identify. The futuristic "Soccer Reinvented" campaign revealed "Team Adidas" made up of, among others, the Italian Alessandor Del Piero, the Argentinian Fernando Redondo, the Dutchman Edwin Van de Saar, the Englishman Paul Gascoigne, and the American John Harkes. The ad depicts two teams of identical clones, each kitted out in bland Adidas uniforms, the only difference being that one team dons Adidas "Predator" boots and provides players' names on the backs of their uniforms. Not surprisingly, the "predator" team plays the more inventive, exhilarating, and ultimately successful football. Like Nike's "Good versus Evil," the game is played in a "non-place" (Auge, 1995), a vacuous, neo-stadium resembling an immense bank vault devoid of any signs, symbols, or color. The only spectators "present" within the stadium are depthless simulations of spectators (Baudrillard, 1983); for the "fans" in this campaign are surface representations spatially constrained in television screens adorning a small area of the vast stadium. The ad thus eliminates physical place and replaces it with a spatial ambiguity – or "placenessness – that removes any relational or historical attachment the consumer may have to a particular sport stadium" (Bale, 1998: 268). By removing all referents to place, yet in selecting national football "heroes," Nike and Adidas are able to promote their brands transnationally, effectively engaging and invoking national sensibilities and experiences within a multitude of markets at one and the same time.

The direct successor to Nike's "Good versus Evil" campaign once again emanated from Wieden and Kennedy, Amsterdam, and was timed to coincide with the 1998 World Cup. Nike "Beach" rendered a new assemblage of burgeoning football celebrities (Ronaldo, Ariel Ortega, Christian Vieri, Nankwo Kanu, Ibrahim Ba, Roberto Carlos, Luis Enrique, and Hernan Crespo). Like Adidas' "Soccer Reinvented" commercial, these players were located in a distinctly ambiguous space: a remarkably indistinct beach idyll could quite easily have been located anywhere from the Brazilian beach, to the French Riviera or Australia's Gold Coast. The transnational thematic has been transposed subsequently to Nike's latest band of football celebrities (now christened the Nike "Geoforce") in the 2000 television commercial "The Mission." Within this highly stylized commercial, the Nike "Geoforce" set out to reclaim the new "GeoMerlin" soccer ball stolen from Nike by "Uri," a fictional character who sought to impose a defensive approach to the game. The GeoMerlin soccer ball was seen as a threat to Uri's dour football: a game dominated by standardized and mechanized robots that replaced human players, and thus eliminated irrational and risk-taking individuals from the game (www.nikefootball.com). "The Mission" ad, and its accompanying promotional mechanisms, depict how Nike's Geoforce used their inventive football skills to storm the defensive fortress, destroy the robotic leader of Uri's operation, blow up Uri's headquarters and his soccer playing robots, and return the prototype ball to Nike. The "Geoforce" was made up of Edgar Davids (Holland), Oliver Bierhoff (Germany), Francesco Totti (Germany), Guardiolia (Spain), Figo (Portugal), Lilian Thuram (France), Andy Cole (England), Dwight Yorke (Trinidad and Tobago), and Hidetoshi Nakata (Japan), all of them wearing the latest range of Nike "Mercurial" apparel. According to Nike, these "agents" were selected for this particular mission given their demonstrated "courage," "aggression," "determination," "deadliness," and their "natural athletic" ability (www.nikefootball.com). In selecting these agents and their concomitant skills, Nike is involved in the transnational reconstitution of the cultural experiences of football, yet at the same time, Nike retains elements of particular localities through the selection of sporting heroes whose distinctly different skills evoke distinctly different national (football) cultures. For example, the German, Bierhoff, is defined as a natural leader who brings creativity, intelligence, and determination, while the Japanese Nakata is composed, consistent, and instinctive. As such, Nike incorporates within its transnational campaign the very local differences that global capitalism has attempted to overcome (Hall, 1991). However, rather than romanticize or celebrate the sophistication of such campaigns, it is important to outline that these campaigns point to the ways in which transnational corporations are providing commercially inspired representations of locality. In this case, Nike has done little more than select celebrities who represent a superficial and depthless caricature of national cultural differences, sensibilities, and experiences: modern nation statehood effectively being replaced by late capitalist corporate-nationhood.

Coda

Clearly, the cultural innovators responsible for the marketing and promotional strategies of transnational corporations are keenly attuned to the continued resonance of the nation within the logics of transnational corporate capitalism. In this chapter, we have attempted to highlight these enthusiastic engagements with national sensibilities and experiences within specific advertising campaigns. In exposing the durability and resilience of the nation as a cultural entity – thus problematizing the *end of the nation* rhetoric rooted in the global panic brought about by the instantiation of a globally homogeneous commercial culture – we propose that the nation is of central and prefigurative importance in global promotional imperatives. Moreover, we have suggested that sport is a globally present, but locally resonant, cultural practice that transnational advertisers mobilize to negotiate the global–local nexus. This strategy, which we have termed *cultural Toyotism*, points to the ways in which the reproduction of the nation has become exteriorized through, and internalized within, the promotional strategies of transnational corporations.

These initial interpretations suggest that these commercially inspired reflections are likely to be depthless caricatures of nation that delineate particular national contexts through drawing out, or selecting, stylized signifiers of (sporting) traditions, pastimes, and celebrities. Of interest here is the centrality of sporting forms and sporting celebrities in what Hannerz (1996: 89) described as a "changing" of the nation under the logics of transnational corporate capitalism. Sporting spectacles and celebrities, or perhaps more accurately, a commercially inspired reflection of sport that emphasizes entertainment, glamor and at times violence, are increasingly being incorporated into these transnational campaigns. Of course, this is merely an observation; however, it does point to the problematic nature, for both sporting and national cultures, of a climate increasingly dictated by an external, commercial, locus of control. These corporate reflections of nation are not necessarily any more false, imagined or inauthentic than those constituted internally through the political and economic realm. However, significant questions remain to be answered in respect of the problems posed when national identity becomes externally and commercially constituted.

In this chapter we have focused on the global–local element within the ranks of the culture industries that actively affirm the continued relevance of national cultures. However, there are those whose engagement with the concepts of nation and national identity has been indifferent. In this sense, and perhaps prompted by the hegemonic "borderless world" (Ohmae, 1990) rhetoric of the global marketplace, many advertising agency account directors eschew the utility of national cultures in providing the basis for profitable consumer segmentation and targeting. Instead, they focus on developing what are deemed to be more cost-effective "global" campaigns, that circumvent national borders by creating more expansive global consumer tribes linked by lifestyle values, or preferences, rather than spatial location. This notion of post-national geographies of consumption (Leslie, 1995) clearly underpins the work of *180*, the innovative Amsterdam agency founded by defectors from Wieden and Kennedy (the agency responsible for most of Nike's advertising). *180's* corporate mission speaks to universal traits, experiences, and emotions in a manner designed to appeal beyond the specificities of national cultural boundaries (Hunter, 2000). *180's* placeless universality is perhaps most graphically exemplified within its recent global "Adidas makes you do better" campaign for the sports footwear and apparel giant. In four separate television commercials English soccer player David Beckham (clearing the streets of litter), Trinidadian sprinter Ato Boldon (returning a stolen television), Russian tennis starlet Anna Kournikova (countering cheating at an arcade game), and New Zealand rugby player Jona Lomu (rescuing a suffocating fish), all use their sporting or physical skills for the good of humanity as a whole. By focusing on such seemingly universal moralistic and heroic traits, the campaign transcends the nationality of the athlete in question and the national cultural context within which the ad is consumed. As Larry Frey, creative director of 180, opined, "I think the Adidas we've done prove we can create and cross borders effectively" (Hunter, 2000).

Clearly, then, there are differences within the philosophies of individual advertising agencies in respect of the relevance of the nation as a source of identity and differentiation. Given the *changing context* through which the nation is continually being produced and reproduced, empirically based investigations that concentrate on the nature of the symbolic analytic workforce, their training, values, and their global–local cultural literacy are required to aid scholarly understanding of the production and reproduction of corporate nationalism(s). Such an approach can address the fractured or contradictory strategizing of transnational corporations and highlights the increased importance of comprehending the role of the advertising industry in constituting the contested geographical markets of what Albrow (1996) terms the "global age."

References

Albrow, M. (1996). *The Global Age*. Stanford, CA: Stanford University Press.

Allen, J. (1992). Post-industrialism and post-Fordism. In S. Hall, D. Held and A. McGrew (eds), *Modernity and its Futures* (pp. 168–204). Cambridge: Polity Press.

Anderson, B. (1983). *Imagined Communities: Reflections on the Origin and Spread of Nationalism*. London: Verso.

Appadurai, A. (1990). Disjuncture and difference in the global cultural economy. *Theory, Culture and Society*, 7, 295–310.

Auge, M. (1995). *Non-places: Introduction to an Anthropology of Supermodernity*. London: Verso.

Autoserver.com/newsroom/sports.http://www.autoserver.com/newsroom/sports/oth/1995/oth/soc/feat/archive/112696/soc33262.html. FIFA Slams Nike Soccer Advert.

Bale, J. (1998). Virtual fandoms: Futurescapes of football. In A. Brown (ed.), *Fanatics: Power, Identity and Fandom in Football* (pp. 265–278). London: Routledge.

Baudrillard, J. (1983). *Simulations*. New York: Semiotext(e).

Bell, E. and Campbell, D. (1999). For the love of money. *The Observer*, May 23, p. 22.

Bourdieu, P. (1984). *Distinction: A Social Critique of the Judgement of Taste*, trans. R. Nice. London: Routledge & Kegan Paul.

Castells, M. (1983). Crisis planning and the quality of life: Managing the new historical relationships between space and society. *Environment and Planning D: Society and Space*, 1, (1).

Castells, M. (1996). *The Rise of the Network Society*. Oxford: Blackwell Publishers.

Chadbourn, M. (1999). Why Lara Croft is too hot for the world to handle. *The Independent*, November 1, p. 14.

Dirlik, A. (1996). The global in the local. In R. Wilson and W. Dissanayake (eds),

Global Local: Cultural Production and the Transnational Imaginary (pp. 21–45). Durham, NC: Duke University Press.

du Gay, P., Hall, S., Janes, L., Mackay, H. and Negus, K. (1997). *Doing Cultural Studies: The Story of the Sony Walkman*. London: Sage.

Giulianotti, R. (1999). *Football: A Sociology of the Global Game*. Cambridge: Polity Press.

Hall, S. (1991). The local and the global: Globalization and ethnicity. In A.D. King (ed.), *Culture, Globalization and the World-System* (pp. 19–39). London: Macmillan.

Hannerz, U. (1996). *Transnational Connections: Culture, People, Places*. London: Comedia.

Harvey, D. (1985). The geopolitics of capitalism. In D. Gregory and J. Urry (eds), *Social Relations and Social Structures* (pp. 128–163), London: Macmillan.

Harvey, D. (1993). From space to place and back again: Reflections on the condition of postmodernity. In J. Bird (ed.), *Mapping the Futures: Local Cultures, Global Change* (pp. 3–29). London: Routledge.

Held, D., McGrew, A., Goldblatt, D. and Perraton, J. (1999). *Global Transformations: Politics, Economics and Culture*. Stanford, CA: Stanford University Press.

Hobsbawm, E.J. (1990). *Nations and Nationalism since 1870: Programme, Myth, Reality*. Cambridge: Cambridge University Press.

Hobsbawm, E.J. and Ranger, T. (eds) (1983). *The Invention of Tradition*. Cambridge: Cambridge University Press.

Hunter, S. (2000). Border-bending creative. *Boards Magazine*, March. Available online at www.boardsmag.com/articles/magazine/200003/ideas.html.

Jameson, F. (1991). *Postmodernism, or, the Cultural Logic of Late Capitalism*. Durham, NC: Duke University Press.

Leslie, D.A. (1995). Global scan: The globalization of advertising agencies, concepts, and campaigns. *Economic Geography*, 71 (4), 402–425.

Levitt, (1983). *The Marketing Imagination*. London: Collier-Macmillan.

Luke, T.W. (1996). Identity, meaning and globalization: Detraditionalization in postmodern space–time compression. In P. Heelas, S. Lash and P. Morris (eds), *Detraditionalization: Critical Reflections of Authority and Identity* (pp. 109–133). Cambridge: Blackwell Publishers.

Luke, T.W. (1999). Simulated sovereignty, telematic territoriality: The political economy of cyberspace. In M. Featherstone and S. Lash (eds), *Spaces of Culture: City-Nation-World*. London: Sage.

Morley, D. (1992). *Television, Audiences and Cultural Studies*. London: Routledge.

Morley, D. and Robins, K. (1995). *Spaces of Identity: Global Media, Electronic Landscapes and Cultural Boundaries*. London: Routledge.

Nikefootball.com. The Geoforce. Available online at http://www.nikefootball.com/english/front/index.html.

Ohmae, K. (1990). *The Borderless World*. New York: HarperBusiness.

Perry, N. (1994). *The Dominion of Signs: Television, Advertising, and other New Zealand Fictions*. Auckland: Auckland University Press.

Pietersee, J.N. (1995). Globalization as hybridization. In M. Featherstone, S. Lash and R. Robertson (eds), *Global Modernities* (pp. 45–68). London: Sage.

Prendergrast, M. (1998). *For God, Country and Coca-Cola: The Unauthorized History of the Great American Soft Drink and the Company That Makes It*. New York: Touchstone Books.

Reich, R. (1991). *The Work of Nations: Preparing Ourselves for Twenty-first-Century Capitalism*. New York: Knopf.

Robins, K. (1990). Global local times. In J. Anderson and M. Ricci (eds), *Society and Social Science: A Reader* (pp. 196–205). Milton Keynes: Open University Press.

Robins, K. (1991). Tradition and translation: National culture in its global context. In J. Corner and S. Harvey (eds), *Enterprise and Heritage: Crosscurrents of National Culture* (pp. 21–44). London: Routledge.

Robins, K. (1997). What in the world's going on? In P.D. Gay (ed.), *Production of Culture/Cultures of Production* (pp. 11–66). London: The Open University Press.

Sassen, S. (2000). Whose city is it? Globalization and the formation of new claims. In F.J. Lechner (ed.), *The Globalization Reader* (pp. 70–76). Malden, MA: Blackwell Publishers.

Sloane, A. (1999). *Echo of Europe*. The New Zealand Herald, December 11.

Smith, A.D. (1991). *National Identity*. London: Penguin Books.

Tomlinson, J. (1999). *Globalization and Culture*. Cambridge: Polity Press.

Williams, R. (1983). *The Year 2000*. New York: Pantheon Books.

10 "I'm afraid of Americans"?

New Zealand's cultural resistance to violence in "globally" produced sports advertising

Andrew Grainger and Steven Jackson

I'm afraid of Americans
I'm afraid of the world
I'm afraid I can't help it
I'm afraid I can't

(David Bowie, "I'm Afraid of Americans," 1997)[1]

There seems to be a trend over the past couple of years, originating in America, to have increasingly violent and aggressive sport-shoe commercials and in our view they are inappropriate.

(Winston Richards, Executive Director of the New Zealand Television Commercial Approvals Bureau in 1995)[2]

Introduction

In 1997 singer David Bowie released the hit single "I'm Afraid of Americans." Although wryly described by Bowie himself as being "Not as hostile about Americans as [Bruce Springsteen's] '*Born in the USA*'" (cited in Anon., 2000), the song could be read as a none-too-subtle expression of both trepidation and open hostility toward the purported trappings of American society and its attendant popular cultures. For Bowie – or more precisely the xenophobic "character" through which his narrative unfolds – while America offers the rich promises of freedom, individuality, and success (*No one needs anyone . . . Johnny looks up at the stars*), he actually sees cultural imposition, conformity, and moral decline (*God is an American . . . Johnny wants pussy and cars*). Thus, despite its allure, contemporary America is seen to be a site which evokes cultural apprehension – a warning sign to the dangers posed by commercialism without restriction.

While such sentiments are perhaps, at one and the same time, extreme and ironic – especially given that Bowie continues to both influence, and be influenced by, American musicians – they, in part, reflect much wider fears about the possible threats posed by U.S. economic, political, and cultural dominance. With American media products in particular, and popular culture more generally, increasingly assuming global pre-eminence, the U.S. has ever more come to be seen as the corrosive driving-force of global homogenization – whether such a process is real or merely perceived to be so. This trepidation toward the encroachment of American culture is also symptomatic of broader concerns among a number of nations – at both the "core" and the "periphery" (Lash and Urry, 1994) of "global" culture – who presently confront the outcomes and effects of a world apparently distended from the confines of national or regional boundaries. Although the consequences of cultural, economic, and political globalization remain the subject of debate across a wide range of forums, what is undeniable is that an expanding network of new media and communications technologies – especially those relating to the televisual media – continue to effect a "compression" in the global flow of objects, images, and people (Harvey, 1989). In an era of satellite television, cable TV, e-mail, and transnational corporations, the global continues to increasingly meet the local, the national the international, and the domestic the foreign. And, although geography creates an immutable notion of distance, the ever-evolving technological complexity of contemporary society ensures that countries which had at one time seemed far removed from the global forum, now encounter an escalating range of transnational products and practices as their isolation in space and time diminishes.

However, while there is no doubt that globalizing forces have radically altered the economic, political, and social structures of modern culture, the question of just how globalization impacts on local cultural identity and experience nonetheless remains. Of specific concern in both political and popular realms is the potential threat posed by the expanded, and the sometimes seemingly unrestricted, access to "global" ideas, commodities and images which has been afforded by the rapid advancement of the global communications media. In particular, some critics have argued that unsanctioned cross-cultural consumption of global – more often specifically identified as, whether justified or not, American – products and practices may in fact threaten the political sovereignty and cultural uniqueness of local contexts. The rising tide of foreign media "commodities" which has accompanied the ascension of an American-dominated transnational media thus provides a clear target of critique for those who see "imported culture" as a corrosive force which threatens both cultural autonomy and the assumed integrity of national identity.

One such commodity, which has emerged to become a global focus for such national deliberation and nation state policy debate, is media violence. From cartoons to dramas, from movies to the nightly news, popular representations of violence continue to be scrutinized and criticized by parents, scholars, and "official" censors alike. Significantly, a notable feature of these critiques has been a proclivity toward associating media violence with television, cinema, and advertising originating from the U.S.A.[3] While such an expressed concern with violence in Hollywood cinema and television is typical of numerous national contexts, the small South Pacific nation of New Zealand has increasingly emerged as one of the most fervent critics of "American" media commodities. In fact, New Zealand is rapidly gaining a reputation for upholding one of, if not the, most conservative – and arguably hypocritical and contradictory – state broadcast policies with respect to media violence (Watson and Shuker, 1998; Weaver, 1996).

There is perhaps no better illustration of New Zealand's cautious approach to the censorship of media violence than the country's regulation of television advertising. Numerous bans by local censorship bodies have made it patently clear that violence in advertising remains a sensitive issue – in fact, with a few notable exceptions, it appears to be almost entirely unacceptable. This has been particularly true in the area of athletic shoe commercials and sport-related advertising where, in the past decade, no less than six sport-related commercials have either been officially banned and/or voluntarily withdrawn due to rulings citing the issue of violence. The fact that most, if not all, of these advertisements were judged to be acceptable for continued screening in other countries (such as the U.S.A. and Australia) demonstrates the complexity of the localized consumption of global cultural artifacts. Moreover, the bans reveal that it is insufficient to assume that local cultures will necessarily passively accept the results of transnational production. Thus, it is essential to realize that the process of globalization has created not only cooperation and consensus (or at the extreme, *homogenization*), but has simultaneously stimulated conflict, disagreement, and resistance.

The prohibition of violent, "American"-produced sport-themed advertising in New Zealand represents just one example of such an opposition, and this contested terrain of power, politics, and contradiction in New Zealand can therefore serve as a useful site for analyzing what Appadurai (1990) terms as a global/local *disjuncture* in the contemporary flow of transnational commodities and practices. Hence, in this chapter we provide case studies of several sport-related advertisements banned from New Zealand television screens (because they were deemed to be excessively violent) as a means to illustrate and discuss the politics and contradictions associated with state policy censorship as located within wider debates about Americanization, globalization, and global/local disjuncture. After initially outlining the context of state media policy in New Zealand – including the codes and responsibilities of the two key censorship bodies, the Advertising Standards Authority (ASA) and the Advertising Standards Complaints Board (ASCB) – we aim to show how the bans imposed against several American-produced commercials not only reflect the incongruity and uncertainty of Appadurai's (1990) notion of disjuncture, but further, disguise efforts to demarcate a unique national "identity" in a time of growing intercultural connection.

Global flows, local incongruity: globalization, advertising, and disjuncture

Before beginning any specific analysis, it is worth noting that, while there are numerous examples of the more subtle cultural and linguistic discrepancies and disjunctures that have occurred when global advertisers attempt to locate themselves in local contexts (see, e.g. Howes, 1996; Solomon, 2001), points of vari-

ation and opposition are also often the result of official, state-sanctioned practices. For example, disjunctures frequently emerge as a consequence of differences in legislation and policy between local and global contexts (see de Mooij,
1998; Myers, 1999). A recent example in New Zealand was seen when the local
Ministry of Health began investigating whether the touring Indian cricket team
was breaching local smoke-free legislation by wearing the logo of a cigarette
manufacturer on their bats and uniforms (Stink over logo on gear, January 11,
1999: A4). Although legal advice led the Ministry to abandon the possibility of
prosecution (Smoke-free logo row stubbed out, January 16, 1999: A5), the case
highlights how local policy, legislation, and regulation still provide a way of dif-
ferentiating cultural or political distinctiveness in the global climate.

In broadcasting, these types of divergencies in regulation between global
point-of-origin and local point-of-consumption have been more commonly suggested in variations on the issue of media censorship. This has been particularly
true in relation to media violence where "various countries have come to different conclusions about what should be permitted and at what time it should be
broadcast" (Watson and Shuker, 1998: 168). As noted above, the regulation of
violence *in advertising* can also differ according to national context. For
instance, a recent advertisement for the U.S.-based apparel manufacturer Nike
featuring the company's celebrity soccer endorsers skirmishing with "forces from
hell" (Jensen, 1996: 58), screened regularly on ESPN soccer broadcasts in the
U.S.A., while the same commercial was banned in a number of other countries
because it was judged to be excessively violent by local regulators (Jensen,
1996). The reaction to this commercial reinforces how, despite the expansion
of transnational markets and the growth of cross-cultural image industries, the
reception of global products and services still remains largely dependent on the
historical, political, economic, and cultural specificities of local contexts (Hall,
1991; Lash and Urry, 1994). The acceptance of international commodities and
images is therefore far from uncritical. Similarly, global advertising, driven
largely by American multinationals, may be misunderstood, misinterpreted, or
even subjected to officially sanctioned forms of cultural resistance, when
released in localized settings.

Fearing the foreign? Deregulation and the contemporary New Zealand mediascape

The bans imposed against several sport-related advertisements in New Zealand
provide clear examples of such instances. That is, they demonstrate how global
advertisers may be forced to confront varying forms of public and political resistance at, and within, local cultural boundaries. In the remaining sections of this
chapter, we wish to examine two of these bans in greater detail, as a means to
demonstrate just how complex and contradictory this local consumption can
be, and to illustrate the importance of understanding how particular cultural
values and media regulation impact on the global/local nexus of sport marketing. However, in order to fully understand those global/local disjunctures which

relate to sport, violence and advertising in New Zealand, it is important to first outline the economic, cultural, and political conditions from which these instances of cultural resistance have emerged. Understanding the rapid changes confronting the contemporary media is particularly important in the New Zealand case for, as Hutchison and Lealand (1996: 7) have argued, in the relatively few years since deregulation in 1989, the New Zealand mediascape has "witnessed a . . . revolutionary reshaping . . . that is unprecedented in the rest of the world." Most significantly, there has been a nearly complete conversion of the state-controlled, public service-oriented television network to a fully commercial, market-driven system (Atkinson, 1994). In addition, the number of potential television channels – even when excluding those on the new Sky Satellite system – leapt from two in 1984 to twenty-one in 1999 (Farnsworth, 1996; Smith, 1996). Consequently, over the past decade, New Zealand has seen a fourfold increase in the number of hours broadcast on network television alone (Farnsworth, 1996; Smith, 1996; Watson and Shuker, 1998).

Deregulation may be seen to be of particular importance because it meant that Television New Zealand (TVNZ), the state-owned and operated television network (formerly the New Zealand Broadcasting Corporation), became a State-Owned Enterprise (SOE). In effect, this required, as it still does, TVNZ to be operated as a for-profit business with the expectation of an annual return to its primary stakeholder, the New Zealand government. However, in tandem with this fiscal responsibility, TVNZ was also charged with ensuring that its programming continue to reflect and develop New Zealand's culture and identity (Butterworth, 1989; Spicer et al., 1996). Perhaps not surprisingly, the result is an inherent tension between TVNZ's need to seek and generate capital and its mandate to represent and cultivate New Zealand culture. These seemingly, though not necessarily, mutually exclusive objectives have become increasingly difficult to balance in a domestic deregulated market which has suspended rules concerning foreign ownership and, in addition, produced a need for – and, arguably, a dependence on – increased foreign programming.

The reinvention of TVNZ as an SOE, the emergence of new television networks (including satellite television), and the need for more imported programming has, in turn, raised concerns about both the quantity and quality of New Zealand television (Bell, 1996; Lealand, 1991). In relation to domestic content in particular, growing criticism has been levied at the fact that, while the amount of local programming has doubled since the mid-1980s (due to the rise in the number of channels and extended broadcasting hours), local content as a proportion of total programming has actually dropped (Farnsworth, 1996). With local content declining, imported television has begun to dominate New Zealand screens, and, in a further trend, while the country once looked to Britain for its programming, in recent years there has been a considerable shift toward imports of American origin – over two-thirds of all imported programming is now from the U.S.A. (Laidlaw, 1999; Smith, 1996). Furthermore, the emergence of satellite television in New Zealand looks set to increase the amount of American content on New Zealand screens with new programming options being dominated by U.S. cable channels such as ESPN, HBO, and CNN.

With the tide of foreign programming in New Zealand rising rapidly, the perceived consequences of "Americanization" or "commercialization" – and the potential threats they may pose to local culture and identity – have begun to receive increasing attention from socially concerned critics of New Zealand broadcasting. Certainly, retaining some form of cultural identity on the small screen has become a critical issue to those who see local television as an "independent window" through which to reflect New Zealand society (Smith, 1996). Television is seen by many to be a significant communicator of New Zealand's national identity, and foreign, and more specifically American, programming is consequently viewed as perhaps the greatest threat to the cultural uniqueness of the medium. As local television critic Keith Harrison puts it:

> We, as a tiny country and as a vulnerable and isolated island people, must cling to a system which will help keep our identity and hold the predators of the world at bay ... we are in danger of being swamped ... by imported soaps and dramas of the most vacuous kind, with the great majority coming from the United States
>
> (Harrison, 1999: 74)

Harrison's comments also allude to the fact that it is not only the mere *quantity* of imports that has seen critics decrying a growth in foreign programming: rather, issues of *quality* have also been at the forefront of apprehensive analyses of the changing nature of New Zealand television. Judging by the volume of public debate, one of the main concerns about the content of local programming is the level of violence (Watson and Shuker, 1998; Weaver, 1996). Such fears are demonstrated both in the existence of media watchdog organizations, such as the campaign lobby group Media Aware, and by the establishment of official agencies responsible for developing and administering codes of practice that relate to violence. These latter organizations have been charged with overseeing the development and enforcement of broadcasting codes and policy directed toward maintaining "acceptable" standards for television programming. Two such examples – and it is noteworthy that the policies of both agencies each feature specific codes addressing the subject of violence – include the Broadcasting Standards Authority (BSA), which is responsible for the regulation of general television programming in New Zealand, and the Advertising Standards Authority (ASA), which administers similar codes for advertising.

Obviously, with the regulation of advertising in New Zealand being the focus of this chapter, the emphasis here is on the workings of the latter of these agencies, the ASA – the advertising industry's self-regulatory body. Consisting of members from both advertising and media agencies, the ASA operates as a voluntary self-regulatory organization which attempts to maintain codes of practice that embody "a proper and generally acceptable standard of advertising" (ASA, 1998: 9). The advertisers, advertising agencies, television programmers, radio stations, newspapers, and magazines which form the ASA attempt to direct these standards through the development, alteration, and administration of the Advertising Codes of Practice. These codes are then enforced by the ASA's independent monitoring body, the Advertising Standards Complaints Board (ASCB).

Although it is the primary regulator of New Zealand advertising, with respect to procedure, the ASCB actually functions as the secondary censor of commercials screened on New Zealand television – before going on air, all advertisements are initially screened by the New Zealand Television Commercial Approvals Bureau (TVCAB). If accepted by the TVCAB, an advertisement is then rated, according to content, so that it can be aired at "appropriate" times (TVCAB, 1998). However, despite this screening process, once a commercial is aired it can still be challenged, and any member of the New Zealand public can lodge a formal complaint against an advertisement if they feel it breaches the ASCB's Codes of Practice. Complainants are required to submit a formal written objection, citing the specific code that they feel has been violated, to the ASCB. At this point the Board Chairperson makes a preliminary decision as to whether or not there is a sound basis for the complaint. If it is determined that there is, then the case is turned over to the Board (which comprises nine members, including the aforementioned Chair, four members of the public and four industry representatives) which then makes a decision to reject or uphold the complaint.

Over the past five years, sport-related advertisements have been at the center of a proportionally high number of complaints that have cited possible violations of one or all of the Rules from the ASCB's Code of Practice. Further, at least six of these commercials have either been banned from screening or later been voluntarily withdrawn by the advertiser. Significantly, while in each of these cases the justification given by the ASCB for the ban was that the commercial in question was excessively violent, another notable feature of these rulings is that the commercials, with only one exception, were produced in the U.S.A. for American multinationals. Thus, although the sanctions may reflect an enhanced appreciation – on the part of both the ASCB and members of the New Zealand public – of concerns surrounding media violence, the relationship of these prohibitions to the processes of Americanization and commercialization should also not be overlooked.

In the first instance, it is clear that media violence has been an unmistakable focus of local critiques of the American media – notably attacks on media violence are usually levied against Hollywood cinema, and, though rarely empirically verified, overwhelmingly American programs are assumed to contain the highest levels of gratuitous violence (see, e.g. Watson *et al.*, 1991). In addition, there is little doubt that the deregulation of New Zealand broadcasting in 1989 – which resulted in a marked increase in the level of American television imports – has added to these concerns, as well as raising new ones, about what New Zealanders are watching on their screens. While historically the vast majority of programs and advertisements on New Zealand television have been domestically produced, an increasingly open market has resulted in the emergence of more "global" commodities within the local "mediascape" (Appadurai, 1990) – and the majority of these have, of course, been American-produced. As we suggest, the response to this growing foreign influence has often been heightened by local concerns with the nature of imported programming and commercial messages. One way New Zealand has addressed these issues has been to establish formal agencies such as the ASA in order to maintain standards of acceptability with respect to television programming. Considering this context it could, therefore, be the case that the censorship of media violence may serve to conceal some of the broader issues surrounding the regulation of the global media. More specifically, it may be that the regulation of advertising in New Zealand is not only about sanctioning the use of violence, but rather it may be a useful means to obscure attempts, whether deliberate or otherwise, to reassert a local "identity" which some see as being threatened by foreign, predominantly American, cultural imports.

To examine such a proposition, we now present two specific examples of global/local disjuncture which relate to the prohibition of violence in sport-related commercials. In each case we refer to the specific advertisement which has been banned, the basis on which it was challenged, and, finally, how the ASCB subsequently arrived at its decision. In turn, we also highlight some of the politics, inconsistencies, and contradictions associated with these ASCB rulings. Ultimately, these disjunctures serve to highlight how global media products may be re-evaluated, misinterpreted or even actively resisted and challenged in local contexts, and how such opposition is often rife with contradiction and ambiguity. Moreover, while our analysis is obviously focused on the discrete context of contemporary New Zealand, we suggest that many of the issues examined here have implications for any number of "global locals." For, despite its relatively isolated geographic location, with new technologies making cultural borders increasingly permeable, New Zealand has been but one of many nations forced to confront a rising tide of transnational commodities and images. Hence, while we acknowledge the limitations of generalizability from a specific location, we contend that the case studies here are likely to be of interest to a wide number of national contexts.

Banning American violence? Sport-related commercials and the Advertising Standards Complaints Board

One of the first sport-related commercials to come before the ASCB was a 1994 Nike advertisement featuring a rugby football coach in the process of "psyching" up his team during a pre-game address. He implores his players to "visualize your opponent as your worst enemy. The person you absolutely despise the most . . . the absolute most." Occasionally cutting from the locker room, the narrative is interspersed with scenes of the players tackling the various people who supposedly represent their worst enemies. Among them are a traffic warden, former England cricketer Ian Botham, and a New Zealand "All Black" rugby player.[4]

The commercial ends with the players tackling a final "enemy" – the coach himself. As the screen fades to black, and the Nike "Just Do It" slogan appears, we hear him, in strained tones, telling his players that "You boys are quick learners."

The official ASCB ruling transcripts record that the complainants in this case maintained that not only did the commercial fail to convey the article being sold, but that it also could possibly incite violence, especially on the sports field. There appeared to be at least three aspects to their argument. First, a possible violation of the specific advertising code that addresses the offensive representation of violence.[5] Second, the advertisement is challenged because it does not explicitly feature the product for sale. And finally, they directly confront Nike by questioning the ambiguity of the company's "Just Do It" signature slogan (ASCB, 94/152).[6]

In its defense, Nike contended that the advertisement had received a favorable response both from the public and those directly involved in the game of rugby. More significantly, it also argued that it would not intentionally jeopardize its global profile by producing a violent commercial. As Nike maintained:

> [Nike] have an international reputation to uphold and all advertising produced is carefully scrutinised . . . in fact, we briefed the agency [American-based Wieden and Kennedy] to pay great attention to eliminating any foul play or violence from the advertisement.
>
> (ASCB, 94/152: 1)

However, the argument failed to sway the ASCB, which, while acknowledging that the advertisement was intended to be a "spoof," was firmly of the view that the representation of people being tackled (the majority of whom were not rugby players) was violent. ASCB was of the opinion that the combination of inciting phrases, coupled with tackling, was offensive. Furthermore, it asserted that there was general public concern with violence on and off the sports field and that this added to the inappropriateness of the commercial. Accordingly, the Board ruled that the commercial breached codes for offensive advertising and it was subsequently withdrawn.

Although only one of several sport-related advertisements prohibited from screening in New Zealand, this case is perhaps the most vivid example of just how strict local advertising regulations are with regard to the portrayal of violence. Certainly, it is evidence of wider efforts by local advertising censors to make it clear to advertisers that gratuitous violence of any form is unacceptable, regardless of the way it may be framed or presented. This notwithstanding, however, what may be more significant to note from this case is that, like several other Nike advertisements that have been the subject of complaint, the *Coach* commercial faced no restrictions in other countries in which it screened, including Australia and the U.S.A.. Thus, even when occurring on a regional basis between nations with seemingly very similar cultures (such as New Zealand and Australia), global advertising and marketing campaigns are still subject to local interpretation, legislation, and resistance (see also Grainger and Jackson, 1999; 2000).

The notion of cultural difference as expressed through the distinguishing of New Zealand as a uniquely regulated mediascape is perhaps more apparent – and, certainly, differences are even expressly suggested by the regulatory agencies involved – in a second case of the 1995 banning of a Reebok advertisement featuring former National Basketball Association (NBA) player Shawn Kemp. This particular case received more media attention than any other advertising ban to date, in part because the basis and justification for local censorship codes for violence were brought into question from several sources. The ensuing debate is also especially noteworthy because the vast majority of statements made by local advertising censors readily identify, indeed, accentuate, the assumed dissimilarities between New Zealand and other global markets – in terms of both broadcast audiences and their advertising standards. Moreover, the ban is significant because it not only reveals how notions of cultural difference (in this case, between the U.S.A. and New Zealand) can be expressed through media censorship, but it raises further questions about how commodified images of racial otherness may be implicated in disjunctures occurring at, and within, the global/local nexus of New Zealand.

Submitted to the TVCAB in June of 1995, the commercial in question was closely modeled on the popular video-game *Mortal Kombat*, and featured Kemp (at the time of the NBA's Seattle Supersonics) challenging an animated grim-reaper-like opponent to a game of one-on-one basketball. The advertisement opens as Kemp's antagonist issues the warning that "only those with super-human ability may enter [its] court." Responding to the challenge, Kemp replies "I got next." The reaper-figure then transforms into a large six-armed opponent as the confrontation begins. After Kemp's initial attempts to reach the basket are repelled by his imposing rival, he then secures a "bonus" in the form of a pair of Reebok sneakers. In his new "Kamikazes," Kemp is now able to get to the hoop and slam-dunk the ball over his opponent. He celebrates by delivering a loud "primal scream" which causes his adversary to disintegrate. As the picture dissolves to Reebok's trademark "planet," a computerized voice asks if viewers "dare to continue."

Before being released in New Zealand, the advertisement was first submitted to the TVCAB for screening consent and rating. However, upon reviewing the advertisement, the TVCAB concluded that the commercial failed to meet local broadcast standards. It was therefore banned from screening on New Zealand television before it even went on air, and thus no official complaint was ever made to the ASCB, and there was no need for a Complaints Board hearing. Nevertheless, because the ban motivated several sources to question New Zealand's advertising codes for violence, the case still garnered considerable media publicity. As the official transcript of the TVCAB ruling for this case was not available, these publicly recorded media reports help to surmise the basis of the decision-making process in this instance. One such example is an official memorandum sent by the TVCAB to Reebok New Zealand's advertising agency

MOJO. In it, TVCAB Executive Director Winston Richards explains the Approvals Bureau's position. As he states:

> [The TVCAB's] view, consistent with our previous decisions and with relevant determinations of the Advertising Standards Complaints Board, is that the level of aggression and violence are totally unacceptable in an advertisement for sports shoes . . . the basic concept of a shoe advertisement which turns basketball into a battle is likely to be unduly offensive to a significant section of the community.
>
> (Reebok commercial banned in New Zealand, 1995: 1)

Responding to Richards' statements during a panel discussion on a local television news segment (*Ralston*, TV3 News, June 19, 1995), Reebok New Zealand's Marketing Manager Jeremy O'Rourke maintained that, in contrast, Reebok felt that "in this instance . . . the commercial isn't any more violent than other commercials or programming which is currently on air and we've had similar types of advertising go to air in the past and we just feel there is an inconsistency here." However, Richards believed otherwise, countering that the commercial was in fact "extremely aggressive, and in [the TVCAB's] view violent, and we're quite sure that it does not meet the standards."

On closer examination, there are several interesting features surrounding the banning of the Kamikaze advertisement generally, and Richard's arguments more specifically. First, although the commercial was prohibited from screening on New Zealand television, it was approved for showing in local movie theaters. Such inconsistency was noted by Reebok New Zealand's General Manager Ian Fulton who felt that it seemed "so contradictory to have differing standards for cinema and television" (Reebok commercial banned in New Zealand, 1995: 1). Indeed, there are separate regulations concerning the screening of advertisements on television and in movie theaters. Such a policy seems somewhat misdirected given that the ban's assumed intent is to shield young audiences from unacceptable representations of violence. Of further note is the fact that the New Zealand Cinema Advertising Council is a member of the ASA. Hence, if the commercial had provoked a public complaint, then it would have been subject to review by the ASCB – the agency upon whose codes Richards' decision appears to be based.[7]

A second, and perhaps more pertinent, feature of the Kamikaze ban is that, although it is not stated in the official memorandum sent to Reebok, statements by Richards in later newspaper and television interviews allude to the "American" source of violence in advertising. For example, in an article appearing in one of New Zealand's prominent daily newspapers, he contended that "there seems to be a trend over the past couple of years, *originating in America*, to have increasingly violent and aggressive sport-shoe commercials, and, in our view, they are inappropriate" (Sport shoe advert ban stuns Reebok, 1995: 7, emphasis added). Similarly, when confronted during the aforementioned news segment with the fact that the Kamikaze commercial was playing successfully in almost every other Reebok market except New Zealand, Richards replied:

> It's an American commercial that is certainly played in America and Aus-
> tralia and, I presume, in other countries that accept American standards.
> But we are more conservative when it comes to violence than America ...
> and more conservative than Australia, and that is quite clearly spelled out
> in [Advertising Standards] Complaints Board decisions.
>
> (*Ralston*, TV3 News, June 19, 1995)

Richards thus not only targets the U.S.A. as a prominent source of advertising violence, but he also clearly demarcates New Zealand as different from both America and Australia with respect to local policy on the issue. When later questioned about Richards' comments, ASA Executive Director Glen Wiggs also agreed that American standards were "more liberal," but he was even more explicit in identifying American advertising and, indeed, the American media in general, as violent:

> We don't have problems with New Zealand produced ads being violent. . . .
> We [New Zealanders] aren't into violence. . . . It's an imported thing. *Viol-
> ence is recognized as an American thing.* . . . In the States, when you look at
> the TV programs . . . it's full of people shooting each other and killing each
> other ... very violent. And that reflects in the ads. The Reebok ad is
> typical of the way this comes through.
>
> (Wiggs, 1998, emphasis added)

Advertising standards and the contradictions of conservatism

Evident, then, from the comments of both Wiggs and Richards is the use of the term "conservative" to connote New Zealand's national censorship policy. Wiggs contends that this merely reflects broader social differences between the U.S.A. and New Zealand: "The differences between the U.S.A. and New Zealand advertising standards are more to do with our culture ... we're not into shooting people and things like that," he argues (Wiggs, 1998). Although Wiggs' argument may be undermined by the amount of violence on local cinema and television screens, the adoption of a conservative stance toward media violence is apparent among those directing the censorship of advertising in New Zealand. Moreover, this conservatism is not only evidenced at the level of official regulation, but also in the growth of public critiques of advertising in New Zealand. Indeed, the rapid rise in the number of public complaints made to formal regulatory bodies such as the ASCB has become a significant trend of New Zealand broadcasting in the decade since deregulation (Barclay, 1999: C7).

While the basis of such conservatism is certainly open to debate, some have suggested that both official bans and complaints made by members of the public are due in large part to the issue of "cultural sensitivity" (see Barclay, 1999; Goll, 1995). Notably, as the author of an *Asian Wall Street Journal* article examining New Zealand advertising standards in light of the Kamikaze ban suggested (Goll, 1995), some have argued that cultural sensitivity may itself have much to do with local concerns about the state of racial and ethnic relations in New Zealand. As Goll (1995, p. 1) remarks: "some observers relate New Zealand's advertising sensitivities to the country's recent struggle to compensate its indigenous Maori tribes for colonial-era abuses." When questioned as to how he believed the cultural sensitivity issue may affect the regulation of advertising, ASA Executive Director Wiggs also proposed that:

> While we [New Zealand] have barriers on sex and violence, where we have the biggest barrier . . . is in terms of race. We are very racially aware in this country. Therefore, you have got to be very careful with stereotypical portrayals of people. . . . That's our country. We're going through a time . . . of resolving the wrongs of the past . . . the Waitangi Tribunal [which hears Maori land and resource claims in New Zealand] and so on. . . . Everyone is trying to resolve it.
>
> (Wiggs, 1998)

Thus Wiggs uses a somewhat defensive tactic to explain and justify New Zealand's cultural sensitivity with respect to advertising. As part of that strategy, Wiggs identifies the relatively more enlightened, progressive, and fair treatment of "its indigenous people" compared to the U.S.A. and Australia. In light of such comments, it would therefore be neglectful to completely ignore the issue of race in examining the Kamikaze ban given that Shawn Kemp is an African American. While the possible global/local disjunctures related to the intersection of racial identity and the contemporary global media remain largely outside the scope and aim of this chapter, some commentary here is thus essential.

The global/local disjuncture of race: I'm afraid of (African) Americans?

In brief, the Kamikaze ban suggests that there may be a possibility of a global/local disjuncture within the context of the racialized sporting "other" in New Zealand. At this point it seems premature to make any conclusive statements. In fact, there is some evidence to suggest that African American athletes, as well as other aspects of African American popular culture – including music, fashion, and speech elements – are sources of fascination among New Zealand youth (Allison, 1991; Ihaka, 1993; Jackson and Andrews, 1996; 1999a; 1999b; Lealand, 1988, 1994). More specifically, the authors of a number of recent studies examining the popular presence of American sporting culture in New Zealand (see, e.g. Andrews *et al.*, 1996; Jackson and Andrews, 1996; 1999a; 1999b; Melnick and Jackson, 1998) have contended that, in addition to being attracted to the extraordinary talent of African American athletes, New Zealand youth are fascinated with the points of *difference* offered by African American culture (see also Andrews, 1997; Ihaka, 1993; Lealand, 1994). New Zealand journalist Jodi Ihaka (1993) has noted how this embracement of American culture, and African American culture in particular, has been especially strong among young indigenous Maori and Polynesians in New Zealand. She therefore argues that identification with African American culture suggests an added dimension to the notion of difference:

> For many young Maori . . . there's an extra appeal about the Black elements in the culture the U.S. is exporting. Perhaps there is special sympathy among Maori for another coloured minority, particularly for one that's had such a dramatic, desperate and highly publicized history.
>
> (Ihaka, 1993: 10)

Similarly, Leonard Wilcox (1996: 123) has also maintained that:

> Maori and Polynesian youth in New Zealand tend to identify with the music, dress, and styles of their African-American counterparts. There they find . . . a focal point of resistance, a means of challenging the hegemony of New Zealand's overwhelmingly white power structure through membership of a transnational tribe.

Thus, the consumption of American popular culture among Maori and Polynesian youth may not only be an expression of identification with what they perceive to be their oppressed, trans-Pacific brothers and sisters, but it may also reflect a more serious agenda of racial politics.

Perhaps it is this "black Pacific"[8] which is contributing to some of the unfounded and irrational fears about globalization which have been expressed by particular factions of the New Zealand community. It may be that concerns with issues such as media violence are being exacerbated by local articulations of "American" gang culture within Maori and Polynesian communities (Ihaka, 1993; Wall, 1997). The popular articulation of Maori identity with gangs is perhaps most clearly exemplified in Alan Duff's (1990) novel *Once Were Warriors*, which was later made into a movie (1994, Lee Tamahori dir.) of the same name. Both enjoyed widespread success in New Zealand, with the movie becoming the highest grossing film – inclusive of foreign imports – in New Zealand cinema history. The popularity of *Warriors* may be of particular significance because, as Wall (1997: 44) argues, the phenomenal success of the film version owed much to the fact that it employed "numerous stereotypes which situate Maori experience within the wider discourses of the Black Other." Taking such a social context into account, the ban imposed against the Kamikaze commercial could therefore potentially be interpreted as a form of resistance against threatening images of America, "constructed through the intersection of sport, technology, and commodified images of violence and racial otherness" (Jackson and Andrews, 1999a: 38–39; see also Andrews *et al.*, 1996: 437). In essence, it could be argued that, while the media afford New Zealanders an opportunity to become familiar with elements of African American culture, an attendant consequence may be that local audiences have embraced some of the "reactionary codes, mobilized by the popular media, that [have] conflated racial identity with criminal deviance" (Andrews, 1997: 74; see also Butler, 1993; Clarke, 1991; Feagin and Vera, 1995; Giroux, 1994; Staples and Jones, 1985; Van Dijk, 1987; Wall, 1997; Wilcox, 1996).

One potential consequence, as Wilcox (1996) argues, is that African American culture in New Zealand may serve as a potential target for racial hostility that may otherwise be directed toward other indigenous minorities; in some sense, the African American may:

> [stand] in "generically," for the racial "other" in New Zealand. . . . On the one hand, this articulation deflects and codes racial hostility in ways that are more socially acceptable (hostility toward Maori can be expressed by racial proxy). On the other hand, given the strong connection between Maori and black rap culture, racial hostility against African-Americans . . . can readily be decoded and read as displaced hostility toward Maori.
>
> (Wilcox, 1996: 132)

While Wilcox refers to a wide range of cultural representations which appropriate images of colonialism and reinforce notions of blackness and whiteness, the concept of racial proxy could well play some role in the Kamikaze ban. The challenging of more overt images of racial otherness – such as the physicality of an African American basketballer – could act as a way of deflecting wider cultural apprehensions associated with the "prospect of a new bicultural or multi-ethnic society" (Wilcox, 1996: 132). Obviously, further research is necessary in order to more fully appreciate the potential links between local media censorship and the perceived threats of the racialized other. Nonetheless, while such an issue is undoubtedly complex, it is apparent that resistance to, or censorship of, African American popular culture functions to marginalize the identities of particular minorities or racial/ethnic groups, particularly those of Maori and Polynesian youth.[9]

Conclusion: Conservatism, contradiction and New Zealand advertising standards

Despite a set of established criteria for judging the acceptability of advertising in New Zealand, there seems to be little consistency with respect to either public perceptions, or the application, of rules governing advertising violence. Certainly, there are a number of unanswered questions with respect to the decision-making processes of the agencies involved in the regulation of advertising in New Zealand. For instance, there appears to be some contradiction between banning some advertisements for "commodities" such as athletic apparel on the basis of violence while permitting trailers or promos for violent television programs or movies to be shown (albeit often in late or "adult" viewing hours). Moreover, given the amount of profanity and violence that appears on New Zealand television in other televisual formats, it seems strange that advertising has been the target of such a high level of regulation and critique. Yet, in spite of any inconsistency, it is our argument here that the advertising bans examined in this chapter may nonetheless be viewed as reflective of increasing local concerns about the escalating amount of foreign media imports circulating within the New Zealand mediascape. Given that New Zealand advertising standards are frequently demarcated, and indeed even justified, through reference to other countries – particularly the U.S.A. – there appears to be a complex relationship between the bans and the processes and practices of both globalization and its seemingly more identifiable relation, Americanization. In the Kamikaze ban, for instance, New Zealand regulators define their standards as being "more conservative" than their American equivalents. Moreover, not only do they see local codes as more stringent than in the U.S.A., they further allude to America being the "source" of media violence. Hence, whether intended or not, New Zealand advertising regulation and policy has acted as a means by which the country has marked its own mediascape as unique from other cultural contexts. Advertising as a medium in itself – and, more importantly, its perceived centrality to the spread of American commercial and popular cultures – may also play a significant role in the bans. With New Zealand television having been advertising-free in its nascent years of the 1960s, the opposition to advertising may be symbolic of attempts to resist the emergence of some of the less desirable consequences of commercial television and the deregulation of New Zealand broadcasting.[10] Certainly, given both the contemporary and historical U.S. dominance of the commercial media (see Hall, 1991; Herman and McChesney, 1997; Tunstall, 1977), it would not be entirely surprising if American advertising came to be associated with such profit-oriented restructuring, and, subsequently, advertising may become a visible target for local opposition.

Obviously, such an argument should not be overstated, given that the vast majority of foreign advertisements go on air on New Zealand television without complaint – and only a small number of these commercials have ever been banned. Yet, it could be argued that it is only those commercials which are more likely to arrest viewer attention – often those appropriating images of violence – that are consequently challenged. That is, those practices which most visibly denote U.S.-initiated capitalistic intemperance – for example, the incursion of advertising into a limitless number of cultural spaces and the commodification of violence – may more readily become points of contention for those seeking to mediate the potential threats of American cultural products. Hence, advertisements which embody the more recognizable (mediated) impressions of what America "means" (violent, excessive; see Bogart, 1995; Butler, 1993; Leonard, 1997) are more likely to attract attention or be resisted. If advertising faces opposition because it is perceived to represent the intemperance of American capitalism, then, by extension, it seems probable that those commercials which most clearly denote the supposed excesses of American culture are, in turn, more liable to be the subject of complaint.

It may therefore be that New Zealand's cultural resistance to violent globally produced sports advertisements represents just one way in which it has responded to concerns about the ascendancy of American popular culture. Much the same as its position on nuclear arms, it is possible that the banning of specific globally, and primarily American, produced commercials may denote an expression of the "David and Goliath" stance often adopted by New Zealand toward political, economic, and cultural superpowers such as the U.S.A. (Grainger and Jackson, 1999; 2000). Thus, it may be that the media violence issue – whether intentionally or otherwise – serves to obscure attempts to reaffirm a local "identity" which some see as threatened by global media flows emanating primarily from the U.S.A.

While such a contention is obviously open to debate, regardless of the extent – if at all – to which the focus on media violence conceals efforts to demarcate a distinct "New Zealand" identity, such disjunctures in the global–local flow nonetheless reveal that it is too simplistic to assume that all nations will necessarily passively accept the artifacts of any potential global cultural impetus. Although some have claimed that the hyper-circulation of American commodity signs is contributing to the emergence of globally shared patterns of cultural existence,[11] the regulation of sport-related advertisements in New Zealand underscores that, in the context of globalization, there still remain opportunities for nations to do more than accede to the decisions of transnational marketing. As this example attests, in any specific local mediascape, domestic media, traditions, language, and regulation "still play key, often predominant, roles in determining the media culture" (Herman and McChesney, 1997: 9).

However, New Zealand's ambivalent relationship to media violence also affirms how the global/local relationship often embodies contradictory positions on the part of local cultures. For instance, the popularity of Nike in New Zealand – just as it is elsewhere, Nike's trademark "swoosh" has a seemingly ubiquitous presence in this small nation – reveals that although local contexts may covet the benefits of capitalism, its attendant consequences (such as a violent television commercial) are often seen as less desirable. Likewise, such a notion is certainly evident in the regulation of the New Zealand mediascape where, at the same time that advertising regulators were pointing to the American source of violence in marketing, more Hollywood television filled local screens than ever before (Allison, 1991; Lealand, 1991, 1994; Smith, 1996). Furthermore, there is some evidence to suggest that racial, and more precisely African American, identity serves as a means through which such ambiguous global/local disjunctures may be manifested – while several scholars have proposed that African American athletes, and other facets of African American culture, remain an important source of appeal in New Zealand, the banning of the Reebok Kamikaze commercial featuring Shawn Kemp intimates that some New Zealanders may be somewhat resistant to more overt images of African American otherness.

By way of conclusion, we would therefore suggest that future analyses may benefit by considering these types of instances in which national contexts appear to be simultaneously attracted – if not dedicated – and opposed to the products and practices of American popular culture. Moreover, because both Americanization, and globalization more generally, are not unitary processes, and the form and extent of each are "dependent upon political structures and forces which are specific to national and local states" (Street, 1997: 82), there is also a need to consider how the differing forms and degrees of societal participation in the global cultural economy affect the process of globalization and "make difference[s] to its precise form" (Robertson, 1990: 27). While it is certainly obvious that a single message is not always applicable on a global scale, "because there is not one global culture comprised of people with identical values" (de Mooij, 1998: 61), there is a need to understand the personal and collective politics which underlie the definition and assertion of such cultural standards, expectations, and identities among a wide number of "global locals." Through such cross-cultural endeavors it may be possible to explicate how global or universal conditions may coexist within the differential, the specific, and the personal experiences of the local. By analyzing the localized, and obviously highly politicized, spaces in which global production and local consumption take place, such research may better enable us to understand the complex dynamics which contribute to coincident embracement of, and resistance to, American popular culture.

References

Advertising Standards Authority (ASA) (1998). *Advertising Codes of Practice*. Wellington, New Zealand: Advertising Standards Authority Inc.

Allison, P. (1991). Big Macs and baseball caps: The Americanisation of Auckland. *Metro, 124*, 124–130.

Andrews, D.L. (1997). The (Trans)National Basketball Association: American commodity-sign culture and global–local conjuncturalism. In A. Cvetkovich and D. Kellner (eds), *Articulating the Global and the Local: Globalization and Cultural Studies* (pp. 72–101). Boulder, CO: Westview Press.

Andrews, D.L., Carrington, B., Mazur, Z. and Jackson, S.J. (1996). Jordanscapes: A preliminary analysis of the global popular. *Sociology of Sport Journal, 13*, 428–457.

Ang, I. (1996). *Living Room Wars: Rethinking Media Audiences for a Postmodern World*. London: Routledge.

Anon. (2000). *David Bowie: Biography*. Available online at http://artists.vh1.com/vh1/artists/ai_bio.jhtml?ai_id=973.

Appadurai, A. (1990). Disjuncture and difference in the global cultural economy. *Theory, Culture and Society, 7*, 295–310.

Atkinson, J. (1994). The "Americanisation" of One Network News. *Australasian Journal of American Studies, 13* (1), 1–26.

Barclay, C. (1999). Upholding the nation's complaints. *Sunday Star-Times*, April 4, p. C7.

Bell, C. (1996). *Inventing New Zealand: Everyday Myths of Pakeha Identity*. Auckland, New Zealand: Penguin Books.

Bogart, L. (1995). *Commercial Culture: Media Systems and the Public Interest*. New York: Oxford University Press.

Butler, J. (1993). Endangered/endangering: Schematic racism and white paranoia. In R. Gooding-Williams (ed.), *Reading Rodney King: Reading Urban Uprising* (pp. 15–22). New York: Routledge.

Butterworth, R. (1989). The media. In D. Novitz and W. Willmott (eds), *Culture and Identity in New Zealand* (pp. 142–159). Wellington: GP Books.

Clarke, S.A. (1991). Fear of a black planet. *Socialist Review*, 21 (2), 37–59.

de Mooij, M. (1998). *Global Marketing and Advertising: Understanding Cultural Paradoxes*. Thousand Oaks, CA: Sage.

Duff, A. (1990). *Once Were Warriors*. Auckland, New Zealand: Tandem Press.

Farnsworth, J. (1996). New Zealand advertising agencies: Professionalisation and cultural production. *Continuum: The Australian Journal of Media and Culture*, 10 (1), 136–151.

Feagin, J.R. and Vera, H. (1995). *White Racism: The Basics*. New York: Routledge.

Gilroy, P. (1993). *The Black Atlantic: Modernity and Double Consciousness*. London: Verso.

Giroux, H. (1994). *Disturbing Pleasures: Learning Popular Culture*. New York: Routledge.

Goll, S.D. (1995). New Zealand bans Reebok, other ads it deems politically incorrect for TV. *Asian Wall Street Journal*, July 24, p. 1.

Grainger, A. and Jackson, S. (1999). Resisting the swoosh in the Land of the Long White Cloud. *Peace Review*, 11 (4), 511–516.

Grainger, A. and Jackson, S. (2000). Sports marketing and the challenges of globalization: A case study of cultural resistance in New Zealand. *International Journal of Sports Marketing and Sponsorship*, 2 (2), 111–125.

Hall, S. (1991). The local and the global: Globalization and ethnicity. In A. King (ed.), *Culture, Globalization and the World-System*. London: Macmillan.

Harrison, K. (1999). Political threat to cultural flagship. *Otago Daily Times*, January 30, p. 74.

Harvey, D. (1989). *The Condition of Postmodernity: An Enquiry into the Origins of Cultural Change*. Oxford: Blackwell.

Herman, E.S. and McChesney, R.W. (1997). *The Global Media: The New Missionaries of Corporate Capitalism*. London: Cassell.

Horrocks, R. (1996). Conflicts and surprises in New Zealand television. *Continuum: The Australian Journal of Media and Culture*, 10 (1), 50–63.

Howes, D. (ed.) (1996). *Cross-Cultural Consumption: Global Markets–Local Realities*. London: Routledge.

Hutchison, I. and Lealand, G. (1996). Introduction: A new mediascape. *Continuum: The Australian Journal of Media and Culture*, 10 (1), 7–11.

Ihaka, J. (1993). Why the kids wanna be Black. *Mana*, 3, 10–15.

Jackson, S.J. (1994). Gretzky, crisis, and Canadian identity in 1988: Rearticulating the Americanization of culture debate. *Sociology of Sport Journal*, 11 (4), 428–446.

Jackson, S.J. and Andrews, D.L. (1996). Excavating the (Trans) National Basketball Association: Locating the global/local nexus of America's world and the world's America. *Australasian Journal of American Studies*, 15, 57–64.

Jackson, S.J. and Andrews, D.L. (1999a). Between and beyond the global and the local: American popular sporting culture in New Zealand. *International Review for the Sociology of Sport*, 34 (1), 31–42.

Jackson, S.J. and Andrews, D.L. (1999b). The globalist of them all: The Everywhere

Man, Michael Jordan and American popular culture in New Zealand. In R. Sands (ed.), *Global Jocks: Anthropology, Sport and Culture* (pp. 99–117). Westport, CT: Greenwood Press.

Jensen, J. (1996). Reebok, Nike shuffle execs as "Evil" lurks. *Advertising Age*, April 1, pp. 4, 58.

Kayatekin, S. and Ruccio, D. (1998). Global fragments: Subjectivity and class politics in discourses of globalization. *Economy and Society*, 27 (1), 74–96.

Kong, L. (1999). Globalization, transmigration and the renegotiation of ethnic identity. In K. Olds, P. Dicken, P.F. Kelly, L. Kong, and H. Wai-chung Yeung (eds), *Globalization and the Asia-Pacific: Contested territories* (pp. 219–237). London: Routledge.

Laidlaw, C. (1999). *Rights of Passage: Beyond the New Zealand Identity Crisis*. Auckland, New Zealand: Hodder Moa Beckett.

Lash, S. and Urry, J. (1994). *Economies of Signs and Space*. London: Sage.

Lealand, G. (1988). *A Foreign Egg in our Nest? American Popular Culture in New Zealand*. Wellington, New Zealand: Victoria University Press.

Lealand, G. (1991). Selling the airwaves: Deregulation, local content and television audiences in New Zealand. *Media Information Australia*, 62, 68–73.

Lealand, G. (1994). American popular culture and emerging nationalism in New Zealand. *National Forum: The Phi Kappa Phi Journal*, 74 (4), 34–37.

Leonard, J. (1997). *Smoke and Mirrors: Violence, Television, and Other American Cultures*. New York: New Press.

Melnick, M. and Jackson, S.J. (1998). The villain as reference idol: Selection frequencies and salient characteristics among New Zealand teenagers. *Adolescence*, 33 (131), 543–554.

Myers, G. (1999). *Ad Worlds: Brands, Media, Audiences*. London: Arnold.

Reebok commercial banned in New Zealand (1995). Reebok New Zealand press release, June 19. Auckland, New Zealand: Reebok New Zealand.

Richards, W. (1998). Personal communication with author, November 3.

Robertson, R. (1990). Mapping the global condition: Globalization as the central concept. *Theory, Culture and Society*, 7, 15–30.

Smith, P. (1996). *Revolution in the Air!* Auckland, New Zealand: Addison Wesley Longman New Zealand.

Smoke-free logo row stubbed out (1999). *The New Zealand Herald*, January 16, p. A5.

Solomon, M.R. (2001). *Consumer Behavior: Buying, Having and Being* (5th edn). Upper Saddle River, NJ: Prentice Hall.

Spicer, B., Powell, M. and Emanuel, D. (1996). *The Remaking of Television New Zealand 1984–1992*. Auckland, New Zealand: Auckland University Press.

Sport shoe advert ban stuns Reebok (1995). *The Dominion*, June 20, p. 7.

Staples, R. and Jones, T. (1985). Culture, ideology and black television images. *The Black Scholar*, 16 (3), 10–20.

Stink over logo on gear (1999). *The New Zealand Herald*, January 11, p. A4.

Street, J. (1997). "Across the universe": The limits of global popular culture. In A. Scott (ed.), *The Limits of Globalization: Cases and Arguments* (pp. 75–89). London: Routledge.

Television Commercial Approvals Bureau (1998). *The Role of the Television Commercial Approvals Bureau*. Auckland, New Zealand: Television Commercial Approvals Bureau.

Tunstall, J. (1977). *The Media are American*. London: Constable.

Van Dijk, T. (1987). *Communicating Racism: Ethnic Prejudice in Thought and Talk*. Newbury Park, CA: Sage.

Wall, M. (1997). Stereotypical constructions of the Maori "race" in the media. *New Zealand Geographer*, 53 (2), 40–45.

Watson, C. and Shuker, R. (1998). *In the Public Good?: Censorship in New Zealand*. Palmerston North, New Zealand: The Dunmore Press.

Watson, C., Bassett, G., Lambourne, R. and Shuker, R. (1991). *Television Violence: An Analysis of the Portrayal of "Violent Acts" on the Three New Zealand Broadcast Channels During the Week of 11th–17th February 1991*. Palmerston North, New Zealand: Massey University Educational Research and Development Centre.

Weaver, K. (1996). The television and violence debate in New Zealand: Some problems of context. *Continuum: The Australian Journal of Media and Culture*, 10 (1), 64–75.

Wiggs, G. (1998). Personal communication with author, October 20.

Wilcox, L. (1996). Saatchi rap: The "worlding of America" and racist ideology in New Zealand. *Continuum: The Australian Journal of Media and Culture*, 10 (1), 121–135.

11 Cursed or carefree?

Menstrual product advertising and the sportswoman

Annemarie Jutel

Menstruation has oft been considered an impediment to participation in sport. Medical doctors, educators and women themselves believed, and in many cases, still believe, that women cannot, or should not, engage in vigorous physical activity or sporting competitions during their menses.[1] Menstrual product advertisements, however, responded to this "problem," offering what they claimed to be solutions that would open doors to women's fulfillment in both sporting and social settings. However, I argue that the responses these companies offered did not set women free, but rather crystallized social beliefs about the limiting nature of female biology. I will explore how menstrual product advertising historically contributed to women's physical inactivity from their conception in the early 1900s, through to the 1960s by reproducing fragile femininity incompatible with vigorous sporting endeavors, by portraying menstruation as a pathological condition, and by emphasizing the taboo nature of menstruation.

I will also explore how contemporary menstrual product advertisements reproduce menstruation as a restrictive experience. In the early twenty-first century, women can purchase menstrual products with names such as Libra, Carefree, and Stayfree – conjuring up images of freedom and the potential for a vast number of experiences, presumably including vigorous physical exertion. This chapter demonstrates how contemporary advertisements, although different in style and content, and despite allusions to freedom and liberation, resituate menstruation as a problematic event. Menstruation is socially, rather than biologically, problematic in these contemporary advertisements, but with similarly restrictive consequences. Although these advertisements no longer focus on the pathological nature of menstruation, they promote discourses of restraint, control, and caution. This results in strictly coded rules of feminine behavior that highlight the female body and its social expectations at the expense of embodied physicality.

To develop my argument, I analyze a series of menstrual product advertisements from the New Zealand and Australian women's press in the context of concomitant social and medical beliefs about menstruation. I examine the discursive and symbolic content of these commercial proclamations to identify historical and social continuities relating to women's potential for engagement in physical activity.

Historical background

Despite a marketing bent that described disposable menstrual products as the "modern" emancipating method for dealing with the "problem" of monthly periods, such products are not new; only the commercialization thereof may be considered a modern phenomenon. Egyptian women used softened papyrus as tampons, while in the fifth century BC Hippocrates described a tampon made of lint wrapped around a piece of wood (Bailey, n.d.). Ancient Japanese women used paper tampons, Romans soft wool. African and Australian Aboriginal women used grass or vegetable fiber dressings to capture their menstrual flow. The first commercially available pads were gauze-covered cotton pads produced by Johnson & Johnson in 1896. French nurses during the First World War were impressed with the absorbency of a cellulose pad from which surgical dressings were made, and used it instead of the cloth towels to which they were accustomed (Delaney *et al.*, 1976). Kimberly-Clark, Johnson & Johnson, Scott Paper Products, the Mene Towel Company, and Southalls' Towels were among the industry leaders in the commercial production of disposable products. These pads were either pinned to underpants, slipped into rubber pants, or held in place with a sanitary belt – a simple elastic belt with two garter-like straps to hold the napkin securely in place between the legs. By the 1920s, commercially mass-produced menstrual products were readily available, though as late as the 1970s, many middle-class women in New Zealand were still washing reusable cotton toweling – far later than their counterparts in most Western countries. In the USA, many women were using disposable products as early as the 1920s, and in France, by the 1960s, few women still used washable rags (Jutel, 1998). In the early 1970s, there was an increase in the type and variety of disposable menstrual products, with the advent of sticky tape on the underside of the pad that anchored it to the panty, and of light pads, or panty liners (Berg and Block Coutts, 1994).

Advertisements for these products, not surprisingly, reflected popular beliefs about how women should behave and in which activities they should engage. This is an example of what Wernick (1991) describes as the ideological content of advertising: the deep bias toward conventional and widely diffused social beliefs in the attempt to sell products. Twentieth-century menstrual product advertisements reflected a deep-rooted social belief in menstruation as a barrier to exercise. They achieved this by representing menstruation as a handicap or an illness, by accentuating feminine frailty, and by appropriating feminine physicality. They proclaimed that women required extraneous support – mass-produced menstrual protection – in order to achieve active goals.

This approach was not isolated from a larger social context. For centuries, and indeed up to the present time, health care professionals have described menstruation as an illness, or dysfunctional state; one that variably has mandated withdrawal from, or reduction in, previous physical activities. Early Anglo-Saxons saw menstruation as a state of ill-health: *mōnaðādl* meant monthly illness and *mōnuðseōc*, monthly sickness (Burchfield, 1985; Waite,

2000). But, in more recent times, menstruation signaled not only the arrival of womanhood to women of the leisured class, but also a relegation to more sedate activities due to the havoc that the periods were presumed to wreak on the organism. In 1845, medical physician de l'Isère referred to menarche, or the onset of menstruation, as the "brilliant and stormy crisis," and attributed numerous disorders to menstruation: hysteria, catalepsy, convulsions, spasmodic disease, cardialgia, dyspnea, chlorosis, epistaxis, hematemesis, and a variety of febrile affections (de l'Isère, 1845: 31).

Galbraith (1903: 31) echoed de l'Isère's position, some fifteen years later, in a medical textbook entitled *The Four Epochs of a Woman's Life*:

> With the beginning of menstruation, the equilibrium of the body is very easily disturbed, so that even in the case of the healthy girls some precautions should be taken and a rational régime should be adhered to; while in the case of the delicate girl, a still more careful attention will have to be directed toward her weak points, in order that she may develop into a healthy woman.

Fear that the onset of the menses would bring heretofore-silent pathologies to the surface was a common theme. "The girl's whole system is in a ferment under the stealthy advance of the consciousness of sex," wrote Marion Harland (1882: 99) in a guidebook for young women. Medical doctor George Napheys (1871: 25) confirmed that "at this critical period, the seeds of hereditary and constitutional diseases manifest themselves. They draw fresh malignancy from the new activity of the system." He believed that tuberculosis, disfiguring skin diseases, insanity, and congenital epilepsy could surface at puberty due to the strain on the system produced by the onset of menstruation.

G. Black (n.d.) went so far as to use a euphemism of illness, or "being unwell" to refer to the menstrual periods. His diagnosis of pregnancy was based on the cessation of the menses, and he explains: "A woman who has been menstruating regularly up to the time of her marriage ceasing to be *unwell* shortly after, it is presumptive of her having conceived" (Black, n.d.: 225). Patricia Vertinsky (1994) concludes that Victorian approaches to feminine biology provided the foundation to the position of male medical doctors as the guardians of women's health and behavior. She explains that "doctors judged who was fit and who was not, with these judgements carrying implications of being fit or unfit for particular tasks, physical activities and certain types of sports" (Vertinsky, 1994: 41).

The treatment of menstruation as illness is not just historical. Contemporary anthropologist Elisabeth Martin (1987) has analyzed the medical and popular rhetoric surrounding menstruation in the late twentieth century. She conjectures that menstruation is perceived as illness because woman is seen as Other. Man, with his non-cyclical physiology, is the standard to which woman's function is compared. Deviation from this non-fluctuating model of normality constitutes malady. She concludes that vestiges of the image of menstruation as illness due to its deviant nature still pervade contemporary approaches to the female body: medical textbooks describe the menses in terms of failed conception, while conversely depicting aspects of male physiology in terms of marvel. Martin (1987: 47) writes:

> Perhaps one reason the negative image of failed production is attached to menstruation is precisely that women are in some sinister sense out of control when they menstruate. They are not reproducing, not continuing the species, not preparing to stay at home with the baby, not providing a safe, warm womb to nurture a man's sperm. I think it is plain that the negative power behind the image of failure to produce can be considerable when applied metaphorically to women's bodies.

Seeing menstruation as a dysfunction or illness provides a context for understanding the recommendation of restricted physical activity and limited engagement in sport for women that the menstrual product advertisers exploited to build their claims of feminine requirement for their products. Late nineteenth- and early twentieth-century medical people and physical educators made some challenges to the idea that complete withdrawal from physical activity was required of menstruating women. Many writers, both medical and lay, advised an abundance of fresh air and gentle occupations as a remedy to menstrual ills, but formally discouraged exertion, and by extension, sport. These views, and particularly their guarded tone, allowed menstrual product advertisers a useful window for the promotion of their products. If cautious activity was permitted, then menstrual product advertisers could posit their products as a support or solution without which exercise might be dangerous. Their proposed solution solidified the problematization of exercise for women.

At the turn of the century, Dr. Mary Wood-Allen (1913/1899: 145) wrote: "I do not want you to think yourself a semi-invalid ... I want you take care of yourself at all times, and especially during your menstrual periods." She advised young women to stay active, but she defined the type and intensity of activity quite strictly. Her explanation for the curtailment of sporting activities was purely mechanical. The uterus, she revealed, was engorged with blood both prior to, and during, menstrual periods. This engorgement rendered the loosely suspended organ very heavy. "It is easy to understand," she rationalized, "that long walks or severe exercise at the menstrual period will more easily cause it to sag" (Wood-Allen, 1913/1899: 145).

Another early female doctor, Mary Melendy (1904), also promoted "healthy" exercise in the open air for women, but drew the line at exercise during menstruation. She reminds her readers that "the system is more easily chilled at this time of the month than at any other, and when chilled, suppression results. Over-exertion has equally bad effects, leading to displacements" (Melendy, 1904: 306).

Eulalia Richards (1939), some decades later, advised young women to see menstruation as normal, but she, too, cautioned against excessive exercise. "The average girl would be wise to avoid competitive sport if possible during the first day or two of menstruation," she wrote in the *Ladies' Handbook of Home Treatment* (Richards, 1939: 695). While Richards attempts to convince her readers to consider menstruation as something other than a recurring illness, she provides so many prescriptions and recommendations as to make such consideration difficult (avoid cold baths, keep the feet warm and dry, avoid excessive exercise and constipation). She even describes depression, and "nervous irritability" (Richards, 1939: 695) as universal features of normal menstruation.

Menstrual product advertisements paralleled these beliefs about the nature and consequences of menstruation. Many advertisers referred to the menstrual period as a pathological condition, illness, injury, or state of debilitating dysfunction, that their products would alleviate. It is difficult to fathom how the products could fulfill this role, since further references are oblique and non-specific.

"Thousands of women suffer needless fear and pain because they still cling to old-fashioned unhygienic ways," preached advertisers for Camelia Sanitary Towels. Although the description of the product is quite practical (feather light, as absorbent as cotton wool), the eye-catching title reads "Banish Unnecessary Fear and Pain," and features the worried face of a young woman. It refers to menstruation as the "critical period" in much the same way as de l'Isère did eighty years earlier (*Mirror*, 1928). This advertisement situates menstruation in the context of pathology – both emotional and physical. The product, a simple disposable towel, is somehow linked to the irradication of both.

In contrast to Camelia, Southalls'[2] advertisements show active and apparently carefree women attempting to convey images of physicality; however, the text accompanying the image tells a different story. Despite the image of health, it identifies menstruation as an infirmity, and refers to women as "handicapped both in physical strength and what might be termed Nature's big hygienic handicap" (*Mirror*, 1929). This contradiction is salient. The Southalls' publicists show a woman on horseback, obviously active and capable, to illustrate their publicity claims. Their suggestion is that despite infirmity, and because of Southall, this woman may engage in sporting activity. They have naturalized the notion that a woman is not fit for exertion – without their product in aid. In 1937, Santex refers to menstruation as a "trying time" for women (*New Zealand Woman's Weekly*, 1937b). Although the terms are not medical, Santex's approach reinforces the notion that being a woman encompasses a recurring formidable challenge that may be overwhelming without the support of their pads.

Menstrual product advertisers do not mention menstruation itself, but employ a litany of euphemisms, many making reference to the menses as pathological or abnormal. In the early 1950s, Tampax talks about "difficult days" (*Home and Country*, 1950; *New Zealand Woman's Weekly*, 1951), the "difficult part of the month" (*New Zealand Woman's Weekly*, 1956), or "problem days" (*New Zealand Woman's Weekly*, 1959). This pathologization, or problematization, of the menstrual period underpins the image of ubiquitous feminine illness to which excessive physical activity would pose a dangerous challenge.

While the problematization of menstruation, the transformation of a regular occurrence into a pathological, or at the very least, a troublesome and deviant event, contributed to women's perceived unsuitability for sport, another pervasive theme infused menstrual product advertising and reproduced social perceptions of women's inability to engage in vigorous physical activity. Menstrual product advertisers relied heavily upon the image of fragile femininity; it socialized women to accept frailty as a genetic truth of female biology rather than a historically structured or socially learned condition.

Central to the idea of feminine frailty is anxiety over sex differentiation and a fear of encroaching on the male preserve of physical prowess (Willis, 1974). For sport historian Alan Guttman (1992: 20), "the direct political threat to male dominance posed by physically powerful women . . . was enough to unsettle all but the most confidently masculine men." Moscucci (1993) argues that gynaecologists equated women to children, and made their social dependence explicit through images of physical delicacy and psychological instability.

A prominent advertising ploy that emphasizes the fragility of women in general, and menstruating women in particular, and by extension suggests the unsuitability of women for vigorous physical activity, involves what I call the "Princess and the Pea schema": the representation of exquisite femininity through the use of soft and delicate objects. In the classic fable, *The Princess and the Pea*, a young, handsome prince puts all his potential brides through an unusual trial in order to determine if they are delicate enough to be his bride. He invites each one to sleep upon a stack of twenty mattresses and twenty feather beds under which he places three small dry peas: "They knew that the lady they had lodged was a real Princess, since she had felt the three small peas through twenty mattresses and twenty feather-beds; for it was quite impossible for anyone but a true Princess to be so tender" (Opie and Opie, 1974: 218).

In the same manner, by highlighting the dainty nature of their products, menstrual product advertisers imply that women are fragile. Focusing on the delicate, soft nature of a menstrual towel or tampon confirms that the industry believes in the fragile nature of the "real" woman, or at least believes that a large proportion of the market accepts this as true. Camelia's sanitary towel is "feather light" (*Mirror*, 1928), Santex will keep a woman "fresh and dainty" (*New Zealand Woman's Weekly*, 1937a), and Tampax is "discreet as well as dainty" (*New Zealand Woman's Weekly*, 1937c). Although soft towels may be more comfortable, the choice of descriptors revolves not around comfort, but rather around delicateness, conveying that feature, by extension, to the users of the products: a delicate woman uses a delicate towel.

Furthermore, the iconographic use of a svelte female form to convey delicacy and fragility is present throughout the twentieth century, with all brands of menstrual product. Menex women in 1933 are willowy and slender, wearing only the "flimsiest of frocks" (*Mirror*, 1933). Tampax pencil-line illustrations in the 1940s and 1950s feature women in tightly waisted and sashed dresses, with, in many instances, off-the-shoulder, or strapless bodices, and a choker necklace to accentuate sloping shoulders and an already slender neck. By the 1960s, the

Tampax girl actually supplies her measurements. "I'm 5' 7'', 35-22-35," she proclaims (*New Zealand Woman's Weekly*, 1965). This miniscule waist,[3] though complemented by the ample bosom and hips of the adult woman, accentuates the fragile figure of the delicate woman. A 22-inch waist is unlikely to accompany the musculature of a 5' 7'' active sportswoman.

In the mid-1960s, Johnson & Johnson took out large and prominent advertisements for Modess sanitary napkins in a number of women's magazines. These advertisements focused on royal poise and luxury. The accompanying photos featured exquisitely dressed women in evening attire, often in chateau-like settings. Mink stoles, satin evening gowns, and rustling silk against a backdrop of chandeliers and tapestries reveal decorative, immobile mannequins. The use of Modess products would confer, in the context of the Princess and the Pea scenario, royalty or elegance, rather than the strength and action requisite for physical activity.

We saw earlier the contradictory representation of an active woman in a menstrual product advertisement with a textual message of natural inability. By the late 1920s, some advertisers used the image of the active, and even sporting, woman to promote their products without the accompanying restrictive text. This would seem to be in contradiction with my hypothesis that menstrual product advertising detracts from women's participation in sport. For example, Menex pictures a woman playing tennis to promote "the modern hygiene." "Freedom! of movement and mind" heralds the title (*Mirror*, 1934). Southalls' shows a woman on horseback (*Mirror*, 1929), and in 1936 shows a woman playing a "hard game of golf" (*New Zealand Woman's Weekly*, 1936a). Jumping several decades, in 1966, Tampax exhorts "Go, girl, go!" and coaxes, "Be active! Nothing hampers you, nothing holds you back" (*New Zealand Woman's Weekly*, 1966). A happy young woman in outdoor gear smiles out from the page at the reader.

Although many companies have used the image of the active woman, they have underlined the fact that these levels of activity are only possible because of the use of extraneous support – explicitly from their products. They use the image of sporting women to punctuate what they portray as the technological advantage of their product for solving the problem of menstruation. The text accompanying the 1934 Menex advertisement explains that these disposable menstrual napkins *enable* a woman to "go the whole day through" (*Mirror*, 1934). The word *enable* is key; it implies that the product conveys the physicality that a woman is naturally lacking. In other words, menstrual product technology is solving a natural problem. Tennis-playing is contingent upon the use of disposable napkins. Southalls' reminds women that they "can indulge in the most vigorous of vigorous sports ... when relying on Southalls'" (*New Zealand Woman's Weekly*, 1936b). This reliance on the Southalls' product underlines a woman's natural *inability* to undertake physical activity during her menstrual period without suitable "protection." However, it does open the door to the possibility of physical activity, and even encourages it by the visual accompaniment. The assumption that this is *potential* physicality, actualizable only with an extraneous product, positions female physicality outside of a woman's locus of control – a deterrent rather than an aid to her engagement in sport.

One might argue that the commercialized menstrual product played an important role in allowing women to engage in sporting activities. Surely rags would be bulky and uncomfortable – belts and pins harsh and abrasive? Few contemporary sportswomen would consider competing with a sanitary belt and cotton towels between their legs. However, this argument has serious limitations. Although the design of a sanitary belt in itself seems restrictive – a thong-like strap lodged between the buttocks with an elastic belt around the waist – its design is the same as a G-string leotard or panties, often touted by aerobicists as a technically liberating design that purportedly allows more freedom of movement for the gluteal muscles. Although these items are of like design, and have a similar impact on the anatomy of the user, they have important functional differences that constitute the discomforting factor. This underlines a concern with menstrual concealment, rather than with comfort.

Similarly, the idea of competing or training wearing cotton rags to catch menstrual flow would be strangely alienating for contemporary sportswomen. Most would suggest that the appearance of readily available disposable products made participation in sport possible. The bulky rags would be uncomfortable and would interfere with athletic movement. Yet, competitive female cyclists, triathletes, and duathletes wear cycling shorts with bulky, gel-filled chamois, thicker than most twentieth-century menstrual toweling. These are sport-specific products, and as such are legitimized. They need not, for example, be concealed as evidence of a taboo biological function. The modern, streamlined disposable products did not enhance women's sporting experience as much as they enhanced their ability to conceal a taboo process. Here again, the assumption that liberation from toweling and availability of disposable products was the reason for women's increased involvement in sporting activities is based on faulty foundations. Corseting, boned and under-wired bras, restrictive clothing, and inadequate footwear were far more likely than menstrual pads to prevent women from engaging in sport than cloth toweling and security pads. The attribution of difficulty and hindrance to reusable toweling is related to the persisting need for menstrual concealment denied by the thick napkins. I will discuss the impact of menstrual concealment in more detail below.

The distinct benefit gained by using disposable napkins or tampons revolves around menstrual concealment in a society that sees visual evidence of menstruation as taboo, and convenience, rather than physical liberation. Women eagerly dispensed with the labor-intensive hand washing of menstrual towels when they purchased disposable products.

The taboo nature of menstruation in Western society is an important barrier to women's involvement in active sport. Menstrual product advertising has, in ostensibly proposing a solution to the problematic potential for exposure, reinforced the taboo, and hindered women's physicality.

Most cultures associate strong taboos with menstruation. Delaney *et al.*

(1976: 116) even suggest that the Polynesian word for menstruation, *tupua*, may be the etymological source for the word "taboo." Menstrual taboos take different forms in different cultures, but most are concerned with the potential for contamination of the surrounding area. In the case of menstrual blood, there is an infringement of *symbolic* order that hence impinges upon *social* order (Douglas, in Buckley and Gottlieb, 1988). The anomaly of menstrual blood is that it transcends the limits of the body; blood is normally contained within, and only exceeds these limits in cases of injury, illness, or . . . menstruation.

Western menstrual taboos do not imply withdrawal from society, or isolation from common areas. Instead, they mandate hiding evidence of menstruation, menstrual blood, or menstrual products. Concealment of menstruation requires vigilance. For example, a menstruating woman will plan her clothing and her activities to ensure that nothing "shows." A visible spot of menstrual blood on the back of a white outfit would require an immediate change of clothing, far more rapidly than with any other type of stain. The imperative of menstrual concealment has provided an important barrier to women's involvement in active sport, for menstrual blood is far more likely to spot the clothing of a woman involved in active movement, whose towels can displace and fail to capture all of the flow, or whose exposed positions can reveal a normally hidden area of clothing, potentially imprinted with the evidence of tampon leak. The omnipresent concern of "does it show?" or "does it smell?" constitutes a further mechanism of restriction for active women.

Menstrual product advertising has detracted from women's participation in sport and physical activity not only by, as we saw above, assigning inactive roles to iconographic representations of women, and by suggesting that exertion is only possible with extraneous support, but also by reinforcing the menstrual taboo and mandating the necessity of permanent vigilance. Disposable menstrual products may, in fact, conceal better than bulkier towels, but concealment is only an issue of concern if the menstrual taboo is enforced – a task that menstrual product advertisers have assumed. By enforcing the menstrual taboo, however, they are also enforcing a situation that makes engagement in sporting activities more difficult for women.

The enforcement of the menstrual taboo is not simply concerned with hiding menstrual blood, it also involves concealing discussion of menstruation and menstrual products. Making discussion of menstruation "hush-hush" by referring to it in euphemistic terms reinforces the need to conceal the function. If the process becomes unmentionable, the duty to conceal and to monitor intensifies.

Abundant examples of euphemistic references to menstruation exist in menstrual product advertisements. Euphemism is a rhetorical device for avoiding mention of something that may be seen as distasteful, inappropriate, painful, or perhaps frightening. Using a euphemism implies a negative event or object. We have seen above the array of euphemisms used to describe menstruation, and, by so doing, reinforcing the negative nature of the process. In my survey of over 200 twentieth-century menstrual product advertisements from 1928 to 1970 only one uses the word menstruation; others use euphemisms, and yet others generalize, avoiding any mention of anything that could remotely be related to menstruation. They avoid even mentioning a chronological event. This is a kind of inference by absence. Instead of the formulaic "difficult days" or "trying times," these advertisements might proclaim that Tampax provides a woman with freedom to do whatever she wants "*at all times*" (*Home and Country*, 1948), or that Meds make you free to relax and enjoy yourself "any day of the month" (*New Zealand Woman's Weekly*, 1963). The very issue under reluctant scrutiny is contained in a larger framework that linguistically dodges the point it addresses. To talk about a specific day, they mention *all* days. In so doing, advertisers have circumvented the basic level of linguistic taxonomy. Instead of citing the event they wish to represent, they designate a more general occurrence. The higher the taxonomic level, the further they remove the term from the specific event they intend to identify. By generalizing the function to a higher level, they create obscurity. However, total obscurity, in the context of women's "affairs," implicitly refers to menstruation. This avoidance even of euphemistic or metaphorical reference to menstruation emphasizes the terror of this taboo, and, as we have stated above, such dread detracted from women's potential involvement in sport.

Although I have dwelt thus far on historical examples of menstrual product advertisements reinforcing ideas about the female body that detract from women's potential to engage in active sport, there are important continuities apparent in contemporary marketing strategies. Many late twentieth-century menstrual product advertisements treated menstruation as problematic or pathological, underlined an image of fragile womanhood, insinuated a feminine need for extraneous support, and euphemized the function, reinforcing the duty to monitor the body. In 1995, *Dolly*, an Australian publication for teenaged girls, published an advertisement for Whisper Ultra-Thin. It depicts one girl standing inside her school locker, and another outside, pleading with her. Both are wearing white gym shorts and T-shirts. "C'mon Tania, just tell the PE teacher you've got your period," coaxes the second girl. "Oh sure," replies her distressed friend. "The man who picked 'white' for our sports uniform? He'll understand what it's like to be bloated like a blimp and damp like a wet flannel. The only period he thinks about is lunch period! Tell him I've got swimmer's ear . . . or tennis elbow . . . or athlete's foot. Just don't tell him I've only got my period or he'll make me . . . par-ti-ci-pate!!!" (*Dolly*, 1995). Tania, like many schoolgirls, would have used her period as an excuse not to participate in sport. In fact, her friend is encouraging her to do so. Tania lists external and internal discomfort that she associates with menstruation, and then tells her friend to use swimmer's ear, or any number of other physical complaints as equivalent pretexts to excuse her from her softball practice. She actually fears the attitude of her coach (he'll make me . . . par-ti-ci-pate!!!), which is non-problematizing. The advertisers of Whisper Ultra-Thin, however explain that Tania could in fact go to practice – if she used Whisper Ultra-Thin with Wings. She would feel cleaner and drier, and "wouldn't have to spend the softball season in her locker." Here, menstruation is treated as a condition, and the only way to cure it is to rely on the extraneous support of the Whisper product. Although proposing a technological solution to what it portrays as a problem, this advertisement emphasizes the imperatives of menstrual concealment, and situates woman's physicality outside of her locus of control. It is Whisper that holds the key, and not the sportswoman herself.

Freedom and participation are also the underlying themes in the Carefree advertising campaign. Emma and Kate are two cartoon characters who feature in a series of Carefree Body Contoured Tampon (a Johnson & Johnson product) advertisements. These young women are depicted in a series of liberating activities: fishing, sunbathing, museum going, or reaching for the stars. The sales pitch reads: "Carefree's Body Contoured Tampon Gives you the confidence to do whatever you want ... Whatever that may be!"(*Dolly*, 1999). The iconographic message as well as the accompanying rhetoric is very similar to the Southalls' advertisements from the 1920s and 1930s. The caricaturized line drawings reproduce fragile femininity – pencil-thin images of willowy women with sloping shoulders, and no strength. In contrast, a cartoon man in the Kate and Emma series has thick arms and defined pectoral muscles. Furthermore, the women pictured are engaged in fulfilling physical activities; inaccessible without the support of the advertised product.

Stayfree, also a Johnson & Johnson product, also hearkens back to old menstrual product advertisements which problematize menstruation. "Now, the only period you'll have to worry about is double maths" they proclaim (*Girlfriend*, June 1996). Stayfree will keep a girl "stress free," "takes away the drama," and allows her to "stay completely confident." The theme under consideration here, however, is menstrual concealment and not biological function.

Menstrual product advertising in the twenty-first century

At the turn of the century, there was a noticeable change in the approaches of certain menstrual product advertisements with consequences for sportswomen. The biological "problem" of menstruation was de-emphasized, and a new social problem created. The December 1999 issue of *Dolly* features a two-page advertisement for Carefree Pizzazz tampons. The first page shows four small, brightly printed paper boxes carefully aligned a quarter of the way from the top of a cheerful apple-green page. "New Clicktop packs from Carefree™ keep your tampons secure" is inscribed in white below the boxes (*Dolly*, 1999: 59). Overleaf, the page is reversed; the pretty little boxes are upside down on the same cheery background, the text is above, rather than below, and also upside-down, reading: "even in this position." Finally, at the very bottom of the page, rightside up, is the Carefree logo and the words, "the freedom to be yourself" (*Dolly*, 1999: 61). An intensive media campaign, including television advertising, touts the advantage of attractive click-top boxes. Tampons no longer fall out of their boxes, spilling into handbags and drawers. Competitor Libra produced a "hologram" box which it too plugged vigorously in television and print media with, like Carefree, no reference to the quality or nature of the product contained within. Name recognition was assumed – viewers/readers would *know* the ads were for tampons, but instead of vaunting the tampons, these advertisers praised the boxes in which they were contained. Here, we have another example of euphemism by omission. The very description of the product is absent. The box constitutes a concealment tool *par excellence*; not only is the process for which the tampon is intended hidden from view, so too is the tampon itself. The self-consciousness that the menstrual taboo mandates, and which these advertisements reinforce, albeit under the guise of the solution, is evidence of continuities in approaches to menstruation which interfere with women's engagement in vigorous physical activity.

But furthermore, this approach *accessorizes* the menstrual product. The box (containing the invisible tampons) becomes a fashion imperative, and fashion is a powerful social tool that may also detract from women's experiences of physical activity. As Roland Barthes (1967) explains, fashion fulfills a didactic function, it is a sort of initiation. Fashion texts are the authoritative voice that explain the complex meanings of that which is visible, but that has deeper significance, only obvious to the enlightened. Compliance with fashion is critical, because "for those who do not comply, it carries a sanction: the degrading mark of the unfashionable" (Barthes, 1967: 24). Barthes calls fashion a "phenomenon of initiation," a function that menstrual product advertisers fill as well. Previous advertisements patronize, support, explain, and offer the young woman all kinds of rules of deportment (particularly the teen readers of magazines such as *Dolly* or *Girlfriend*); here the menstrual product advertisements endow their products, through the fashion discourse, with the further ability to sanction or embrace. To be unfashionable is also to reveal feminine biology – to produce the evidence of menstruation through the visible presence of menstrual paraphernalia. Taboo even in its suggestion of menstrual potential, the stray tampons are a source of embarrassment that must be camouflaged; womanhood remains an infliction, a deviance, a liability.

Twenty-first-century Libra advertisements also focus on the taboo nature of menstruation. "New Libra Invisible stops leaks, so you'll never get caught out," whispers one advertisement, text in small font over a large image of a garden hose that has just been run over with a lawn-mower, now patched with sanitary napkins. "Now there's a superior ultra thin pad, with an anti-leak core that holds fluid better than any other ultra thin pad." *Woman's Day* (2000) shows another Libra advertisement featuring a young woman's body from waist to knee, with a stylish belly button piercing and ornament. She is wearing five pairs of panties. "You'll feel even more secure with our liners" (*Woman's Day*, 2000). There is no mention of illness, no evidence of the Princess and the Pea schema, but a persistence of the need to conceal menstruation at all costs, one that will contribute to continual awareness of the body and its functions rather than awareness of intentions and goals.

These advertisements take an interesting departure from examples of the 1940s, but also provide evidence of certain continuities. Carefree is no longer explicit about conveying freedom to the user, though the implicit suggestion is quite obvious in "the freedom to be yourself." There is no mention, or suggestion, of illness or of pathologization of menstrual function. These features do not place the same limitations on physical activity as those surreptitiously imposed by previous advertisements. However, the new angle nonetheless contains persistent indications of menstrual taboo, instilling other limiting perspectives. Associating menstruation with fashion practices fosters intense preoccupation with the body, its presentation, its concealment and revelation, in a way that interferes with other meaningful activities such as exercise.

Menstruation is not a limiting or restricting function in a majority of cases. For it to be so represented by menstrual product advertisers, and for such representations to be replaced with, or accompanied by, fashion imperatives is to reduce women's biological cycles to embarrassing, restrictive, and dreaded occurrences with strict rules of behavior. By purporting to solve problems, these marketing strategies recreate and reinforce social beliefs about the female body that often leave women on the sidelines, or as the *Dolly* advertisement ironically suggested, in the locker.

References

Bailey, R.H. (n.d.). *Small Wonder: How Tambrands Began, Prospered and Grew*. Internal document, Tambrans, Inc.

Barthes, R. (1967). *Système de la mode*. Paris: Editions du seuil.

Berg, D.H. and Block Coutts, L. (1994). The extended curse: Being a woman every day. *Health Care for Women International*, 15, 11–22.

Black, G. (ed.) (n.d.). *The Family Medical Advisor*. London: Wardlock and Co.

Buckley, T. and Gottleib, A. (eds) (1988). *Blood Magic: The Anthropology of Menstruation*. Berkeley, CA: University of California Press.

Burchfield, R. (1985). An outline of euphemisms in English. In D.J. Enright (ed.), *Fair of Speech: The Uses of Euphemism*. Oxford: Oxford University Press.

Dolly (1995). May, p. unknown.

Dolly (1999). December, pp. 59, 61.

de l'Isère, C. (1845). *A Treatise of the Diseases and Special Hygiene of Females*. Philadelphia, PA: Lea & Blanchard.

Delaney, J., Lupton, M.J. and Toth, E. (1976). *The Curse: A Cultural History of Menstruation*. New York: E.P. Dutton & Co.

Galbraith, A. (1903). *The Four Epochs of a Woman's Life*. London: W.B. Saunders & Co.

Guttman, A. (1992). *Women's Sport: A History*. New York: Columbia University Press.

Harland, M. (1882). *Eve's Daughters, or Common Sense for Maid, Wife and Mother*. New York: John R. Anderson and Henry S. Allen.

Home and Country (1948). May, p. 13.

Home and Country (1950). December, p. 45.

Jutel, A. (1998). I can't I've got my period!: Menstrual mythology and the production of feminine movement. *Avante*, 4, 72–91.

Martin, E. (1987). *The Woman in the Body: A Cultural Analysis of Reproduction*. Milton Keynes: Open University Press.

Melendy, M. (1904). *Vivilore: The Pathway to Mental and Physical Perfection*. Place unknown: Vansant.

Mirror (1928). October, p. 31.

Mirror (1929). May, p. 51.

Mirror (1933). November, p. 36.

Mirror (1934). January, p. 56.

Moscucci, O. (1993). *The Science of Woman: Gynaecology and Gender in England 1800–1929.* Cambridge: Cambridge University Press.

Napheys, G.H. (1871). *The Physical Life of Woman: Advice to the Maiden, Wife and Mother.* Philadelphia, PA: George Maclean.

New Zealand Woman's Weekly (1936a). 20 February, p. 58.

New Zealand Woman's Weekly (1936b). 15 October, p. 57.

New Zealand Woman's Weekly (1937a). 18 February, p. 35.

New Zealand Woman's Weekly (1937b). 4 March, p. 61.

New Zealand Woman's Weekly (1937c). 14 October, p. 52.

New Zealand Woman's Weekly (1951). 15 November, p. 4.

New Zealand Woman's Weekly (1956). 11 October, p. 7.

New Zealand Woman's Weekly (1959). 2 May, p. 36.

New Zealand Woman's Weekly (1963). 11 November, p. 72.

New Zealand Woman's Weekly (1965). 4 October, p. 96.

New Zealand Woman's Weekly (1966). 19 September, p. 115.

Opie, I. and Opie P. (1974). *The Classic Fairy Tales.* London: Oxford University Press.

Richards, E. (1939). *Ladies' Handbook of Home Treatment.* Warburton, AU: Signs Publishing.

Stayfree (1996). *Girlfriend*, June, p. unknown.

Vertinsky, P. (1994). *The Eternally Wounded Woman: Women, Doctors and Exercise in the Late Nineteenth Century.* Urbana, IL: University of Illinois Press.

Waite, G. (2000). Personal interview. Dunedin, New Zealand.

Wernick, A. (1991). *Promotional Culture: Advertising, Ideology and Symbolic Expression.* London: Sage.

Willis, P. (1974). Women in sport. *Working Papers in Cultural Studies,* 5, spring.

Woman's Day (2000). 6 March, p. unknown.

Wood-Allen, M. (1913/1899). *What a Young Woman Ought to Know.* London: Vir Publishing Company.

12 Generational marketing

Fitness, health and lifestyle formations

Jeremy W. Howell

Americans living in the United States aged 50+ are 27% of the population, yet they account for 50% of all discretionary income, 80% of all money in U.S. savings and loan accounts, 77% of all financial assets, 66% of all stockholders, 58% of all healthcare spending, and 41% of all new car purchases.

So reported Maddie Kent Dychwald of Age Wave LLC[1] during a two-hour-long Presidential "closed door industry leadership" meeting at the 1998 International Health, Racquet and Sportsclub Association's (IHRSA)[2] Annual Conference held in Phoenix Arizona. Designed as a forum to discuss the impact of emerging market forces on industry opportunities and possibilities, the "closed door" seminar is one of the key annual business services that IHRSA, as a trade association, provides to its leading North American and International corporate members. During the meeting Dychwald meticulously pointed out that America is in the midst of a massive demographic shift of immense political, economic, and cultural consequence. She noted that between the years 1995 to 2005 the 0 to 17 age category of the American population would increase by 13 percent. In contrast, the 18 to 34 age group, the market so coveted by current advertisers, would decrease by 8 percent. Alternatively, the 35 to 54 age group would increase by 29 percent while the 55+ age group would increase by 13 percent.

These figures were especially interesting to the industry leaders in attendance. IHRSA research was already showing that for the period 1987 to 1995 national U.S. health club memberships had risen 118 percent for the 55+ age group and 63 percent for the 35 to 54 age group but only 26 percent for the 18 to 34 age group (IHRSA, 1995). For Dychwald the challenge for health club owners and managers was extremely clear: how should they adapt and strategically develop marketing and business plans that respond to this unique and powerful "Age Wave?" Specifically, how should industry leaders prepare for the marketplace power that will be exerted by an extraordinary and maturing baby boom generation?

With specific reference to contemporary health and fitness practices, this chapter questions what the term "generation" actually means in our mediated promotional culture. Exactly what does the "baby boom" actually signify when it comes to health and fitness? What are the key sensibilities that have created, and continue to create, a cultural space in which the fit and active body is given economic and symbolic value to such a degree that it is seen to define a particular lifestyle formation? And, perhaps most importantly, how does this lifestyle formation turn around and impact upon future industry fitness and health promotional practices?

The baby boom generation

> Lifestyle is the social relations of consumption in late capitalism, as distinct from class as the social relations of production.
>
> (Lowe, 1995: 67)

In marketing circles, the baby boom generation is normally referred to as a cohort market segment; a relatively stable consumer group that, by experiencing important external events during their formative years, develop a common culture, history and value structure which produces a shared set of consumption habits and tastes. The baby boom generation is commonly split into two separate cohorts. The former cohort, born between 1946 and 1954, has as its pivotal moments of formation the social turmoil and upheaval associated with the Vietnam War, the John F. Kennedy and Martin Luther King assassinations, and Woodstock. The latter cohort, born between 1955 and 1965, has as its defining features the broken idealism of the post Watergate era and the narcissism associated with the personal consumption culture of the 1980s (Rice, 1997). Taken together, both cohort segments have been the focus of an incredible amount of market attention as American companies analyze these shared formative values, preferences, and behaviors so as to develop strategies by which to target market certain products or groups of products.

For instance, take the popular 1998 "Woodstock" Pepsi-Cola commercial, a classic example of generational marketing and one showed by Dychwald during her IHRSA industry leadership presentation. To the music of Canned Heat's "Going Up the Country," the commercial begins with what appear to be two local farmers looking out towards a long line of cars driving along a narrow lane leading to the site of the 1969 original Woodstock music festival held on Max Yasgur's farm outside White Lake in upstate New York. "Here come those damn hippies again," mentions one farmer as the subtitle "Summer of Love Reunion (25 years later)" comes into screen view. The cars, the majority being Mercedes or BMW Sports Utility Vehicles (SUVs), pull into designated parking areas on the actual Woodstock site. They are met by uniformed valet staff. The camera pans to a middle-aged, spectacled, balding man wearing a sports coat and tie, as he faintly recognizes a middle-aged woman whom he inquisitively refers to as "Sunflower?" She looks at him and, as if astonished, states "Pigpen?" They embrace while the commercial cuts to another corporate attired balding man dancing and strumming his air guitar. As a distant voice is heard performing a microphone check over the speaker system, the commercial cuts to the image of a dozen men swinging golf clubs as if on a driving range. Each is dressed in a collared pastel-colored sports shirt as if warming up for a weekend round at their country club. As the song "Going Up the Country" continues to frame the commercial, one concert goer turns to another and states, "this place hasn't changed in twenty-five years," while his partner, dressed as a Payne Stewart lookalike and pointing to the surrounding countryside, ironically replies, "Yea, it's a shame. They should have put in some condos by now." At this point in the commercial, we are taken to the actual sound stage and meet the original members of Jefferson Airplane as they are discussing their "low-fat low sodium" diets, only to be immediately drawn back into the audience as we see another balding, middle-aged man in suit and tie speaking into his cell phone shouting, "The green marble goes in the upstairs bathroom." In the background are a number of women in classic Jane Fonda workout clothing, exercising as if in an aerobics class.

It is at this point that we see the first reference to Pepsi-Cola the product. On a distant hill there are four young teens watching the proceedings sitting atop their mountain bikes with Pepsi-Cola cans in hand. As they watch stunned, one teen pronounces, "And this is the anniversary of an historic event?" When asked which one, the teen replies, "Watergate!" As the commercial moves to the conclusion, we return to the sound stage to see John Sebastian and Country Joe McDonald in discussion. When asked if he remembers doing this twenty-five years ago, Country Joe, with a dumbfounded look, replies, "No." With the images of golfers and more business-attired people playing frisbee and dancing wildly, a voiceover simply asks the viewer, "Wouldn't it be nice if your youth was as easy to hold on to as an ice-cold Pepsi."

In marketing terms, the Pepsi-Cola commercial is not so much about the selling of a soft drink as an actual product as it is about the way in which maturity and lifestyle is commodified, glamorized, and ultimately marketed as brand identification. The Pepsi-Cola commercial articulates, distributes, places, and connects events, human practices, subjects, and products into a particular generational formation. It provides the cultural landmarks, narratives, images, and statements that connect a particular product meaning to a particular market segment. After all, at 77 million strong with spending power of $1.7 trillion, it is hard to ignore an aging generation that in 1998 accounted for 29 percent of the total population and 39 percent of all adults in the U.S.A. The commercial makes generational sense because we know that over the next fifteen years, four million Americans will turn 50 each year. Similarly, marketers recognize that 10,000 people will turn 50 each day for the next ten years, a rate of one every eight seconds, and that there are more Americans over age 50 in the U.S.A. than there are people living in Canada.

I introduce this commercial to make the five key marketing points that frame this entire chapter. First, a commercial is never simply a recording of Madison Avenue hyperbole but is rather a process whereby an individual is positioned into a consumer market segment. Here, as consumers, we not only purchase the objects of production, but also come to see ourselves, particularly our bodies, as commodity signs in which we invest. Second, the actual meaning of a product is never fully determined ahead of the cultural context into which it is immersed. How particular products are connected to particular practices, events, consumers, and market segments is never an historical given. Rather it is an ideological, material, and affective articulation. Third, this articulation is formed within the dominant sensibility that every cultural formation puts into place, a sensibility that "defines its effects in people's lives and thus the way in which a particular formation is lived" (Grossberg, 1992, p. 72). Fourth, while a generational market segment may have an element of formative stability, its identity is never quite as rigid as we might like to think. The meaning of any given "generation" itself does not exist outside of the very cultural signs, products, and practices to which it is articulated. Last, and as a consequence, the actual meaning of a generation is constantly in flux and constantly formed, de-formed and re-formed.

Lifestyle formations

> First came the baby-boom generation, 77 million Americans born between 1946 and 1963. They created the modern health club industry. They *were* the market. They were also the industry's entrepreneurs.
> John McCarthy, IHRSA Executive Director (2000: 18)

This process by which the term *lifestyle* is articulated to the re-formation and de-formation process has clear implications for those of us involved in the fitness and health club industry. For, while the emergence of the fitness and health club industry has clear historical connections to the physical cultural movements of the late nineteenth century, the physical education reform acts of the 1950s, and the Cold War national debate over military efficiency and readiness of the 1960s and 1970s, it is only with the 1980s re-formation of the baby boom audience that the industry begins its path to institutional maturity (see Howell and Ingham, 2001).

Nowhere is this more evident than in the marketing of fitness and health club products and programs to the Young Urban Professional (the Yuppie) market segment that first won widespread notoriety during the 1984 U.S. Presidential elections. According to Hertzberg (1988), the Yuppie, as a re-formation of the baby boom generation, became associated with two politicians – Liberal Gary Hart and Republican Ronald Reagan. The Hart campaign had actually highlighted the existence of a block of voters who were young, upwardly mobile professionals. For instance, in 1955 just 2.7 million Americans enrolled in college. By 1968, at the height of the counter culture-movement, one-third of the U.S. population was receiving some form of schooling, and college enrolment had increased by as much as 50 percent. Almost four years after Jack Weinberg's famous "Don't trust anyone over thirty" statement, *Time* magazine, with a cover title of "Twenty-five and Under," had made the baby boomer their 1966 Man of the Year. Baby boomers were, according to the introductory letter from the publisher, "well-educated, affluent, rebellious, responsible, pragmatic, idealistic, brave, 'alienated' and hopeful" (Auer, 1967: 11). As the "Man of the Year" lead story stated,

> they are a highly independent breed, and – to adult eyes – their independence has made them highly unpredictable. This is not just a new generation, but a new kind of generation. . . . Untold adventures awaits him. He is the man who will land on the moon, cure cancer and the common cold, lay out blight-proof, smog-free cities, enrich the underdeveloped world and, no doubt, write finis to poverty and war.
>
> (Jones, 1967: 18)

Yet, despite that liberal social consciousness and popular discourse, the identity and practices of the Yuppie increasingly become aligned to the 1980s redefinition of social conservatism as it functioned alongside extreme voluntarist and marketplace lines of force. In this sense, it was the Reagan campaign that, in part, articulated itself to that audience. After all, by the 1988 Democratic Convention in Atlanta the top-selling badge was "Die Yuppie Scum," and the *Wall Street Journal* had inscribed Reagan with the title of "Most Aged Yuppie" (Hertzberg, 1988).

That this serves as an odd contradiction given the dominant sensibility by which the baby boom generation is usually articulated is self-evident. It clearly put Yuppies in a structurally ambiguous position in a political sense. By 1989 Paul Lyons was writing in *Socialist Review* that the term had become one of the key words of the time. For Lyons (1989: 11), the Yuppie had become:

> part of a critical conversation taking place over the past fifteen or so years about, among other things, the meaning and legacy of the sixties . . . the nature of the American Dream, the integrity of being affluent, the nature of work and its relation to reward, the system of social class and status in America, and the present political conservatism.

From a marketing perspective, the Yuppie was the exemplar of the new way in which the provision of commodities and techniques produced a more loosely textured, more diffuse and diverse measurer and definer of lifestyle. If an earlier baby boom formation had taught us anything it was that the essential meanings attached to traditional identities of the 1940s and 1950s were no longer as stable as might be presumed. Now, the baby boom generation was enveloped by a new cultural sensibility defined by a logic of consumption that increasingly persuaded individuals to not only purchase the objects of production, but to also recognize themselves and their bodies as commodity signs in which they materially, ideologically, and affectively invest.

Whether Yuppies could be defined by what they produced was questionable.

But they could be defined, in part, by what they consumed. Yuppies, as the special end-of-year *Newsweek* (1984, December: 28) edition entitled "The Year of the Yuppie" put it, simply "Live to Buy" and they "define themselves by what they own." For as far as the Yuppie was concerned, status and style had become a commodity resulting in a sensibility and attitude to life that could not be contained by sociological categories and statistical parameters (Howell, 1991; Howell and Ingham, 2001).

It is in this context that the 1980s saw some of the most rapid redefining and expansion of fitness and health club products and programs. For instance,

> By the eighties, the B.A.'d professional high earning Yuppie as a social type was numerous enough ... to sustain thousands of chic restaurants and shops, aerobic clubs, organic products lines, therapy centers, clinics, boutiques and alternative weeklies wobbling increasingly between investigative reporting and shopping tips.
>
> (Gitlin, 1989, p. 431)

What was clear in this new lifestyle formation was that one was no longer a marginal faddist and crank to preach against good old American enriched white flour products. No longer were quality-of-life issues the private property of ecological movements and responses from a counter-culture concern with some form of impending environmental apocalyptic nightmare (see Howell, 1991). When Adelle Davis introduced her book *Let's Eat Right to Keep Fit* in 1954, she was regarded as nothing more than a village crank (Reed, 1981). Yet, similar concerns took Jane Brody's *Nutrition Book* to best-seller status in the 1980s. The book was a lifetime guide to good eating for better health and weight control written by the Personal Health columnist of the *New York Times*. Even Continental Baking Company, producer of such wonderful American culinary delights as Wonderbread and Twinkies, introduced oatmeal bread for "oatmeal goodness" (Ruggles, 1989). As Bing (1989: 32) put it:

> Today, with Oat Bran by my side, I can continue to live the vigorous lifestyle that is the only way I can do business. My cholesterol level reads about 180 right now, and by next summer, through determined consumption of Oat Bran, I plan to have it down in the single digits. Then I'm going to buy a convertible.

Even the beef industry was impacted by this new cultural sensibility. Its Food Style '89 campaign pamphlet showed a young man pedaling a stationary bike with the words "Lifestyle" and "Countdown to a better health" embossed in red and black lettering respectively. The leaflet also showed a plate with a strip of lean beef nicely arranged among uncooked or steamed vegetables. As the beef industry's pamphlet stated: "Health, nutrition, fitness, exercise – these are the watchwords for today's lifestyle. And as we move into the '90s, they're becoming even more important."

Of course, what all this indicates is that signs, goods, and commodities "can be discursively re-articulated to construct new meanings, connect with different social practices, and position social subjects differently" (Hall, 1988: 9). Yesterday's radicalism could become today's common sense. In the final nightmare of this commercialization of bohemia (Hertzberg, 1988), Nike Inc. introduced its "Revolution in Motion" advertisement campaign to the sound of the Beatles 1968 song "Revolution." Termed an "emotional documentary" by directors Paula Greif and Peter Kagen (White, 1987), a counter-culture signifier ironically became re-articulated and acted as a signifier of a new lifestyle formation (see Howell, 1991).

Not surprisingly, many industry promotional campaigns were based on this dominant sensibility, none more pertinent than Jane Fonda's workout series. Fonda's first fitness book, *Jane Fonda's Workout Book* (1981), was on the *New York Times* best-seller list for two years. She followed that success with *Jane Fonda's Workout Book for Pregnancy* (1982) and the release of her original *Workout* VHS tape, which went on to sell over a million copies before being taken off the market. This was a remarkable feat in a time when movie rentals accounted for 80 percent of most video shops' revenues. From "Barberella to barbells" (Levine, 1987), the transformation of Hanoi Jane into a fitness icon became a cultural marker of the times.

The metaphor of transformation was evident in a variety of health club advertising strategies. The Chicago Health and Racquetball Club produced an innovative *Chicago Sun Times* print advertisement featuring Glenn Fry of the Eagles rock band. The late 1990s advertisement contained two photos of Fry. The first was a photo of a droopy-eyed Fry with long, flowing hair, Fu-manchu-style moustache, and loose-fitting clothing. Anchoring the image in place was the block-lettered text, "Hard Rock." In the contrasting frame, Fry appeared clean-shaven with close-cropped hair and wearing a tight-fitting sleeveless T-shirt. The side-on view showed him performing a bicep curl with dumbbell in hand. Underneath the toned image of Fry was the title, "Rock Hard." The translation of the Eagles Glen Fry from a 1970s "Hard Rock" performer into a new commodity sign of the emerging 1980s "Rock Hard" culture was clear.

Such a transformation was also at the heart of the popular 1985 health and fitness film *Perfect* (Bridges, 1985). The story of the film involved an exposé that was to be written by Adam Lawrence (John Travolta), a *Rolling Stone* magazine reporter, on The Sports Connection, an actual Los Angeles health club. The focus of the exposé was Jessie Wilson (Jamie Lee Curtis), the number one aerobics instructor at the club. In an early interview, Lawrence was told by one member of The Sport's Connection that the club is all about "good times . . . a totally new concept in athletic club. We're more than a club, we're a lifestyle." Lawrence went on to give an astute analysis of that lifestyle:

The baby boomers are the physical great awakening comparable to the spiritual great awakenings that have gripped America about every one hundred years. I think people want to take responsibility instead of leaning on institutions. For instance, the government; do you believe anyone thinks the government will take care of us anymore . . . or big corporations, or doctors. So you have to take care of yourselves. So there's a hell of a lot of people out there trying to get in shape, as you well know. I think I feel we've gone full circle back to this Emersonian America as self-reliance. . . . So what could be more American, more All American, more Old Fashioned All American, than institutions like the "Sport's Connection." Little capitals of Emersonian America scattered from sea to shining sea.

Of course, none of this was lost on a new breed of baby boom entrepreneurs who were themselves positioned within this new lifestyle formation. For instance, the website of The San Francisco Bay Club notes that it:

> has been a San Francisco tradition since October 1977. When the Club opened, 1,500 members were presented with a dynamic, new concept: a multi-purpose, co-ed, and high quality club that catered to the emerging baby boomer market. The goal for the Club was to be a community unto itself where friendships were forged, professional networks created and good citizenship was fostered; a tradition to which we are still committed. . . . The Bay Club was the first downtown co-ed, multi-facility club in the country. We also created the first center for aerobics in the Bay Area, and provided the first downtown shuttle service bringing members from the financial district to the Club.
>
> (http://www.sfbayclub.com/history/history_home.htm)

Health clubs as secular cathedrals full of technological devices with which to develop the bronzed, muscular, Adonis-like body sprang up in many major American cities. Having the right kind of body signified that we somehow had our lives under control. The non-fat, non-smoking, physically toned body became as much a sign of status as an Armani suit, a Karan shirt, and a Jaguar XJS.

Glorification of the body, absorption with physical beauty, pursuit of a self-betterment lifestyle, and an increased passion for youth were having a massive effect on what Americans expected and hoped for in their everyday lives. As Claire Schmais, coordinator of the dance/movement therapy program at the City University of New York's Hunter College, stated at the time: "how you act and how you think are one and the same. The way you use your body is a metaphor for your life . . . there is no separation between your body and yourself" (Steinbaum, 1989: 113).

The Chicago Health and Racquetball Club also used World Champion body builder Rachel McLish to advertise its twenty-eight stores (*Chicago Tribune*, 1988, August 15). The advertisement showed a full-length visual of a sultry-looking, oiled-down McLish, dressed in a tight-fitting half-cut top and high hip-cut bottoms. She was standing beneath the large block-lettered header, "All the right equipment." Each part of her body had an arrow pointing to the name of the equipment that was used to develop that particular muscle group: the

Polaris Chest Press, the Eagle Bicep/Triceps, the Eagle Wrist and Forearm, the Keiser Hip Abductor, the Stairmaster, the Universal Leg Press, the Nautilus Leg Extension, the Eagle Standing Calf Raise, the Banked and Cushioned Indoor Track, the Nautilus Side Leg Curl, the Paramount Power Squat, the Universal Crunch Bench, the Lifecycle, the Keiser Military Press, the Nautilus Four-Way Neck, and last, but not least, relaxing saunas and whirlpools for the mind. But of course, having all the right equipment can take on another meaning, especially when the text of the advertisement encouraged the reader to "come by today. And we'll make you look good in all the right places."

This desire to be all that you can be, whether a possibility or not, was also played out in the popular image of the health spa. The spa used to be a place where rich women were pampered, massaged, and prudently exercised; an elite boot camp for aging wealthy women. By 1989 most spas catered to women between the ages of 25 and 50, with 60 percent of these women undergoing an "experiment in lifestyle re-education," and while "no spa can promise that one will live happily ever after you depart, some do provide a toll free hot line number to call should a woman feel herself fall from grace" (Cullerton, 1989: 177).

According to Mel Zuckerman, owner of the now infamous Canyon Ranch Spa in Tucson, Arizona, people went to spas because they had to, or because they wanted to beautify themselves: "today, a significant number who come here do not need to lose weight. They want to use their vacation time to learn something that will help them for the rest of their lives" (Wells, 1989: 76). Similarly, Julie Anthony, Director of the Fitness and Sports Medicine Institute at the Aspen Club in Aspen, Colorado, stated: "ten years ago what was being printed was to slim your thighs in ten days – things that were Band Aid approaches, not lifestyle approaches" (*USA Today*, 1988, September 14: 2D).

The Canyon Ranch Spa was also featured on one of the first *USA Today* television shows (1989, January 17). Regarded as the "ultimate holiday," people were told they could learn, for $3,000 a week, a lifestyle where calorie counting, exercise and meditation were an everyday experience: Slim down, shape up, and recharge for a successful quality of life. And of course, if Yuppies couldn't get to the Canyon Ranch Spa, they could always purchase the total video program, *Canyon Ranch: The Complete Workout*.

Even upmarket department stores hopped on to the health spa bandwagon. Marshall Field's offered the EPI-SPA for the body beautiful: "This Summer let the spa come to you. It's easy (no appointment necessary) with the revolutionary EPI Product line." Its Body Conscious '89 Program was similarly promoted: "O.K. This summer, you're going to shape up! You're going to stop neglecting your one and only body and start recognizing its beauty needs. It's easy with the Works, our version of the 'spa in the city'" (*Chicago Tribune*, 1989, July 15).

This was also the marketing decade that brought us Nike Inc.'s "Just Do It" and Reebok International's "U.B.U." lifestyle advertising campaigns. As the innovative Reebok commercial put it, "We're not just selling sneaker's, we're selling an attitude." As the *Boston Globe* (1988, October 3) commented, the

Reebok advertisements plug a theme of "personal freedom." The commercials implore the audience to find "modern ways of expressing ourselves" (48 Hours, CBS News, 1988, September 22). Indeed, both Nike and Reebok spent much of the 1980s competing for the athletic footwear market pole position. For instance, in 1988 Nike Inc. increased its advertising costs by 36 percent, spending a total of $34 million. That same year, Reebok International spent between $35 and $40 million in advertising (USA Today, 1988, July 26). While these figures may not appear remarkably high today, consider the fact that between 1983 and 1988 Reebok International's revenue increased by over 10,000 percent. And between 1984 and 1988, the U.S. athletic footwear market itself had gone from annual sales of $2 billion to $4.3 billion with Reebok International and Nike Inc. holding 27 percent and 23 percent of the share, respectively (New York Times, 1989, February 14).

Such lifestyle marketing meant that product and service marketing, formerly two relatively distinct fields, became more and more of a single hybrid. As McKenna (1988) notes, the Yuppie catalogue Land's End unconditionally guaranteed its clothes emphasizing that they would arrive within 24 to 48 hours. Its mail order revenues grew by 35 percent in 1988 (USA Today, 1989, May 5). As audiences increasingly took their world news from the instant information offered via network and cable television, daily newspapers increasingly took to a magazine format to increase sales. Just as in magazines ranging from The New Yorker to The New Republic, Newsweek to U.S. News and World Report, Glamour to Vogue, Cosmopolitan to Elle, Christianity Today to Rolling Stone, and Esquire to Advertising Age, features on health and fitness became a permanent staple in many national newspapers. Even a reader of The New York Times could turn to "Fitness" every Monday and "Medical Science," with research findings that "could affect your life" every Tuesday. Wednesday brought a maze of food, safety, health, and nutrition tips in "Eating Well." On Thursday, the reader learned about trends and developments from the "Health" page. The week was rounded out with Jane Brody's "Personal Health" column, Daniel Goleman's writings on psychology and emotional well-being, and the Sunday Magazine's "Body and Mind." As a 1989 advertisement concluded, "To keep up with good health, keep up with The Times."

That the emergence of the fitness and health club market was articulated to this new lifestyle formation is, then, hardly surprising. The Yuppie was the vanguard of the "Revolution In Motion." The words and images associated with a whole myriad at health and fitness products and practices saturated American airwaves. Yet words and images do not work in isolation. They are articulated across many sites of daily life, from jogging, to workout clothes, to fashion, to diet, to everyday social relations. They are articulated to an attitude of a new look, to a new aesthetic of self-betterment, to a new quality of life. And that quality of life was played out within a model of mood and fantasy that provided people with a space to invest, make sense, and stabilize their own fragmented and mobile identities. As a USA Today (1989, May 5) full-page advertisement header for DP fitness equipment put it, "Excuses are a dime a dozen – results are under $400." The advertisement leaves the reader with the thought, "Discover how good it feels to be fit for life."

"Circa 2000": a generation on the move

For the past twenty-five years, the industry has been chasing the baby boomers relentlessly. Their interests, their needs, and their issues have controlled the marketplace. Nearly every industry development – from yoga, to day spas, to hospital-based clubs – have all focused on bringing an ever greater percentage of baby boomers into health club facilities (McCarthy, 2000: 18). In April 1998 BT Alex Brown Research produced a report on equity leisure services and products for its investment customer base. Entitled "Leisure Trends into the New Millennium," the report focused on the way in which boomers are reinventing middle age and redefining the concept of aging in America. Thinking of themselves as being ten or fifteen years younger than their chronological age, boomers are defined increasingly by a youthful sensibility regarding middle age: "Freed from the responsibilities of their 40s, boomers will create an adventurous life stage we call mid-youth that will redefine the traditional notions of the mature market" (IHRSA, 1998: 41). The report also made reference to the fact that health club memberships increased to 20.8 million in 1996, up 9 percent over the prior year and 51 percent since 1987. Total club revenues grew to $9 billion in 1996. These figures are supported by industry trade reports. In 1983 there were 6,309 commercial health clubs in the U.S.A. By 1998 that number had more than doubled to 13,799. As of January 2004, IHRSA statistics show that there are now 23,500 commercial clubs in the U.S. with a membership base of 39.4 million and annual revenues of over $14 billion (http://www.ihrsa.org).

Similarly, according to American Sports Data, frequent sports, fitness, or outdoor activities were radically impacted by the maturing baby boom generation. Between 1987 and 1996 there was an age participation increase of 39 percent for the 35 to 44 segment, 51 percent for the 45 to 54 bracket, and 28 percent for the 55+ population. As the BT Alex Brown report again emphasizes, "Just as they have changed every stage of life they have lived through, the baby boomers are likely to create a new second middle age market, this altering the very nature of the mature market" (IHRSA, 1998: 43).

By 2000, fitness and health club programs and products were immersed in this new formational moment. Realizing that the age range of the baby boom generation in 2000 was 36 to 54 and that 42 percent of households were headed by people in this age group (Mitchell, 1998: 190), those in the health care industries, including hospitals, HMOs, and health and fitness organizations, were recognizing a new cultural sensibility where physical and mental therapeutic modalities join together to form a new lifestyle of longevity consumerism (Howell and Ingham, 2001). Take, for instance, the massive appeal of Dr. Deepak Chopra and Dr. Andrew Weil. Since the publication of his best-selling book *Ageless Body, Timeless Mind*, Deepak Chopra has been the most visible proponent of the mind/body relationship. After a 1993 appearance on *The*

Oprah Winfrey Show, "130,000 copies of his book were sold in one day" (see Leland and Power, 1997: 54). Similarly, Andrew Weil's nationwide best-sellers *Spontaneous Healing* and *Eight Weeks to Optimum Health* have helped in alternative medical therapies increasingly becoming part and parcel of an integrated medical approach to the total well-being of the individual. But perhaps the most remarkable transformation of this lifestyle consumerism has been the general acceptance of the "Integral Transformative Practice" (ITP) methodology of George Leonard and Michael Murphy by many in the health and fitness industry. With the publication of their book entitled *The Life we are Given: A Long-term Program for Realizing the Potential of Body, Mind, Heart and Soul*, many fitness and health professionals have paid increasing attention to their research into integral transformative practices. Again, this is an interesting transformation given the historical connection of both authors to the baby boomer Human Potential Movement and the world-renowned Esalon Institute[3] in California. The marketplace is increasingly looking for innovation that can deliver a broad range of goods, services, and experiences that *integrate* concepts of exercise and fitness into a more complete definition of health.

In a Garry Trudeau-drawn *Newsweek* cover page entitled "The *New* Middle Age: A Boomer's Guide to Health, Wealth and Happiness" (April 3, 2000), the editors position the volume by displaying three other Trudeau-designed cover pages, namely the "Year of the Yuppie" (December 31, 1984), "The 80s Are Over" (January 4, 1988), and "The Overclass" (July 31, 1995). Referring to Trudeau as "someone who has long chronicled the arc of the baby boom for *Newsweek*," the 2000 edition was a continuation of their attempt at describing the formation, de-formation, and re-formation of a generation. Nowhere is this more evident than in the excerpt from David Brooks' book *Bobos in Paradise*. Brooks, a senior editor of *The Weekly Standard* and *Newsweek* contributing editor, sees the baby boom defined increasingly by a cultural sensibility that blends the rebellion of the 1960s with the materialism of the 1980s. The result, for Brooks, is the emergence of a new lifestyle formation: the Bourgeois Bohemians (BOBOS) (Brooks, 2000: 63):

> Again and again I found the same thing: bohemian attitudes from the hippie 1960s have merged with the bourgeois attitudes of the Yuppie 1980s to form a new culture, which is a synthesis of the two. For a time we had a culture war between people who loved the Woodstock 60s and the people who loved the Reagan 80s. But while the culture warriors were arguing with each other, regular Americans were adopting attitudes and lifestyles from both. The people who dominate our culture now are richer and more worldly than the hippies, but more spiritualized than the stereotypical Yuppies. Our attitudes toward work, sex, pleasure, ambition, politics, intellect and even God are shaped by this weird synthesis between the bourgeois and the bohemian.

Whether we are seeing the actual re-formation of a generation along such lifestyle lines is debatable, but there is no doubt that we are seeing the articulation of the baby boom generation to a new cultural sensibility in which the meaning of middle age is moving into the political, economic, and cultural epi-center of everyday life. For instance, a 2002 Harris Poll conducted for the National Council on Aging found that almost half the people currently between the ages of 65 and 69 now considered themselves middle-aged. The same report indicated that this was true for one-third of people in their seventies. In a *New York Times* editorial on the subject Dudley Clendinen asked what exactly should we call this "new, longer, more leisured and apparently enjoyable late stage of life? These older people who do not feel old" (2000: 10).

This returns us to the Maddie Kent Dychwald "closed door industry leader-ship" presentation at the 1998 International Health, Racquet and Sportsclub Association's (IHRSA) Annual Conference held in Phoenix Arizona. As both academics and marketers we can clearly question the whole theoretical premise behind the idea of a large generational market segment waiting to be targeted by clever advertising campaigns such as the introductory Pepsi-Cola commer-cial. We now actually know that markets are both theoretically and practically infinitely fragmentable, and consumers can be clustered in a variety of ways. Using innovative software programs and data-mining technology, market researchers, consultants, and organizations can develop an array of market seg-mentation profiles.

Nevertheless, we should not lose sight of the theoretical way in which mar-keting is involved in the actual construction of generations as lifestyle forma-tions. We must remember that generational categories cannot pre-exist the cultural elements that make it up. Generational categories are prevalent not because their referent is some coherent stable market segment but because, when articulated to lifestyle formations, they are effective in surrounding and invading the bodies of various populations, incorporating them into their own spaces, making them a part of the formation itself (Grossberg, 1992: 72). Gener-ational categories do not exist outside of lifestyle formations; they are incorpo-rated into them via particular cultural sensibilities.

IHRSA has a current strategic intent of realizing one million health club members by 2010. To reach that number necessitates mapping ways in which particular cultural sensibilities are effectively articulated to different exercise populations and products so as to open up empowering health and fitness opportunities and possibilities of investment. While this mapping of sensibilities may not be the language of the marketplace, it is most certainly the underlying theme of current industry strategic thinking. As John McCarthy, IHRSA Exec-utive Director, has clearly stated, the industry must now begin to focus on a new generational opportunity: "72 million echo-boomers, sometimes called Gen Y, boys and girls born between the beginning of 1980 and the end of 1985. Now age 5–20, they represent our next bull market" (McCarthy, 2000: 18). In the end, we can ignore and dismiss the construction of generational categories or market segments as the fanciful thinking of social engineers. Or we can engage them to help us to better theorize the way in which we make sense of the images and signs that flow unceasingly within the circuits of promotional culture. The way in which exercise, fitness and health events, texts, symbols, and activities overflow into the channels of our everyday world, in all their forms and regularities, tells us a great deal about the ways in which meanings, values, and social relations therein are produced, represented, and lived.

References

Auer, B. (1967). A letter from the publisher. *Time*, January 6, p. 11.

Bing, S. (1989). Man at the trough. *Esquire*, September, pp. 147–148.

Bridges, J. (Producer, Director) (1985). *Perfect* [Film]. Los Angeles: Columbia Pictures Inc.

Brooks, D. (2000). Bourgeois bohemians, *Time*, April 3, pp. 62–63.

Clendinen, D. (2000). What to call people who used to be old. *The New York Times*, July 2, section 4, p. 10.

Cullerton, B. (1989). The spa and the single woman. *Self*, April, pp. 175–178.

Gitlin, T. (1989). *The Whole World is Watching: Mass Media in the Making and Unmaking of the New Left*. Berkeley: University of California Press.

Grossberg, L. (1992). *We Gotta Get Out of this Place: Popular Conservatism and Postmodern Culture*. New York: Routledge.

Hall, S. (1988). *The Hard Road to Renewal: Thatcherism and the Crisis of the Left*. London: Verso.

Hertzberg, H. (1988) The short happy life of the American Yuppie. *Esquire*, February, pp. 100–109.

Howell, J.W. (1991). A revolution in motion: Advertising and the politics of nostalgia. *Sociology of Sport Journal*, 8 (3), 258–271.

Howell, J.W. and Ingham, A.G. (2001). From social problem to personal issue: The language of lifestyle, *Cultural Studies*, 15 (2), 326–351.

IHRSA (1998). *1998 IHRSA Report on the State of the Health Club Industry*. Boston: The International, Health, Racquet and Sportsclub Association.

Jones, R. (1967). Man of the Year. *Time*, January 6, p. 18.

Leland, J. and Power, C. (1997). Deepak's instant karma. *Newsweek*, October 20, pp. 52–58.

Levine, S. (1987). Jane Fonda: From Barberella to barbells. *Women's Sport and Fitness*, December, pp. 24–28.

Lowe, D. (1995). *The Body in Late-capitalist USA*. Durham, NC: Duke University Press.

Lyons, P. (1989). Yuppie: A contemporary American keyword. *Socialist Review*, 19 (1), 111–122.

McCarthy, J. (2000). The next bull market: 72 million echo boomers. *CBI Magazine*, July, p. 18.

McKenna, R. (1988). Marketing in the age of diversity. *Harvard Business Review*, 88 (5), 88–95.

Mitchell, S. (1998). *American Generations*. Ithaca, NY: New Strategist Publications.

Reed, D. (1981). The fitness craze: America shapes up. *Time*, November, pp. 94–106.

Rice, F. (1997). Making generational marketing come of age. In J. Richardson (ed.), *Marketing 97/98* (pp. 112–114). Guildford: McGraw-Hill.

Steinbaum, E. (1989). Fear of fitness. *Self*, April, p. 113.

Ruggles, R. (1989). Wild oats: America's bran new obsession. *Self*, April, pp. 210–212.

Wells, L. (1989). Spa life. *The New York Times Magazine*, May 7, pp. 75–77.

White, A. (1987). Running on recall. *Film Comment*, July/August, p. 75.

13 Staging identity through consumption

Exploring the social uses of sporting goods

Fabien Ohl[1]

Broadly speaking, sport, and its associated events, stars and commodities, are forms of communication. The interest in, and success of, communication, including advertising, through sport can be explained, in part at least, by its powerful and pervasive symbolic efficacy. However, to date there has been little analysis of the relationship between the representational aspects of sport advertising and the equally important practice of sport consumption; that is, how particular sporting commodities are used within everyday lifestyle. This chapter aims to analyze more precisely the social context and ramifications of the symbolic efficacy of sport by focusing on the consumption and uses of sporting goods. More specifically, using France as a case study, I attempt to provide some rare empirical data. However, although France serves as the site of analysis we cannot ignore the impact of globalization and its role in shaping consumer markets and the meaning of commodities in everyday life. To this extent France is one of many "global locals."

Using Goffman's notion of the presentation of self in everyday life, we will see that changes in the nature of our relationships with objects and people are evident in and through a contemporary reading of sport consumption. Moreover, as I hope to demonstrate, differences in cultural patterns of sporting goods consumption reinforce the fact that the same standardized product can be purchased and used by very different people, for different reasons and with resultant different meanings. Clearly, sport consumption is dependent on wider socioeconomic changes, especially the expansion of the media industry. Through the lens of Pierre Bourdieu's analysis of the media field, we can see the increasing influence of the media and its impact on sport consumption. Arguably, sport is both an ideal commodity and a vehicle for media marketing. This is due, in part, to sport being a dynamic, unpredictable, emotionally charged public performance facilitating spectator and fan identification, and, in turn, targeting strategic market segments.

Still, the importance of sport consumption cannot be limited to the effects of the media field. Sport consumption is also embedded in other cultural changes that help to explain a process of "sportivization" of physical appearance emerging in the 1960s, particularly in youth culture. Youth over-consumption and the conspicuous wearing of sporting goods needs to be understood in this cultural frame and will be discussed in relation to the quest for identity and the presentation of self (Goffman, 1959). I aim to show that consuming sporting goods contributes to an illusion, one exploited by advertisers, of acceding to an authentic, genuine, and valorized culture. Arguably, the quest for authenticity through consumption is not necessarily juxtaposed with the increasing globalization of markets because, as previously noted, even for standardized sporting goods, their ultimate meaning is rooted within specific contexts and conditions of use. The study of consumption and identity is gaining increasing importance because of the rising tendency to conflate and legitimize "the consumer" as the model of social actors and citizenship.

Sporting goods as sacred

> A society cannot create itself or recreate itself without at the same time creating the ideal.
>
> (Durkheim, 1960: 603)

The consumption of sporting goods has to be understood with respect to changes in mainstream society. For example, beyond broader political and economic changes, shifts in belief systems may help to explain the central place that consumption now holds in our everyday lives. Notably, the boundaries between the sacred and the profane are no longer as clearly differentiated as they once were. Our customs, habits, and appearance "crystallize into action sequences of roles, values and communication with an emotional and a strong symbolic responsibility" (Rivière, 1995: 264). Understanding the strong ritualism of sporting goods use and display is one way of approaching the significance of consumption. In Goffman's (1967) analysis the body is the essential matrix of ritual production, and the rites of interaction provide many opportunities to reaffirm the moral and social order. Thus, the positive rituals expressed by a great respect toward objects are also celebrations of individual and group achievement. Within sport, objects such as trophies and medals are integral parts of rituals of honor and celebration. However, even within everyday life sport commodities such as racquets, skis, kayaks, or cycles are the subject of great deference. Although those practicing sport as a form of leisure are less likely to consider objects as sacred, they still retain meanings beyond simple utility. They are often personalized by an elaborate system of choices related to colors, signatures, or other marks of distinction. The careful handling of sporting objects is a sign of respect for the value of practice and practitioners (Fottorino, 1996). Notably, profane goods of capitalism are often regarded as sacred (Featherstone, 1991: 121) such that the most important objects of consumption, both sport and non-sport, constitute an extension of the person and the collectivity. Moreover, modern forms of animism can be read into our relations with sports objects. Athletes display concentration and emotion as they engage in sporting activity. In many ways attachment to sporting objects is also an attachment to a way of life. Commodities punctuate the sport, the participant, and his/her consuming biography. Objects, connected with events, are treasured as the relics of a glorious past. The first pair of sport shoes bearing a brand, the first safety binding with cables for skis, the wooden racquet or the first ski pass constitute a sort of archaeological treasure chest. They are symbolic markers of sporting challenges, victories, and memories of the past. Indeed, our relationship to the consumption of sport commodities reveals a type of social itinerary. Discussions about the origins of the first sailing board, the advent of fiberglass in kayaks, skis or rackets, recall the values of a past life and provide an opportunity to critique the boorish consumer materialism of our times. Likewise, discourses about sport objects are a means of remembering and an important source of information about past conditions of practice (Löfgren, 1996). Unfortunately, the symbolic aspects of consumption are too often neglected because of the dominance of economic approaches that give priority to quantification. Yet, in most cases, the consumer is not a *homo-economicus* purchasing with rationality; even the shopping experience is a social experience (Falk and Campbell, 1997), and there are social uses of goods at stake that involve a variety of cultural patterns.

Sporting goods use and cultural patterns

The notion of social determinism is still strong if we consider the statistical databases of consumption in each country or at an international level (e.g. INSEE, Statistics Canada, U.S. Census Bureau). Factors such as income, occupation, or educational attainment are strongly correlated with all types of consumption, including leisure and sport. However, the understanding of social practices needs to be analyzed at a micro level. Social reality cannot be limited to a so-called objective statistical analysis, because the subjective aspects are often the most important with respect to understanding behaviors. Furthermore, there are serious problems in trying to reconstruct a particular sport consumer identity from aggregate social or economic statistics. Such a hypothetical consumer is the result of the average of very different and contradictory purchases and uses of goods and services; it is not a real person but rather an artifact. Ethnographic or sociological observations of real behavior, rather than constructed on statistical bases, helps to explain the complexity of consumption. For example, while there is clear evidence of the globalization of fast-food chains and the mass consumption of sporting goods, this should not be interpreted simply as the homogeneity of culture. Thus, in the case of France, eating in a fast-food restaurant once a month doesn't mean an Americanization of French lifestyles.

Similarly, although 90 percent of people buy sport goods at least once a year, they are using them in very different ways. The uses of sporting commodities are so diverse that they cannot be easily compared. Indeed, the persistence of cultural patterns in consumption remains strong, linked to the social context and the identity of particular social groups (Usunier, 1996). Consumption involving strong cultural habits, like food, are not changing very fast even if we can observe an important growth of fast-food chains; on the contrary, products are redesigned to respond to the demand of traditional and so-called authentic food. Consumption that involves cultural patterns, or habitus in Bourdieu's axiomatic, are more linked to local culture and local difference, although goods such as clothes can be used in different ways and contexts not directly linked with habitus. Notably, habitus is also at stake in sport practice, uses of the body, sexuality, or language. It is also important in the presentation of self; but goods are very arbitrary social signs that change relatively quickly, and objects and brands are not necessarily linked to a particular social category. People from different countries, classes, and cultures are increasingly practicing the same sports and using the same commodities. For example, sport shoes are mass consumed in Western countries; an underprivileged teenager as well as a businessman can buy the same pair of Nike's. However, the "meaning" of the commodity and its use may vary widely. The meaning of goods depends on their use. Some previous research suggests that the upper classes generally use them for sports while the lower classes often use them in everyday life as part of their ongoing participation in a valorized culture (Desbordes *et al.*, 1999). Significantly, the use of a commodity does not imply the involvement of fundamental properties of the habitus. Wearing Reebok or Adidas clothes is not, of course, a question of habitus, even if the goods used are nonetheless signs of social conditions. Thus, although French and American consumers are buying the same sport shoe, the use and meaning may be vastly different. In the U.S.A. you will often meet women wearing sport shoes with a suit as they travel to the office but you will rarely see such a practice in France or in Italy. That is why comparisons must be made relative to both uses and purchases. It is definitely not the same practice to use sporting goods while training, shopping, working, dining out, or going to the cinema; the signification of consumption depends on cultural patterns and social interactions inscribed and expressed in a diversity of places. For example, although 80 percent of Adidas advertising for youth is the same all over the world, it does not translate into the same uses and meanings of sporting goods (Tribou and Madec, 1999). The appropriation of sport clothing and symbols by U.S. inner city gangs – or by many European youth living in the poorest suburban peripheries – to express their identity have little or nothing in common with the sporting use of older people from completely different backgrounds and positions. While both may use the sporting commodities to demarcate particular identities and social standing, the latter group has a greater opportunity to actually use the goods in everyday life, though they may not choose to do so.

The significance of consumption is also concerned with its relationship to other goods and with the specificity of context in which it is used. Wearing a Lacoste polo shirt under a suit to play tennis, to go to school or to go to a disco are not the same forms of consumption. It is a mistake to think that habitus is able to explain all behaviors without taking into account the context and the system of roles inscribed in social spaces and institutions. As a consequence, there could not be a direct, clear, and systematic relationship between the consumption of athletic goods and social patterns. That is why, despite an undeniable homogenization within the process of supply, the consumption of goods and services is still rooted in local culture and local struggles (Jackson and Andrews, 1999).

Nevertheless, despite local resistance, the impact of powerful global forces on societies cannot be ignored. The media in particular are transforming the social context of local cultures and local struggles. Arguably, the media are decreasing the autonomy of many other social fields (Bourdieu, 1996), including sport, and having an increasing influence on youth culture, consumption, and social representations. In many ways the media frame the way in which most behaviors, including sport consumption, occur and must be understood.

The increasing influence of media on sport consumption

There is an increasing influence of media, particularly television, on the symbolic organization of society. As a consequence, the autonomy of other social fields (e.g. intellectual, political or sport) is decreasing (Bourdieu, 1994, 1996). That is why the value of commodities often depends on their place on television (marketers often attach the label "Seen on TV" to increase the credibility of their products). The influence of television is quite significant to particular categories of people because their access to other forms of culture is often limited, and television holds quite a dominant position. Indeed, some argue that this is why their cultural autonomy against television is lower. Young people often find heroes and role models for identification in the media (Duret, 1993). Sport stars have now taken their place among movie and music celebrities because sport has become a powerful vehicle in the media business (Andrews and Jackson, 2001). Thus, it is not surprising that identity confirming sport consumption by youth is valorized by the dominance of television.

The transformation of the media field and its main social role, added to the specific characteristics of sport events, feeds the symbolic efficacy of sporting goods (explaining its high level of consumption). Sport events make for good television because of their entertainment value, ease of scheduling, and, at least in relative terms, lower cost of production. But their economic efficiency is also linked to a symbolic one. The interest in sport comes from its capacity to put on stage *action situations*, or in Goffman's terms, "fateful situations" (Goffman, 1967; Birrell, 1981). Sport is one of the few remaining real social contexts in which character can be demonstrated as well as social and moral assessments conducted. Even if it is obvious that the conditions of ordinary life don't imply such clear competitive action situations, the sport narrative gives sense to everyday life during a period in which the meta-narratives of Western modernity (science, humanism, socialism) are unable to provide it (Lyotard, 1979). It affords the opportunity to compare and express its own values and behavior (Ohl, 2000). The sport narrative is also often a description of ways of acting and interacting, and refers to established social codes of behavior. Similar to a guide of *savoir-vivre* (Picard, 1995), discussions of sport behavior recall and update the social codes of everyday life including those linked to gender, race, sexuality, and class divisions.

Sports embody numerous characteristics that turn them into events capable of generating stories, and the resulting analyses and comments contribute to the spread of sport consumption. For example, the simplicity of sport events and the uncertainty of the result help to generate intrigue and excitement. Sport provides a context, like a theater, within which people from different cultural backgrounds meet and interact. The engagement of body and values linked to action accentuates the possibility for a spectator to feel the intensity and emotions. In an era revealing a relative pacification of society, sports provide symbolic "fateful situations" which contribute to the regulation of emotions (Elias and Dunning, 1986). Sport events put heroic people on stage (Ehrenberg, 1991; Duret, 1993), and it is probably because sportspersons are from different social classes, but often from lower classes, that the interest in events is so intense (Leite, Lopes and Maresca, 1989).

The above factors outline why narratives and images of sport provide a set of social codes and figures useful for the construction of "self." The success of sporting goods is embedded in ordinary people, the emergence of heroes, symbols of nation, success and wealth. In this symbolic system, commodities refer to sacred heroes with valorized identities and buying and owning these goods is, more often for young consumers, a means to accede to a recognized culture. In the abundant comments on sport events and heroes – on television or in newspapers – there are descriptions of social frames (Goffman, 1974), on how people interact, and on the relations between identity and behavior (Ohl, 2000). The success and understanding of sporting rhetoric can be explained by its capacity to represent our behavior in various circumstances. Identification with sporting heroes provides newspapers, magazines, and television with a role in the construction of identity. Comments are important because they give a description of heroes with which people can identify; furthermore the emotional dimension of sport events accentuates the probability of affective affiliation. Another advantage is that, unlike more fixed aspects of identity such as gender, race, or nationality, sport provides heroes that are continually changing and thus each generation can have its own role models. The transformation of media contributes to the spreading of sporting appearances, but the trend is at first inscribed in wider social changes related to the question of appearance. In other words, mediated sport offers an external resource to validate identities in the process "of the internal–external dialectic of identification" (Jenkins, 1996: 20).

The sportivization of appearances

Fundamental changes in the organization and regulation of the global economy have contributed to the emergence of new social categories, new definitions of identity, and changes in belief systems. And, while economic forces certainly play an important role, they cannot be isolated from other parameters. Beliefs, for example, also play a major role in the economy (Weber, 1958), as do other factors such as technology and science. Moreover, these combined transformations have facilitated the development of a mass market creating a culture of consumption. Among the effects of these developments is the popularity and expansion of sport. This trend is not the sole result of the increasing number of people practicing sport. In fact, the majority of sports commodities are not used for the practice of sport per se. Indeed, for sporting goods retailers, for every purchase by a serious sportsperson there are an equal number of purchases made by consumers who don't actually practice sport. In France, like most countries, clothes (66 percent), accessories (58 percent), shoes (54 percent) and equipment (24 percent) are not necessarily, and indeed rarely, used to practice a sport (Pouquet, 1994). Furthermore, people interested in many types of sport commodities are more sensitive to the sport labels and brands than to their actual function. Often they are interested in large or at the very least "authentic" logos. Conversely, many "real athletes" prefer inconspicuous sporting signs (though their sponsorship deals may require their display). Their legitimate position in the sport field and the opposition to people's conspicuous use of sporting goods explains their apparent distance to the material signs of sport identity (Desbordes *et al.*, 1999).

The importance of the need to display sporting goods can be explained by their symbolic function. The concern for the sign, the sporting and relaxed appearance is often more important than the performance or the technical merit of the products. At the same time we should consider some of the wider social changes in the relationship between fashion and various cultural practices. Since the 1960s, there has been a decline in the need for formal clothing partly because of price but also because of the reduction in the number of formal ceremonial occasions that demanded their specific use. Sport clothing, among others, emerged to fill the gap in the market. For example, from 1953 to 1984, the consumption of men's suits dropped from 26 percent to 7.7 percent and women's suits from 12.7 percent to 6.4 percent, whereas sport clothes consumption increased from 0.9 percent to 12.8 percent for men and 0.9 percent to 11.8 percent for women (Herpin, 1986).

However, the decline of ceremonial clothing doesn't mean the end of social ceremonies; they are not disappearing, rather they are changing. With adults often making different choices, young people are creating new ceremonies that replace, and, in some cases, oppose traditional ones. For example, there are new fast-food and casual dining styles and practices (using hands versus cutlery) that are challenging traditional patterns. Notably, although these are often less formal, they are still very ritualized and affirm new social codes.

Arguably, the popularity of sport helped inspire today's "sporting style" of fashion. This style has been further popularized by movie and music stars wearing, and thus legitimizing, sport fashion. For example, during the 1980s, the hip-hop movement spread the sporting style in specific music cultures. Many sport brands benefited from this tendency without any specific marketing plan (e.g. Helly Hansen, Fila, Nike, Fubu). Today, sporting brands exploit this trend by producing specific goods and developing strategic partnerships with musicians (e.g. the Reebok "team rap").

The image of sports people and their diverse ways of expressing their identities are increasingly being exploited by modeling agencies. For example, the Marylin agency created a department whose job it was to recruit athletes for advertising campaigns. Athletes from football (R. Pires, D. Trezeguet), rugby (R. Ibanez), athletics (J. Galfione), and boxing (E. Holyfield) were recruited because of "the positive image he (the sportsman) gives and his attitude as well during competitions and in daily life" (chief of Marylin agency quoted in *La Lettre de l'économie du Sport*, 4 March 1998: 4). This ad agency comment suggests that athletes are not only models of behavior when competing; they are also considered as models of projection and identification for everyday life. It is their human qualities, as much as their physical ability, which are at stake.

Sporting brands also influence a wider clothing style with other brands often inspired by sport innovations. Sporting brands offer the most readable and recognizable logos, clothes, and shoes. Lacoste placed his first crocodile on an item of clothing in 1933, at a time when labels were only discreetly fixed under the dress or inside the shoes. Other sporting brands, notably Adidas and Puma, contributed to the spread of this tendency. Today, many brands put their logo on clothes (e.g. Billabong, Chevignon, Paraboot, Benetton). In addition, technical materials, like Gore-Tex, which was first used in the sport industry, is now being adopted for other clothes and shoes. The increasing consumption of sport clothes has also contributed to a blurring of the relations between clothing and social status. The rigid boundaries that once existed have given way to more complex avenues for expressing identities associated with age, gender, and status. These changes help to explain why sporting goods figure so prominently in the process of self-presentation in youth culture, as will be illustrated in the case study of France.

French youth culture and sporting goods

In France, the post-war period was accompanied by significant economic growth with the emergence of a "new bourgeoisie" of professional managers (Boltanski, 1982). The rise of new social groups explains, in part, the quest for new symbols of status. Opposed to the established bourgeoisie in terms of age and social origins, they demanded recognition of their identity. During the 1960s, this demand was expressed not only in social conflicts associated with work or education but also symbolically through consumption.

The image of success represented by the American way of life, including blue jeans, Coke, chewing-gum, music, sport, and Hollywood movie stars, was embedded in these struggles. In a changing social and economic context, particularly with the creation of many new jobs and the arrival of a new generation of baby boomers, commodities became symbols used to stage new social status. During 1960s France and particularly the events of May 1968, cultural consumption and, paradoxically, the distrust of consumption, were among the most visible expressions of opposition to traditional culture. The presentation of self was also used to express political opposition to capitalism. But these cultural changes were not limited to France. In numerous countries, the consequences of economic development, like the transformation of the labor force (decline of agriculture and industry) including the rise of female employment, had relatively similar consequences. Commodities were used to affirm new styles as opposed to established ones. This helps explain the focus on appearance, including that inspired by sport, as well as the development of values related to comfort and leisure versus traditional, rigid codes of *savoir-vivre* and self-control. This is not to suggest that class-based consumption disappeared; however, new global forces were emerging to influence both what and how people consumed.

Without neglecting the diversity of uses and meanings still strongly linked to social class, we cannot underestimate the homogenizing effects on youth in the more economically developed countries. Transnational corporations like McDonald's, Disney, Sony, EMI, Coca-Cola, and Nike strongly contributed to the development of a global youth market. In part, this was achieved by trying to cultivate youth consumerism among the wealthiest groups. This does not suggest a universal consumer given that there is not a common youth culture; however, in some cases there are enough common references to use the same, or similar, ads when selling particular products. Some have argued that the globalization process is the background of a homogenization of some aspects of culture and social conditions. Considering culture, particularly youth culture, each generation seems to seek its own autonomy and identity while expressing its own values and behavior. The 1960s sacred values of peace and love were rejected by the 1970s preference for hate and outrage (e.g. the anarchy of the Sex Pistols). The political conservatism and consumer conformism of the 1980s served as a deliberate distancing from the rebellious punk attitudes. Even dominant images of the body can be contrasted across eras: the pale and sickly look of the punk period versus the shaped and muscled body of the 1980s. Later eras of youth consumption continued to demonstrate elements of contradiction. For example, hip-hop and rap music are based around identity politics and a critique of society, yet are often closely linked to the values of consumption (e.g. wearing of sport brand clothing) and the display of wealth.

Moreover, social changes often impact on young people first because they have to adapt more than other people. New technologies, new job categories, increased education, and a new focus on the body through exercise, sport, and diet are all enabling and constraining factors influencing the current generation. Moreover, in the new social context, this generation, often acceding to the middle or upper classes (social mobility was high in France during the postwar period because of central changes in employment structure), does not want to reproduce the established bourgeois codes. The new lifestyles included all sorts of cultural elements from underground culture in music, theater and art, to the consumption of jeans, cigarettes, and/or the emergence of new sports. The rising sale of sporting goods is partly inscribed in this cultural transgression. In this context global sport companies such as Adidas and Nike were strategizing with respect to the new markets. Adidas focused on formally instituted sports, whereas Nike was responding to the new physical pursuits beyond the boundaries of traditional sports. In part, Nike's success was due to its innovative advertising and its sponsored athletes. In addition to star athletes and idealized role models, such as Michael Jordan, Nike also engaged in a strategy of transgression by using "athletes with an edge," for example, Eric Cantona. Nevertheless, transgression must not be overestimated. Transgression in advertising is symbolic, and in many cases reproduces rather than challenges the social and moral order. As a consequence there is often no opposition to the consumption process and market forces. As Goldman and Papson (1998: 54) note, Nike intentionally garners "media attention when it occasionally transgresses bourgeois moral boundaries." Even the recent success of Adidas can be explained by a "transgressive" use of clothes and shoes both within new sports (snowboarding, skateboarding), and within other realms of popular culture including music (e.g. Madonna and various rap stars). Despite a great diversity of uses, sport heroes or stars often create a global reference point opposed to the established order. In many cases the reference to sport and its associated heroes, heroines, and events provides a source of identification with particular movements of resistance. This opposition is very different from those during the 1960s; it has very few political or ideological connotations and has more to do with generation struggles and the creation of a specific culture that mixes sport, music, and other cultural practices.

The rise of the school-leaving age, the difficulties associated with finding and securing a job, and the challenges of gaining financial autonomy, have all increased the emergence of specific values that oppose adults and dominant representations of the establishment. It helps explain why young people are very receptive, and sometimes involved in, the creation of new fashions and new practices. The wish to affirm their own values explains their desire to consume and, as a consequence, they are a major target of sport companies. Sport is a culture of youth, and sport consumption depends on structuring youth experiences. That is why sporting goods are linked to youth biography. Sport and sport commodities function in important ways with respect to youth experiences including: achievement and awards, learning experiences, gifts and memorabilia (Desbordes et al., 1999). Thus, it is not surprising that sporting goods consumption is used by many as a way of affirming and staging identity.

Consequently, sporting goods are not only commodities, they are identity markers used to affirm autonomy. Because financial independence is rarely available before age 20, young people struggle, in different ways, for a symbolic autonomy. The use of sport clothes also contributes to the creation of symbolic barriers, which help to delimit a culture through appearance. Nonconformist and provocative appearance is also a way to limit contact with adults. Face-to-face rituals are more difficult when sharing little common references and behaviors.

Rules, attitudes, self-presentation, language or images are often opposed to what is supposed to be the established social order. The functions of sporting goods are relatively similar to the role of language or music. Goods create differences between members of the group and others. It is a kind of coding, to affirm one's own culture against an inaccessible or non-desired culture. Sport is a more valorized culture, particularly in the media, than traditional cultures of public institutions (school or cultural centers). Pleasure derives, in part, from playing with the commodities; young people combine colors, materials, and logos, and often make jokes about themselves. In the construction and the affirmation of identity, sporting goods are one of the elements of a wider system of hybrid social identities. Language is also a key element; it is often used to define insiders and outsiders. However, while linguistic interactions are important, youth culture is centered around the visual and imagery, and that is why the presentation of self is so important. It requires clothes defining both similarities and differences, it confirms that the visibility of brands is essential, and in some cases it is complemented by particular music. In sum, sporting commodities provide a powerful, expressive, and accessible vehicle for youth to define themselves.

Affirmation of identity and the quest for authenticity

The consumption of objects is in many ways a "laboratory of identity games" (Lögfren, 1996). Sporting goods, unlike traditional ceremonial clothes or shoes, enable people to engage in new forms of behavior as distinct and original experiences. In France, reference to American culture is important because it includes heroic anti-establishment figures such as Muhammad Ali (Fantasia, 1994: 70). The links with its ancient colonies and the process of migration explain some unique features of the French situation compared to other countries such as Germany, the U.S.A. or Australia. There is an important segment of the French youth population that is of North African descent. This group tends to be from lower socio-economic categories and to experience difficulties in trying to affirm a positive identity. As racial/ethnic "others" within France, their strong need for recognition may explain their highly visible affirmation of identity. This process is very similar to the one that prompts minorities to use consumption, especially that of valuable brands, to shape their collective identity (Lamont and Molnàr, 2001). For young people in general, this period of uncertainty demands that they also express a strong identity through their use of particular clothing styles, language (slang), and attitudes. Thus, for a lot of French youth, American culture is reconstructed and appreciated in opposition to the established tradition, although it doesn't have the same meaning, habitus or behavior. Reference to the imagined American way of life is used as a kind of symbolic struggle linked to age and values. The highly publicized destruction of a McDonald's restaurant in 1999 by French farmers[2] fighting globalization is, conversely, a fight against what is supposed to destroy French cultural diversity and identity. The valorization or the stigmatization of the dominant culture has both to do with the domination of an international culture standardized by marketing processes and with the social struggles between groups. The threat to the diversity of cultural practices is real but complex. In many cases,[3] the symbolic aspects of culture are more at stake than its reality: "in terms of the consumption of culture, fast-food represents no threat to *haute cuisine*, any more than blue jeans are a threat to *haute couture* or Tupperware a challenge to Limoges porcelain" (Fantasia, 1994: 80). Furthermore, French restaurants and *haute cuisine* are often exported all over the world.

The construction and display of identity around sport can be explained by the fairly wide spectrum of uses, styles, heroic figures, and champions with whom to identify. It may be a key reason why teenagers with uncertain identities appreciate sporting cultures. The relative autonomy of adolescent culture explains their propensity to transform objects from their original purpose and to react to corporate strategies. Hence, as previously mentioned, sport items are often used for purposes other than the practice of sport. Nevertheless, the "game" of identity is complex, and even within sport the established codes can be rejected (Catani, 1996). For example, marketing that is too conspicuous can disturb and produce negative reactions from young people or sportsmen (Desbordes *et al.*, 1999). Consider the case of D. Vincent, organizer of the "Big Mountain Snowboard Contest" who warned that: "the main danger is the men wearing suits and ties, the ads in sport." As a result he made a deal with Rusty (a Californian surf brand) because he felt that a different, less commercial sponsor relationship was preferable (quoted in Desbordes *et al.*, 1999).

The quest for identity is expressed through the recurrent question of authenticity associated with sport commodities. This question is important on at least two levels. First, sport brands help organize youth to position themselves against casual brands within the vast clothing market. Second, it operates as an internal reference in the competition between sporting goods corporates. Youth sensitivity to the question of identity explains their demand for authentic and genuine values (versus those of the establishment). The success of sporting goods is linked to their ability to provide identity through perceived authenticity. Corporate discourses take into account this youth demand by promoting themselves through recognized champions. For sporting brands, the question is not only to respond to the demand, they also have to defend and define their own identity within the competitive marketplace. The consumption of these goods is clearly related to fashion; thus, their competitors are not only other sport brands but casual fashion as well. Consequently, sport brands need to maintain a strong identity that is highly recognizable, which helps to sell the product at a high price, and which preserves a space for consumption for the highly fluctuating youth market. The rhetoric around authenticity and genuine values corresponds to a demand for references. Moreover, it helps to mask the contradiction between the sport brands as fashion and sport brands associated with top-level athletes. The opposition between authentic and casual fashion is reflected in the symbolic struggles of corporations. For example, former CEO of Adidas, Robert Luis Dreyfus, declared that: "Swank is finished. Nike-type show off is no longer the trend: young people want authenticity" (*L'Essentiel du Management*, January 1995: 48).

The new leitmotiv of fashion specialists is authenticity. According to T. Cornet from "Who's Next," "Street tendency is an authentic movement" (in

Sport Première Magazine, 163, 1997: 45). Likewise, the title of a recent article in *Sport Première Magazine*, a French professional review for sport producers, was "Authenticity to survive." Thus sport consumers and sport corporations are forced to negotiate a paradox. On the one hand, consumers seemingly seek authenticity, and corporations therefore need to signify and market their brand through the creation of "authentic" sport products. On the other hand, the reality is that most consumers are using sport commodities for fashion and display, and this further propels the fashion element of sport commodities rather than sport performance use per se.

For small retailers, authenticity is one of the best ways to survive. To fight against the concentration of retailers, small shop owners are resisting with "authenticity above all" (*Sport Première Magazine*, 179, 1998: 10). The search for history, patrimony, and authenticity is a strategy to compete within the sporting goods market. Market standardization is a problem for brand identity; affirming authenticity is both a response to the demand and a way to dominate new competitors in the market and to set off the sporting goods market. A 1998 Adidas advertisement illustrates these strategies well. The advertisement states: "Do you remember your studs? In 1954 we created the first 'screw-on studs,' then, everybody else did too. Today, we have created Traxion . . . Soon, everybody else will do the same." Reference to history through advertising is a marketing strategy to challenge Nike and other brands. The strategy of staging history may also be observed in smaller markets like the surf-wear market. Harry Hodge, Quiksilver and Na Pali co-founder, argues that "what makes us different from other brands is our long history in sport and in surf . . . many brands in this sector don't have the heritage and the authenticity of Quiksilver" (*Sport Première Magazine*, 179, 1998: 35). In some cases, transgression can bring authenticity: for example, R. Harnie-Cousseau, organizer of Glissexpo (a big sport show specializing in snowboard, surf, skate, roller, and so on) declared that to succeed, the show must "create an authentic atmosphere" and recover "the touch of madness that made it a past success" (*Sport Première Magazine*, 189, 1999: 20).

Thus, the "economic" competition within the sporting goods market is largely a battle fought out within the symbolic realm because the products are quite similar. Moreover, the notion of authenticity, largely and paradoxically because its meaning is so generic, is used within global marketing strategies to construct particular identities (e.g. age). To reiterate a previously stated point, my intention is not to suggest that youth around the globe are the same because they wear the same goods or listen to the same music. Differences of use are still strong between and within each country, but the *processes* are very similar because of a trend towards the homogenization of production and supply, and the similarity of social conditions of the middle and upper classes of the wealthier countries.

To increase profit, producers try to be efficient through standardization (of product, communication, production or design); it costs less and allows one to offer more goods in each country. Standardization is accompanied by an increasing number of goods available in each market. The relative homogenization of purchases can also be explained by the standardization and concentration of retailing. And, while consumer behavior and demand is not standardized, it nevertheless operates within an increasingly standardized context.

Sport as a means of acceding to a valorized culture

The development of the media is a primary factor in the success of sport consumption, but it is certainly not the only one. For example, though there is evidence to the contrary, there remains a general perception that sports are more openly available to everyone compared to other cultural forms and practices such as concerts, theater, cinema, and restaurants (Donnat, 1998). The strong economic valorization of sport culture provides a key source of legitimacy in society, and this strengthens the propensity of social actors to justify their identification with it. Wearing particular brands of sport clothes or shoes is a way of taking part in a culture valorized by heroic media figures, and it is also a way of adopting a highly legitimated pursuit of particular styles. For example, following the success of the 1998 soccer World Cup, a lot of French people bought the official jersey of the winning team, and many men shaved their hair to look like Barthez or Zidane.

The success of sport in the media explains the importance of consumption of sporting goods by young people, particularly those from underprivileged environments. For them, the point is to have access to a culture that is not labeled or perceived to be a cheap culture. They shun the less expensive, less exclusive retailers' brands and those not associated with sporting champions (Ohl, 2001). Excluded from most cultural institutions, they over-valorize the sporting culture, using sporting signs to provide a positive identity. Sport clothes and shoes used outside the arena of actual performance are worn to affirm a specific identity, different from traditional bourgeois identity, but nonetheless valorized by our society.

The image of Nike, a key factor in its economic success, is often based on an anti-establishment position. Undoubtedly creative and unique, Nike advertising campaigns are often cynical and self-mocking, constructed against the traditional brands offering moralized accounts of the social world. For example, in one Nike advertisement, NBA star Charles Barkley is used as an intelligent "bad boy," declaring that: "I am not a role model, I am not paid to be a role model. I am not paid to wreak havoc on the basketball court." In its ads, Nike also uses W. Burroughs who wrote an anti-bourgeois novel (*Naked Lunch*), and music by the Beatles ("Revolution") and Iggy Pop's "Search and Destroy" which is an anti-middle-class and an antisocial song (Goldman and Papson, 1998). The main cultural and economical changes[4] which started after the Second World War and spread during this period imply difficulties for a part of the new generation to construct its identity in society. Rebelliousness against established values could be explained by the difficulties in acceding to the valorized bourgeois model.

For the French lower classes, difficulties are both economical and cultural. For example, in urban areas, young people from the lower classes are often excluded from shops because they are perceived as social problems: unemployed, delinquent, criminal, and violent. Pinçon and Pinçon-Charlot (1992) noted that it is difficult for the lower classes and lower-middle classes to go into the luxury shops of Paris. Even if they go into different small shops to look at the goods without being willing to buy, they avoid the most expensive shops because they don't feel at ease. To this extent the commercial doorstep is both objective and symbolic. For these lower-class French youth, shopping in prime retail centers is problematic. Economic factors often relegate them to being window shoppers and, as previously noted, they are often excluded because of their appearance. At the same time their quest for identity propels them to purchase commodities that they cannot afford and which they tend to wear and display in highly visible ways in order to affirm their identity and to differentiate themselves from those bourgeois groups that they resent and resist. Wearing sport clothes in an ostentatious way in conjunction with particular manners of behavior and speaking are signs of their desire to exist in public spaces. As such, public space becomes a contested terrain because for these youth it is an important site of performance. Through the presentation of self, young people seek to meet friends who share the same values, to express an identity, and to participate symbolically in the control of public space (Ohl, 2001).

For many young people, the sporting commodities used in the presentation of self are considered as sacred – they symbolize access to a valorized culture. Yet, although they are sacred, their meaning and value are temporal and fleeting and are continually scrutinized. Sport, and its heroic figures, respond very well to this demand because athletes must perform on a stage (or arena) of uncertainty that represents aspects of the human condition. Sport, more than all other domains, demands that, whoever you are, even if you are a world champion, you must train and fight to stay at the top. From a symbolic point of view, sport is the antithesis of the culture of inheritance and privilege.

Sport brands are using this type of opposition to establish codes and traditions. For example, the advertising agency that handles most of Nike's campaigns, Wieden and Kennedy, deliberately set out to shock and challenge the status quo. Examples of this transgressive style include ads featuring scenes of athletes vomiting, perpetuating violence, and challenging authority. However, given the nature of sport and the high status of the athletes involved, they reinforce "the belief that success is the consequence of trying harder" (Goldman and Papson, 1998: 157).

The images circulated through Nike and other sport advertising campaigns are seductive, and help to explain the seemingly contradictory consumption patterns of youth. They want to have signs of relative wealth for the purpose of status but need those signs to represent some form of resistance against the established order. Enter brands like Lacoste, Adidas, Fila and Nike that provide a range of images to accommodate various consumers. For many youth in France it is a conspicuous use of sport commodities that helps facilitate their affirmation of identity. Their ceremonial use of sporting clothes can be easily replaced as they mature and obtain new social and economic status. One question that remains however, is how these French youth localize and rationalize their use of global sport commodities.

Sporting goods, local identity and globalization

In France, Nike, Adidas, and Reebok are the favorite brands of 11 to 17-year-olds and now supersede brands like Hollywood, Coca-Cola, and McDonald's; other sporting brands like Quicksilver and Oxbow also hold a high rank (Inquiry by Teen Generation 1997, quoted in *Sport Première Magazine*, March to April 1998: 113). The international reputation of sport brands is very strong, so they are particularly visible and important consumption items from a symbolic point of view. Notably, there is a vast difference between the real economic impact of the sporting goods industry compared to others and its public visibility.[5] This is partially explained by the capacity of sporting events to become very desirable media commodities. The overestimation of sporting brands with respect to their economic turnover is also associated with powerful positive social representations that are, while increasingly more difficult to accomplish, distanced from the unpleasant side of commercialization. Clearly, top sportspeople earn a lot of money but their effort and ability are visible, and as such they can be differentiated from the establishment and those who inherit privilege and position.

The expansion of world trade and global markets, professional uncertainty, imaginary social mobility, growth of media, extended longevity, and the increasing number of years spent at school, are all contributing factors to young people using sport commodities (and others) as new markers of identity. Numerous sporting goods operate as identity markers, including those developed by various sport clubs and associations. These contribute, in various ways, to the maintenance of social bonds between their members. The visible display of sporting emblems and logos demonstrates loyalty and commitment, and symbolically separates out the true supporters from the casual fans. In a more systematic way, European professional football and basketball clubs have developed the sale of identity-related sporting goods. For example, the Naples' Football Club sold more than a million souvenirs in 1990 (Bromberger, 1994); in 1997, Manchester United offered 1,500 items in its catalogue and earned $33 million profit; and the Bayern Munich Club has sold 350,000 jerseys per year. From this point of view, France is relatively different, since the supply of accessories is more limited. The organization and history of strong state centralization in France accounts for why football clubs are less likely to function as the agent of local identity than other European clubs.

Thus, the consumption of sporting commodities enables the affirmation of local and national identities. However, the increasing globalization of the market does not spare any field of modern societies. As various local sports seek to survive, they are increasingly dependent on global television and corporate sponsorship. As a consequence, they are commodified, and local control is either lost or greatly reduced.

Today, most sport brands have a global strategy. Sport, as noted throughout this chapter, is used as a common culture through which to unify consumption. Consider the following extract from an Adidas document distributed to its employees in 1997:

> The consumers Adidas is targeting are the athletes. These consumers care about their sports. They care about performance. They are physical. They are competitive. They expect the best for themselves and their athletic products. There is no difference anywhere in the world. This is our core message ... and the message must be the same anywhere in the world. If it is not the same, it is not Adidas.
>
> (Adidas Corporate Objectives and Mission, 1997: 9)

Several European clubs also partly changed their identity from a status club full of references to a local identity to a make, source of benefit in an international-ized market. Sport pictures have turned into products negotiated in an interna-tionalized market in which local differences diminish. The spreading of consumption and the rationalization of the supply involve the standardization of goods and, to a lesser degree, of services. Within the process of globalization the search for identity is not necessarily connected to a town or a region. In many cases local identities are not directly at stake. Objects don't necessarily emphasize the individual or national identity, and the created bonds have no affirmed historic dimensions. Social bonds appear to be organized around the emotion and the passion for a sporting activity and are often short-lived and superficial. For instance millions of people buy jerseys, sashes, and so on of the (football) World Cup. The French, winners of the World Cup or the New Zealand All Blacks rugby team are related to a nation but as well often work as a brand. When young Americans or Brazilians are buying the World Cup winner T-shirt, they don't purchase the French tradition and history but the winning brand.

Paradoxically, there seems to be a contradiction between the embeddedness of goods in local or national culture for some consumers and the simple use of goods as commodities for others. Even if contradictions exist, the roots are not so different. Consumers buy sporting goods because they have a visible and readable identity whether it is national, local or a brand. The global and the local are interacting in social uses of supply. French consumers appreciate global brands because of their international, particularly "American," image. Nonethe-less, the success of local brands like "64" in the Southwest of France, of ethnic clothes or retro fashion are rooted in the opposition to the mass market (64 is also the number of Pyrénées-Atlantiques, a French administrative local territory called "département." The combination of goods, global or local, ethnic or retro, conspicuously or discreetly used, gives the impression of attempts to build a singular presentation of self.

Styles, as systems of difference, have to be analyzed in relation to the diversity of social positions and conditions. But, if we consider the uses of objects, the point is no longer just a matter of explaining consumption by socio-demographic parameters alone. The postmodernist approach helps us to understand the genesis of these new social bonds established around the aesthetic dimension of social life (Maffesoli, 1990). These bonds seem to develop thanks to new forms of grouping around hedonistic, aesthetic, and consumer needs. Sport consumption finds its logic in the creation of social bonds and in the visibility of new identities. To simplify, one could say that individuals give the impression of belonging to a great football family rather than to the working class. This simplifying vision corresponds to social representations that are spread and in which socio-political stakes are more structured around consumption than around class struggles. The sporting ideology is spreading, and imposes sport and its events as a social conquest. For example, the Spanish conservatives (The Aznar political party) referred to the football show on TV in the following words: "this social conquest football is for the Spanish consumer" (quoted in M.C. Decamps, *Le Monde*, 1997: 33). It signifies that consumption, particularly sport events on media, has a central place in society and can be compared to other social issues such as democracy, human and child rights, abortion, and so on. Considering these social changes, particularly in consumption, some sociologists like Maffesoli made a break with traditional deterministic explanations. The idea is that sport or other types of consumption are not only reflections of social class but form the basis of new groupings (Maffesoli, 1990). Sports, clothes, and music are sufficient to define a style and to bring together people through the ephemeral bond of appearance (Maffesoli, 1998). Consumption is changing our society, particularly through the deconstruction of the social (e.g. classes, work, conflicts). But it seems that, even if these sporting groups work in a relatively autonomous way, the billions of TV viewers watching the World Cup or wearing sports gear share few interests apart from television or goods. Furthermore, this sharing is limited to the objective dimension of behavior, and fails to take into account the subjective aspects of use. The cultural diversity which explains the various uses of sport goods, practices or events also helps explain the symbolic efficacy of sport advertising or advertising through sport.

Symbolic efficacy of advertising and ideology of consumption

Advertising and the discourses of sport brands are developed around the sporting uses of commodities. Despite the reality of consumer (mis)use, sport brands wish to associate their goods with a very athletic use. The following extract from a document distributed by Adidas to its personnel in 1997 gives us an illustration:

> Our brand strategy is to be associated with any activity that is *Physical* and *Competitive*. In short, if it is not physical and competitive, it is not sport.

And if it is not sport, it cannot be representative of the Adidas brand. The Adidas brand must not appear on or be associated with any product or competitive activity that does not have its roots in a physical or competitive activity.

The consumers Adidas is targeting are the athletes. These consumers care about their sports. They care about performance. They are physical. They are competitive. They expect the best for themselves and their athletic products. This is not different anywhere in the world. This is our core message ... and the message must be the same anywhere in the world. If it is not the same, it is not Adidas.

(Adidas Corporate Objectives and Mission, 1997: 6–7)

Sporting brands are merging with top-level sport to differentiate their identity from the fashion brands, which are too dependent on changes in young consumers' tastes.

There are social roots of sporting goods brand efficacy. They depend not only on the work of sharp communicators or marketers, but are above all based on central cultural changes within societies. Discourses around mass consumption, the role of emotion or age in the explanation of behavior contribute to the understanding of the changes. But it also appears that the question of symbolic social struggles is at stake. Sport consumption provides social markers that help to transform and euphemize social struggles (Bourdieu, 1979).

The socio-demographic data and the various uses of goods show that the mass consumption of sporting goods is not a democratic access to sport (Desbordes *et al.*, 1999). The lower classes are using sporting goods as a symbol of social integration and participation in a valorized culture, while the upper classes are more often using them for sport.

Goods may also be used to delimit a territory or to recall symbolic domination in a practice. For example, during the diffusion of golf in France, old players were buying new and more expensive goods to differentiate themselves from the new players (Ohl, 1991). Moreover, their very participation in golf may have been stimulated by the rising popularity of another sport: tennis. In response to the democratization of tennis during the 1980s, many, in their quest for symbolic distinction, either shifted to or reinvested in golf, a more expensive and exclusive sport.

Moreover, key social questions like those linked to politics, equality, education or economics seemed to be worn away by the less essential questions concerning fashion and sport culture (winners, cheaters, scandal). Through its contribution to the pacification and transformation of social struggles, the important communication and advertising processes around sport culture fit very well within the ideological processes of a consumer society and served to maintain the symbolic order. The emerging messages reinforce the mythical belief that everyone can be a winner in the consumer society (Miles, 1998).

As consumption becomes the main reference of citizenship, ads help global companies to spread the idea that social changes are less linked to political choices than to consumer choices. Consequently, political projects seem to be limited to abstract ideological struggles often with little relevance to society. Effectively, there has been an objective and symbolic victory of the economical field over the political field, which has become too disconnected from real life. Sport consumption, arguably, plays a role in this process; sport victories are celebrated though they are devoid of politics, while the purchase and display of sporting goods provides people with rather fleeting notions of access to a valorized culture.

Thus, international advertising campaigns developed by global companies to standardize their image and to achieve economies of scale can be analyzed as a way to reify the consumer as a specific asocial, ahistoric figure. But this idea of a new consumer, far removed from traditional patterns, does not resist analysis. The social construction of an uprooted consumer gives support to a liberal neo-classical analysis of society (Ohl, 2002). The main struggles, which are not limited to class struggles, are still expressed in social spaces through consumption. What looks like a question of fashion or even of self-identity is at first a sociological question. Despite the complexity of uses and meanings of consumption, marketing communication on the global mass market provides a sense of the substitution of social actors or citizens for consumers. Thanks to the increasing role of the media, this stereotypical discourse has emerged as the privileged rhetoric of late capitalism. However, despite the reality of today's "consumer culture," it does not mean that social actors can be reduced to a kind of *homo-economicus*.

The increasing place of consumption brings important changes in society, but the inflation of discourses around a new consumer culture should not incite one to abandon all social determination perspectives. Thus, the struggles around appearance and identity affirmation dissimulate other important social struggles. Class or generation conflicts are euphemized in fashion discussions and in debate around the legitimate way to use clothes. Even with the diffusion of consumption, the bourgeois uses of sport clothes are still opposed to the more popular uses as ceremonial clothing. Social positions and conditions are integral to the genesis of tastes (Bourdieu, 1979). The diffusion of sporting goods, as mass commodities, does not fit with the idea of equal uses and significance of sporting goods (the old idea of sport without inequalities, barriers, and so on) because even if people of different social categories are buying the same commodities and are sensitive to the same advertisements, the way and the place they use the commodities are often contradictory. In many areas of social life oppressed social classes are more sensitive to the social codes of success. This helps to explain why sporting goods for men and fashion for women are very often considered by particular social groups as important signs through which to differentiate themselves from the very group to which they belong. People for whom integration or success is less recognized have to make consumption visible. For them the importance of clothes, for example, often has more to do with social relations: the normality of appearances is a kind of necessity. The harmony of style recalls the social bonds and thus maintains what Bourdieu calls the "social capital" (1979: 225).

Economic or marketing approaches that only take into account the actual purchases can be efficient, but are far removed from the signification of consumption. Finally, the analysis of sport allows us to grasp the contradictions of our societies and to understand the complexity of consumption. Sport concentrates numerous characteristics, altering our relations to objects and to services. Based on the different approaches outlined above, it is difficult to justify the use of the term "consumer" with respect to all actions of purchasing or using commodities. The behaviors of consumption alone do not reveal any distinctive characteristics, values or ethics; nonetheless, sport consumers are, first and foremost, social actors.

References

Adidas Corporate Objectives and Mission, 1997.

Andrews, D.L. and Jackson, S.J. (2001). *Sport Stars: The Politics of Sporting Celebrity*. London: Routledge.

Birrell, S. (1981). Sport as ritual: Interpretations from Durkheim to Goffman. *Social Forces*, 60 (2), 354–376.

Boltanski, L. (1982). *Les cadres. La formation d'un groupe social*. Paris: Minuit.

Bourdieu, P. (1979). *La distinction, critique sociale du jugement*. Paris: Minuit.

Bourdieu, P. (1994). L'emprise du journalisme. *Actes de la recherche en sciences sociales*, 101/102, 3–9.

Bourdieu, P. (1996). *Sur la télévision*. Paris: Liber.

Bromberger, C. (1994). *Le match de football. Ethnologie d'une passion partisane à Marseille, Naples et Turin*. Paris: MSH.

Catani, M. (1996). Basiques imparables, yaourts, jeans, blousons et mode de la rue. *Ethnologie française*, 26, 180–193.

Desbordes, M., Ohl, F. and Tribou, G. (1999). *Marketing du sport*. Paris: Economica.

Donnat, O. (1998). *Les pratiques culturelles des Français, enquête 1997*. Paris: La Documentation française.

Douglas, M. and Isherwood, B. (1979). *The World of Goods. Toward and Anthropology of Consumption*. London: Allen Lane.

Duret, P. (1993). *L'héroïsme sportif*. Paris: PUF.

Durkheim, E. (1960). *Les formes élémentaires de la vie religieuse* (4th edn). Paris: PUF.

Ehrenberg, A. (1991). *Le culte de la performance*. Paris: Calmann-Lévy.

Elias, N. and Dunning, E. (1986). *The Quest for Excitement, Sport and Leisure in the Civilizing Process*. London: Blackwell.

Falk, P. and Campbell, C. (1997). *The Shopping Experience*. London: Sage.

Fantasia, R. (1994). Everything and nothing: The meaning of fast-food and other American cultural goods in France. *The Tocqueville Review*, 15 (2), 57–88.

Featherstone, M. (1991). *Consumer Culture and Postmodernism*. London: Sage.

Fottorino, E. (1996). Obut, les boules qui se prennent pour des planètes. *Le Monde*, September 3, 9.

Goffman, E. (1959). *The Presentation of Self in Everyday Life*. New York: Anchor Books.

Goffman, E. (1967). *Interaction Ritual: Essays on Face to Face Behavior*. New York: Doubleday Anchor.

Goffman, E. (1974). *Frame Analysis: An Essay on the Organization of Experience*. New York: Harper & Row.

Goldman, R. and Papson, S. (1998). *Nike Culture: The Sign of the Swoosh*. London: Sage.

Granovetter, M. (1985). Economic action and social structure: A theory of embeddedness. *American Journal of Sociology, 91* (3), 481–510.

Herpin, N. (1986). L'habillement, la classe sociale et la mode. *Economie et Statistiques, 188,* 35–54.

Herpin, N. (1987). L'habillement et le corps, *Economie et Statistiques*. Paris, INSEE, *196,* 55–63.

Irlinger, P., Louveau, C. and Metoudi, M. (1987). *Les pratiques sportives des français*. Paris: INSEP.

Jackson, S.J. and Andrews, D.L. (1999). Between and beyond the local and the global. American sporting culture in New Zealand. *International Review for the Sociology of Sport, 34* (1), 31–42.

Jenkins, R. (1996). *Social Identity*. London: Routledge.

Lamont, M. and Molnàr, V. (2001). How blacks use consumption to shape their collective identity. *Journal of Consumer Culture, 1,* 31–45.

Leite Lopes, J.S. and Maresca, S. (1989). La disparition de la joie du peuple. Notes sur la mort d'un joueur de football. *Actes de la recherche en sciences sociales, 79,* 21–36.

Löfgren, O. (1996). Le retour des objets? L'étude de la culture matérielle dans l'ethnologie suédoise. *Ethnologie française, 26,* 140–150.

Lyotard, J.F. (1979). *La condition postmoderne*. Paris: Minuit.

Maffesoli, M. (1990). *Au creux des apparences*. Paris: Plon.

Maffesoli, M. (1998). *Le temps des tribus*. Paris: Klincksieck.

Miles, S. (1998). *Consumerism as a Way of Life*. London: Sage.

Ohl, F. (1991). *Pratiques économiques, pratiques sociales: étude de la genèse sociale du coût financier des sports*. Thèse de doctorat en sociologie, Université de Strasbourg II.

Ohl, F. (2000). Les commentaires journalistiques sur le sport ont-ils un sens? *Recherches en communication, 14,* 185–213.

Ohl, F. (2001). Les usages sociaux des objets sportifs: le paraître "sportif" en ville. *Loisir et société/Leisure and Society, 24* (1), 111–136.

Ohl, F. (2002). La construction sociale des figures du consommateur et du client. *Sciences de la société, 56,* 24–41.

Picard, D. (1995). *Les rituels du savoir-vivre*, Paris: Seuil.

Pinçon, M. and Pinçon-Charlot, M. (1992). *Quartiers bourgeois, quartiers d'affaires*. Paris: Payot.

Pouquet, L. (1994). *Le comportement des consommateurs d'articles de sport*. Paris: Crédoc.

Rivière, C. (1995). *Les rites profanes*. Paris: PUF.

Tribou, G. and Madec, I. (1999). L'image de la marque Adidas auprès des adolescents, un entretien avec I. Madec, directrice du marketing de la société Adidas France. *Décision marketing, 18,* 37–39.

Usunier, J.C. (1996). Consommation: quand global rime avec local. *Revue Française de Gestion, 110,* 100–116.

Weber, M. (1958 [1947]). *The Protestant Ethic and the Spirit of Capitalism*. New York: Scribner's.

Notes

1 Model behavior? Sporting feminism and consumer culture

1 Another magazine that serves as a hybrid form is *Sports Illustrated for Women/Sport Magazine* which premiered in April 1997. Each issue was sent to 450,000 identifiable female *Sports Illustrated* subscribers and 60,000 people on a Time-Warner database. An estimated 100,000 issues were sold at newsstands. Close inspection of the inaugural issue reveals considerable space devoted to discussions related not only to sport but also to issues of sexuality. Article titles such as "The phallic fallacy," "Sex, lies and softball" and "Is it O.K. to have sex before the game?" suggest that narratives of sexuality exist as integral content. *Sports Illustrated for Women* has also ceased publication.

2 "Knowing" the hero: The female athlete and myth at work in Nike advertising

1 Although Nike was advised of the potential of the women's market, there were no Nike advertisements marketed to women prior to 1987 (Cole and Hribar, 1995: 359).
2 Nike's discursive practice of erasing race in this context is much more complicated and deserves much more space than we can give it within the bounds of this chapter. It is something we hope to take up further elsewhere.

3 Women's sports in Nike's America: Body politics and the corporo-empowerment of "everyday athletes"

1 According to findings released by the Women's Sports Foundation in a report entitled "Health risks and the teenage athlete," athletes are less likely to use illicit drugs, less likely to be suicidal, and more likely to have positive body images than their counterparts who did not participate in sports (http://www.womenssportsfoundation.org/cgi-bin/iowa/issues/body/article.html?record=771). However, such findings are highly suspect (cf. Lafrance, 1998) and often do not take into account race, class, ethnicity, and other socio-economic issues. See also Cole *et al.* (2001) for a discussion of girl athletes that links citizenship and consumption within late modern America to popular understandings of sport, feminism, and nationalism.
2 *Sports Illustrated for Women* has since ceased publication due to a downturn in circulation in the post-9/11 economic downturn period, a trend mirrored across the board in magazine publishing.
3 Part of the 1972 Educational Amendments Act, § 901 of Title IX states in part: "No person in the United States shall, on the basis of sex, be excluded from participation, be denied the benefits of, or be subjected to discrimination under any education program or activity receiving Federal financial assistance."
4 As is frequently noted in discussions relevant to Title IX, 1998 saw 39 percent of all

collegiate athletes as women, a considerable increase from 1972, when women accounted for only 2 percent (National Coalition for Women and Girls in Education, 2002). Unfortunately, as Cole (2000: 5) reminds us, "Title IX has been, and is at best, unevenly instituted and enforced. Most universities have made minor and symbolic compromises while few have been penalized for persisting disparities." Despite such poor enforcement – and its highly controversial ramifications from the point of view of collegiate men's athletic programs – Title IX is still widely regarded as the turning point in women's athletics. However, rather than pronounce such endeavors as the WNBA and W*USA as a victory for Title IX, it is much more revealing to state that this victory lies squarely with adidas, Hyundai, McDonald's, Nike, Reebok, Sears, the NBA, and the whole host of multinational and transnational corporations who have invested in, shaped, and benefited from women's sporting "success." For a discussion on the relationship between Title IX and the popular acceptance of women's sport in the 1990s, see Cole (2000).

5 Regarding the *X-Files*, Meaghan Morris (1997) has shrewdly observed that, while the character of Scully is "a highly trained, impeccably professional, and immaculately groomed bimbo" (p. 367), her "cool acceptance of an incommensurability between reason and faith simply confirms the contrast between her post-Enlightenment progressivism and Mulder's [her FBI partner in the show] more romantic, New Age drive to reconcile the two" (p. 374). This is particularly revealing of the popular view of mainstream postfeminism inasmuch as Nike's female-centered ad campaigns – especially "Everyday Athletes" – acknowledge both a bio-political fashioning of the self in concert with a New Age, self-reflexive spirituality as a means of self-actualization and self-improvement. It would seem, then, that Denzin (1991), invoking Foucault (1982: 25), had already anticipated such a move by Nike – that is, the coalescing of post-Enlightenment and New Age ideals of the body within commodity-sign culture – when he stated that:

> [U]nder cultural logic of late capitalism, knowledge is progressively centered in modes of scientific discourse which focuses on the bio-politics of control. This regime of power turns each postmodern subject into an object to be manipulated by the state and its various control apparatuses. . . . What started as a colonization of representations by the commodity form (that is the ideological commodification of objects) has now turned into a situation where the postmodern culture colonizes the commodity.

6 In short, Grossberg (1992: 252) views the rhetoric of popular conservatism as overlapping with Cold War conservative ideologies in focusing on the "world mission of the U.S. and the need to reinscribe powerfully nationalistic feelings in order to recapitulate the 'traditional' values of the nation . . . which were undermined by internal forces in the 1960s."

7 It is unfortunate to note that, while the mainstream press has heaped praise upon Girl Power! *en masse*, scholars have been noticeably absent and/or uncritical on the subject. Notable exceptions, however, include Heywood (1999, 2001) and Baumgardner and Richards (2000).

8 Explaining their conceptual understanding of "popular feminism," Cole and Hribar (1995: 356) go on to state:

> Postfeminism can be characterized as the process through which movement feminism was reterritorialized through the normalizing logic . . . governing 1980s America. While movement feminism generated spaces and identities that interrogated distribution and relational inequalities, meanings, differences, and identities, the postfeminist movement includes spaces that work to homogenize, generate conformity, and mark Others, while discouraging questioning. . . . In other words, a normalizing discourse.

9 For highly informative and exhaustive critiques of the P.L.A.Y. campaign, see Cole (1996); Cole and Hribar (1995); and Lafrance (1998).

4 Enlightened racism and celebrity feminism in contemporary sports advertising discourse

1 This chapter is a revised version of an article that was entitled "Just Do It": Corporate Sports Slogans and the Political Economy of "Enlightened Racism," which appeared in *Discourse: Studies In The Cultural Politics of Education* 16: 191–201 (1995).

2 African American women were excluded from the protests at Mexico. According to Tyus, who dedicated her gold medal to Smith and Carlos, "It appalled me, that the men simply took us for granted. They assumed that we had no minds of our own and that we'd do whatever we were told." Carlos' response was that "They should have been involved. It just wasn't done, but it was not meant to be denigrating. So many things were happening, and there was so little time. It was an inadvertent oversight" (Moore 1991b: 72; also see Moore 1991a and Spivey 1985).

3 Nike has also used African Americans Mike Powell and Ken Griffey Jr. and Sr. in similar advertisements.

4 Some readers who saw the Australian band Midnight Oil perform at the closing ceremony of the 2000 Olympics may have noticed that its members had the word "Sorry" displayed prominently on their clothing.

5 Phillip Ruddock, former Minister for Reconciliation, recently said that Aborigines were handicapped partly because they came into contact with Europeans relatively late, and were hunter-gatherers who had not even been familiar with the wheel when they encountered Europeans.

6 In September 2003 Nike agreed to pay US$1.5 million to settle a lawsuit alleging it lied about conditions at its low-cost Asian suppliers.

7 In October 2003, Smith and Carlos were the guests of honor at a day of events to commemorate the thirty-fifth anniversary of their protest which was organized by the student association at SJSU. The event also raised funds for a statue of Smith and Carlos which the association plans to erect on campus in 2004. Smith is now head coach of the men's cross-country and track and field team at Santa Monica College, California, and Carlos is a track and field coach and a suspension supervisor at Palm Springs High School, California (Bartindale 2003; Dilbeck 2003; Steele 2003).

5 Race, representation, and the promotional culture of the NBA: the Canadian case

1 The 1995 to 1996 season was the teams' first as active participants in the league, although the franchises had been granted approximately two years before.

7 Fitting images: advertising, sport and disability

1 This is a substantially revised version of a similarly titled conference paper (Aycock and Duncan, 1998).

2 Neither Turow (1997) nor Sivulka (1998) mention it in their detailed analyses of niche advertising.

3 Each of three recent textbooks – Davis (1997); Barnes *et al.* (1999); Shakespeare (1998) – includes a brief summary of the literature, but none of the data are more current than the early 1990s.

4 To save space we have not reproduced an appendix in which our sample keying is more specifically identified. Those interested may contact the authors for this appendix.

8   Close encounters of another kind: nationalism, media representations and advertising in New Zealand rugby

1 This chapter forms part of a larger, multi-authored project on 'Television and National Identity in New Zealand' undertaken by the Centre for Film, Television and Media Studies at the University of Auckland. The project is supported by a Marsden Fund of New Zealand grant.

2 As Australian critics such as Graeme Turner (1993) and others have pointed out, the (gradually unraveling, yet still) dominant predisposition in British cultural studies is that 'Britain ... is the unquestioned category which never needs to be spoken ... nationality seems utterly naturalised, always already in place' (p. 9). This is notwithstanding the fact that Britain's Industrial Revolution was founded upon the spinning of cotton from India and its culture symbolized by the drinking of tea from Ceylon. Perhaps, as a Salman Rushdie (1988) character puts it, 'The trouble with the English is that their history happened overseas, so that they don't know what it means' (p. 337). Or perhaps this remark is itself rather too close to being complicit with that easy, exasperating conflation of 'English' and 'British' that is at once a more overt indication of Graeme Turner's general point and a semiotic inflection of what Michael Hechter (1975) has called 'internal colonialism'.

3 Perhaps, then, it might be said that the trouble with the Americans is not that their history happened overseas, but that it happened in Hollywood.

4 Consider, for example, that imperious tone displayed by Fredric Jameson (1995) in assessing Australian contributions to Grossberg et al. (1992) cultural studies collection. He suggests that these 'noisiest detractors of "grand theory" ... may owe something to the idiosyncratic and anarchist roots of Australian radicalism'. This is, however, home to 'an even more sinister variant of this otherwise harmless anti-intellectualism' (in the shape of a British, but at that time expatriate, Tony Bennett!) that 'may have some relevance in a small country with socialist traditions, but is surely misplaced advice here' (Jameson, 1995, pp. 624–625). This collapsing together of a particular version of 'here' with a purportedly general conception of theoretical work foregrounds the distinctive form of marginality available to left intellectuals in the USA. What it thereby effectively privileges is that culturally specific blending of cognitive autonomy and professional insulation which is made possible by the sheer institutional density of the US higher education system (and which at once encourages theory to be 'grand' and 'Marxist' to be an adjective but rarely a noun).

5 The Maori are New Zealand's indigenous peoples.

6 The Japanese electronics firm NEC made use of the same Japanese actor in two formally similar, but locally inflected, commercials that were shown on both sides of the Tasman. In Australian screenings he was always identified as Mr Ockermura, in New Zealand he was referred to as Mr Kiwimura. In one commercial he was shown as a member of a surf lifesaving team, in the other he became a trout fisherman. The former tends to signify 'Australia' and the latter 'New Zealand'.

7 Such otherwise very different film directors as Lee Tamahori and Vincent Ward have both made New Zealand commercials that embody sporting themes.

8 A 1999 Adidas' All Black commercial makes use of the song 'Bless 'em All' in order to solemnly invoke the lineage of All Black captaincy (see Jackson et al., 2001). The song was a popular anthem among troops during the war. A recently recorded version by the eponymous World Cup Supporters Club was entitled 'Fuck 'Em All'. It too was commercially mediated, of course – but altogether closer both to the spirit and sentiments of the (much-censored) original and to Speilberg's conception of dialogic imagination. It climbed to seventh place in the local hit parade.

10 "I'm afraid of Americans"?: New Zealand's cultural resistance to violence in "globally" produced sports advertising

1 "I'm Afraid of Americans" appeared on Bowie's 1997 album *Earthling*.

2 See Reebok commercial banned in New Zealand (1995).

3 For instance, both Watson and Shuker (1998) and Watson *et al.* (1991) have noted the criticism of "American" media violence in New Zealand. Moreover, in a survey of New Zealand audiences, Watson *et al.* (1991) found that "it was American programmes that generally had the higher scores on the 'likelihood to cause concern' scale" (cited in Watson and Shuker, 1998: 86).

4 Despite its release in New Zealand, the inclusion of Botham (a much reviled opponent in Australian cricket circles) and an unidentified All Black (the name given to New Zealand's national rugby team) suggests Australia was actually the primary market for the commercial.

5 Interestingly, despite referring to the code for violence in this instance, it has more often been codes for *offensiveness* which have been examined by the ASCB in adjudicating complaints against violence in television advertising.

6 Within this chapter I have referenced information and quotations from individual ASCB case studies according to their designated complaint number. In most cases the ASCB rulings do not include page numbers.

7 According to the TVCAB its decisions are governed by relevant legislation such as the Broadcasting Act, as well as the more specialized Codes of Practice developed under the auspices of the BSA and ASA (see TVCAB, 1998). In particular, the TVCAB employs the ASA's Codes of Practice for screening and classification of commercials prior to their transmission. Obviously, commercials banned by the ASCB have been previously approved by the TVCAB, so there are signs of discontinuity in terms of how each organization applies the same Codes of Practice.

8 The term used here is borrowed from Andrews *et al.* (1996), although the concept is actually developed from Paul Gilroy's (1993) notion of the *Black Atlantic*, and its more specific use by Ben Carrington in his analysis of sport and black youth in Britain (see Andrews *et al.*, 1996).

9 For further discussion of how opposition to American popular culture may obscure class, race, and ethnic divisions in local contexts see Ang (1996), Hall (1991), Jackson (1994), Kong (1999), and Kayatekin and Ruccio (1998). Many of the issues raised by these authors are explored in the New Zealand case by Lealand (1988; 1994), and, particularly in relation to racial and ethnic identity in New Zealand, by Wilcox (1996).

10 Indeed, Horrocks (1996: 55) argues that, since deregulation, advertising has become the "biggest bone of public contention" among New Zealand television audiences.

11 For discussion in regard to New Zealand culture and identity specifically, see Allison (1991), Laidlaw (1999), and Lealand (1988).

11 Cursed or carefree? Menstrual product advertising and the sportswoman

1 One high school principal reports that physical education teachers in her all-girls' school in New Zealand must keep track of her students' periods simply to ensure that they don't use the excuse "I can't I've got my period!" to sit out of gym classes more than once a month.

2 Southalls' was written with an apostrophe in 1928 print advertisements, but became simply "*Southalls*" (without the apostrophe) by the early 1930s.

3 A 22-inch waist is some two inches below the fifth lowest percentile in waist girth according to the 1993 *Size and Shape of New Zealanders Study*.

12 Generational marketing: fitness, health and lifestyle formations

1 Age Wave LLC is a development company based out of Emeryville, California that is creating a portfolio of business ventures addressing the specific needs of the aging population. Founded by internationally known gerontologist, psychologist and best-selling author Dr. Ken Dychwald, the name "Age Wave LLC" refers to the title of his 1988 best-selling book *Age Wave: The Challenges and Opportunities of an Aging America*.

2 The International Health, Racquet and Sportsclub Association (IHRSA) is a non-profit association dedicated to the growth, protection, and promotion of the health club industry, and represents more than 5,600 clubs worldwide. IHRSA is an international leader in health club industry education, research, and advocacy. IHRSA will celebrate its twentieth anniversary at its annual international convention and trade show held March 21–24, 2001, in San Francisco, CA.

3 Esalen was founded in 1962 as an educational center devoted to the exploration of unrealized human capacities. It quickly became internationally known for its blend of East/West philosophies, its experiential/didactic workshops, the steady influx of philosophers, psychologists, artists, and religious thinkers, and its breathtaking grounds blessed with natural hot springs.

13 Staging identity through consumption: Exploring the social uses of sporting goods

1 I make a point of thanking Steven Jackson for his help as an editor and for rewriting my "French English." It goes without saying that all the text is completely my responsibility.

2 At the head of the group, J. Bové, from "confédération paysanne," a union opposed to the more conservative FNSEA. J. Bové is not a typical farmer: speaking very good English (he spent three years in Berkeley with his parents as teacher and researcher), he was also involved during the 1970s in many French social movements. His installation as a farmer in Larzac is the symbol of a choice, a way of life, and it is a transgression to the social order and its institutions (in Larzac one of the most important demonstrations against the French nuclear military base took place there).

3 But it is not always the case. For example, the domination of only a few TV and cinema producers is an important threat to the diversity of culture. The stake is less their national identity; we too often focus on American domination than their monopolistic position in the market which forces the smaller producers out of the market (they cannot compete with the marketing of large companies and are not distributed in cinema auditora).

4 Main changes in economy and work, new definitions of feminine and masculine roles, changes in the definition of age, apparition of new lifestyles, the decline of social classes as a reference, the decline of the confidence in institutions, the spreading of consumption or the globalization process are some of the most important parameters which accentuate difficulties in the construction of social identity.

5 Sport industry weighs very little compared to other industries (bank, chemistry, motor industry). If we compare the turnovers and reputations, the margin is enormous. The biggest firms in the richest countries often weigh as much (if not more) as the whole of the firms producing sport goods. Nike, the leader of the market, represents four times less than Peugeot, a car manufacturer absent on the North American market. GM alone is twice as big as the whole sport market put together.

Index